SEATTLE'S HISTORIAN AND PROMOTER

Seattle's Historian and Promoter

The Life of Edmond Stephen Meany

George A. Frykman

Washington State University Press
Pullman, Washington

Washington State University Press, PO Box 645910, Pullman, Washington, 99164-5910
Phone: 800-354-7360 Fax: 509-335-8568

First printing 1998

Publication of this book was made possible in part by the financial assistance of the Washington State University Department of History and the Sherman and Mabel Pettyjohn Endowment.

Front and back cover photos courtesy Special Collections Division, University of Washington Libraries. Front: #UW 17999. Back: #NA620.

Library of Congress Cataloging-in-Publication Data

Frykman, George A., 1917-   .

Seattle's historian and promoter : the life of Edmond Stephen Meany / George A. Frykman.

p. cm.

Includes bibliographical references (p.   ) and index.

ISBN 0-87422-168-4 (pbk.)

1. Meany, Edmond S. (Edmond Stephen), 1862-1935. 2. Historians—Washington (State)—Seattle—Biography. 3. Businessmen—Washington (State)—Seattle—Biography. 4. Seattle (Wash.)—Biography.

I. Title.

F899.S453M434 1998

979.7'772041'092—dc21

[B] 98-26213

CIP

Dedicated to Elizabeth "Betty" Frykman for encouragement and devotion to the cause all these years.

CONTENTS

Acknowledgments

In the first place, this biography could not be written until the late Charles M. Gates, of the University of Washington, introduced me in 1957 to the rich collection of the Meany Papers at the University of Washington archives. His objective was to find a historian to write the life of Edmond S. Meany. I gladly seized the opportunity, beginning by applying for research aid to the Graduate School at Washington State University, where I was a member of the Department of History. For several years I received substantial aid from the Graduate School for travel and subsistence while away from home in Seattle, engaged in research at the University of Washington.

In the researching years I had much assistance and encouragement from Richard C. Berner, director of the University of Washington's Manuscript and Archives Program. Such assistance extended from reaching out the hand of friendship to supplying a typewriter and a work desk in his own overcrowded office, as well as in helping me when he brought the last of the Meany Papers to Seattle from Cape Cod, the home of Edmond S. Meany, Jr. Robert E. Burke of the history faculty at the University of Washington, and reference librarians at the same institution were generous with their encouragement, and with their archival and editorial assistance.

Heavy teaching schedules and administrative duties produced long delays in finishing the biography but writing began in earnest in 1990 after publication of my institutional history: *Creating the People's University: Washington State University, 1890-1990* (WSU Press).

The "Life of Meany" evolved from a one-dimensional figure to that of a multifaceted late Victorian gentleman under the critical gaze of fellow scholars and the requirements of fairness and integrity in dealing with documents and the subject of this study. In this regard, special thanks are extended to Richard Maxwell Brown, of the University of Oregon, for his sympathetic evaluation of the first full rendition of the manuscript and to

Carlos A. Schwantes, of the University of Idaho, for discerning remarks on the general orientation of the study.

My departmental chairmen have my thanks for their unfailing encouragement of this and other projects—scholarly, teaching, and research. They are (in order of service): Herbert J. Wood, Raymond Muse, David H. Stratton, Richard Hume, and Roger Schlesinger. I am also grateful to the department for its financial assistance—through funds made available from the Sherman and Mabel Pettyjohn Endowment—to the WSU Press for this book. I thank my editor at the Press, Keith Petersen, for his close attention to detail and for his genuine interest in the book.

Norman Forness, a premier research assistant (and for many years since a professor of history at Gettysburg College) has my gratitude and admiration for his research assistance in the early years of this project. Alice E. Marong, my daughter, typed the first, provisional draft, for which I am very grateful. Liza Rognas brought preparation of the manuscript to a close with her typing of the revised draft and assistance with its editing. Finally, Betty Frykman, my wife, provided immeasurable help by critically reading the entire revised draft with me, improving both style and clarity of thought.

George A. Frykman, Professor of History, Emeritus
From the Palouse Hills at Pullman and Washington State University

PROLOGUE: A LIFE IN MINIATURE

SEATTLE AND THE STATE of Washington were young communities in the years down to World War I. As such, they offered special opportunities for achievement to two generations of pioneers. Businessmen not only dominated the material life of these communities but also sought to replicate late nineteenth century middle class society and its code of values, subsumed under the rubric "survival of the fittest." With that Social Darwinian philosophy went the avid practice of individualism and *laissez faire* attitudes in social and cultural life as well as in the marketplace. Success generally was measured in material wealth. Since attainments in other endeavors gained for their possessors less esteem, most aspiring young men counted upon gaining leadership in a commercial field.[1]

Edmond Stephen Meany (1862-1935) was one of those young men: bright, eager, and competitive. He began a business career in Seattle seeking profits briefly in the retail garden plant and flower market, with his business dying quickly. Then, having served an apprenticeship in reporting for local newspapers, he began publishing a newspaper and magazine in partnership with other young men as impecunious as himself. Again he failed. He also speculated in real estate, an avenue to riches for many of Seattle's leaders whom he admired but could not emulate.

In 1890 Meany became involved in press agentry, promoting local fairs and Washington's participation in the Chicago World's Fair of 1893. At the same time he served two terms in the lower house of Washington's legislature, becoming a leading member of the Republican-dominated King County (i.e. Seattle) delegation and a prime mover in the development of the fledgling University of Washington. His success in this matter put him in position for a role as a mentor to those individuals planning Seattle's Alaska-Yukon-Pacific Exposition of 1909.

While serving in the 1893 session of the legislature Meany drew the attention of Will L. Visscher, a Tacoma journalist, who wrote that Meany as a youth had been forced to shoulder the full responsibility for his family.

The "simple story of his struggle for education," wrote Visscher, "is one of the highest encomiums that may be uttered in praise of American institutions, and at the same time stamps him as an exemplar of the doctrine of the survival of the fittest." Visscher also found that Meany possessed a sterling integrity and zeal, employed above all else in seeking the welfare of his city and state. Visscher concluded his praise by stating that Meany ranked among the "foremost in the councils of his party [Republican]...and merits the confidence and esteem of the most prominent men of our new state."[2]

Meany possessed the moral character, ability, and dedication needed to become a leading recorder and historian of the growth and progress of Washington institutions and society. He began early in life to preach pioneer values and to "rejoice" (his own word) in the evidences that pioneer achievements remained useful and honored in his own day. In Meany's later years he commemorated patriotic events and heroism through civic exercises and symbolic acts which drew in not only Seattle's business leaders and populace but also those of the international community.

In between, in the years of his prime, Meany taught and wrote history at the University of Washington, providing the first scholarly work on Washington's past. That volume served students and the public for a half century before being superseded. More important for future scholarship, Meany edited and published the *Washington Historical Quarterly* from 1906 to 1935, providing a forum for regional historians through which they might circulate new ideas, themes, and topics needed to revise the Washington story. Under Meany's direction, the *Quarterly* also became the journal containing what historian Robert E. Burke has called the "systematic publication of an amazing variety of sources of Pacific Northwest history." It was clear to Meany that pioneer history was an essential aspect of the evolving story of the state and its people and that the task of collecting and publishing documentation—which he did avidly—was worthy of a historian's best efforts.[3]

CHAPTER ONE

A Pioneer Youth in Michigan and Washington (1862-1885)

EDMOND STEPHEN MEANY was born on December 28, 1862, in East Saginaw, Michigan, the son of an immigrant Irish seaman and his American wife of Scottish ancestry. Family tradition holds that shortly before the birth his father—Captain Stephen Meany—"stamped" into his living room on a snowy day to announce tearfully to his wife that Edmond, his brother, had been killed and robbed on his way out of the Idaho gold mines the winter before. They gave their child the name of the murdered uncle.[1]

When the child grew to manhood he professed to have little knowledge of his father's family, and none of his maternal ancestors. The information that remains points to a history somewhat different from the experience of the hordes of Irish peasants who had been forced off the land by the potato famines of the 1840s. Stephen Meany, Edmond's father, had been born in 1833 in Fermoy, County Cork, Ireland. His parents possessed a comfortable home with a "stone house and barn" and "grounds terraced to the banks of [a] creek." James, Stephen's father, had established an academy and for years had served as its principal.

In the end, the Meanys did not prosper in Ireland and James' family fled to America. Of their eleven children, one had been lost at sea, and four had died in infancy. The remaining six migrated to America. For reasons listed only as "politics" principal James Meany lost his academy and home in the 1850s and he, too, migrated to America to live with his son John in Pennsylvania. In 1865 he visited Stephen, then living in East Saginaw, and in the family tradition was remembered as a "cultured Irish gentleman of great dignity and refined taste."[2]

Years earlier, the thirteen year old Stephen attended school in his father's academy but longed to go to sea. His father acceded to his wishes—as he apparently did in the case of another son, James, who later drowned off Australia—placing Stephen as an apprentice under an old friend.[3]

The succession of events is unclear but Stephen experienced two shipwrecks, one off the southern coast of Africa where, according to family tradition, he was nearly eaten by survivors. The second came off Borneo while on a whaling expedition. Service in 1854-1855 as a petty officer, "Captain of the Main Top," aboard H.M.S. *Majestic* in the British navy's Baltic Campaign during the Crimean War probably was the high point of his naval career.[4]

Only three years after the Baltic Campaign concluded, Stephen Meany migrated to the United States, settling in the central Michigan lumbering country of the Saginaw Valley. There Alexander English hired Stephen to captain his river and Great Lakes vessels, sailing to ports such as Chicago and Buffalo. It was a golden age for river and lake transport in Michigan, where at first no railroads competed for the shipment of lumber from that forest-rich frontier. By 1858 or 1859, English had formed a close business and personal association with Meany. Putting down roots, Captain Meany applied for citizenship (obtained in 1867) and on May 27, 1861, married Margaret Ann, the daughter of English. Some nineteen months later, their first child Edmond Stephen was born.[5]

Stephen's steady employment was accompanied by other marks of respectability. He joined the Independent Order of Odd Fellows in 1865, and received the adulation of three river communities (and a watch and chain) in 1866 when he displayed "courage and generous self-forgetfulness" in rescuing three people from drowning. He also acquired a house and lot in East Saginaw which he had difficulty selling when he once again pulled up stakes and headed for the West Coast.[6]

The booming lumber industry of the Saginaw Valley apparently failed to bring prosperity to Captain Meany, for he took his family on the Union Pacific Railway to San Francisco in the spring of 1870. Although the Meanys stayed in California for more than a year there is virtually no information available concerning their activities. Later, Chicago served as their home while the captain presumably worked in Great Lakes shipping.[7]

By 1873, the family was back in the Saginaw Valley, at Bay City, Stephen then commanding his father-in-law's steamer *Wright.* Subsequently, the captain worked in Muskegon, Michigan, and once more moved to Chicago. Finally, he journeyed out to San Francisco again in 1875. Whether the family accompanied the captain on all his changes of place and jobs is not known, but young Edmond spent some time in Iowa and Illinois during those years.[8]

When the captain once again traveled to San Francisco in 1875 he may have journeyed alone but it is clear that the family was with him within a year and that Benedict and Smith, merchant tailors of that city, employed son Edmond, presumably after school and on Saturdays, for almost a year, finding him "industrious, apt, and strictly honest." Captain Meany's fortunes did not improve; at least one venture failed when he staked a claim to a mine in Winnemucca, Nevada, which yielded no return.[9]

Captain Meany's final change of location took him to Seattle, Washington Territory, where, on February 19, 1877, he signed the register at the American House, advertised as the "first housing above the Steamboat Landing," at the head of Yesler's Wharf. The Seattle he saw as he stood on the shore of Elliott Bay was a small clearing with about 3,000 inhabitants, nestled at the base of heavily timbered hills which sloped steeply to a first-rate harbor.

Part of a new and largely untouched frontier, Seattle must have seemed promising to a man of the captain's talents and experience. The town's livelihood consisted largely in supplying California with lumber and coal, shipped by means of coast-wise vessels. In addition, Seattle dominated the water transport network of Puget Sound, the unchallenged means of local transportation. Indeed, Captain Meany lost little time in qualifying for a master's license to operate "upon the waters of Puget Sound and its tributaries and all waters between Olympia and the sea."[10]

He was a tug-boat operator when he went down to the pier not quite five months later, on July 10 or 11, 1877, to welcome Margaret, his wife, and their two children. Edmond was fourteen and Mary Mildred thirteen as they arrived from San Francisco on the S.S. *Dakota*. The captain took his family to a "comfortable" house that he had rented on Third Avenue, between Pike and Pine streets. Though only three blocks above the waterfront, Third Avenue was a part of the residential area of the small port. In later life, Edmond recalled that his first Seattle home had had a few attractions, one being a well in the front yard from which he hauled water in a bucket.[11]

Seattle, of course, was still crude in appearance, a frontier town in the scale of its amenities. Recently stripped of its forest cover, it yet showed stumps on its outskirts. The streets for the most part remained badly graded earthen routes which ran off as trails into the woods. Such sidewalks as existed were planked. Most residences were simple and unadorned but many had ample, fenced yards containing fruit trees, if also "outside plumbing." Class distinctions were minimal, as evidenced by the situation of Arthur A. Denny, Seattle's founding father, who lived within a few blocks of the Meanys. That austere, aging pioneer entrepreneur kept a cow, chickens, and a barn at his home long after signs of urbanism rose all around him.[12]

Within a few months, the Meanys moved to the edge of town, a half dozen blocks east at Eighth Avenue and Union Street, where a large barn was a special attraction. Purchasing four cows on credit, Edmond became a herdsman and milk distributor, serving customers along a regular route. Pasturing was easy as he simply turned the cows loose in nearby fields and woods, but the roundup each evening proved tiresome as the cattle roamed considerable distances. Edmond cultivated a garden too, picked cherries from trees in the front yard, and cut stove wood from adjacent stands of trees. Seattle, in those years, offered him a life typical for a boy in small-town America of the nineteenth century.[13]

In September of that first year in Seattle, Edmond's parents had a serious decision to make regarding formal schooling. Edmond was almost fifteen, a time for decision in that day. Should he go to work, become an apprentice, seek training for business, or prepare for college? Seattle—indeed, the Territory of Washington—offered no fully developed public high school instruction. The best hope would be to find ambitious teachers or a set of school board directors who might tack high school courses onto the eighth grade curriculum.

The first decision was that Edmond would attend the nearby Central School, which had two teachers. The choice seemed promising since Major E. Ingraham, the twenty-five year old principal, graduate of a Maine normal school, was an enlightened and vigorous teacher who became a fast friend of Edmond. Unfortunately, the school was overcrowded, uncomfortable, and lacked equipment or facilities for high school studies. Morale undoubtedly was low, for school funds ran out after only two months of operation and classes remained open only because the teachers agreed to wait until January for their pay.

Edmond's attention soon shifted to the University of Washington Territory, located a few blocks to the north on a prominent knoll. Housed in a rustic version of a Greek temple, the institution had a shaky history, but now seemed more stable with the installation of Alexander J. Anderson, a capable leader. Edmond excitedly asked his father for permission to enroll. The latter was "thoughtful," according to Edmond's later recollection, for the tuition charges seemed high to one with a tug-boat captain's wages. Nevertheless, they worked the matter out, with Edmond entering the preparatory department of the university, undoubtedly understanding that he would have to work his way through.[14]

His feet were now set on the path that he would never really leave. For the remainder of his life Edmond would be associated closely with the University of Washington. The enthusiasm of this red-headed, blue-eyed, skinny youth—who would be more than six feet tall when he graduated—grew quickly into a love for and faith in the institution which at that time ill repaid him because of its poverty and lack of resources. Poorly supported by the legislature and the public, it had never enjoyed outstanding teachers nor had it taught more than a handful of college students. Only one student had earned a collegiate degree before Meany enrolled and the great majority had studied in the primary and secondary departments.[15]

In the winter and spring of 1878, Edmond was one of 126 students enrolled, most of whom, as usual, pursued sub-collegiate studies. Meany's academic record for those terms is not extant, but it is clear from the *Annual Announcement* of June 1878, that he studied such fundamentals as reading, geography, arithmetic—possibly elementary algebra—United States history, and perhaps began the study of Latin.[16]

He continued preparatory studies during 1878-1879, but probably enrolled in some collegiate courses as well, a privilege accorded about forty prep students. His parents' hearts must have been warmed by his academic performance, for he scored an average grade of 94 percent in all subjects. In the closing exercises for the year, on June 13, 1879, in mixed preparatory and college student competition, he debated the question, "Resolved, that the purchase of Alaska was a good investment for the United States," arguing for the losing team, which had taken the negative position.

Already, at this early date, Edmond Meany had formed numerous associations which were to mark his adult life. On the same platform with him at the academic exercises was J.E. Chilberg, later a prominent banker, who along with Meany promoted Seattle's Alaska-Yukon-Pacific Exposition of 1909. Other classmates and close friends included J.B. Denny and C.C. Denny, sons of Arthur A. Denny, Seattle's founder. Present, in addition, was Elizabeth ("Lizzie") Ward, also a member of a prominent pioneer family, whom he would marry after they graduated from college.[17]

The Sunday School of the "Brown Church," the Methodist Protestant congregation, was also a source of fruitful associations. Clarence B.

Bagley, in his *History of Seattle*, claimed that by 1880 this Sunday School "had become the largest in the territory with 171 officers, teachers, and pupils." At least as early as April 1878, "Eddie" Meany and "Lizzie" Ward were classmates, along with Clarence Ward, later Meany's short-term business partner. Dillis B. Ward, father of "Lizzie" and Clarence, was the assistant superintendent, and a strong advocate of temperance and strict morality.

Dexter B. Horton, Seattle's first prominent banker and Meany's benefactor on at least one occasion when he was in need of school funds, was the superintendent. "Eddie" remained a regular participant in the Sunday School throughout his college days. The Reverend Daniel Bagley, a vigorous and influential pioneer, who had organized the church and was still its leader, held Meany's affection but when the latter recalled their relationship in later years he made no reference to religion, discussing instead their mutual concern for "the upbuilding and strengthening of the University of Washington."[18]

Edmond continued preparatory studies in the fall of 1870 and in the public exercises at the end of winter term, March 19, 1880, with 200 guests present, he debated the question, "Resolved, that Napoleon was a greater general than Julius Caesar." The reporter for the *Seattle Daily-Intelligencer* complimented the four debaters for their knowledge of history, which probably gave Edmond small comfort as he again was on the losing side.[19]

Nevertheless, the Gnothautii Literary Society, sponsor of the debate, made Meany its president that term and a further mark of esteem and achievement came with his election as secretary of the Young Naturalists' Society, which was devoted to the study of natural history. These organizations had the sanction of the faculty for introducing studies that went beyond the formal curriculum. Although Meany's grades at the year's end were less satisfactory than for the previous year, dropping from 94 percent to 89 percent, they still placed him in the upper third of the students. In addition, he profited substantially from the extracurricular forays into literature, history, and natural science.[20]

Tragedy visited Edmond's family during the spring of 1880, however, striking at its stability and fortune. Gold discoveries at Ruby Creek, high in the Cascades' watershed of the Skagit River, had drawn Captain Meany and more than a thousand men to the diggings, approximately 100 miles north of Seattle. If the captain found any gold, he lost it along with his life on the return trip. On April 26, 1880, he joined nine other miners and two crewmen for the trip down the Skagit in a large, badly over-crowded canoe. Almost immediately after the launching, the craft overturned in turbulent waters, drowning the forty-seven year old Stephen Meany and five other men. Meany's body was never found in spite of diligent searches. The *Daily Intelligencer* for April 29, 1880, concluded its report on the accident with these words which barely suggested the extent of the tragedy for the family: "Captain Stephen Meany, an old steamboat man of this city...leaves a wife and family to mourn his untimely death."[21]

The seventeen-year-old Edmond now took charge of a virtually destitute household, which included Mary Mildred, his sister, and his mother, both of whom were frequently invalided the remainder of their lives, and an infant brother named Jay. When relatives in California offered assistance, Edmond abandoned his studies and, on October 7, 1880, boarded the S.S. *Dakota* with the family, bound for San Francisco. They settled on an uncle's ranch near Los Gatos, a small town about sixty miles south of San Francisco. Some relatives may have resided in nearby San Jose, as Edmond received some mail there. Lonely and frequently homesick, Edmond worked at humble ranch chores, though he seized some opportunities to hunt in the hills above Los Gatos and learned to dance.[22]

After a year in California, the family returned to Seattle. Edmond found work to sustain the family and to continue his studies. The mercantile firm of Densmore and Johnson hired him to keep its books and for good measure he became janitor for two churches—the Plymouth Congregational and the Trinity Episcopal. On Sunday mornings he just had time to light the fire in the furnace at Plymouth before rushing seven blocks to ring Trinity's bell. He soon gave up the Plymouth job in favor of sweeping out Dexter Horton's bank mornings and evenings and on Saturdays. Some time later he lost the bank task to relatives of Horton. It was a worrisome time for Meany as tuition fees were due, but his concern vanished when an anonymous benefactor made the payment. Years later he learned that Horton had befriended him in this matter.[23]

Little is known of Meany's educational experiences during the 1881-1882 school year, his academic record having been lost. Nor can it be assumed that he followed the formal course requirements listed for the Bachelor of Science degree, his announced preference. He regularly participated in the activities of the Young Naturalists' Society, reading an elementary paper on "The Bear" to the membership on January 20, 1882, and later debating the characteristics of the *crustacea*, as well as serving as vice-president.[24]

For his second collegiate year, 1882-1883, the catalog listed Ed S. Meany as a freshman in the classical curriculum. He studied Cicero, took lessons in Greek, and pursued geometry, rhetoric, and botany. Meany's interests continued to broaden during the 1883-1884 school year in which he studied the classical historians Herodotus, Thucydides, and Livy and read general history for half a year. He also tackled analytical geometry, zoology, and spelling, the latter once again revealing that the presence of preparatory students diluted the quality of the collegiate program.[25]

Nevertheless, the appointment of Leonard J. Powell as president in July 1882, raised the intellectual horizons of the school and infused the classes with a new spirit of learning. Powell, who had been superintendent of public schools in Oregon and before that professor of science and mathematics at Willamette University, praised the classics as "the standard by which one should measure an education." That philosophical standard may explain in part Meany's choice of courses. His attraction, too, to Miss Mattie L. Hansee, his Latin teacher, also played a role in his interest in classics.

At the same time that Powell praised the classics, he strengthened the scientific curriculum, recognizing its increased popularity among the students and its usefulness to society. New courses were added and Powell's appointment of O.B. Johnson as science professor provided Meany with his greatest inspiration and role model. A lawyer, Johnson had trained himself in natural science. He had taught at Pacific University in Oregon and when attracted to the University of Washington, brought with him the finest natural history collection in the region, containing some 20,000 specimens.[26]

Meany decided in his senior year, 1884-1885, to complete the work for the Bachelor of Science degree, enrolling in classes in astronomy, geology, chemistry, mechanics, logic, and moral science. Professor Johnson kindled Meany's lifelong enthusiasm for nature and for frequent field trips around Puget Sound to collect flora and fauna. As an adjunct to his teaching, Professor Johnson provided strong guidance to the Young Naturalists' Society, assisting the members in organizing sections on botany, conchology, entomology, ichthyology, mineralogy, ornithology, and paleontology. Though the Young Naturalists' Society was small its value for education was considerable. The members fell to their work enthusiastically, collecting, classifying, and mounting specimens as well as organizing a course of lectures which, if all proposed were actually given, certainly represented "the strenuous life."

The artificial barriers and formal activities of the regular curriculum were not found in the Society, as the members framed their course of study and designated Meany, the curator of the botany collection, to confer with Professor Johnson about it. In addition to conducting field trips the Society slowly developed a museum. The Young Naturalists reached an important milestone in September 1883, when they furnished a collection of mounted birds and animals and a case of Indian arrowheads and implements for an exhibit held at Yesler's Hall celebrating the completion of the Northern Pacific Railway.[27]

In later years, history was Meany's great passion—the collecting of documents, teaching, writing, and publication of historical materials—but he must have found the college's offerings rather thin fare, even when the classics courses were included. Teaching was by means of recitation, even though the 1888 catalog claimed that "History is taught by outlines. The best texts are consulted and quoted" and "discussions are held upon causes of events, laws, locations, climate, [and] famous men, which make or destroy nations." The suspicion remains that there was little joy in such recitations, especially when compared with a field trip to a beach or island in the Sound. The meager resources of the University's library prevented serious research and hindered critical reading and writing. No member of the faculty, furthermore, specialized in teaching history. It was, of course, probable that Meany drew considerable interest and knowledge from debates and oratorical contests since their subjects often were historical or political.[28]

The course on moral science may best illustrate the character of Meany's formal education. Widely taught to seniors in the typical nineteenth century college, classes in moral science generally were conducted by the president, especially if he was a clergyman. Such classes reinforced the Protestant ethic and morality, placing heavy emphasis upon the dictates of conscience while equating revealed religion and natural religion (science) as diverse paths to God's truth. Meany listened to typical moral science lectures delivered by the Reverend J.D. Pierce, a local Baptist minister. Pierce advocated women's suffrage, but on biblical grounds rather than political, and in his ministerial capacity conducted several revival meetings "on the character and mission of Christ, grappling with the skepticism and doubts of the present day." Francis Wayland's *Elements of Moral Science* was required reading. Ten years later Meany recalled he had been less impressed with Wayland's earnest exhortation to accept "revealed religion" than with claims of "natural religion." The latter, Meany wrote, "seemed to me sufficient that all my thought on such subjects since then has been in accord with that plan." Wayland's benign cosmos and salutary laws of nature clearly supported a comfortable world view for Meany and other students in late nineteenth century Seattle.[29]

Meany and fellow students eagerly courted opportunities for leadership, which their extracurricular organizations gratified. Meany became the president of the Young Naturalists' Society in October, 1882, and in the next fall term gained the same position in the Erosophian Literary Society. In October 1883, he helped merge this literary organization with another to form the Philomathean Lyceum and became its first president. Meany thus plunged into the intricacies of parliamentary procedure and campus politics.[30]

Dabbling in campus politics may have caused him briefly to dream of a law career and to dip into *Blackstone's Commentaries on the Laws of England,* the celebrated work on English jurisprudence. That interest proved ephemeral but politics did not, for in the summer of 1884 he joined the Young Men's Independent Political Club, which collaborated with several other so-called "law and order" groups to oppose dishonesty in local government, especially lax enforcement of liquor, vice, and gambling laws in Seattle. The city's voters did not knuckle under to these neophytes, electing instead a businessman's ticket which promised to sustain the traditional "easy virtue" policy, which they believed necessary for prosperity. Meany's interest in this avowedly non-partisan club continued for two years while he served in several of its positions.[31]

Journalism, not politics, was the first career opportunity arising out of Meany's student experiences. The chance to smell printer's ink came when President Powell asked him to write newspaper stories for the *Post-Intelligencer* concerning three special university lecture-demonstrations of electricity and magnetism. These brief but clearly written reports, which appeared March 8, 9, and 10, 1883, evidently impressed owner-editor Thomas J. Prosch so much that he hired Meany in October to substitute for Sam Crawford, his city editor, who had gone to Olympia to fill a patronage post as the clerk for enrolling bills in the Council of the Territorial Legislature. Meany served for at least a week, until Crawford unexpectedly returned early.[32]

After that, Meany became supervisor of carriers and collections for the *Post-Intelligencer* north of Cherry Street, encompassing somewhat more than half of the city's territory, including much of its newer residential area. Edmond received more than a smattering of business experience, for he purchased the papers from the publishing company, hired, trained, and paid carriers (many of whom were university students), and supervised collections of subscription fees.

On March 7, 1884, he extended his supervision of newspaper circulation to the entire city, which then possessed some 7,000 inhabitants. Business took him south of Skid Road, to the restricted districts where saloons, vice, and gambling flourished. His regular trips to that area undoubtedly broadened his education in ways foreign to the university experience. Because his profit margin was small, he also distributed the popular Portland *Oregonian*. Ever alert to journalistic possibilities, he also relayed news items to city editor Crawford, sent dispatches to the *Oregonian*, and for a time also telegraphed news items to the *New York Herald*.[33]

In the midst of final examinations for the autumn term, in the first week of January 1885, Meany kept a diary in which he revealed that a busy newspaper schedule did not seriously interfere with his student life. On Saturday, January 3, he noted that he had had "a busy day with my collections and boys [carriers]. Rained hard all day and collections were light." In the evening, preparing for Sunday church services, he noted that he "was the only male at choir practice."

On Monday, the first day of examinations, he stayed home "writing, reading, studying, and posting my books [on newspaper circulation]. The usual 'office work' was done." On Tuesday he was "successful" in his geology examination and then spent the evening at Judge Greene's home reviewing moral science with daughter Hettie, while her even more attractive sister "Agnes sat at the same table offering suggestions and making the evening pleasant generally."

Unfortunately, on Wednesday Meany also had a test in chemistry for which he had not studied. The results were predictable. He passed moral science with high marks but made a low, though passing, grade in chemistry. "Prof. O.B. Johnson," he granted, "was guilty of marking high in order to pass me and the rest of us seniors. I could not pass on a fair count of my paper."

In any case, in a mood reminiscent of countless generations of students, Meany immediately resolved "to study so hard this coming term as to leave no chance of...failing in any other study." Newspaper work forced him to postpone the good resolution until 6 a.m. the next morning, when he rose early to prepare for a test in mechanics. A few hours later, he emerged from that examination with good results.

That day, however, had just begun. He had a spelling test on Friday to think about, the ever-present newspaper work, and a paper to read at the Young Naturalists' meeting. Finishing those matters, Meany attended a campus "entertainment" and concluded the evening with a "lunch" at which he chatted with Judge William D. Woods. The seeming seriousness of this last activity was marred by some of his peers who spoke boisterously of "Ed Meany" in loud tones.[34]

Commencement that spring loomed large in community affairs as well as for Meany and five other students who received the degree of Bachelor of Science. One additional student earned a Master of Arts degree (awarded to an experienced teacher). In addition, four young women received teaching diplomas. Since only ten collegiate degrees had been awarded in the history of the University, it is not surprising that the Class of 1885 should have been accorded special attention at graduation ceremonies on May 22. The enchanted reporter for the *Post-Intelligencer* described the graduation scene as follows:

> The spacious stage of the Opera House was set to its full depth in a sylvan scene....On the right of the stage sat the grave and reverend Board of regents; on the left the bright young graduates; in the center the faculty and Governor [Watson C.] Squire, while dispersed about were parents and friends of the new alumni....Orchestra, parquette and gallery were filled with the best people of this goodly town, and all things seemed auspicious for a pleasant evening; and the promise was fully kept.

It was Meany's hour of triumph. As valedictorian, he declaimed on "America's Nationality," the reporter noting that Meany

> possesses in a marked degree the making of an orator. Apart from his delivery of his own well rounded sentences, his recital of Webster's celebrated allusion to the English drum beat following the sun in its daily course was illustrated with grace and power of gesture which brought down the house.

Later, Meany had the honor of cutting the class cake and handing it around, amid congratulations and genial conversation. At twenty-two years of age the slender, tall, red-headed, and blue-eyed college graduate stood poised on the threshold of a career. The question was: what career? He had not been trained for a profession, but his education, youthful experiences, and acceptance by the community prepared him to grapple with life enthusiastically and with initiative. Indeed, graduation was not the only event of the commencement season which molded his future. The evening before these ceremonies the two-year-old Alumni Association made him president and orator for the ensuing year. In all this, Meany was not only well prepared to meet the challenges of life but was committed to service to the University as well.[35]

CHAPTER TWO

Searching for a Calling and Starting a Family (1885-1890)

ONE SUMMER DAY, six weeks after graduation, a young lady friend traveling in Australia wrote to Meany in reply to his description of that event: "So you were the Lion on Commencement Day—of course I supposed you would be." She wondered about the aftermath: "Don't you have a dreadfully gone feeling now, as though you had nothing of importance to do—that is unless you are going to start east right away....I wonder if you will go to New Orleans as you said you might."[1]

If Meany had once thought of seeking his fortune in New Orleans, or elsewhere in the "east," the strong tug of circumstance, interest, and association kept him in Seattle. Instead of fleeing to a metropolis, he stayed at home to try to win success in journalism and business. He also indulged in artistic activities and social club functions which reinforced the beliefs and practices of the governing middle class, which he shared. Equally important for middle class identification, Meany became interested in the "fair sex," which produced some sentimental outpourings and at least one sorrowful experience of rejection. He married, however, before his twenty-seventh birthday and soon founded a family.

Almost immediately upon graduation Meany responded to the challenge thrust upon the community by riots instigated against the Chinese minority in the region and the city. Racial antagonism against the Chinese was compounded when, in a depressed economy, they found work while large numbers of white men were unemployed. The hop fields of Squak Valley, east of Seattle, experienced the first violence on September 7, 1885, when gunfire from angry whites killed and wounded numerous Chinese workers. Violence spread to Tacoma, where on November 3, a mob drove scores of Chinese from the city.[2]

Seattle's blue collar workers, employed as well as unemployed, harbored the same resentments against the several hundred Chinese in their midst. A mass meeting on November 7, sponsored by anti-Chinese forces—including labor union agitators—revealed a growing class consciousness in addition to a strong sinophobia. Sheriff John H. McGraw and other business and political leaders formed a Law and Order League advocating the protection of the Chinese as the threats of violence grew. In addition, the sheriff, urged by Governor Watson C. Squire, helped assemble and equip a troop of Home Guards which served in the city's defense forces along with several other militia units. Together they numbered approximately 425 members.

Edmond Meany joined the Home Guards immediately, taking his place in Captain George Kinnear's company, which had approximately 125 names on the muster roll. Many prominent men signed on with Kinnear's unit, including banker Dexter Horton, railroad promoter Thomas Burke, Judge Orange Jacobs, and the Rev. Clark Davis, of the Brown Church. The opposition between management and labor implicit in the lineup of opposing forces seemingly was obscured in the hour of impending conflict and in contemporary accounts. Certainly, Meany required little reflection concerning the justification for creating special law and order forces before he joined the Home Guards. As an undergraduate he had served in the University Cadets, a group also found in Sheriff McGraw's camp, and he had, since the previous year, supported other law and order political groups in elections.[3]

Agitation erupted into violence on February 7, 1886, when an anti-Chinese mob herded some 350 Chinese—virtually all in town—to the waterfront, preparatory to shipping them to San Francisco. Judge Roger Greene thwarted those plans for the moment, however, by issuing a writ of *Habeas Corpus* to Captain Alexander of the *Queen of the Pacific*, the ship on which they were being loaded. Nevertheless, after their appearance in court, the Chinese were escorted back to the dock and some two hundred boarded the ship, their passage being paid by onlookers, including Law and Order supporters. The mob became even more angry than before as Meany and other Home Guards escorted the remaining Chinese—perhaps one hundred and fifty—back to their quarters to await another ship which would sail in a few days. A scuffle ensued in which gunfire from the Home Guards killed one of the mob. The Home Guards and all other militia were relieved of duty on February 10, being replaced by regular army troops dispatched from the Vancouver Barracks.[4]

Private Meany left no contemporary record of his thoughts regarding the morality of Home Guard actions, but, in 1909, in the first edition of his *History of the State of Washington*, he defended the claim that the hastily organized "citizen soldiers" had been needed. They "had been organized by the responsible citizens to protect life and property and enforce the laws." Their presence had been justified when the mob attacked them while they were protecting the Chinese. "Captain George Kinnear, a veteran of the Union army, was not to be trifled with," wrote Meany. "His order to fire was promptly obeyed." After one man fell, mortally wounded, "the mob dispersed" and "law was supreme in Seattle."[5]

Meany remained in the militia when, on March 9, 1886, the Home Guards became Company E of a battalion and later the First Regiment of the National Guard of Washington. Subsequently, although he paid little heed to the social activities and often missed drill, Meany earned corporal's stripes and served on active duty during Seattle's great fire of June 6, 1889. The flames leveled most of the commercial and industrial sections of the city while missing the better residential areas. Corporal Meany and his cohorts of Company E guarded the city's prisoners, removing them from the jail when fire threatened it. He also took his turn at preventing looting in the burned area.

Duty was boring most of the time during the two weeks of service, relieved occasionally by the camaraderie evident when his captain, E.H. Carr, loaned his long overcoat to the "shivering" corporal while the latter did sentry duty. Meany recalled one tense moment which relieved the tedium. He raised his gun one night to fire at an indistinct object in the murky waters of Elliott Bay, only to discover that it was a stump, not a potential looter or escaped prisoner.

In retrospect, in 1909, Meany exuded the optimistic attitude of pioneers toward fires in their crowded, inflammable cities. He reported later in his *History of the State of Washington* that there had been great fires in Spokane and Ellensburg in 1889, as well as in Seattle. He concluded the description of the fires by quoting Governor Miles C. Moore, the territorial chief executive, whose 1889 report to the secretary of state affirmed that "these calamities, seriously felt as they are, in no degree threaten the prosperity of the new state.... Not a word of discouragement is heard, but everywhere there is evidence of renewed energy and ambition."[6]

Meany was ready in the mid 1880s to share in the rewards of energetic and well-directed ambition, but fortune did not turn rapidly in his favor. He continued to supervise *Post-Intelligencer* carriers and collections until January 11, 1887. At that time Leigh S.J. Hunt, who two months before had taken control of the newspaper with an eye to transforming it into a metropolitan daily, brought Meany into the editorial room as night editor. The title was a bit pretentious, however, for Meany could hardly specialize in one task. He edited the national and international news, read proof, clipped other papers for additional news items, and helped load early editions on Puget Sound boats in the small hours of the morning.

Meany wrote news items and editorials as a matter of course, but also initiated a want ad department and pleased Hunt when he started printing local commercial news. When he sought to include lumber mill statistics for the Puget Sound area, however, he met with obstruction and learned something of the jealousies and suspicions of business competitors. The mill reports ended abruptly when one manager refused further information on the grounds that data supplied by other companies was "anything but true and given out evidently in a Spirit of Braggadocio."

Not daunted by such rebuffs, Meany soon sought an opportunity to publish his own newspaper. He was getting anxious, in addition, to move to another situation because he was carrying "too heavy a load" with the *Post-Intelligencer*. So firmly planted in his memory was that conviction that years later he asserted without a trace of self-consciousness that the owner had had to hire five men to replace him.[7]

Finally, in August 1888, he joined Alexander Begg and David B. Murray to publish the Seattle *Trade Journal* as a daily and weekly newspaper. Meany and Begg handled publication while Murray supervised business affairs. For some weeks the *Trade Journal* remained exclusively a commercial paper, devoted to market reports, stock quotations, real estate transactions, banking and shipping items, and the like. Gradually, however, the editors began to publish general news, local and national, and to promote Seattle in ways other than commercial, such as campaigning to obtain a United States naval station on Lake Washington.

Meany and Begg also published the *Puget Sound Magazine*, intended as a literary periodical. Actually, Begg had launched this publication earlier as the *Puget Sound Gazetteer*, but the new name appeared before Meany joined as co-editor with the second number of volume two, published in August 1888. They edited at least three more numbers of this slim publication before it died for lack of literature to publish and probably too few subscribers. Even a cash prize competition to ferret out local Indian legends proved disappointing.[8]

Meany and Begg had no better luck with their newspaper. Meany, in fact, dropped out of the partnership sometime before March 27, 1889, when Begg sold the paper to the Journal Publishing Company. In a hastily-written note he optimistically informed Meany that he would liquidate his debts on the coming Saturday. When that happened, he would be "like yourself out in the bitter cold. But I'll warm up again as I know you will." Unfortunately his forecast was inaccurate. Dexter Horton's bank had claims against the partners which were not paid until Christmas of 1891, and Begg, in addition, owed money to L.H. Griffith, probably rent, for which he asked Meany's help in getting a postponement of the due date.[9]

On April 6, 1889, Begg announced plans to start a new magazine and newspaper but Meany decided to explore another type of enterprise. He joined with Clarence C. Ward, who would soon be his brother-in-law, to establish the firm of "Meany and Ward: Growers and Dealers in Seeds, Bulbs, Plants, Trees, and Shrubs." They operated from a greenhouse at the northern edge of town, where Mercer Street would later be developed. Meany and Ward conducted their business at least until January 1891, and perhaps longer since it is clear that they were being billed for operating expenses as late as November 28 of that year. Meany, however, had ceased activity in the firm, probably in the early months of its operation when he became a politician and once again practiced journalism.[10]

In August 1889, if not earlier, Meany became treasurer of the *Seattle Press*. He was attracted by the enterprise of new owners Leigh S.J. Hunt and William E. Bailey, who sold their first issue on August 1 for two cents a copy and paid out change from stacks of bright new pennies. The two-cent editions did not last long, but the *Press* offered Meany new experiences and expanded opportunities. Hardly confined to keeping the company's books, Meany avidly collected and published banking and clearing house statistics and helped put the editions on the street.[11]

No later than the fifth day of publication, the circulation manager failed to deliver the stack of papers for Snohomish to the depot in time for the departing train. As Meany recalled many years later, publisher William E. Bailey chartered a train of the Seattle, Lake Shore, and Eastern Railroad to haul the papers to the small town twenty-five miles north of Seattle. Meany and a boy loaded the papers on the train and climbed aboard. They found excitement when the train encountered a forest fire while steaming through Lake Forest Park in northern King County. "The engineer put on steam," Meany reported. "They pulled thru [*sic*], clinging to the swaying seats, watching trees fall with thunderous roars as the train flashed by." When Meany dropped off the train with the papers and a supply of new copper pennies for making change, "Clayton Packard, publisher of the Snohomish *Eye* exclaimed, 'that's what I call enterprise with a big E.'"[12]

The *Press* managers' streak of romanticism loomed larger than their sense of practical enterprise when, in 1889, they sponsored an expedition to explore the Olympic Mountains. Not yet penetrated by white men, the massive bulk of the Olympics intrigued Washingtonians as enticing, beautiful, and mysterious. Popular interest had been heightened in 1888 when Territorial Governor Eugene Semple wrote a "poetic and striking description" of the mountains in a report to the United States Secretary of the Interior. The *Seattle Press* reprinted the account, which included Indian legends depicting a supposed idyllic and luxuriant valley in the interior of the mountains. The *Press* continued to excite the public and its own managers, publishing an interview in which the State of Washington's first governor, Elisha P. Ferry, on October 23, 1889, called for an exploration of the Olympics and repeated some of the Indian legends.[13]

The *Press* soon was flooded with inquiries from newspapers all over the nation. Treasurer Meany plunged into a new promotion when he read a letter from James H. Christie, a self-proclaimed explorer of the arctic regions of northwest Canada. Christie proposed that the *Press* underwrite an expedition which he would lead into the mysterious Olympics. Favorably impressed, Meany introduced him to William E. Bailey, who quickly agreed to sponsor Christie's exploration. Meany then offered his greenhouse—conveniently empty at that time—for use as Christie's headquarters. The latter accepted with alacrity and, anxious to beat rivals into the Olympics, moved into the greenhouse with five companions (later reduced to four), and in a few days assembled and packed his equipment. On December 7, 1889, Christie received final instructions and the party was on its way to the Strait of Juan de Fuca and the Olympic Peninsula.[14]

Christie's romantic spirit dominated the exploration, a matter signified by the fifty pounds of "colored fire" carried for signaling Seattle from Mount Constance, which supposedly was visible from the city. Meany joined the fun, sitting up two nights in the cupola of the University building armed with Arthur A. Denny's telescope, waiting in vain for a glimpse of the flare. Unfortunately, the party lost the "colored fire" along the way and, in addition, the explorers did not make it to the top of Mount Constance.[15]

Meany visited the party in the first stage of the trek, while the members were struggling up the Elwha River, south of Port Angeles. He did some fishing, which he enjoyed, but concluded upon close observation that Christie's party was ill-prepared for the tasks ahead, which made a somber report for his superiors back in Seattle. The *Press* staff could only wait anxiously for spring and for the party to emerge from the mountains. A telegram that broke the silence on May 21, 1890, brought great relief. Christie's party was in Aberdeen and had wired for expense money for the return trip to Seattle.[16]

His party had discovered a route through the mountains running from north to south (a main trail for backpackers today). The party returned to Seattle with photographs, maps, and reports which revealed that the legends of a "promised land" were unfounded. Furthermore, it was the first group to learn that the Olympics were not simply a ridge or range in the ordinary sense, but rather a cluster of spurs and snowy peaks scattered in all directions. On the other hand, Christie insisted, quite incorrectly, that geysers existed in the mountains.[17]

Christie named many mountain peaks and other geographical features after Seattleites, newspaper publishers and editors, his sponsors, and Meany. Three-fourths of the names attached to peaks have vanished, but that of Mount Meany remains. The *Press* treasurer's personal rewards were eminently satisfying. As Floyd Fessler reported regarding Meany in the *Seattle Star* on February 8, 1930: "tall, slender, and red-headed, he was honored by the explorers when, as they gravely told him later, they found a tall, skinny mountain peak, with red rocks on top" and named it after him. Mount Meany, as Edmond discovered years later when he climbed it, did not have the colored rocks, but measured up to Christie's description in other respects. It proved to be 6,790 feet high, being several hundred feet taller than nearby Mount Seattle and Mount Queets. The three peaks form the watershed for the Queets, Quinalt, and Elwha rivers.[18]

Other newspapers in Seattle and Tacoma exhibited little interest in the expedition or its results, regarding Christie's work simply as a means of promoting the *Press*. By the time Christie returned to Seattle, numerous other explorations were being prepared which also diminished interest in the *Press* party. Nevertheless, in mid-June 1890, Meany rode the railroad to San Francisco to have zincograph engravings made of maps and illustrations for a special edition devoted to the expedition. When published on July 16, 1890, Meany mailed copies to a host of newspaper editors, which resulted in numerous requests for free use of the engravings and reports. After a brief period of interest, the *Press* party's exploits disappeared from public consciousness.[19]

Meany's fishing in the Elwha suggests that the necessity of making a living did not prevent him from pursuing avocations begun as a student or from seeking new leisure time activities. Indeed, he had obtained a racing shell in 1885 and had become something of a sportsman, a new role in life. He confided in his diary on September 21, 1885, that "I went rowing in my newly acquired shell this evening and enjoyed myself very much."

He greatly prized his sleek craft, which not only gave him exercise but also opened a new perspective on the city and the surrounding area. In his diary entry for September 21, Meany stated that "the scenery never appeared more beautiful." After describing the Olympic Range and the broad expanse of green water, he noted that "at unequal distances from my shell and the Kitsap shore moved the quaint though graceful Indian canoes on their way from the hop fields of the White River Valley."

One September day three years later he felt a thrill of sports competition—perhaps for the first time—when he encountered a boat load of Indian hop pickers and challenged them to a race. As Floyd Fessler reported the matter later,

> Soon all were paddling [several Indians in a canoe], but the skinny young white man drew closer and closer. Faster and faster the Indians' paddles flew. The tiny racing shell still gained. Then, as he drew alongside, Meany "put on steam" and shot past, ignoring the waves that were breaking over his rail.

In retrospect, Meany "smiled" and stated that he had "felt like another [Ned] Hanlan," a Canadian generally accepted as the greatest single sculls racer of that day.[20]

As beguiling as an athletic victory might be, rowing did not replace nature studies as a serious recreational interest. Only two months after college graduation in 1885, he attended the Chautauqua summer assembly on Vashon Island, in Puget Sound, where he, according to one reporter, "gave a practical talk on botany, urging greater attention to the science which scatters myriad forms in our pathway." Within a few months he sought assistance in developing an herbarium and in collecting plants, seeds, trees, and economic minerals for the Young Naturalists' Society.[21]

He again spoke at Chautauqua's "Science Day," July 29, 1886, reporting on "The Trees of Puget Sound." He imparted information on the economic aspects of local forest industries but candidly acknowledged that he had not yet learned to identify some species of pines and willows. The following July he went to Chautauqua fully armed with a "well prepared paper" on botany, which an appreciative reporter mentioned as giving clear distinctions between the "three kingdoms of nature" and outlining the principles of plant classification.[22]

Such summer exercises before uncritical Chautauqua audiences might simply have inflated Meany's ego while leaving him no wiser than before except for one person: professor O.B. Johnson. The latter still directed activities of the Young Naturalists, participated with them in Chautauqua meetings, and joined their field trips. He and Meany spent a week in the summer of 1888, for example, dredging for "unique specimens" of submarine botanical and animal species along the beaches of Vashon Island, a task worthy of serious students.[23]

Not content with nature studies alone, Meany joined the new Seattle Art Association shortly after its organization in late April 1885. Its members sought to improve their knowledge of arts and artists, staging exhibits, entertaining visiting artists, and sketching. Meany helped plan programs and held positions in the organization for a time.[24]

Meany possessed a fine bass voice, which led him to perform on various occasions. One such moment came on November 25, 1885, when he sang a solo at a literary and musical program of the Avon Club. Shortly after, he acted in the Club's production of Shakespeare's *Cymbeline.* He also made inquiries about the study of *Faust* in English translation. His inquiry into Goethe's work was bound up with a deeper attraction. He wanted to read *Faust* in the company of a young lady.[25]

Interest in the opposite sex had begun much earlier. An anecdote he told, later related by his son, described young Ed joining with other boys in serenading young ladies, a pleasure he fitted in with milk deliveries one evening. According to the story:

> There was a place in the wooden sidewalk...where it was high enough to hide the empty milk cans underneath. Then he could join the singers and make the rounds. They would see upstairs lights go out, and the curtains part a crack so the fair eyes could peer down on the nocturnal warblers.

Probably as a junior, Meany fell in love with Martha (Mattie) L. Hansee, his Latin instructor. Only three-and-a-half years older than he, Mattie apparently returned his tender feelings and they became engaged. For some undisclosed reason, however, she returned to her family's home in Ellenville, New York, at the end of the summer of 1884. Meany was not daunted, for he did not expect her absence to be permanent and they had not broken their engagement. But, she did not return. The glories of his senior year were mingled with melancholy moments because of her absence. He greatly enjoyed the New Year's holiday season following her departure, for example, but paused in the midst of a round of courtesy calls to confess to Mrs. O.B. Johnson that he missed his "Hansee," feeling "a deep longing and a craving for a look or at least a word about the Queen of my affections who has my heart in her keeping at the other extreme end of our Union."[26]

Twice in the first week of January 1885, he wrote letters to Mattie, and after the second he further indulged in youthful romantic daydreams, walking in the woods where they had wandered. Five days later, he attended a party at which two young ladies flirted with him. He resolved, however, to keep them at arm's length because of his "true devotion to my darling Mattie." He confided further in his diary that he hoped that before he should meet these young ladies again that there would be a Mrs. Mattie Meany.

As the months passed, though, his thoughts did not all center on Mattie. He rowed his shell, rode horseback, and sometimes sailed with the Young Naturalists in the *Sappho*, a boat the Society had acquired. He liked to sing the latest songs, to play croquet, and to attend the theater. In a rather self-conscious way he read Victor Hugo's *Les Miserables* by himself, apparently after trying, without success, to interest a lady friend to join him.[27]

He turned eagerly toward Agnes M. Greene of Olympia, a classmate earlier and one of his "dearest friends," when she wrote in June 1886, urging him to vote the straight Prohibitionist ticket in a local election. Responding after the event, he assured her that he had been repelled by the party's rigid dogmatism and only her postal card had persuaded him to vote for Prohibitionist candidates. He asked her to wear his pin, but she firmly refused his advances.[28]

The hopeful young man even persuaded a postal clerk to let him search through the Olympia mail, looking for a letter from Agnes. Finding none, he went home, took out a box of school day programs and mementos of youthful triumphs they had shared, and poured out his thoughts in a letter to her:

> Program of the "Prize Contest." I remember that night, our position, our voting,—all. Well why should I not remember? Are such things ever forgotten?...What a quantity this box contains! How fruitful of

> thought is it! How sacred the memories it suggests! Were this house to burn, this box would be saved, if possible, even at the sacrifice of articles of more intrinsic value.[29]

Later, when Agnes thanked Edmond for sending some newspapers to her "and Roger" his emotions threatened to transform his feelings into a cloying, overbearing friendship, when he wrote:

> Did I ever tell you of the pleasure that the running of such errands gives me, when done for friends who are away? . . . I expect that I am just a trifle different from other people in that respect, but I deem him under obligations who is made to feel the confidence that his friends impose upon him.

Corresponding ceased, however, when on May 21, 1888, Agnes informed him in a stiff note that he should not write again.[30]

In the meantime, Meany's long-distance courtship with Mattie Hansee slowly ground to a halt. They had not been together since September 1884, when, almost three years later, they agreed to break off the engagement. Nevertheless, when Meany learned she had joined the faculty of the Women's College in Salem, Oregon, he apparently asked her to reconsider. Replying on September 17, 1888, she declined to change her position, reminding him that "we found once that our decision in the affirmative was a mistake."[31]

Apparently she had a more lively sense of their unsatisfactory relationship than did he. Mattie had remained the teacher, Edmond the pupil. He told her proudly of his strivings and successes and she responded approvingly as a mentor might. In particular, she had commended him for his concentration on business and church work when formerly he had been "so fond of society." She still esteemed his friendship and promised never to forget "the many pleasurable incidents" and "delightful recollections" of the earlier days.[32]

When Mattie wrote a final letter on December 7, 1888, she congratulated Edmond for his recent engagement to Sarah Elizabeth (Lizzie) Ward. No other correspondence sheds light on the betrothal of the two. The Meany and Ward families had been acquainted for many years, of course, and Edmond and Clarence Ward had recently joined as business partners. The young couple married at a family gathering on the evening of May 1, 1889. Both had graduated from the University in 1885, although Lizzie had taken an abbreviated teacher's diploma. Edmond, at twenty-six, was almost two years older than his bride. At six feet, three inches, he also towered above the attractive Lizzie, who was approximately five feet tall. She had just finished four years of teaching at Seattle's Denny School, where she "taught with a degree of genius," according to Joseph Hazard in his *Pioneer Teachers of Washington*.[33]

The young couple immediately set up housekeeping at the old "Mercer homestead" in the undeveloped area near Lake Union, where "Meany and Ward, Florists" already operated its greenhouse. They were fortunate in selecting that remote spot since the great Seattle fire of June 6, 1889, did not reach it. Edmond moved all his personal property from downtown except his beautiful racing shell, which was consumed in the flames that destroyed its dock-side boat house.[34]

Married life began on a shoestring. Edmond had recently lost his financial interest in the *Trade Journal* and the *Puget Sound Magazine* and owed money. He soon paid his debts, but Alexander Begg, his former partner, was slow in liquidating his obligations, providing Meany further anxiety. His most recent venture into the florist business, in addition, showed few signs of success in a small community which already possessed seven other florists.[35]

Lizzie's role in this marriage was succinctly stated by Hazard in his pietistic *Pioneer Teachers of Washington* when he wrote that she "typifies the woman who graced the teaching profession for a few years, and then devoted the rest of her life to her own family." He concluded his characterization with the highest praise he knew: "She was a true daughter of the pioneers."

Lizzie immediately shared the burdens of the extended Meany family that Edmond had labored under since his father's sudden death a decade earlier. She had not merely to control the slim budget, but also had to help care for her mother-in-law, invalided part of the time, and for Mildred (called Birdie), her husband's sister. Mildred suffered from a recurrent, incapacitating illness that necessitated numerous trips to San Francisco for treatment. She had, in fact, married a Californian in the fall of 1887 but he proved to be irresponsible and unable to assist in caring for his wife or in providing a home for her.[36]

Horizons brightened when Meany became treasurer of the *Seattle Press*'s publishing company, and then great joy prevailed when Lizzie gave birth to Elizabeth Lois—called Bessie. First mention of the birth is contained in a note of congratulation dated September 22, 1890. Almost a month later, Dillis B. Ward, the grandfather, wrote delightedly to Edmond, who was in

Spokane Falls on business, that "Lizzie and the baby are getting along nicely. They have been with us for a week or more."[37]

Meany had gone to Spokane Falls representing King County in a public relations capacity at the Northwest Industrial Exposition. For the next three years he would often be away from home, either serving in the state legislature or acting as a press agent and promoter of local and state enterprises. But Edmond was a proud father who loved to play with Bessie when he did get home.

Dillis B. Ward and the closely-knit Ward clan supported Ed and Lizzie warmly. Dillis's status as a pioneer leader was as legitimate as that of Arthur A. Denny and the Rev. Daniel Bagley, both much admired by Meany. Dillis had traveled over pioneer trails to Oregon in 1853 as, indeed, had his wife, though in other company. Both had later moved to Seattle where they met and were married.

Dillis Ward's influence on his son-in-law had begun as a teacher in the Sunday School of the Brown Church. In fact, Meany continued as his pupil and co-worker on Sundays until the year after his college graduation. At that time, Meany succeeded Dexter Horton, the banker, as superintendent. He also joined Ward and Horton on the board of directors of the Seattle Young Men's Christian Association (YMCA) in 1887, and in succeeding years continued in that post.

Of strong Protestant faith, Ward began each year by devoutly inscribing in a private journal, using well-worn biblical phrases and paraphrases, his gratitude for God's grace and evidence of his own good works. His faith had led him to embrace prohibition and to fight for it by joining the Prohibitionist Party. His son-in-law, too, embraced that movement, but resisted pressure to join the Prohibitionists' political party. Although in his later years Ward was best known as a real estate dealer, he had taught school in Seattle for more than two decades and later served on the school board.[38]

These varied activities certainly suggested to Edmond Meany that a busy man of affairs should also answer a Christian calling to public service as well as a call to faith. Ward, too, had earned the affection and respect of the community toward which Meany was striving. Ward was a middle class gentleman who lived by the rules of society and strove mightily to succeed by individual enterprise, but always respected the public's welfare. He remained serenely confident about his way of life, although never affluent. In exemplifying such pioneer and Christian traits Ward provided lessons not to be lost on his sensitive son-in-law.

CHAPTER THREE

Press Agentry and Politics: Meany as Promoter and Legislator (1890-1892)

IN THE FALL AND WINTER of 1890-1891 Meany found events moving rapidly and offering numerous opportunities for press agentry and for public service on a larger scale than he had experienced previously. Seizing these chances gladly, he became first a promoter of Washington's participation in the World's Columbian Exposition, to be held in Chicago in 1893, and then an advocate and creator of a new campus and enlarged mission for the University of Washington. He also loaned his talents and energies to land promotion ventures in Douglas County and on Orcas Island.

The start was inauspicious when Meany appeared in Olympia on September 3, 1890, to report on a special session of the first legislature for the *Seattle Press*. Immediately after adjournment a week later, he took up the tasks of a press agent for the privately organized Washington World's Fair Association. He was to persuade Washingtonians to support participation in the Chicago World's Fair through a state appropriation and by local cooperation.[1]

Meany's role quickly became larger than that of press agent. On September 25, 1890, he joined a special committee, along with F. Lewis Clarke of Spokane and J.M. Hill of Pullman to draw up plans for the Association's operation. Three weeks later the committee recommended that twelve departments be set up and that the chairman of each should form the body of commissioners controlling the state's exhibit at Chicago.[2]

Even before the leaders could give him direction, Meany made himself indispensable to the Association. He was greatly heartened when Dr. Nelson G. Blalock of Walla Walla, a prominent member of the body and a well-known man of affairs, sent him a note stating that "I feel confident that you are the right man in the right place." Before the end of September Meany justified that confidence with a deluge of news releases which were published in many of the state's newspapers.[3]

As a prelude to Chicago, Meany turned his attention to advertising Spokane's Northwestern Industrial Exposition, scheduled to run through the month of October 1890. The World's Fair Association expected Spokane to serve as a testing ground for the later Chicago exposition. As early as August 20, C.W. Robinson, general manager of the Spokane Fair, had complimented Meany for a number of articles he had written concerning this local event. Soon thereafter, Thomas W. Prosch, a vice-president of the Seattle Chamber of Commerce, testified to Meany's success by seeking his advice on Seattle's and King County's participation at Spokane. He assured Meany that "you are my chief dependence and you must not fail me in any particular."[4]

Meany did not disappoint his old friend Prosch as they visited Kent, a few miles south of Seattle, on September 16, to inspect a local fair. They were successful in arranging to transport the whole exhibit from that fair to Spokane's meeting. Thereafter, Prosch collected and shipped other exhibits from King County to the Spokane site. Meany departed for the Northwest Industrial Exposition in late September to supervise King County's exhibit and to keep it open for the thirty-four day schedule. For him and for the World's Fair Association, the Spokane event provided triumphs but also frustrations and disappointments which would make them more realistic in preparing for Chicago. On September 30, for example, a day before the exposition opened, the *Kent Journal* reported that some of Kent's farming and horticultural exhibits had spoiled through carelessness in shipping. In addition, other exhibits had not been delivered by the Northern Pacific Railroad, although they had been shipped in plenty of time.[5]

The fair, nevertheless, was a success for the King County delegation as well as for Spokane County. Seattle Day, October 11, brought a delegation of 150 civic leaders from Puget Sound and some 3,000-4,000 visitors to the King County exhibit. Prominent Seattleites extolled their city's growth and its promise of future prosperity. Generously, they also praised Spokane and its rich hinterland. The exhibit that day certainly lived up to Prosch's admonition that Meany should "make our quarter shine....I hope to find it the popular resort of the crowd, admired by all, and the center of sociability and information."[6]

For the evening of Seattle Day, Meany arranged an informal dance to which he invited all the prominent people present at the fair. That occasion was only a brief respite from his almost unceasing round of fair duties, for he increased the publicity of the Association's activities while maintaining the King County exhibit. In that connection, he interviewed all available legislators to find out what work was being done around the state on behalf of the World's Fair Association. He then made the results known through press releases.[7]

Shortly before Meany took up his duties at the Spokane Fair, King County Republicans nominated him to run for the state's House of Representatives from North Seattle's forty-second district. He was absent from the city at the time, a matter which did not affect his prospects in the slightest. Newspaper publisher Fred J. Grant, his mentor and friend, guided his nomination through a harmonious caucus. Indeed, Meany, characterized by one writer as "a young pioneer of this city," was a very popular choice at the convention, obtaining the highest number of votes accorded in the meeting.[8]

Grant wrote two weeks after the convention to assure Meany, who was still in Spokane, that he need not worry about the campaign. "Everything is going along well and the result of the city election [held earlier] has almost assured victory in the county." Nevertheless, John R. Kinnear, Republican senatorial candidate from the twenty-eighth district, and G.E. De Steiguer, Meany's running mate for the two House seats in the district, nervously urged Meany to come home to campaign. Both men professed to believe that the elections would be close. At the same time, De Steiguer, acknowledging Meany's popularity, characterized the district as so small "that personal acquaintance goes a long way" toward winning.[9]

Grant disagreed with Meany's running mate, pointing out that his district traditionally was strongly Republican. Prosch too observed that the Democrats were demoralized and, hence, not a problem. Grant in addition noted that Meany would probably capture the Prohibitionists' votes. It remained, however, for the Rev. Clark Davis to put the matter most trenchantly when he chided Meany, the teetotaler:

> You are just too green to be in politics. Now dont [*sic*] you know that had the Prohis [Prohibitionists] endorsed you it would have Lost [*sic*] two votes where it gained you one? besides your Friends, and most Prohis are your friends, will vote for you any way. [*sic*][10]

Meany finally managed to get back to Seattle for a "grand rally" of Republicans in his district. The election on November 4, 1890, swept him and the entire King County Republican delegation into office. Meany received 417 votes while De Steiguer gained the second House seat in the district with 373 votes. The nearest Democrat, James C. McKilroy, had only 268 votes. The Republicans in sum held overwhelming majorities in both houses of the state legislature.[11]

Meany had little time to savor his victory or that of his party. He spent most of November visiting Puget Sound counties to promote the work of the World's Fair Association and its allies, the chambers of commerce and the boards of trade. Beginning in late October, and continuing until December 27, he traveled to all parts of Washington. Well received in most places, he discovered that the Farmer's Alliance and the Populists, who had opposed Washington's participation in Chicago's fair, had gained supporters. R.J. Neergard, Adams County auditor, for example, told Meany that with wheat at forty-one cents per bushel he could give no assurance that his constituents would not all become Populists and oppose an appropriation for the exposition.[12]

Perhaps because he already sensed political trouble, Meany in late November had sent a questionnaire to each legislator asking his view on Washington's participation at Chicago. The responses came in slowly but by mid-December it was clear that most respondents thought Washington should make a substantial appropriation. Furthermore, they wanted an exhibit separate from Oregon or any other state. Representative Frank R. Spinning, a farmer from Puyallup and a Republican, warmly supported a good appropriation and struck a chauvinistic stance when he wrote: "Independence is my choice. If Wash. can not command attention and even admiration by a thorough exhibit of her advantages and wealth, God pity our sister states."[13]

By the time he returned home for Christmas, Meany had traveled in all except two of the state's thirty-four counties and he felt that it had been a successful tour. A reporter for the *Post-Intelligencer* found him enthusiastic about the potential and resources of each county, anticipating that each would make a good showing in Chicago. Travel had deepened Meany's love for his state, promoting an invincible optimism, as seen in these words:

> Talk about your tours around the world and trips abroad, I would not exchange for one moment my experience in the recent World's fair trip I have made around our own state of Washington for all the vaunted pleasures of travels in far lands. Scenery unsurpassed, resources unheard of and people unequaled in generosity and enterprise have been among the tangible and valuable proofs that have fallen my way.[14]

Shortly after New Year's, Meany joined the House of Representatives in Olympia at the opening of the second legislature. Editor Erastus

Brainerd of the *Seattle Press* hired him to report the legislative proceedings. When the *Times* scooped the *Press* in publishing Acting Governor Charles E. Laughton's message to the legislature, Meany's reporting tasks were reduced to commenting on House activities, providing gossip on personalities, and obtaining bills for reporting in the *Press* when they were introduced.[15]

Meany responded by filing stories regularly which limned the personalities of his fellow legislators and recounted anecdotes of the session. Brainerd, however, again criticized him for "being a day after the fair" and failing to "use your position as legislator to acquire information and get beats for the newspaper." The editor had earlier made up his mind to assist Meany's advance in newspaper work. His strictures, however, "that legislatures and world fairs are ephemeral compared with the life work of journalism" made it clear that Meany had not measured up to Brainerd's standards. The editor continued to criticize Meany for a short while but external developments soon brought Meany's political reporting to an end. On February 10, 1891, Brainerd informed Meany that the *Press* had purchased the *Times* and that under the reorganization of staff his services no longer were required.[16]

The first order of business for Representative Meany and his King County cohorts was to re-elect Watson C. Squire as United States Senator. They had to defeat Judge W.H. Calkins, a Tacoma Republican. To insure Squire's victory, the King County delegation arranged a caucus to take place in the Hotel Olympia on the evening before the election. To Meany, with his strong voice and tall figure, went the duty of announcing the caucus. A fascinated reporter for the *Post-Intelligencer* recorded the subsequent developments. When Meany appeared on the middle landing of the hotel's grand staircase, "holding in his left hand a paper, extending his right arm over the crowd and commanding silence," he gained the attention of the assembled people.

In a resounding voice Meany then announced the meeting of the Squire forces and began to read the names of participants. Almost immediately, the Calkins supporters—aided by the Democrats—tried to outshout him. "Meany persisted, and raising his long right arm toward heaven, emphasized each name with an unmistakable shake of his clenched fist." The Calkins men rushed the staircase "with a great howl," but several of Meany's supporters, including John H. McGraw, Squire's campaign manager, protected Meany and his paper. "Then...Mr. Meany shoved the paper under his coat...and escaped into one of the rooms on the second floor." The caucus duly nominated Squire and the next day, January 21, 1891, a joint session of the legislature elected him to succeed himself.[17]

A victory celebration held two weeks later at the Rainier Club in Seattle honored McGraw as the architect of the triumph while hailing Meany as the "hero of the staircase." Although the latter could not contribute to the magnificent silver service presented to McGraw, his admirable toast to McGraw identified Meany with leaders of the business community and with the Republican leadership. Under less pompous circumstances, in a private letter, a longtime Seattle associate wrote about the staircase melodrama in the following terms: "I see by the mornings [*sic*] post that Meany of Seattle has held his own grandly against the Tacoma toughs, good for you, Shake [*sic*]."[18]

A few days before the tumult over the Squire caucus Meany had quietly launched the Washington World's Fair Association campaign to obtain a legislative appropriation for a state commission which would develop the state's exhibits at the World's Columbian Exposition in Chicago. The exhibit would focus on "illustrating its [Washington's] history, progress, moral and material welfare and future development." In a later statement, the Association unveiled a broad plan to attract capital and immigrants to the state. As the first step, Meany introduced a concurrent resolution in Washington's House of Representatives to establish a joint committee of three senators and five representatives which would be responsible for framing world's fair legislation. The resolution passed quickly in both houses. Meany and Senator J.H. Long, Republican of Chehalis, became co-chairmen.[19]

Each co-chairman introduced the bill proposed by the World's Fair Association in his branch of the legislature. The measure contained a one-fourth mill tax on property for 1891, 1892, and 1893 to fund participation in the exposition. Supporters believed the levy would yield $250,000. That sum became a stumbling block, however, when even the supportive editor of the *Post-Intelligencer* argued that the levy would overburden the taxpayer.[20]

Even before the bill had been introduced chapters of the Farmer's Alliance and Patrons of Husbandry stated their opposition to the proposed appropriation. In some instances, farmers opposed an appropriation of more than $100,000 for the biennium. In other cases, they resisted any taxation at all for the benefit of the exposition. By January 19, 1891, Meany, still reporting for the *Seattle Press*, wrote that a proposal for a reduced sum of $100,000 might be well received, provided the proposed World's Fair Commission contained at least one farmer.[21]

When the joint legislative committee met on February 13 to analyze the bill for the exposition, it adopted the compromising spirit that Meany had suggested. It dropped the one-fourth mill tax provision, substituting an appropriation of $100,000 to be drawn from general revenues. Vouchers for printing and publication would, in addition, increase the appropriation.[22]

For the next three weeks the House debated the bill. It had one additional provision, since farm leaders insisted that a "dirt" farmer be added to the ten-member commission. Representative R.A. Hutchinson, Democrat of Mondavia, Lincoln County, moved to add Edward Ramm, a farmer from his own district, and the House complied. Before the vote, Meany objected, pointing out that Dr. Nelson G. Blalock, an incumbent commissioner, was a farmer. Hutchinson would have none of that argument, citing Blalock, a Walla Walla physician and rancher as only "a city sidewalk farmer."[23]

The conviction was widespread, apparently, that the ten stipulated commissioners were self-appointed and did not represent all the people—particularly not the farming, mining, and timber interests. To quiet such objections, the House amended the bill to increase the commission from ten to thirty-four members, one for each county. That amendment later met Senate approval. However, just before the measure went to the Senate, W.D. Tyler, Republican of Tacoma, in the words of the *Post-Intelligencer*'s reporter, made a "direct thrust at Meany of King" with the proposal to forbid legislators from employment under the commission. Tyler's amendment failed, but the House accepted a second proposal to cut the appropriation to $25,000 for each year of the biennium.[24]

Meany failed to rally support for the committee's financial proposal and could only hope that the Senate would be amenable. Those expectations were met as Senator Long led the movement which restored the total appropriation of $100,000. The measure finally went to Acting Governor Charles E. Laughton who signed it into law on March 7.[25]

Meany's other major concern in the second legislature was to establish a new and enlarged campus for the University of Washington. The ten-acre downtown tract on which it had been located since its founding in 1861 no longer provided sufficient space for the number of students enrolled nor facilities for a scholarly and scientific institution. The rapid growth of the city's business section in the 1890s also threatened to stifle campus expansion. The first serious consideration of removal to a new site had come in 1889 when a committee of the legislature investigated the matter and recommended seeking a new location, remote from downtown.[26]

University authorities responded positively to the proposal, as Meany learned on January 21, 1891, when President Thomas M. Gatch wrote to him that "I wish we could get the [public] school section on Union Bay [off Lake Washington]." He urged Meany to "confer with Capt. [P.B.] Johnson, one of our Regents," who shared Gatch's concern. A few days later, the state legislature established a committee to examine the existing campus and several state-owned public school tracts in or near Seattle as the site for a new campus. Meany, as the legislature's only graduate of the University of Washington, joined the special committee and quickly became its leader.[27]

Meany's committee met with civic leaders at the headquarters of the Chamber of Commerce on Friday evening, February 6. W. Lair Hill, chairman for the meeting, called on Meany, who promptly urged the creation of a modern university. It should, he said, be modeled on the University of Michigan, the "apex" of a "pyramid" of which the common schools would be the base. The University should be a place where a poor boy could acquire a full education. Chairman Hill ably seconded Meany's thesis, arguing that every branch of learning must be cultivated at the University, including poetry, science, and outdoor sports. For that curriculum he proposed a 160-acre campus.[28]

The recommended acreage had not been agreed upon when, the next morning, several civic leaders escorted Meany and his four legislative colleagues to view the school lands. They agreed by sundown to recommend President Gatch's choice, a fraction of a beautiful, wooded, public school tract on the shore of Union Bay. That evening the Board of Aldermen, of the city's bicameral council, approved an ordinance requiring Seattle to give a quit-claim deed to the state for the University's downtown tract. Such a transfer would only be completed if a new campus contained 100 acres and was located within six miles of the old site.[29]

The ordinance went immediately to the House of Delegates, the second house of Seattle's City Council, where a festive spirit prevailed, as reported in the *Seattle Press*. "About eleven o'clock the ordinance came in from the other house, and as Representative Meany entered with the sergeant-at-arms he was greeted with cheers. The bill was read and passed under suspension of the rules."[30]

Two weeks later, while reporting the Seattle Council's action to the legislature, Meany expressed confidence that the University bill would "be rushed through to its final passage." On February 23, 1891 he introduced the House bill for relocation of the University. The rules were suspended and the measure quickly passed. The next day, Senator L.F. Thompson, Republican of Tacoma, introduced a similar bill in the Senate. On March 4 the Senate's version was substituted for that of the House with Meany's approval. One important change was the final decision on the size of the campus. Senator Long moved that it should contain 160 acres. This amendment passed and was inserted in the statute, which became law on March 7, 1891.[31]

Meany played only a minor role in another matter of concern to King County Republicans—sufficiently regulating the railroads to prevent the defection of eastern Washingtonians from their customary Republican ranks to the Democrats or the rising Populist Party. This issue, in fact, was one of the most serious in the state's politics since no effective regulation had been imposed in the first legislature. The farmers of eastern Washington demanded numerous curbs on railroad activity, particularly on rate discrimination against grain shippers.

The King County Republicans walked a narrow line in seeking to mollify their eastern Washington compatriots with modest regulation while precluding serious interference with the transcontinentals which had been favoring Seattle over Spokane and other inland points through discriminatory freight charges.[32]

Although Meany did not lead in developing railroad regulatory bills, he faithfully sought the welfare of his party and Seattle's business community in debates and roll calls. He leaped into the fray on February 17 when Representative W.D. Tyler proposed an amendment to the Fellows bill, which would have prohibited all railroad rate discrimination within the state. In a "strong and eloquent speech," Meany objected to the amendment on the grounds that denying rebates on goods shipped to Seattle would be "a direct blow at the prosperity of that city," handicapping it in its competition with other West Coast ports. He appealed successfully to the "Friends of Seattle from Eastern Washington" to oppose the amendment. His view prevailed and the amendment failed.[33]

Subsequently, the Fellows bill fell by the wayside, superseded by the Wasson bill, which provided for moderate freight rates on farm products. Eastern Washington legislators accepted the bill as the best they could hope for, while the King County delegation felt that Seattle would not be injured by it. In the end, Acting Governor Charles E. Laughton incurred the wrath of Meany and many other Republicans, as well as the *Seattle Post-Intelligencer*. Several bills to regulate the railroads, including the Wasson bill, were placed on Laughton's desk for signature but he vetoed all of them.

When interviewed, Meany stated "If we cannot do something to show that Mr. Laughton is not in accord with his party or that his party repudiates his action, the next election will go hard with us."[34]

In summing up "Mr. Meany's record" for the legislative session, the *Seattle Press-Times* reported that he "was one of the most active members of the second legislature of Washington." In addition to matters already discussed, Meany was credited with a major role in obtaining the largest regular operating budget the University had ever enjoyed—a figure of $25,000 plus $1,600 for Regents' expenses. He also introduced a measure providing for the election of Washington's members of the Electoral College. That bill quickly became law. An additional measure which Meany sponsored provided for dividing the state into two congressional districts, separating King from Pierce County and insuring both Seattle and Tacoma a member of the United States House of Representatives. It did not come to the floor for a vote, dying presumably because the state as yet was entitled to only one member in the House. Meany had introduced these bills to satisfy his political mentor, editor Fred J. Grant, whose newspaper, the *Post-Intelligencer*, invariably was friendly to him.[35]

Meany's leadership in steering the world's fair bill through the legislature produced the expected reward. Three weeks after the legislative session ended he became press agent and secretary to the executive committee of the World's Fair Commission. He needed to visit the exposition headquarters in Chicago soon, particularly to select a location for Washington's building. Personal business intervened for the moment, however. Meany had invested in two real estate propositions as a result of his travels around the state on World's Fair Association business. Both deals came to a head before he could leave for Chicago.

The first enterprise concerned land and fruit development on Orcas Island in the San Juans. The island had experienced its first significant settlement in the 1880s and by 1890 Seattle businessmen were selling land to prospective fruit ranchers. Meany became interested in Orcas Island while soliciting apples for exhibit at the Northwestern Industrial Exposition. He invested in the Orcas Island Fruit Company and became its president on March 18, 1891, amid grandiose talk of expansion, but in the face of inadequate financing. The company expected to plant 5,000 prune trees and 2,000 apple trees on its 290 acres during the coming year. Calculated yields and income were impressive and the company even drew up plans for a summer resort. Meany had little to do with subsequent developments.

The firm fell on hard times very soon as Orcas Island's speculative boom collapsed in the panic of 1893.[36]

While visiting Waterville in Douglas County, east of Wenatchee, Meany became involved in land speculation with Seattle financiers. News that two different railroads, the Central Washington and the Seattle, Lake Shore, and Eastern, had been surveyed through Waterville stimulated speculation, as did rumors that one or both might build tracks through the fledgling town.[37]

In November of 1890, Meany joined with Charles Liftchild, a real estate operator, in a plan to purchase land near Waterville for speculation. They would hold it until prices rose or perhaps plat a town and then sell it to "the outfit," meaning Seattle capitalists. Some of the latter had organized the Waterville Improvement Company to provide a water system and electricity for the town of 700 people, most of whom apparently thought that a railroad and other amenities, including a national bank, would insure Waterville's status as "The Coming City of Central Washington."[38]

On December 5, 1890, Meany became associated with Fred Ward, who represented a number of Seattle financiers, in promoting the First National Bank of Waterville. Meany became, in effect, a broker selling stock in the bank. He took an option on some stock himself and became a director of the bank. When he could not pay for the stock, his dreams of a banker's income were shattered. On March 26, 1891, he was ordered to resign as a director and assign the capital stock to Ward.[39]

Meanwhile, Liftchild and Meany sought to gain control of Waterville town lots. Details are lacking but it is clear that they and Charles A. Briggs, Meany's Seattle real estate associate, sank funds into their scheme and that Meany and Liftchild, at least, were losers. Meany wrote to Briggs on May 15 "very much surprised and not a little chagrined" that the latter would not honor his moral commitment to the partnership by sharing Meany's loss on a financial bond. "The miserable failure that resulted from our venture," he wrote, left him in desperate straits. "I have no money. I am overdrawn at the bank, I have notes to meet with an empty purse. My current bills are three months behind and my household must be sustained. I cannot pay you until I get some money."[40]

He learned, as months passed, that little hope resided with the Waterville Improvement Company. The bargain made with Waterville authorities was not working out satisfactorily. The local people had promised to grant 700 acres to the company in return for a water system and electrical generation to supply all homes and businesses. There were engineering problems and misunderstandings. The townspeople withheld 120 acres and those granted to the promoters seemed of less value than had been anticipated. In the end, the town had fewer than 500 people and the Seattle promoters were trying to "get out even."[41]

Meany, of course, had continued working for the World's Fair Commission. Indeed, since the executive commissioner had not yet been chosen, Meany worked through March, April, and most of May 1891 largely on his own. Before traveling to Chicago he wrote to many of the thirty-four commissioners, soliciting ideas for exhibits and information which he might use in press releases and magazine pieces. Once in Chicago, in early April, he ingratiated himself with director general George R. Davis at the exposition headquarters, obtaining a publicity coup when Davis advised young men to migrate to the State of Washington. Meany also gained favorable consideration for an advantageous site for Washington's exposition building.[42]

When the Commission met at Ellensburg on May 20, 1891, the members chose Ezra Meeker as the executive commissioner. A pioneer settler in Puyallup and a well-known hop farmer, Meeker had been endorsed by Seattle's Chamber of Commerce. Meany reported that everyone at the meeting had seemed pleased with the choice and in at least two press releases he praised Meeker as a busy and competent leader. Meeker, however, launched a hectic campaign of publicity, collecting, and planning of exhibits with little attention to Meany's work or consultation with the executive committee.[43]

Meeker, in fact, touched off a controversy on May 30, complaining to Dr. N.G. Blalock, president of the Commission, that he had been denied access to the appropriated funds. This, he wrote, made it impossible for him to develop the exhibits. The issue was joined a month later when Meeker again insisted upon his prerogative, arguing that under law he had sole authority to spend the appropriation. Furthermore, he found the nine-member executive committee unwieldy and demanded that it be reduced to three, including himself. Meany, too, soon drew Meeker's criticism for allegedly failing to keep him informed of the proceedings of the executive committee.[44]

The committee members responded by depriving Meeker of final authority in making staff appointments, pointedly keeping that power in their hands. President Blalock also asked Meany to stop off at Puyallup to learn from Meeker whether he intended to work in harmony with the committee. Meeker, in turn, stubbornly claimed full authority for collecting the exhibits. Once again, he complained that the Commission's funds were being wrongfully withheld from him and that Meany was uncooperative. The *Seattle Press-Times*—at that time directed by an editor unfriendly to Meany—printed Meeker's accusations in full detail, including a charge that Meany had spent $500 of commission funds improperly.[45]

The climax of the quarrel came on August 22, when president Blalock took the place of the flamboyant Meeker as executive commissioner. The latter waged a losing battle to retain his position, and to censure the executive committee. The wilder charges he made about improper handling of funds were toned down as he "disclaimed any intention to insult anybody." Nevertheless, he repeated an oft-stated claim that it was unconstitutional for Meany to receive pay from the Commission since he was a member of the legislature which had put through the appropriation. Meeker's resolution to dismiss Meany was simply laid on the table and forgotten.[46]

Readers of the *Post-Intelligencer* on September 6 learned from a long letter to the editor that Meeker still accused the executive committee of assigning funds for purposes not proper under law. He was not speaking of criminal liability or civil indictment, but rather of "reprehensible" and "unbusinesslike" actions. The old animus remained, in any case. He refused to condone any situation in which more money was spent for committee meetings and planning than for collecting exhibits, a final outburst against the fact that the purse strings had never been in his hands. As for the press agent, Meeker concluded that the money paid Meany was "a perfectly useless expenditure."[47]

Executive Commissioner Blalock moved the headquarters from Seattle to Walla Walla, his home town, necessitating Meany's transfer there in the first week of September, 1891. Meany left his family in Seattle for the time being. Working conditions improved under Blalock, restoring Meany's normal optimism. He liked Walla Walla, too, and applied familiar criteria to it when he wrote to J.W. Dodge, of Seattle's Chamber of Commerce:

> This is a fine country but I believe that if some of the Seattle elixir of trade were infused into this body commercial great transformations would at once gather over this pleasant valley like a cloud....A cloud would not hurt, taken in any sense you wish. The weather is hot, the brick blocks are mortgageless and the people are by far too serene and contented. The first impulse that enters a Seattle man's mind on getting acquainted here is "oh for some Puget Sound rustling to stir things up here!"[48]

The cloud metaphor may have arisen from Meany's concern over the shadow cast by Meeker and the *Seattle Press-Times* upon his career and the legitimacy of his employment. Meeker persisted, according to some rumors, in seeking Meany's dismissal, and other information suggested that some Tacoma people were aiding him. Meany called these developments an annoyance, not serious accusations. The shadows began to disappear when the "imported editor" of the *Press-Times*, who was disposed to "knife" Meany, departed and was replaced by the latter's friend, E.B. Piper. Nothing further came from Meeker or the *Press-Times* to irritate Meany.[49]

On the contrary, Blalock gratifyingly heaped work and responsibilities on his assistant. When Meany departed for Seattle on October 21, 1891, to bring his family to Walla Walla to live, Blalock asked him to come back quickly as the work was piling up. In a jocular vein he offered an inducement: "You will miss your Pears and Apples [*sic*] if nothing else. I notice that a box lasts longer now than it did a few days ago." Then, as if to cinch his argument about work and to speed the Meanys on their way, he reported that "We are getting some very fine Specimens of Fruits [*sic*] now for preservation."[50]

A week later Meany had settled his family in Walla Walla, where it would remain until April before returning to Seattle. The satisfactions of family life once again assured, he buckled down to his many office tasks. Answering correspondence was only the beginning. He processed invoices and vouchers, planned exhibits, took on numerous speaking engagements, and, of course, wrote publicity, including magazine articles. Not only did Meany collect information on a possible exposition building, he also gained a significant role in the selection of the architect. The State Board of Trade and its local chapters, supposedly valuable agencies for obtaining displays and providing other kinds of assistance, had to be constantly cajoled and encouraged to carry out projects. He also had to maintain valuable contacts as well with Chicago exposition officials.[51]

The task which perhaps tried Meany's patience and persistence most sorely arose from the Commission's decision to publish a souvenir book to be distributed at the exposition. It was to contain a history of the state and to present a variety of statistics on resources and prospects pertaining to the growth of Washington. It should express the pride of Washingtonians in their state and also serve as a magnet to attract outside capital and immigrants who were willing workers and producers. Meany, as editor, without staff and with few other resources, had to collect fresh statistics on a variety of subjects. The network of personal relationships he had built up in his public relations work, especially among the World's Fair commissioners, politicians, and newspaper editors, undoubtedly saved the project from disaster. He asked the commissioners to aid him by encouraging county assessors and auditors to collect the required data and by monitoring their work in some cases.

Meany's persistence was required in most counties, especially in the more sparsely settled portions of eastern Washington. In one instance the collected data was lost; in others the gathering was slow and sometimes incomplete. Meany asked newspaper editors—most or all of whom had received exposition "copy" from him—to write and publish articles on the history and development of their counties and then forward copies which he might use in compiling the souvenir book.[52]

In the midst of heavy duties at Walla Walla, Meany accepted an invitation to speak at the 1892 Fourth-of-July celebration in Pullman. That small southeastern Washington town was a center of wheat and fruit farming as well as the home of the recently established Washington Agricultural College, the state's land grant institution. Meany seized the opportunity to promote local contributions to Washington's exhibit at the Chicago fair in the following terms:

> from Whitman, the famous banner county of the State, we expect a prize acre of wheat...many bushels of threshed grain, many interesting exhibits from the Agricultural College and hundreds of specimens of your luscious fruits. Other counties will produce coal, and iron and fish and timber and stone but none of them can hope to excel you in grains and your choicer fruits.[53]

Only then did Meany switch to the fervid patriotic oratory expected on that day. Speaking in terms familiar to nineteenth-century America, he recounted the Anglo-Saxon story of civilization. It began four centuries before when

> a prophet would indeed be called mad [sic] who would have asserted to that world of Latins, Teutons, Britains, and Norsemen that in the far west over the rim of the unknown watery horizon of the Atlantic there existed a cradle in which should be rocked the first true child of human liberty; that *there* should be found the home of the greatest nation of the globe.[54]

Then, borrowing the conventional wisdom from James A. Garfield, the martyred president, Meany pointed out approvingly that "the course of Empire is still taking the way westward....When the circle is complete, the Pacific will be the theater of civilization. Our domain is, therefore, washed by the ocean of the present [the Atlantic] and the greater ocean of the future; and this last we shall command."[55]

After an incantation to the flag and praise for American culture, Meany returned to his plea for cooperation in developing Washington's exhibit. It was true, he acknowledged, that a former generation undervalued farming and showed disrespect for the farmer. The land-grant colleges, such as the fledgling Pullman institution, had revolutionized attitudes and agricultural production. "How different now!" he exulted. "On every hand is recognized the sturdy worth of the farmer, the miner, the mechanic and all other producers." Americans are a people, he told his audience, who would respond bravely "to [their] country's call to protect her honor and her flag." In the fortunate time of peace which Americans enjoyed they had another mission, the one which he was preaching: "This brave people of Washington have other great works to claim their immediate attention." Thus did Meany put a high value on the display of the fruits of peace and civilization in the Chicago exposition.[56]

The glowing optimism Meany expressed from the patriotic platform contrasted sharply with his growing anxiety about Blalock's handling of Commission matters. The doctor, seeking more time for his medical practice and business affairs, increasingly delegated work to Meany, sometimes failing to inform him of decisions made. When, in early December of 1892, Blalock mentioned that he might resign as executive commissioner, Meany urged him to do so.[57]

Meany's anxiety arose from his own ambition to succeed Blalock and because of a rumor circulating of "a mean, underhanded scheme of Dr. Blalock's to attempt to thrust me aside," which he communicated to commissioner William L. LaFollette of Pullman. Meany labored under a heavy strain as his infant daughter, Elizabeth Lois, had died at Thanksgiving, and his wife was very ill. He felt that in his bereavement he "should expect nothing but warm support and sympathy from those whom I have always supported with loyalty."[58]

Stories had circulated that Blalock had docked Meany's salary when the latter attended his wife and daughter. Meany, apparently, never made such a claim and Blalock vigorously denied the rumor. The latter, however, did not deny the story that he, as a staunch Democrat, wanted to replace Meany with Percy Rochester, a Seattle Democrat. Meany reacted vehemently to that threat, confiding to a friend: "Trust to this...I have my war clothes on and if my wife lives I will remain on deck and fight among the rigging until I win or go down."[59]

His wife survived, giving birth to a son, Thomas Mercer, on December 10, 1892, and Meany remained a candidate. The *Seattle Press-Times*, in discussing the Commission meeting of December 15, predicted that Meany would be elected executive commissioner. It also expressed confidence he would be a "superior officer" to Blalock. The outcome of the meeting was unhappy for Meany. Dr. George V. Calhoun, a Republican of LaConner, in Skagit County, was chosen executive commissioner. Meany's disappointment undoubtedly was tempered by friendly past contacts with Calhoun. In a story Meany had filed with the *Seattle Press* well before these events, he had described Calhoun as "one of the handsomest men in the whole state," and acknowledged that "No man in Washington has a cleaner record as a consistent, conscientious and hardworking republican [*sic*]." Harmony was restored once more, as Calhoun indicated that he planned to spend much of his time at Commission headquarters in Tacoma while Representative Meany served in the sessions of the third legislature in Olympia.[60]

CHAPTER FOUR

Springboard and Goal: The World's Fair and the University (1892-1894)

MEANY'S SUCCESSES AT THE SECOND legislature whetted his appetite for more politics. When he moved to Walla Walla at Dr. Blalock's order he seized the opportunity to visit United States Senator John B. Allen, who made his home there. Sometime later, on January 29, 1892, he wrote to the senator in Washington, D.C., confessing that he had a growing interest in seeking re-election to the House of Representatives in Olympia. "I am," he continued, "strongly in earnest about furthering the best interests of our State University and goodness knows it needs help badly." He then added significantly: "I have been assured of the strongest kind of help if I should wish to run again."[1]

Correspondence with Senator Allen continued, with Meany reporting that in a recent trip around Puget Sound "no opportunity of saying a good word for my friend in the Senate was allowed to escape." He then sought to ingratiate himself further with Allen by reporting "an amusing and pleasant fact" he learned while visiting in Seattle. As a young lawyer Allen had boarded in the home of Meany's father-in-law, Dillis B. Ward. "You used to bring the ladies pretty boquets [*sic*] of flowers early mornings. You used also to play with one of the babies of the family....That baby...is my wife. When you come home you will have the opportunity of fondling her baby whose name is also Elizabeth but her pet name is the other diminutive—Bessie."[2]

Meany soon disclosed to Allen his fears for his own future, probably emboldened by the newly formed ties of friendship. "I am beginning to wonder what I will do for a living after the World's Fair work is completed," he wrote on April 7. "The newspaper profession has lost its charm. It is not profitable." Furthermore, it offered little chance for "permanent advancement." Once more, he thought of moving to Washington, D.C., "to get some kind of work...and devote myself evenings to the study of the law in one of the famous law schools there." Then, with a law degree, he might return to Seattle, "equipped to start work where there are many chances for advancement, profit, and keen enjoyment."

Unfortunately, his next statement dissolved that dream. He had to admit that at thirty years of age his opportunity for lengthy study had almost certainly vanished. "I am loaded with expenses. My family—wife, baby, mother, invalid sister and little brother—must all be cared for while I am studying." No evidence remains that Senator Allen tried to answer the question that followed: "Can you advise or encourage me at this turning point in my career?"[3]

He reported the same hopeful plans three weeks later to a friend in Philadelphia, indicating he would take advantage of an undisclosed "promising opening" in the nation's capital in order to obtain law training. Though burdened by family ills, he revealed his own ebullient, resilient spirit: "As for me, I am as hale, and long legged as of yore. I sport a most beautiful Van Dyke beard. Some day I will get a picture taken and send you one." To all this he appended a shrewd and realistic observation: traveling around the state he had made "valuable acquaintances and friendships in all the counties. This will be of value to me in my future business and more especially if I retain my present apetite [*sic*] for politics."[4]

Speculation about law studies vanished as Meany practiced more assiduously the politics which were based upon his strong party loyalty and pride of place. He grieved when disaster struck the local Republicans in the city elections of March 8, 1892. The Democrats captured every elective office and a majority in the House of Delegates. Five days later, the blow was tempered when the King County Republican Convention nominated John H. McGraw as state delegate to the national convention. Word also came that Senator Allen's supporters had won an important victory in Walla Walla County. Together, these triumphs thrilled Meany, as he wrote to McGraw: "Your victory and his [Allen's] victory make me feel so good that I can almost forget the Seattle landslide disappointment."[5]

In April, Meany took steps to win re-election to the state's House of Representatives. At the same time, Meany informed Senator Allen he would be able to solicit support for the Senator's re-election in the Puget Sound country. As for his own prospects, Meany asserted renomination by the King County Republicans would be tantamount to re-election. Allen accepted his offer to help, later asking him to talk to Grant, McGraw, and

Leigh Hunt, publisher of the *Post- Intelligencer*, about winning Republican support in Snohomish County.[6]

Stump speaking played little or no role in Meany's campaign. Instead, he sought more federal and state patronage for Seattle and King County. Specifically, he tried to take advantage of an 1891 state law setting up Washington's agricultural college and main experiment station in eastern Washington. The law required that at least one station must be established west of the Cascades. On March 3, 1892, he urged the Seattle Chamber of Commerce to lobby for location of that experiment station on the new campus of the University of Washington. The University of California, Meany thought, had set an indisputable precedent when its chief experiment station was located at Berkeley. Meany had no possibility of success: the agricultural college authorities placed the station in Puyallup, Pierce County.[7]

Equally unsuccessful was Meany's suggestion to the Chamber of Commerce that the small, underfunded normal schools being established should be disbanded in favor of one consolidated teacher training program at the state university. He knew that the next legislature would have to deal with more requests for small normal schools, widely scattered, as part of their "log-rolling" practices. His efforts to counteract those tactics in order to provide better training met with little response.[8]

More transparently political was Meany's suggestion that the Seattle Chamber of Commerce seek to have the office of the State Board of Horticulture moved from Tacoma to Seattle. John T. Blackburn, of Vashon Island, a member of the Board, had alerted Meany, about October 1, 1892, that for a short time it would be possible to make that move because of the particular membership of the Board. Blackburn argued that such a move was needed to provide important services to local horticulturists. Meany responded by urging the Seattle Chamber of Commerce to find space for the state agency. Shortly after January 1, 1893, the Board moved its office to the Haller Block in downtown Seattle, where it remained for about two years before returning to Tacoma. In retrospect, the biennial reports indicated no advantage to Seattle had resulted from the move: horticultural services were distributed impartially over the state but a small budget severely limited their value.[9]

Meany responded quietly on August 6 to his own renomination for the lower house of the legislature. He was greatly elated a few days later when John H. McGraw was nominated for governor on the first ballot in a state Republican convention dominated by supporters of Senator Allen.

Meany rejoiced to see his friends rewarded but was incensed when he learned that Tacoma delegates tried to injure McGraw's candidacy by attacking his character and criticizing his advocacy of federal financing for construction of a canal to connect Lake Washington to Puget Sound.[10]

Meany responded earnestly to what the *Post-Intelligencer* characterized as "attacks...by malicious and worthless enemies" by joining a number of well established citizens in recounting numerous anecdotes and testimonials to McGraw's rise to success over adversity and "his strict integrity as a man." Speaking to a hostile Tacoma audience, Meany illuminated McGraw's character in terms of service to young men starting out in life, stating that "almost nine out of ten of the young men who have struggled for advancement in Seattle have been helped in one way or another by Mr. McGraw." That sweeping claim was supported by only one case, but it was highly personal. Meany spoke eloquently of his own plight when left penniless at the head of his family at seventeen years of age:

> One day this boy without money or influence was met by Mr. McGraw, who said, placing his hand on the boy's shoulder: "Young man, I knew your father and I know something of the struggle you are having now, and if there is any way I can help or befriend you, I want you to let me know of it, and don't hesitate to call on me."

Meany then reported that he had turned to the scoffers and concluded: "Gentlemen...I am that young man, and there is no man in the State of Washington that I would sooner fight for as a leader than John H. McGraw."[11]

Meany spent little time campaigning but his earlier prediction had been correct—nomination was tantamount to election. He led eight candidates for the two House seats in the forty-second district with 866 votes. His running mate, L.H. Wheeler, won the second seat with 840 votes. The leading Democrat, Lee B. Hart, gained only 558 votes and was followed by a second Democrat, two Populists, and two candidates from the Prohibitionist Party. Meany again would be surrounded by friends when he went to Olympia—the King County delegation numbered six Republicans who were senators and thirteen representatives, all but one being members of his party. McGraw, elected governor by a comfortable margin over Democrat H.J. Snively, led the King County delegation.[12]

The day before his re-election, November 7, 1892, Meany telegraphed Charles V. Piper, a classmate in college and colleague in the Young Naturalists Society, asking tersely, "Do you want entomological professorship at Washington Agricultural College? Answer." The Board of Regents of the new agricultural college was organizing its first faculty and "distributing positions in the college among themselves as a matter of patronage," according to a historian of those early years.[13]

When Piper applied for the position, Meany treated his task as that of helping a friend or close political associate. He wired his beloved Professor O.B. Johnson, now retired, to write a strong endorsement of Piper. In addition, however, he invoked the support of a large number of his political friends, beginning with Governor McGraw and even working down to Representative L.C. Gilman, the only Democrat in the King County delegation. Meany commended Piper to one politician as "a loyal young man." His own statement to the regents was short and scarcely concerned with scholarship. Piper, he stated, was well trained and a man of rectitude. When Piper feared problems after attaining the position, Meany assured him that he would have "an abundance of loyal friends when you need them." Among Meany's "true friends" available to Piper were Pullman politicians Will LaFollette and Oscar Young.[14]

Meany's support of Piper proved to be fortunate as the latter became a distinguished scientist and outstanding member of the faculty. Unfortunately, Meany's other political endorsement to the Pullman college yielded bitter fruit. Meany offered Ernest L. Newell, once employed by the World's Fair Commission, as a paragon who would organize an orchestra, teach music or history, serve as a civil engineer, or coach athletics. The regents elected Newell as a "civil engineer and teacher" but eventually tried him at numerous tasks, including teaching history.[15]

Newell heaped praise on Meany for his helping hand in obtaining a position. When the young man soon expressed fears for his tenure, Meany could only advise him in a kind of ritualistic way that he should "brace up," for he had a bright future and loyal friends. Newell quickly became an embarrassment to the college, resigning in February 1893, after proving unable to perform any of the tasks put to him. Though Meany later wrote privately that he was "sorry for Mr. Newell," and that "my interest in his case does not extend beyond desiring that he have a good, fair trial," that disclaimer did not free Meany from vitriolic newspaper attacks.

Criticism of Meany came from the pen of Joseph French Johnson, editor of the Spokane *Spokesman,* as an off-shoot of his very sharp competition for subscribers with the better-entrenched Spokane *Review*. Newell's failure, of course, provided an opportunity for Johnson to portray Meany as representing all that eastern Washingtonians found objectionable in Seattle politics. Johnson labeled Newell incompetent and accused Meany of authoring multifarious difficulties at the new agricultural college.[16]

Johnson claimed that the "Pullman College ought to become one of the greatest industrial and scientific schools in the country, but it will never be the equal of a small denominational college if it is to be made the football of ward politicians." As political problems mounted concerning the Washington Agricultural College, Johnson did not content himself by explaining them solely in terms of patronage. In his mind a conspiracy grew which linked Meany with the college's Regent A.H. Smith of Tacoma. In Johnson's view, Smith and Meany intended not only to control the college, but also to bring together political leaders from King and Pierce counties in order to control a large share of the state's patronage at the expense of Spokane County.[17]

When Meany became chairman of the King County delegation in its preparation for the legislative session of 1893, Johnson chose to represent that appointment as a sign of Meany's prominent rise to power in Seattle politics. Meany made reference to the "nice compliment and high honor paid him" but, in actuality, he was not the political head of the delegation but rather the "whip," who scheduled agendas, briefing sessions, and so forth. Editor Johnson next named Meany responsible for all the problems of the World's Fair Commission as well as those of the agricultural college. From that stance, the editor then leaped to the conclusion that Meany aimed "to be the all controlling power in the state, and even has his eye on the governorship."[18]

Caught up in the whirlwind of propagandizing in news columns as well as on the editorial page, Johnson descended to sarcasm. On December 22, 1892 he wrote that "the revelation of Mr. Meany's ambition will cause a terrible fluttering in the hearts of King County's less powerful and less sagacious politicians, particularly those who have ever dared to smile when this unsuspected Caesar among them sneezed. John H. McGraw should be warned."[19]

Two days after Christmas, Johnson reprinted an editorial comment from the *Yakima Herald* which paralleled his own thought: "The press is after the scalp of E.S. Meany, of the World's Fair Commission, and the probability is that it will soon have it dangling from its belt. It is claimed that he is the political autocrat of the [World's Fair] Board." Then, three days later, the Spokane *Spokesman*'s editor commended the appointment of John D. Hendricks as professor of agriculture at Pullman. Johnson found that one of the professor's best attributes was his criticism of Meany's handling of a World's Fair exhibit in which Meany proposed to display Indian relics more prominently than educational exhibits. Once more, Johnson ridiculed Meany over the appointment of Newell.[20]

Meany's highest priorities for the session of the third legislature, which started in January 1893, were to obtain more money for the World's Fair Commission and additional legislation to establish the University of Washington on its new campus. He was also prepared to support incumbent John B. Allen for the United States Senate. The session did not promise to be a love feast in spite of strong Republican majorities in the legislature. The Northern Pacific's stubborn and effective fight to prevent adequate regulation in the first two legislatures remained a strong threat to sideline major bills.

Indeed, the U.S. senatorial election absorbed a great deal of energy and attention during the entire session. Both Republican candidates, the incumbent Allen, Seattle's choice, and George Turner, of Spokane, were anathema to the railroad since they favored regulation. Other issues divided Seattle, Tacoma, and Spokane in various sectional animosities, making it possible for the railroad lobby to gain its ends. The senatorial election in the legislature required an incredible 101 ballots, all of which failed to produce a winner.[21]

Even in the most absorbing maneuvering and debating over the senatorial election, Meany could not forget editor Joseph French Johnson's charges that he had intervened improperly in the affairs of Washington Agricultural College. Johnson, in fact, reached a climax of unfounded accusation when he wrote in the *Spokesman* that "Representative Meany has declared, if rumor be true, that he would run the college and the state university, and he certainly has been particularly active with his endorsements of his friends; and Regent Smith has been equally complacent in making appointments on Meany's endorsements. If professors are chosen solely for political reasons the public should know it." The editor was about to get his wish: the legislature had appointed a joint committee to investigate the affairs of the college.[22]

The committee's report completely absolved Meany and other outsiders of wrong-doing in their relations with the agricultural college. No employee had been hired "for or through political influence," in the committee's judgment. On the other hand, the regents were found solely responsible for the difficulties in Pullman. Shortly after the legislature adjourned, Governor McGraw removed the entire Board of Regents.[23]

Representative Meany had hurried to Olympia on January 5, 1893, being one of the first legislators to arrive. His haste resulted not from impending attacks on his integrity, but rather because he carried the bulky report of the World's Fair Commission for presentation to Governor Elisha P.

Ferry, the out-going executive. Meany was not a mere courier, but author. The report needed to be publicized as soon as possible to assist the Commission in obtaining another appropriation for the display in Chicago.[24]

Hanging like a dark cloud over these considerations, however, were the familiar accusations by Ezra Meeker that Meany and various commissioners had either wasted or wrongfully spent the previous appropriation and destroyed Meeker's work as first executive commissioner. By early February, the *Seattle Press-Times* leaped into the fray with few facts, reporting that a big fight was brewing between the World's Fair Commission and the legislature on the grounds that the Commission's expenses were appallingly high. Meany, too, must be fired before additional money would be appropriated, according to some of the rumors.[25]

Although there had been some preliminary examination of witnesses, a full investigation was launched on February 9, when Senator A.T. Van De Vanter, Republican of Kent in King County, introduced a concurrent resolution to establish a joint House-Senate investigating committee, which quickly received Senate approval. Meany moved its passage in the House, which followed without delay.[26]

The *Press-Times* reported that Meany had protested the Senate's resolution before presenting it to his own house. The editor of the *Spokesman* once more became scornful of Meany's actions. The latter, however, had reason to be confident of the outcome. Tacoma's Chamber of Commerce already had given its support to a $50,000 appropriation. Samuel Collyer, too, treasurer of the World's Fair Commission, testified to Meany's outstanding work.[27]

Meeker held the stage at the hearings long enough to repeat familiar charges. His most incendiary statements had been made several days earlier in preliminary hearings when he charged wildly that Meany's services as press agent "were not and never have been needed...his acts soon became obstructive and meddlesome....Meany has drawn as salary $3000, and approximately $900 additional expenses which should be returned to the state treasury."[28]

In the next few days, the mercurial Meeker changed his mind and absolved Meany of blame:

> I have recently examined more closely into the work done by Mr. Meany...I find that he has performed very valuable service.... Since August, 1891, he has done the bulk of the work connected with the executive office, and I have no doubt that his services have been worth all that the state has paid for them.[29]

After Meeker's astonishing performance, and following the testimony of a variety of other witnesses, the joint investigating committee completely exonerated Meany of all charges. The commissioners, too, were found innocent of dishonesty or intentional neglect of obligations. Some extravagance had resulted from "utter lack of sources of reliable information pertaining to the work." The committee concluded that the Commission should be permitted to continue its work.[30]

The investigating committee also sponsored a measure to appropriate an additional $50,000 for participation in the Chicago fair plus $5,000 for the women's department. The nine member executive committee established by the 1891 legislature was continued and charged with administering the $50,000, while the women managers of the women's department would expend the smaller appropriation. The Senate approved the bill without incident.

In the House, however, Meany had to rise once more to put down the Meeker nemesis. Representative Stephen Judson, Democrat from Pierce County, sought to renew Meeker's criticism of the Commission by proposing to reduce it to three members. Meany, incensed, made a "strong speech" against the "outrageous attack." Judson was defeated and thereafter joined the majority as it passed the measure 67 to 5. Governor McGraw signed the measure into law without reservations.[31]

Meany was the sole graduate of the University of Washington in the third legislature, as he had been in the second, and once more the King County delegation singled him out to introduce a bill to relocate that institution. That congenial task was made even more satisfying for Meany by the absence of sectional jealousies concerning the welfare of the University. Even Joseph French Johnson of the *Spokesman*, vigilant supporter of the agricultural college, insisted in terms Meany might have accepted, that "Washington needs a university that will rank with Ann Harbor [*sic*, Ann Arbor], the University of Pennsylvania or Wisconsin, not a mere high school, as it is at present." Another noteworthy sign of close relations on the issue came late in the session when the *Tacoma Ledger* joined the call for a university at Seattle which would be "the peer of any in the land."[32]

The problem faced by the legislators was that the 1891 law authorizing the creation of the new campus had not worked out. Due to a depressed economy, the old campus could not be sold at appraised value, so it was not sold at all. In addition, the Board of Land and Building Commissioners had cleared land at the new site and undertaken unauthorized building expenditures. After that, the matter was back in the hands of the legislators.[33]

As chairman of the House Committee on the University and Normal Schools, Meany joined a five-member joint legislative committee to visit the old campus and assess the University's needs. The legislators found the main building neat and tidy but otherwise inadequate for all teaching and learning activities. Ruefully, they concluded that many cities could boast better conditions for their public schools.[34]

Taking up his responsibilities, Meany carefully drew up a university bill, even consulting with members of the state supreme court as to its adequacy. Once satisfied, he introduced it to the House on February 27. His hope for laying the foundation of a great university was represented in fine disregard for the 160 acre limitation stipulated in the 1891 law. Section one of the new bill directed the governor to purchase the whole of fractional section 16 of the school lands lying between lakes Washington and Union. That tract totaled 350 acres of beautiful timbered land. For a university endowment, Meany wrote a provision assigning 100,000 acres of school lands to the University from those available under the Enabling Act of 1889 which had admitted Washington into the Union. Of great significance was a provision that "tuition shall be free to all graduates of the public high schools of the state, whose course of study is approved by the faculty of the university and the superintendent of public instruction." Meany also entered the sum of $150,000 to cover the expenses of clearing the new campus, erecting a building, and selling the old campus. Finally, the Land and Building Commission was to be abolished, leaving the Board of Regents in charge without question.[35]

Meany's bill was referred to the joint university committee which analyzed it closely and made alterations, but did not substantially change any of Meany's seminal provisions, except to liberalize somewhat the tuition provision. An amendment made explicit the charge that education must be equal for both sexes. In addition, it provided that graduates of Washington's private schools might have the privilege of free tuition. The $150,000 appropriation was dropped, with the intention of placing it in the general appropriation bill. Meany very likely supported the alterations as none changed the philosophy behind his bill.[36]

After that, Meany's bill received swift and favorable treatment. The House passed it on March 9, 1893 by a 66 to 3 vote—nine absent or not voting; the Senate voted favorably on the same day, 23 to 2—nine absent or not voting. Meany also played a leading role in obtaining appropriations.

He strongly supported the recommendation of the joint university committee that $39,000 be appropriated for the University's ordinary operating budget. He also rose in the House to amend the general appropriations bill by adding the $150,000 desired for building the new campus, the item dropped from his original university bill. Both grants became law.[37]

When the issue was decided, the *Post-Intelligencer* exulted over Meany's bill: "Its provisions are such as to establish the state university in the most substantial manner possible." Members of the King County delegation and the joint university committee were given full credit for the achievement. In the end, though, Meany's attention to the University's appropriation was singled out for special mention and he was called upon to express his feelings.

He reported that his first thought had not been about creating a University of Michigan of the Far West, although the *Post-Intelligencer* drew that comparison. Nevertheless, it was an idea he probably had begun to covet. At that moment he "took the keenest kind of delight" in the fact that Washington's residents would be able to attend the University of Washington without paying tuition. He linked his "hard struggle" as a student with that "of a lot of young men who are now going through exactly the same trying experience."[38]

If the University of Washington had been elevated above partisanship and political log-rolling, the normal schools had not. Meany's hope, expressed in the spring of 1892, that all teacher training might be concentrated at the University vanished once the new legislative session began. As a matter of fact, he wrote some years later in his *History of the State of Washington:*

> The Enabling Act had used the plural in granting one hundred thousand acres of public land for [support of] normal schools. There was a perfect scramble for normal schools on the part of counties desiring some good State institution. The schools at Cheney and Ellensburg were created by the first Legislature [1889-1890]. Senator Henry Long, of Chehalis, was about to secure the third one when it was changed by amendment from a normal to a reform school, and the senator, in disgust, voted against his own bill as amended.[39]

As chairman of the House Committee on the University and Normal Schools in the 1891 and 1893 sessions, Meany felt overwhelmed by the many requests for normal schools. Most of the petitions were pigeon-holed but on February 4, 1893, his committee reported favorably on a bill to establish a normal school in Whatcom County. It passed both houses and Governor McGraw signed it into law.[40]

Thereafter, matters were taken out of Meany's hands. A joint committee, of which he was not a member, uncovered evidence of mismanagement at Cheney and poor organization of the normal schools generally, arousing the wrath of Governor McGraw, who decided that the legislators were shirking fiscal responsibility by voting extravagant normal school budgets and putting the responsibility for negative action on him. Meany's standing committee had seen the passage into law of its bill to systematize and hence run normal schools economically and efficiently, but that law was forgotten in the wake of the governor's devastating action: he vetoed the entire budgets for the Cheney and Whatcom normal schools, delaying the opening of the latter until 1899 and forcing the former to operate virtually on a starvation basis with local funds until 1895. He did, however, permit the budget for the normal school at Ellensburg to stand.[41]

In the language of the day, McGraw had wielded the "pruning knife" and Meany probably defended his friend's actions at the time. Clearly, he did so later in his *History of the State of Washington* when he applauded McGraw for "heroic efforts at retrenchment." Meany's loyalty to McGraw, though sharply tested by these developments, seemingly remained steadfast even though the *Post-Intelligencer* vacillated. The latter, normally friendly to the governor, "hastened to assure the people of Eastern Washington that McGraw had acted 'unwittingly'" in vetoing the Cheney budget, but at one point called his action malicious. Other papers across the state joined the chorus of condemnation.[42]

So much attention fell upon Meany in the press on more important matters that when he became involved with labor legislation the Spokane *Spokesman* sought to divert its readers with sarcasm: "Representative Meany is amusing himself between investigating committees [by] opposing delegations from the labor congresses. It is wonderful how versatile Mr. Meany is." That effusion followed the appearance of a delegation from the newly organized Washington State Labor Congress, a body of untested strength. Its leaders requested the privilege of the House floor in order to recommend labor legislation. When Meany objected, "the house somewhat severely sat down on Mr. Meany," according to the *Tacoma Daily Ledger*, overruling his motion that the delegation should instead submit to committee hearings. Then, when a labor leader accused a legislator of being "a tool of corrupt capitalists and corporations," Meany leaped to his feet in protest. This time he prevailed as the House accepted his resolution to expunge the aspersions cast upon their colleague. Members of the Senate had the same experience and also passed a motion of censure.[43]

Meany actually sympathized sufficiently with labor's objectives that he introduced two bills in the House on behalf of the Western Central Labor Union of Seattle, a body which had united craft unions with assemblies of the Knights of Labor. The first bill required employers to pay wages to their employees within a week of the time the work was accomplished. It also proposed that unpaid employees be given liens on the firms' property for wages due them. The second, more controversial, measure forbade employers from restraining their employees from joining labor unions. Both bills died in House committees without any visible effort by Meany to extricate them.[44]

When the third legislature adjourned, the Republican Party had split over important issues, particularly the senatorial fight, but Meany's main objectives had been achieved. He must have been pleased to read the Spokane *Review*'s unequivocal statement regarding educational advance: "The most important work in this direction being that accomplished by a bill introduced by Meany of King appropriating $150,000 for state university purposes."

Meany, still only thirty years old, wrote privately that he had been "placed under a stronger fire of criticism and fault-finding than probably befell any other young man in the State." He savored his achievement "in coming out from all this unpleasantness with colors flying and a good measure of success as the result of my work in the legislature and for the World's Fair Commission." At that happy moment he permitted himself to exult that he had "satisfactorily proven that the criticisms of my enemies were entirely without foundation and when this fact was proven it simply redounded the more to my credit."[45]

Far from having time to enjoy his legislative triumphs, however, Meany had to rush back to Tacoma to finish preparations for the World's Fair. Statistics had to be compiled and the souvenir book, entitled *The State of Washington*, had to be seen through the press. As late as March 20—less than three months before the opening in Chicago—many county officials had not delivered their data for the book's statistical compilation. Even the King County statistics were incomplete and carelessly prepared. A trying situation was rendered almost desperate on April 1 when Percy Rochester, the assistant executive commissioner, heaped all the remaining local tasks on Meany and departed for Chicago. At that point, Meany had only ten days to complete everything before he too had to leave for the fair.[46]

He reported to Dr. G.V. Calhoun, the executive commissioner, that everything was going well, calling attention to the fact that all contracts for publishing *The State of Washington* had been signed. All the contractors were Washington firms, which he probably thought would enhance the reputation of the state. Certainly, editors Meany and Elwood Evans emphasized the home production when writing the book's preface. Meany's elation was shattered, however, when Dr. Calhoun ordered him not to leave Tacoma (Calhoun's headquarters) until he received further orders. Meany found that directive so disturbing that he turned to his friend Will LaFollette, one of the exhibit directors in Chicago, pouring out his fears rather frantically that the commissioners might dismiss him:

> I declare Will I am in awful condition financially. I have gone steadily behind for the past two years. I consolidated some of my debts Friday $1700 and now I must raise $1000 more and I will be in shape to leave home. So for Heavens sake dont [*sic*] let them lop off my head or my salary or any part of it. I will be willing to do two men's work and expect to do so. I have fine plans for our "Publicity and Promotion" department and I know our State's work will reap good results through this department if my plans are permitted to mature.

His anxieties proved groundless and twelve days later he informed Dr. Calhoun that he had read the last page proof of the souvenir book, constructed its index, and would be off to join Calhoun in Chicago shortly, as soon as he raised some money.[47]

The first notice of the book appeared in the *Tacoma Daily Ledger* on April 25, when a hasty perusal of the proof sheets suggested to a reviewer that the history of the state, written by Elwood Evans (noted pioneer politician and orator), was good. The reviewer described Meany's statistics as "peculiarly rich." The most "notable feature," according to the story, was a description county by county, "giving minute and valuable information, particularly to immigrants." Two days later, after he had studied the proof sheets more closely, the editor of the *Daily Ledger* provided a more critical statement. The history, he concluded, was admirable and would interest future generations of Washingtonians but not immigrants or investors. A careful examination showed that some of the statistics were "incorrect, and palpably so, and there is much that might have been left out with profit." Nevertheless, he congratulated Evans and Meany "upon having done so much in the [time] given, and done it no worse."[48]

Certainly the book lacked attractiveness when compared with other evidence of Washington's energy, creativeness, and industry exhibited at the exposition. Even Meany admitted, when writing the final report of the Washington World's Fair Commission, that "many of the illustrations [in the book] were blurred and thus rendered worse than useless." He must have been disappointed too in the drab appearance, inferior paper, poor typography, composition, and printing. One could hardly brag that it was a Washington product.[49]

Edmond and his family arrived in Chicago on May 1, 1893, the opening day of the World's Fair. Work on the fair grounds would not be completed for several weeks nor would Washington's exhibits be ready for some time. Nevertheless, the Washington state building had already attracted a great deal of attention. The *New York World* had commented in early April that "the [hall of the] new state of Washington is an unexpected second" to New York's premier structure. "A good many people do not yet know just what spot on the map Washington occupies yet it is showing up at the world's fair with such states as New York and Illinois." The *World* concluded by noting that the building featured gigantic logs in the foundation and lower portion which constituted a "timber exhibit." The fact that all the building materials came from Washington proved "unique and interesting."[50]

Meany sat at a desk in the front gallery of the Washington state building, greeting visitors and singing the praise of his state. He did much more than that, however. He also supervised the register of persons interested in Washington, gathering a list which ultimately totaled 13,760 potential immigrants or investors. He also solicited complimentary subscriptions, reportedly to 200 Washington newspapers. They filled a large public reading room. Lizzie Meany took charge of the *Post-Intelligencer*'s section and also supplied news items to that paper.[51]

Meany never ceased pouring out publicity releases and magazine articles designed to educate Easterners about Washington, but also to reassure the residents of the state that the exhibits were bringing the desired results. In his first on-the-spot release, written May 8, he drew attention to the fact that Washington boasted the largest flag waving over the exhibition grounds. He also proudly related that

> Every Washingtonian points to that great flag as he travels about this "white city" [the exposition], and his love for his good home state grows firmer and stronger, and he knows that beneath that flag is an exhibit of natural wealth that is not equaled by any other state on the grounds.[52]

Later releases had more substance, if no less provincial boasting. By June 1, he had managed to find time to finish an article begun on the train trip to Chicago. Armed with a Kodak and notebook, he had made a pictorial record of the pleasures of traveling from Spokane Falls to St. Paul,

Minnesota, over the Great Northern Railway. He celebrated the beauties of nature he had photographed in "Snapshots in the New Northwest," an article which appeared in *The Graphic* of Chicago on July 15, 1893. Later in the summer he was pleased to find his short illustrated piece on Washington's exhibition hall, "The Home of this New State at the World's Fair," published in *The National Builder* (Chicago).[53]

The steady stream of press handouts reached a climax in "Beating the Whole World," released October 21, near the end of the exposition. In it Meany achieved a press agent's coup: he was able to cite evidence of Washington's splendid resources and progress, as published in an earlier article he had sent to *American Tid-Bits* of Chicago. That earlier piece was built upon half a dozen press releases that had come from his pen.[54]

Meany went on in "Beating the Whole World" to offer his optimistic prophecy of the exhibition's effect upon his state:

> We now know to a certainty that the results to Washington will be many times greater than what the state has expended. Over seven thousand people have declared their intentions of locating in Washington, all, or nearly all, the direct result of what they have seen from the state here at the exposition. Suppose these people bring to Washington an average of $100 each, and it would be fairer to suppose that ten times that amount, you see that it means at that very low figure, over $700,000.

Persuaded by his arithmetic, Meany forecast that "these seven thousand addresses are only a small portion of the tide that is turned toward Washington by this exposition." Later, when his tally of all interested persons exceeded 13,000, he no doubt was overjoyed. The publicist, thus, was carried away by the enthusiasm of the moment and understandably forgetful of economic realities. The exposition occurred in the midst of a depression which discouraged movement of either people or capital to a new state. Only when prosperity returned, after the Yukon and Alaskan gold discoveries poured wealth into Seattle, did Meany's beloved state become attractive to settlers and investors.[55]

Though the World's Columbian Exposition closed its doors on November 1, 1893, the Meanys stayed on at the request of Governor McGraw to pack up the exhibits. By Thanksgiving, however, the family headed for Seattle. The holidays were bleak that year as the Meanys were suffering from what Edmond called, "these frightful Democratic times." He wrote to an old friend in January 1894 concerning an old debt, "I have one single dollar in my pocket and current expense bills [are] raining in on me from every where [*sic*]." He estimated that working for the World's Fair Commission had set him back over $2,000. Plans to pay his debts by touring the state presenting an illustrated lecture on the fair collapsed in the deflationary spiral of the depression.[56]

Meany still had the official World's Fair Commission report to prepare but that would yield little or no income. He tried, in the meantime, to take advantage of contacts made with Chicago businessmen, offering to find them real estate for investment or to sell their products, but nothing came of these forays into business promotion. "As yet I have been unable to secure employment since the World's Fair," Meany wrote on April 2, 1894, to his college classmate, Professor Charles V. Piper. "I declare, Charles, it is awful. My upper lip is kept stiff soley [*sic*] by the support of the lower jaw, which if you will remember, is rather well developed in this specimen of the genus *homo*."[57]

That attempt at humor was quickly followed by a plunge into despair as Meany awaited the outcome of another chance for advancement. In February he had applied for the post of secretary to the Board of Regents of the University of Washington. Though he had the active support of editor Fred J. Grant and Governor John H. McGraw, he professed bewilderment when the latter seemed to be consulting his enemies and not his friends regarding the application. The horizon brightened and Meany's energies were once again concentrated on hopeful developments with the birth of a daughter, Margaret, on April 18, 1894. About the same time he was elected secretary to the regents. This position, though only half-time and paying about $600 per year, immediately occupied most of Meany's working day and future plans.[58]

He quickly became an exemplary secretary, as Frederick E. Bolton wrote in 1950, in an unpublished history of the University. Before Meany's appointment, the regents' records were meager and incomplete, but "Meany compiled model records and that pattern has prevailed to the present," according to Bolton. In reality, Meany became an executive assistant, budget coordinator, and spokesman for academic policy, as well as lobbyist. President Thomas M. Gatch's inability or disinclination to assume the burdens of an institution on the verge of transformation permitted Meany to share in the leadership devolving upon the regents.[59]

Thus, Meany did not simply keep records and make arrangements for ceremonial tasks, such as laying the cornerstone for Denny Hall on the new campus; he also acted as the business agent for the regents in negotiating contracts for constructing that building. He soon made recommendations to the regents for starting professional training in pharmacy and law.

Then, addressing the students in their newspaper, *The Pacific Wave*, he took the role of prophet, usually reserved to the president. Meany predicted that the University would quickly become the "apex" of Washington's educational system in the new century and one of the chief institutions of the "Great West." Love for the old college (he signed the article as a member of the "Class of 1885") did not conflict with his joy at the possibilities for developing professional schools. Above all, he saw the State of Washington—with a great research center—as a prime field for the study of the natural sciences.[60]

In fall 1894, the regents instructed Meany to compile data for the budget request to be presented to the legislature in January. Because he could not attend the next faculty meeting, Meany asked President Gatch to assist him in gathering faculty budgetary requests. In mid-November Meany took to the regents requests amounting to $80,000. He also submitted detailed recommendations for additional faculty along with proposals for a mechanical engineering department and a geological survey.[61]

Meany also assumed a function which later would be assigned to a dean of students when he appealed to Seattle's citizens to help students:

> Citizens of Seattle, can you help students in the university? Every year there come to the University of Washington a number of students who desire to pay their living expenses by securing work that they can do at spare hours while in attendance at school. You who have had to struggle for your education can appreciate this, and if you know of any opportunities of securing such work please notify the undersigned.
>
> Edmond S. Meany, Sec.

This appeal, which also included a request for private housing for students, disclosed that the University's attraction for Meany included its paternalistic concern for the individual in his struggles to rise in the social scale.[62]

In the autumn of 1894 the Meany family moved to the newly opened Brooklyn Addition, located near the new University campus. There Meany purchased a seven-room house and five lots, to which five more lots would be added in 1900. The special levies for paving, sewer, and other necessities stretched the family's resources to the limit the next few years. Thus, it may have occasioned little surprise to Meany's colleagues that he might consider an offer of a staff position with the *Post-Intelligencer*. In the end he accepted only part-time press assignments, remaining resolved to make a career with the University of Washington. But what career?[63]

CHAPTER FIVE

An Academic Career? The Years of Trial (1895-1898)

As the session of the fourth legislature in 1895 approached, Meany, who had not sought re-election to the House of Representatives, served as the chief lobbyist for the University of Washington. He met with the King County legislative delegation on January 5, 1895, to explain the University's requests. In addition to seeking funds to finish construction on the new campus, the regents asked for appropriations to establish professional programs and a geological survey of the state. The total request amounted to $174,000.[1]

Meany, the lobbyist, made an auspicious record. On January 25 he reported to Major J.R. Hayden, president of the Board of Regents, that he had blocked introduction of an anti-drill and uniform bill he thought inimical to the welfare of the University's cadet corps. The exact nature of the proposal remains unknown since it was not printed in either the Senate or House journal. Meany's action fitted with his determination to protect the University at all costs from foes known and unknown. The depth of his feeling can be seen from the fact that he persuaded Governor McGraw to veto any such measure which might reach his desk. The bill to establish a geological survey, Meany also reported to Hayden, had been introduced and printed and he was ready to take a "small sized wagon load of statistics" to the hearing to support its passage. Though Meany took seriously the frequent cries for economy in funding state institutions, he assured Hayden the outcome would be favorable to the University.[2]

Such assurances rested on a firm base of lobbying. February 21 was a typical day: Meany rushed four times that day between the legislative chambers and various state offices, with great results. He was confident that the University would get approximately $170,000 as its appropriation, including operating and capital funds. Furthermore, he told Hayden with no little satisfaction that a King County delegation caucus had pledged to support the regents' requests. Three days later, his optimism declined when he reported that legislators in the House had demanded reductions in the budgets for state institutions. To placate University critics, Meany drafted a bill to reduce the Board of Regents from seven to three members, a measure which died along the way.[3]

Meany also obligingly composed resolutions to form a legislative delegation to visit the University. Adopted without question, these resolutions sent a cadre of legislators and Meany to Seattle on February 28. He had telegraphed to Hayden before departure, asking the regents to meet the delegation and "see they are not euchred out of supper." Hayden and his fellow regents responded bountifully with dinner followed by the theater. The next morning, Meany escorted them to the old campus to attend a student assembly and to review the Cadet Corps. In the afternoon, they took the trolley out to the new campus to confer with the regents and the contractor regarding the new building and financial matters. Favorably impressed with the site, the legislators permitted Meany to write "a good, strong report" for presentation to the legislature.[4]

Meany also drew up a bill forbidding introduction of saloons at the edge of the campus—to avoid the social evils which marked the downtown area of Seattle. Undoubtedly he acted with the full support of the regents and, indeed, of the middle class of the city. Years later historian Norman Clark described those middle class fears as concerned with "the debauchery of their most cherished values through drunkenness, prostitution, narcotic addiction, and violence....And the more saloons there were, the worse they would become." The measure, which became law on March 15, 1895, prohibited selling liquor within two miles of the campus and provided stiff penalties.[5]

To aid Meany's lobbying, the regents authorized Judge William D. Wood, one of their members, to join Meany in Olympia. The judge played an important role in scuttling efforts to reduce the Board of Regents to three members. Wood also persuaded the reluctant legislators to retain the existing $3 per day compensation for the regents until construction of the new campus was completed. After that, the board would have only per diem allowances. Other budgetary matters went smoothly. "All our other bills are passing as though they were greased," Meany reported, "and though I am on the 'go' night and day I am happy as one of those tremendous clams at high tide. We couldn't ask for anything better if the blooming legislature was made to order."[6]

Major Hayden congratulated Meany on his good work, but continued to seek additional compensation for the Board of Regents, a request lost in the hectic activity at the end of the session. Meany stayed in Olympia until the end to safeguard University interests. His assistant, Virgil A. Pusey, was a "daisy" Meany acknowledged, but Pusey, a senator, "has frequently said he could not get along without my help in keeping track of our measures. We haven't missed a point yet but things are traveling lively enough about now to keep a fellow busy."[7]

Regent John Gowey, who also supported the University's bills at Olympia, told Hayden that "the University came out of the 'grind' in good shape, more thanks to Ed Meany than anyone else." The only significant defeat for the University came when a bill to establish a state geological survey did not get out of committee. For his part, Meany commended the King County delegation for its effective aid, saying "our boys from King County are rapidly developing good qualities of successful rustlers." The regents, with justification, looked optimistically to the future, as they received $90,000 for operations, $50,000 for additional construction, and a reappropriation of $39,000 of unexpended capital funds from the preceding biennium.[8]

Meany's reward was immediate. On April 1, 1895, he became the University registrar. Not only was he employed full time, he carried the responsibilities of a business manager and the duties of a buildings and grounds supervisor along with the usual tasks of a registrar—registering students, preserving records, and editing bulletins and the University catalog. He was supervised directly by the Board of Regents, leaving President Thomas M. Gatch in an anomalous position.

Meany's delight overflowed into a letter he wrote to a Chicago correspondent. "You never saw a red headed, long legged fellow more busy during the last three months than I have been. It has been a night and day rush but not a point was lost in the tedious game." He disclosed that he and his family had moved to the Brooklyn Addition, adjacent to the new University campus. Here he hoped to seek election to the state senate in a newly formed legislative district. He confidently assumed that the new district "will always be conceded one legislator for the University and my new neighbors seem to rejoice...that hereafter they can send me." He repeated his desire to U.S. Senator Watson C. Squire but never found encouragement for a candidacy—and perhaps did not seriously seek it.[9]

Meany's passionate devotion to alma mater proved once again to be his greatest source of strength as a community leader. When student editors of *The Pacific Wave* in May 1895, turned to him for a message in their commencement number, he reminded the graduating class of its overwhelming indebtedness to the old school when facing life's battles:

> You stand alone and perhaps have no other weapons in your hands but those given you by your alma mater. Filled with the spirit of brave endeavor you begin the battle and soon test the temper of those weapons. You are not a stranger in the use of the arms of a trained intellect and you soon find that you can win those serious struggles of life, much the same as you won your laurels at school, by vigilant application.

The autobiographical note in this homily waxed strong and vibrant when he reflected that with success came a growing obligation to his school. "You become her champion and you cast about for some way, small or great, in which you can help advance the interests of the institution to which your mind will ever turn as to home, sweet home." For Meany, personally, the search for success turned more and more to his growing interest in natural science, history, and scholarship.[10]

Through his association with U.S. senators J.B. Allen and W.C. Squire, and Congressman W.H. Doolittle and other politicians, he obtained various files of federal government reports useful for both science and history. On January 29, 1892, after asking Allen for a long list of documents, he wrote, by way of apology, "you remember Aunt Betty, don't you? She once gave some famous advice: 'Git a plenty while you're gittin.'" Meany applied that advice in all quarters. He asked B.E. Fernow, chief of the Forest Service, for example, not only for forestry publications but also for the best sources of information on teaching the subject. He made the same request of Harvard professor C.S. Sargent and inquired how he might obtain the sumptuous twelve-volume set of Sargent's *The Silva of North America*. What may at first have been merely an avocation became transformed into a firm resolve to teach history and forestry, perhaps as early as his appointment as registrar.[11]

Meany's interest in pioneers had been stimulated when he met Henry H. Kitson, a Boston sculptor, at the Chicago World's Fair. They had discussed creating a statue of Isaac I. Stevens, the first territorial governor of Washington, architect of the 1850s Indian treaties, and a Civil War general for the Union. This was the beginning of a campaign to place such a work of art in Statuary Hall at the nation's capitol. On November 27, 1894, disclosing a patriotic impulse to Kitson, Meany wrote:

> I have long cherished a thrilling picture of Gen'l Stevens to be reproduced in a heroic statue....it is this: while cheering on his men in battle [in the Civil War] with sword uplifted the color bearer was shot down. Quick as a flash the General caught the falling banner in his left hand and dashed on with a sword in one hand, the banner in the other [shouting] "on my men!"

Meany then went on to ask rhetorically: "Don't [*sic*] it heat up your American blood? Can't you see him there? To my mind such a picture properly reproduced in a fine statue would be as good as a police force, especially in any city of the State where his name is revered."[12]

As he progressed in his investigation, Meany went beyond this simple romantic view of his hero. He pressed Hazard Stevens, son of the governor, for precise details of the Indian treaty meetings conducted by his father in the 1850s, and for recollections on the battle in the Civil War in which Stevens was killed. There is no evidence that Hazard, author of a eulogistic biography of his father, acceded to Meany's request, phrased as follows: "Some day I want to take two maps [of Washington] and sit down with you and have you mark all you can of the sites of the powwows where the various treaties were drawn, the camps made, and the routes taken in those memorable trips. We may be able to adjust dates on the maps which can probably be verified by the records when I get them from Washington City." Though he assured Kitson that the contract for a statue would be completed when the depression of the 1890s disappeared, it did not happen.[13]

Meany had learned that each state was entitled to place two statues in Statuary Hall, Washington D.C., so he began his campaign to include Marcus Whitman, the missionary martyr. A few weeks after initiating the drive for Stevens, Meany sought information from numerous sources on the life and appearance of Whitman. It soon became apparent that no portrait existed. Nevertheless, Meany believed that he could use reminiscences to produce a "composite likeness that under the circumstances will forever stand for Whitman." Subsequently he abandoned his quixotic scheme to produce a portrait where none existed, only to adopt an unreliable reconstruction by Oliver Nixon in his *How Marcus Whitman Saved Oregon*, a pietistic work published in 1895. Meany never lost his extravagant admiration for Whitman, but the statue now standing in Statuary Hall was largely the work of others.[14]

Meany's interest in history grew rapidly, soon transcending efforts to create statues. On March 18, 1895, he sent copies of syllabi for two proposed courses of college lectures to John F. Gowey, a sympathetic regent. Four months later, he asked Gowey to try to locate a book printed in 1857 which contained a message of Governor Stevens and correspondence on the Indian wars of the territorial period. At the time, Meany acknowledged that he hoped to devote his life not only to the University but also to "such historical and scientific work as shall, at the same time that it furnishes me with agreeable occupation, be of use to the University."[15]

President David Starr Jordan of the recently established Stanford University in California provided Meany with fresh inspiration for a career in scholarship and teaching. Meany met Jordan in the spring of 1895 when the latter visited Seattle. Jordan made a deep impression, causing an outpouring of Meany's fervent regard:

> I can never express my keen appreciation of the many visits I enjoyed with you during your recent visit. A young man's life, full of ambition, is like a sort of camera. It catches the light of its chosen luminaries and holds the impression until the plate is shattered. I feel as though I had obtained you for a friend and I mean to hold you as such if it is in my power.

Meany concluded with a familiar declaration of his esteem: "please remember that a friend's chief compensation in this world is found in the opportunity of rendering service to his prized friends."[16]

The opportunity for service primarily belonged to Jordan, however. A celebrated ichthyologist and an educator of note, Jordan met with the Young Naturalists' Society and agreed to classify several fish that its members had discovered in the waters of Puget Sound. Meany nominated Society members who might be honored with the names of the fishes, beginning with the "nestor" of the club, Charles L. Denny. Not only had Denny "collected most of our fish and many other specimens," wrote Meany, but he was also "pure gold as a loyal friend." An added reason urged was that "his father, Hon. Arthur A. Denny, was our patron when we were first organized as boys about fifteen years old." Friendship and scientific activity were rewarded when Jordan responded favorably. The fish was named after Denny, and Jordan honored Meany as well, naming the *Neolipanis Meanyi* after him.[17]

The Stanford influence seemed pervasive. Meany reported to Stanford's registrar, O.L. Elliott, that he modeled the University of Washington catalog for 1894-1895 on that produced by Stanford. He also affirmed to Elliott his intention to continue as registrar and secretary to the Board of Regents for many years while also beginning to teach and engage in research. He asked Elliott: "Do not college men usually look down upon efforts at lecturing or research by a man in charge of the business end of an institution of learning?" He hurried on to justify his intentions, writing "I have expected to meet such a sentiment but the field is here with no workers in it and I have the vigor and enthusiasm of a young man who has had to make his own way so I am going ahead with my plans."[18]

Searching for ways and means of establishing scholarship in local history occupied much of Meany's time and energy during the summer and fall of 1895. He began corresponding with professor Mary Sheldon Barnes, who taught Pacific Coast history at Stanford, and recommended topics in early Northwest history which needed investigation. While searching for publication outlets, he tried unsuccessfully to interest the United States Bureau of Education in underwriting a history of the state of Washington's educational development. He called upon the Library of Congress to answer detailed bibliographical questions. These requests revealed the paucity of such information in Seattle and suggested a measure of Meany's growing familiarity with historical literature.[19]

Never one to hesitate to call upon friends and acquaintances, Meany wrote to local collectors and historians for bibliographical information. Congressmen and senators were hardly immune; they had stacks of government documents to distribute gratis. On August 9, while asking Senator Watson C. Squire to help him find a copy of the government publication *United States Treaties with Indian Tribes*, Meany exulted that he was having great success in collecting materials:

> I am searching high and low for old books...and you would be surprised to see what progress I am making almost without any money whatever. When I get a trace of an old book or a set of books I manage to squeeze the price out of my salary and keep right on searching. There are many old publications to be had but they are becoming rarer each year.[20]

Collecting historical documents and rare books provided Meany with a special kind of intoxication. Perhaps no experience did more to reinforce his passion for collecting than his visit in August to the library of Columbia Lancaster, Washington's first territorial delegate. A fever of excitement gripped him when he received permission to take such materials as he pleased. Meany reported later that he claimed fifty volumes dealing with the "earliest territorial history."[21]

The harvest of his many inquiries about historical materials paid off so handsomely that he began to make plans for a private depository. In the midst of thanking Senator Squire for a volume of Stevens' Indian treaties, Meany reported that he was trying to figure out how he might build a little fireproof room for his library at home—a structure that might cost $300.[22]

He ultimately had to abandon his hope of building a private vault. He enjoyed success, however, in developing the University's library. A special opportunity arose when a group of Seattle's business and political leaders established the Frederick James Grant Memorial Association on September 30, 1895, to promote scholarship in American history at the University. Meany became its secretary and promoter. Although the members at first thought of establishing a chair of American history or political economy, by November the trustees decided instead to create a fund of $2,500 for purchasing books on American history for the library. Meany drew up a list of prospective donors and also solicited a list of the hundred best books in American history from professor George E. Howard of Stanford. Meanwhile, Meany continued to purchase numerous authoritative works out of his own pocket to make up for the deficient University library budget.[23]

Professor Mary Sheldon Barnes of Stanford opened Meany's eyes to the problems of teaching local and regional history when she sent him a copy of her extensive syllabus on Pacific Coast history. It covered major topics of exploration, conquest, diplomacy, and settlement from the sixteenth century to 1846, and contained a bibliography of the most important sources as well. Meany began immediately to fit more details of Pacific Northwest settlement and later history into Barnes' bibliography for his own use.

He also responded eagerly to professor Barnes' suggestion that teachers should create a Pacific Coast Historical Society. That wish did not materialize but Meany took an even more ambitious step when he sought and gained election to the American Historical Association—a tribute to his ambition since the organization was a small, exclusive, eastern club. He also inquired as to whether he might study for the degree of doctor of philosophy in absentia at Johns Hopkins University, the most prestigious graduate school in the nation. That inquiry symbolized a longing which could not be fulfilled. Obligations to his extended family and the University prevented lengthy graduate study, and, of course, earning a doctorate in absentia was impossible.[24]

Meany began teaching in January 1896, under the title of lecturer, offering courses in "The Development of Washington" and "Forestry." Since each course had a small enrollment and met only once a week through the third week of May, teaching did not seriously interfere with his administrative work. The five students in his forestry course wrote "theses" according to his class book. The reports probably were simple term papers, as is suggested by the titles, which included "Oak," "Spruce," and "Fir." His classroom procedures were not disclosed in the classbook, nor is the syllabus available today. He did, however, send a copy of the syllabus to B.E. Fernow, chief of the Division of Forestry in the U.S. Department of Agriculture, acknowledging aid already received and asking for criticism.[25]

In history, sixteen students out of the original twenty-two enrolled completed the course. Each student wrote a paper on such topics as "Indian Wars of the Washington Territory, 1855-56," "Hudson Bay Company and Northwest Company," "Early Settlement of Elliott Bay," "Chinese Riots in Washington Territory," and "Women Suffrage in Washington Territory." Meany sent the syllabus to numerous individuals, including members of the Board of Regents, but only in his letter to professor Barnes did he describe his classroom procedures. Three weeks after opening his courses, he wrote her:

> This work with me is original. I had no systematic training and never heard a class lecture. Up to the time I graduated from the University of Washington in 1885 our work was all from textbooks except a very little laboratory and field work in Botany. In the transformation we are undergoing I find myself in charge of two lecture courses: History and Forestry. It has called into action faculties I [didn't] know I owned and I am really proud of the progress being made.[26]

He concluded with an expression of hope: "I think my classes look upon me as a veteran and I take good care that they do not loiter or dose [*sic*] on the road." His expectations were met at least once that first term. On April 23 *The Pacific Wave* carried a student's reaction to his lecture on territorial days. Affirming that "Mr. Meany has a thorough and exhaustive knowledge of the early history of Washington," the reporter stated that Meany was "in his element when portraying the dramatic scenes," especially those involving Isaac I. Stevens. As "the central figure of the lecture," Stevens was depicted as adopting "wise and energetic measures," for the protection of the white community, and also received an "eloquent tribute" for "his valor and final death in the defense of the Union."[27]

The warmth and generosity of the student's evaluation was matched by Meany when he attempted to compensate for the scarcity of instructional materials by loaning his own books, so laboriously gathered, to students and colleagues. *The Pacific Wave* also acknowledged that the

University's library holdings were inadequate in all fields. The regents' fourth biennial report, issued in December 1896, supported that opinion, revealing that its 5,909 volumes placed the University of Washington far below the University of California and all major eastern institutions. Nevertheless, Meany found satisfaction that some of "the tall oak book-cases with the glass fronts" which he had brought back from the World's Fair were being pressed into service as "the first home of the Frederick James Grant Library of American History." They would have at least 100 volumes available at the beginning of the next term.[28]

Meany's venture into teaching history quickly brought invitations to lecture off campus. On May 30, 1896, for example, he spoke on the history of Washington to a historical society in Olympia. Then, on July 5, he addressed the Washington State Teacher's Association meeting in Spokane where he advocated teaching Washington's history in the public schools. Happily, he was able to report that the Committee of Ten of the National Education Association had recommended a major role for history, particularly American, in the curriculum: "It must be refreshing to the patriotic spirit of the American teacher," he orated, "to realize through the most casual perusal of the educational journals and the catalogues...of the American institutions of learning how great is the revival of zeal in the subject of history, and how prominent is the rank being given to the study of American history."[29]

Meany acknowledged to the Spokane audience that little had been accomplished in the study of local history. There was no textbook and few collateral readings had been published. For the most part he could only lecture, listen to rote memorization, and supervise preparation of term papers on a limited number of topics. Nevertheless, he urged teachers to arouse interest and to guide their students into a subject for which "the opportunity is here; and the material rich, abundant, and important." For his own part, Meany reported that he expected to accumulate quickly the materials needed for serious work.[30]

Though the public schools could hardly hope to proceed even at the University's slow pace in accumulating library materials and trained teachers, local school administrators quickly responded to Meany's interest in their problems. Leaders of the Pierce County Teacher's Institute invited him to speak in August and the Snohomish County teachers followed suit with an invitation for a September speech. Meany accepted both invitations enthusiastically, but refused to accept payment for the appearances. His explanation to Snohomish authorities revealed a deep sense of duty:

> I had not thought of making any charge for the address before your Institute but if you wish to pay my railroad fare and hotel bill...I will not object. My time belongs to the State of Washington and I am very glad if I can be of use in any way in addition to my regular duties.[31]

Meany might have wondered, at least privately, at his progress when the college registration for fall 1896 proved disappointing. His growing reputation off-campus had not attracted large numbers of students. Only six enrolled in his "Development of Washington" course as opposed to twenty-two the previous term. In "Forestry" he had five, the same number as before. Of course, those once-a-week classes, meeting only until Thanksgiving, were interludes in Meany's busy schedule. His administrative duties gave him much greater opportunities for contact with the 300-member student body than did his classes.[32]

Meany's prime historical interest continued to be focused on Isaac I. Stevens. He concentrated on gathering documentation in order to publicize Stevens in oratory and biography. A chance to demonstrate his sincerity, dedication, and historical acumen came when he addressed the Stevens Chapter of the Grand Army of the Republic in Seattle on January 26, 1897.[33]

Meany faithfully recounted Stevens' life from birth to death. A reporter stated that Meany quoted "messages and documents too numerous to be more than alluded to in a brief report," though in fact some were discussed rather fully in the news story. Style, eloquence, and sentiment characterized his address, captivating the reporter who found that his "manner was easy and forcible, rising at times to real eloquence and profound pathos."[34]

Six months later, on July 4 and 11, 1897, Meany published an extended article in the *Post-Intelligencer* entitled, "Ten Indian Treaties: Greatest Work of Gov. Isaac I. Stevens." There he applied the results of his research in the form of a detailed description of the terms of Stevens' treaties with Indian tribes in the region (which Stevens made in his capacity as Superintendent of Indian Affairs for Washington Territory). Though Stevens' actions and policies had sharply divided his contemporaries into supporting and opposing camps, Meany did not hesitate to accept Hazard Stevens' view of his father's treaty-making in the most sympathetic terms. "We are constrained," Meany concluded, "not only to vindicate the treaties but to pronounce their author the greatest man our commonwealth has known."[35]

When the January 1897 term opened, Meany was absent from the campus, once again serving as lobbyist at the biennial legislative session.

This legislature, the fifth since statehood, was dominated by Populists whose farmer and eastern Washington adherents showed little interest in supporting higher education in the face of depression and government deficits. Lobbyist Meany, in addition, received little assistance from the demoralized regents, who expected to be replaced soon by the Populist governor, John R. Rogers. The governor had been swept into office by the Populist landslide at the polls in November 1896. In addition, University President Mark Harrington proved incapable of coping with his institution's problems, rendering Meany's work especially difficult.[36]

Meany soon experienced anxiety about his own future at the University, becoming aware that the Populists looked upon him as a partisan and his office as political. Writing to Hazard Stevens on January 21, 1897, he expressed an enthusiasm about his historical investigations which contrasted sharply with his "greatest dread...that the new state administration may find it necessary to dispense with my services in the University. This would prove a serious blow to my historical researches so I hope the street corner threats and rumors so often reported to me may prove without foundation."[37]

The Populists, by mid-February, had killed a bill to support high schools and Meany despaired of getting a fair hearing for the University. The Populist administration—actually a fusion of Populists, Democrats, and Silver Republicans—took a step in late February to curb Meany's authority, as well as that of the regents, when state auditor Neal Cheetham refused to honor Meany's expense vouchers as lobbyist. In vain, Meany protested that his mandate to represent the regents was clear and that strong precedents existed for payment. In the end, he was out-of-pocket $80 in hotel and transportation charges, expenses which forced him to borrow money which he could not repay promptly.[38]

When it was learned that perhaps no more than $60,000 might be appropriated for the University's operating budget, several of Meany's young friends on the faculty consoled him with the thought that they could manage with that amount by reducing salaries and consolidating positions. They must have been relieved later to find the actual appropriation of $78,000 was only $12,000 less than the regents had desired. The equipment budget, however, dropped to an infinitesimal sum, with the legislature granting only $2,500. As a bit of solace, Meany was able to insert a section into the codified school laws recognizing the University as "the capstone of the State's system of Public Schools."[39]

Though Meany was back on campus by March 9, 1897, he could scarcely concentrate on his work. Governor Rogers had appointed four new regents, all Seattle Populists. Forming the majority on the board, they lost no time in abolishing Meany's administrative post, leaving him insecurely attached to the University through his lectureships. On April 22, however, a new board appointed Meany professor of American history and lecturer in forestry for one year, a role he would assume May 1, 1897. With a sense of relief, he rationalized that the new regents had been moved to such action because they were impressed with his faithful service to the University.[40]

"I see before me a long, hard struggle of good work and I intend to be successful," Meany wrote to David Starr Jordan. "As soon as the University closes I hope to start east as I want to take the Summer work offered by Professor Hart at Harvard. This is a life work that challenges all of my ambition and energy." Due to his financial plight, Meany did not get the opportunity to study under Albert Bushnell Hart, one of the leading American historians. His salary of $1,300, although standard rate for full professors at the University of Washington, did not permit fulfillment of his plans. Nor did a patron come forward after his diligent solicitation of support from several affluent friends. After that, he inquired as to whether professor George E. Howard of Stanford might be teaching that summer. Whatever the reply, the inquiry made on June 14 probably arrived too late. For the summer of 1897, Meany had to be content with the free advice given by one of his correspondents that he engage in home study to prepare himself for the new professorship.[41]

In response to a cordial greeting from Governor Rogers on July 3, he promised to stay out of politics and devote the rest of his life to scholarship. He would refrain from partisanship, Meany affirmed, except to cast his vote. Meany must have winced when he read that Rogers' only objection to him had been that he was "an offensive partisan." The Governor seemed pleased that Meany pledged to be a pure scholar. Rogers also disavowed any intention to interfere with the actions of the Board of Regents, a matter which gave Meany a false sense of security.[42]

At any rate, the sanguine young professor buried himself in the "home study" of history and forestry that summer of 1897, apparently delighted to leave politics to others. He worked diligently to encourage donations of books and funds to the Frederick James Grant Memorial Association. As a result, he acquired an impressive list, including the historical works of Francis Parkman, John Fiske, James Bryce, Theodore Roosevelt, Washington Irving, Hubert Howe Bancroft, and a large number of books recommended by A.B. Hart and other leading scholars.[43]

When classes resumed on September 7, 1897, Meany taught five courses which met for the ten-week term at the rate of seventeen hours per week. The heavy burden, a typical schedule for professors in American colleges, was mitigated by the fact that he had a total enrollment of only fifty-two students. Little may be learned about his course in "General History," beyond the information that its five students met daily with their professor. The four students enrolled in "Problems in American History" appear to have been engaged in a colloquium for which they wrote papers on topics such as "Pre-Columbian America," "Causes that Led to the American Revolution," and "Adoption of the Constitution."

The "American History" course, on the other hand, was extensively documented. Thirty-one students met Meany daily to study the colonial period, using as a textbook Reuben Gold Thwaites' *The Colonies, 1492-1750,* a volume in the well-known *Epochs in America* series. Meany required daily recitations from Thwaites, reports on collateral readings, and term papers suggested in the textbook. He employed debate, recalled from his student days, to point up special issues and interpretations. Debates were held for example, on "Resolved, that Virginia contributed more to our national life than Massachusetts," and "Resolved, that in American colonial life the hardships fell more severely upon the women than upon the men."

"Northwest History" occupied a minor place in Meany's schedule; he lectured twice a week to only seven students. Lacking a textbook, he did not require a final examination. Instead, the students wrote "theses" on some aspect of exploration of the region. Meany also taught "Forestry," but gained only five students, three of whom finished the course. Meany lectured on topics dealing with tree classification, their reproduction and growth, and their economic uses.[44]

Meany's enthusiasm for forestry remained high, a feeling undoubtedly fed more by his extra-curricular projects than by his classroom achievements. On November 20, 1897, he published an article on "Scientific Forestry" in the *Seattle Times* in which he pointed out that the entire University of Washington campus, 355 acres, was virtually an arboretum which as yet had only native trees and foliage. He wrote that "It is the purpose [of the University] to make it a scientific botanical garden by introduction and care of other species and plants." To launch the project, Meany established exchanges of seeds with the Arnold Arboretum at Harvard University, the Missouri Botanical Gardens, the Department of Agriculture's Division of Forestry, and with George W. Vanderbilt's experimental forest at Biltmore, North Carolina. He sought other exchanges avidly, and tried to persuade editors of various forestry journals to assist him with publicity. Meany also proposed an extensive experiment with filberts and hoped to induce some wealthy men to finance the scientific work.[45]

None of these ventures came to fruition, but Meany's interest continued unabated and broadened to include publicizing developments in other branches of natural science. In the winter of 1898, the Portland *Oregonian* carried seven articles on fishes of Idaho and Oregon, which Meany had drawn from reports of the United States Fish Commission. After that, Meany presented fifteen popular reports on botanical, zoological, geographical, and ethnological investigations conducted by others. This series, entitled "The Year in Natural History," appeared in the *Seattle Post-Intelligencer* from February through September, 1898.[46]

About the time that Meany was gathering material for his reports on science, he turned his attention to preparations in Walla Walla for commemorating the fiftieth anniversary on November 29 and 30, 1897 of the Marcus and Narcissa Whitman massacre. Meany's studies of the Whitmans had reached the point at which, on November 21, the *Seattle Post-Intelligencer* published his account, entitled "In Memory of Marcus Whitman and Narcissa, His Wife." In it Meany wholeheartedly supported the prevailing Protestant missionary thesis that Marcus Whitman, Henry Spalding, and their cohorts had not only established missions in the region's interior in the 1830s, but also had, in the process, "saved" the Oregon Country for the United States.[47]

The missionaries' saintliness became interwoven with their heroism in Meany's characterization, a view shared by many contemporaries. Meany, in contemplating a tall memorial shaft to be dedicated at Waiilatpu, compared the Whitmans' courage and dedication to that of Leonidas and his 300 Spartans holding the pass at Thermopylae against the vast Persian army. Meany declared that the monument should be inscribed, "Stranger, tell the people of Christ that we lie here in obedience to His commands." Meany then became lost in his admiration for the Whitmans:

> The lives and deeds of Dr. Marcus Whitman and Narcissa Prentice Whitman will forever remain a brilliant, impressive and instructive chapter in the history of America....Their lives and deaths were packed with events that will prove a flowing fountain of inspiration so long as man shall admire the earnest struggles of true Christian men and women.

When he contemplated the tragedy at Waiilatpu, he felt revulsion typical of his contemporaries. Speaking of the perpetrators of the murders: "My blood fairly boils with indignation over the treachery and ingratitude of those miserable Cayuse fiends." They stood convicted by Meany without thought for the fact that they had been victimized by the presence of whites.[48]

Meany went on confidently to state that Whitman had "saved" the Oregon Country for the United States from Great Britain when he made his famous ride to the East in the winter of 1842-43:

> I have long since gleaned sufficient evidence on this subject to convince me that the famous ride was made for political, as well as for missionary reasons, and that it did play a very important part in the subsequent negotiations that saved to the Union the three whole states of Washington, Oregon, and Idaho and parts of Montana and Wyoming.

Meany found it "incongruous to ascribe to Whitman all the heroic qualities possessed by mankind and withhold from him a patriotism of the highest order." He accepted without proof the notion that the missionary had met with and deterred Secretary of State Daniel Webster from trading away the Oregon Country to the British in return for cod fisheries off the East Coast.[49]

Meany's fervent plea was ill-timed, for within a short time Edward Gaylord Bourne of Yale, one of the first critical scholars of the "Whitman saved Oregon" story, began demolishing it as a legend without foundation. Bourne wrote: "never were confiding scholars and a more confiding public so taken in." The myth of saving Oregon from the British flourished largely because it was connected with a campaign to raise funds for Whitman College in the 1880s. Meany, after further study, reduced his belief for Whitman's greatness to claims that Whitman was a true American patriot.[50]

When Meany began to teach in the winter term on December 6, 1897, the mere handful of students in his classes produced foreboding that he might yet lose his position. He confided a month later to a correspondent in Chicago that "My red Republican head is a target." To ex-President Mark Harrington of the University of Washington then living in New York City, he confessed, "Much has happened and the clouds refuse to clear themselves of threatening storms of whose downpourings no one can estimate as to date or volume." Though deeply interested in the coming municipal elections in which the Populists would try to capture the city government as they had the state, Meany dared not engage in active politics. His forced vow of "pure scholarship" exacted a heavy price, and, with the criticisms of the Populists ringing in his ears, he concluded not to attend the convention of Seattle Republicans.[51]

Meany did little to strengthen his case for reappointment, beyond discharging his campus obligations, before the regents met to consider his case on May 11, 1898. Nevertheless, the next morning the newspapers reported "the welcome news" that he had been reinstated. "Wife and I were correspondingly happy," he wrote later. After breakfast he started for the campus "feeling like a big man," when Acting President Charles F. Reeves hailed him and said it was a "sad mistake," for Meany had not been brought back to the faculty. Later he reported

> Then, I fell out of a seven-story window, so to speak. With a brave front I heard my classes until the climax came with the last class at 3 p.m. A young man came to the door to inform me that I was down for a toast at the Alumni Banquet for May 24, and that the subject was [the] "Future of the University." "All right, sir, I will respond [he replied], and I will do the very best I know how."[52]

In spite of these developments, Meany's hope of reinstatement was not dead. Though Governor Rogers apparently led the Populists in opposition to Meany, he wrote to a regent that "I have never requested his dismissal, feeling that it was a matter entirely within the province of the Board of Regents." Meany, perhaps aware of Rogers' ambivalence, now began to write letters to friends who might bring influence to bear on various regents, stressing his service to the school. He failed to gain reinstatement, however, when the regents met on July 26, as two members of the board, thought to be friendly to him, were absent. The vote was 3-2 against him.[53]

Showing signs of discouragement, Meany began to talk of returning to newspaper and magazine work and possibly seeking to gain a seat in the state senate. Colonel Alden J. Blethen, a regent and owner of the *Seattle Times*, told him that he still might be reinstated if he could persuade Judge James Z. Moore of Spokane to vote for him. Moore had been absent from the meeting of July 26. Meany wrote directly to Moore and asked friends and acquaintances to put subtle pressure on the judge. He "mended his fences," too, by thanking L.D. Godshall and John P. Hoyt for their loyal support on the board. Governor Rogers, indeed, was not overlooked as Meany asked Arthur A. Denny, Judge John McGilvra, and J.T. Ronald, prominent Seattleites, to write the governor.[54]

Meany's struggle for reinstatement became engulfed in a larger contest for control of the University. The greater issue became abundantly clear when Frank P. Graves arrived on campus in August 1898, and assumed the duties of president. Graves immediately recommended that Meany be rehired, arousing Rogers' anger. The latter remonstrated that after pledging to keep the University out of politics, Graves had taken a partisan step on Meany's behalf. Rogers repeated his condemnation of Meany as "a slick citizen," a member of one of the worst political rings in the state. He threw down the gauntlet: If Graves did not withdraw Meany's nomination it would be evident that the new president wished "to enter the field as a political partisan and defender of the worst political methods." An exchange of letters did not soften the differences. Rogers lectured Graves again on his partisanship but then fell back upon his previous position, insisting that the decision was that of Graves and the regents.[55]

Meany visited the governor to plead his case, but to no avail. Rogers told Graves, "I told him I was very sorry he had come to see me; that I was quite willing to admit that he might be qualified to teach history but...that while some injustice might be done him yet I was of opinion that the best interests of the University demanded his withdrawal." Earlier Rogers, when referring to the "slick citizen," had judged harshly and perhaps vindictively that probably "hundreds of people in this state [are] fully as competent to teach history as Mr. Meany."[56]

At that moment, the question of Meany's authority as a scholar and teacher was secondary to the matter of how and by whom the University was to be governed. Should the governor and partisan politics prevail? Or should the new president and his Board of Regents operate the school in a non-partisan, independent fashion? Meany was not simply a pawn. On the contrary, he was a significant part of the larger game, since much of the University's recent development was identified with his career. The decision on these issues was given on September 14, 1898, when the regents reinstated Meany by a 4-3 vote.

The battle for non-partisan operation of the University was not completely decided by this vote, but Graves had achieved a triumph necessary to his service as a real president. Meany's achievements were recognized and he now could concentrate on becoming a professor in the fullest sense of the word.[57]

CHAPTER SIX

Advanced Academic Training and Staking a Claim to Northwest History (1898-1905)

On June 8, 1898, the venerable members of the Washington Pioneer Association gathered "in a grove of tall, slender firs" in Seattle's environs "to enjoy the hearty fellowship and good cheer which comes with breaking bread between friends and neighbors." Before their repast, however, professor Edmond S. Meany toasted them in the following words: "All honor to you, our patriarchs! May the evening of your lives be filled with joy, and comfort, and love, as was the morning filled with sorrow, and danger, and savage hatred." Other speakers on the program recited the perils of the trek to the Oregon Country and retold stories about fighting the Indians. Meany, on the contrary, interpreted pioneer history to his audience in the light of Lewis Henry Morgan's theories of race and the doctrines of Anglo-Saxon superiority. The Indians, according to Morgan, were lodged near the top rung of barbarism on the ladder reaching toward civilization, fated to die out at the advance of the superior white man, and overwhelmed by their inadequate response to the challenge of higher culture.[1]

Accepting Morgan's deterministic explanation as absolving the pioneers of guilt for the anticipated extinction of the Indians, Meany reminded the pioneers of their heroism with these words: "So the pioneers looked to their own little settlements and hoped on. They were few in number but great in pluck. As they looked on their brave, self-reliant neighbors they could well interpret the words of Whittier" as promising a new civilization:

> The rudiments of empire here
> Are plastic yet and warm;
> The chaos of a mighty world
> Is rounding into form.

In closing, Meany soared into his own realm of prophecy. He drew a comparison between the pioneers' warfare with the Puget Sound Indians in 1855 and the Spanish-American War, then raging. The Indians in 1855 had been "greatly surprised to see the 'King George' or English men giving arms and munitions of war to 'Boston men,' or Yankees. They did not realize," Meany explained, "that in the face of savage danger the Anglo-Saxon helps his kin." Then, in a highly romantic vein, Meany exulted that in the midst of war in 1898, "you have seen across every ocean and across every continent the hands of Anglo-Saxons clasped as plighted brother's hands." In the end this would mean creation of a "union of the English speaking nations" which would destroy oppression around the globe.[2]

The prospect of such a salutary outcome of the evolutionary process did not dwell unchallenged in Meany's mind. A few days after speaking to the pioneers, he happened upon an Indian with "bent form and wrinkled face," while tramping in the woods around Lake Union searching for botanical specimens. He tried to imagine, then, not world conquest but what the fate of the Indian might be. He wondered: what might the Indian know of his own history? If such information could be elicited, he thought, the interviewer might "write for the aborigines of Puget Sound a story like Cooper's matchless 'Last of the Mohicans.'"

Meany's sympathy for the aged Indian (whom he called John Cheshison) and his wife "going down life's hill together," was joined equally with his regard for the vanishing pioneer era and the growth of civilization. He imagined the two Indians' lives:

> From their lakeside home they have witnessed a mighty transformation. Along the shore where they gathered berries or shot grouse with bows and arrows there now thunder a dozen times a day huge trains of loaded cars...while all around them are the homes of the white man, any one of which homes would have seemed like a fairy palace if [they] had come across it in their childhood rambles.[3]

For most of Meany's fellow Washingtonians, the events of the Spanish-American War and the gold discoveries in Alaska and the Yukon Territory were more exciting than philosophical musings on Indians. Gold did not greatly interest Meany, but the war stirred his patriotism mightily. As he recalled in his *History of the State of Washington*: "it is a fine commentary on the enthusiastic patriotism of Washington's citizens that thousands of them should ignore the luring temptations of the gold fields and clamor for a chance to volunteer for service under the Stars and Stripes." Indeed, for Meany the war represented close personal ties. Colonel John H. Wholley, his friend and colleague at the University of Washington, commanded the First Washington Volunteer Infantry, which saw action in The Philippines. That regiment was manned in part by young men from the University, Meany's students.[4]

Meany's personal interest in the war grew when he tried to help his brother Jay enlist in the Navy, only to learn that he had joined the Army. The elder brother's sentiments also became mingled with a Christian sense of mission reminiscent of Manifest Destiny doctrines espoused by such popular figures as Theodore Roosevelt and Senator Albert J. Beveridge. Meany's adherence to that commingled religious and patriotic spirit became apparent when he congratulated the preacher of the University's baccalaureate sermon in June 1899. He added these words: "As long as I live there will be in my possession the picture of 'Old Glory' with its folds kissed by Easter Lilies and just below an earnest Christian Minister uttering the words 'Know God!' and 'Victory!'"

Edmond sensed the possibility of personal triumph for the participants in the war. To brother Jay, he gave fatherly advice—which he had already tendered to the new University graduates: "act in this world; theorize in the next." He also sought to strike up a pact of mutual helpfulness with Jay, writing, "I believe that we will yet be more helpful to each other in our upward struggles." To "Frank W. Smith and the other U. of W. boys in Washington Volunteers," who were still training, but would later fight in The Philippines, he expressed pride in their service and confidence "that an opportunity is all you need to win the glory [you] deserve."[5]

Although that "splendid little war," as Secretary of State John Hay called it, began as an exciting and popular crusade, it later became a protracted struggle against the people of The Philippines. Meany, however, did not lose faith in its salutary effect. In 1909, he cited the statement of the official historian of the Washington Volunteers regarding the war's outcome: the soldiers would come home prepared to be better citizens. The typical volunteer "feels more keenly than before the full value of his personal freedom and his rights of manhood, and these returned volunteers...will not only protect the law and order of the land, but they will help build for the future generations a better and grander State."[6]

On October 8, 1898, while the Washington Volunteers prepared to depart for Manila, Meany decided to collect war memorabilia. He asked Colonel John H. Wholley to send souvenirs and letters that represented and detailed camp life, volunteer training, and war experiences. Disclosing a plan to develop a historical museum, Meany urged haste in collecting items, for the "specimens...will soon become precious historical relics." He then stated gratuitously that "I want our own Regiment generously represented."[7]

In the next three days, Meany launched a veritable avalanche of letters. In one he reported to President William McKinley that he wanted "to increase the love of country by inspiring more study of history." The first step in such an education would be collecting "interesting exhibits" concerned with the war. "Will you," he asked President McKinley, "please send to me for the University some photograph or other [souvenir] of the late war and also kindly send a letter signed by yourself giving your hope of the Nation's future under the changed conditions?" He asked other leaders like Secretary of War Russell A. Alger, Colonel Theodore Roosevelt, Admiral George Dewey, and Speaker Thomas A. Reed for their favors, along with medal winners. He asked Lieutenant Richard P. Hobson, for example, to describe his experiences in sinking a Spanish ship in the Harbor of Santiago de Cuba.[8]

On October 10, Meany raised his sights and broadened his inquiry by writing a most revealing letter to Queen Victoria of England. He wrote as a man of action burning the midnight oil, undeterred by protocol in the salutation, or by the deeper question as to whether she would respond to his parochial interests:

> Most Reverent Queen: The State University of Washington is the chief institution of learning in this portion of the United States. As Professor of History I am anxious to increase the love of historical studies by making a collection of autograph letters showing what the rulers of the world think will be the chief result of the Hispano-American war as far as the future of the United States as a nation is concerned. Will you please contribute such a letter?

He sent duplicates of the request in this letter to twenty-five additional heads of state in Europe, Latin America, and Asia. Although Meany continued for some weeks, at least, to enthuse over the project, there is no evidence that he received any of the material he asked for or that an archive resulted.[9]

In perhaps one of his last attempts to elicit historical materials concerning the war, Meany asked a Lieutenant Winslow of the United States Navy for a letter and souvenir. It was more than a simple request, however, for Meany understood as he wrote, "that you once signalled to your commander that you were going in closer [to the enemy] because you were afraid that you would strain your guns." This report of a heroic action had to pass muster with the critical historian, and Meany thus asked for confirmation: "If this story is true and if you would give the particulars in your letter it would be greatly appreciated." There is, unfortunately, no evidence that Winslow ever responded.[10]

As professor Meany entered upon the academic year of 1898-1899, his enthusiasm for teaching was kindled by great expectations arising from signs of strong leadership from President Graves. The contentions of the past two years had disappeared, he confided to an editor, with faculty and students united in support of the new University head. Meany was not daunted by the terms of his reappointment, which had set his salary below the standard for professors. The regents rectified the situation in February 1899, when they raised his salary to $1,500 per year, the "going rate" for professors.[11]

Meany even found inspiration in the simple act of good will expressed by the Macmillan Company when it sent him the second volume of Albert Bushnell Hart's *American History Told by Contemporaries.* Meany's reply offers the only extant testimony concerning his classwork that fall. He reported to Macmillan that he had already begun to use that source book in his American history class, and furthermore, acknowledged that he was also using volumes from Hart's *Epochs of America* series, employing all the aids, guides, and suggestions wherever possible. In doing so, Meany took full advantage of some of the best materials available in that day.[12]

There is additional evidence of the progress Meany was making as a scholar and of its consequence for his critical attention to local and University history. It came to light when Mrs. Richard Winsor, wife of a regent, asked Meany for information on the history of the University. He replied generously with a sketch which emphasized the New England contribution to both public schooling and higher education. His explanation would have delighted the whole school of New England writers who insisted upon their cultural dominance of the nation. Washington's educational development, Meany argued, was founded on New England's Puritan beginnings. He also gave credit to Governor Isaac I. Stevens' influence upon the development of education in the early territorial days.

At that point, however, Meany departed from his pietistic attitude as he contemplated the problems which had been faced by the territorial University of Washington. He wrote to a correspondent that

> There is ample evidence in the old Territorial law records to show that the pioneers had much trouble over their University but one looks in vain for any evidence that they gave a dollar for its support. They

> evidently went on the theory that the lands [endowment] and tuition fees must furnish the means to maintain the school while they passed the laws to regulate it.

Two deeply embedded loyalties clashed within Meany: first to the University and second to the pioneers. His choice on this occasion was unequivocal—the University had suffered at the hands of the pioneers. There is no evidence that the latter, he wrote, made any appropriation for the institution from its inception in 1861 until 1875, when $1,500 was allotted for repairs. Still, Meany's criticism of the early settlers was softened as he acknowledged that between 1875 and 1889 the territory spent $35,000 on the school. Since statehood, however, a period of only ten years, the legislature had appropriated $473,492.38, a figure which promised a glorious future.[13]

There was much to dazzle and impress Meany on November 30, 1898, as he, along with Governor John R. Rogers and a crowd of about 1,000, witnessed the inauguration of President Frank Graves. David Starr Jordan created a sensation by telling the audience that political influence on higher education must no longer be tolerated and that the Board of Regents should permit President Graves to run the institution. This sentiment fitted Meany's expression of confidence in the new administration. Graves created a good public impression by acknowledging that scholarship in Washington had to be practical in order to solve the problems inherent in a relatively new community.

Jordan, however, captivated the audience and Meany in particular by arguing that the highest function of the university should be "the formation of character, the training of men and women in purity and strength, in sweetness and light." Jordan also criticized American higher education for tolerating poorly qualified professors who obviously could not adequately serve the great functions of the institution. His phrase referring to such educators, "professors tied in bundles," preyed on Meany's mind. Some days later he wrote a letter to Jordan praising his address before admitting that some of Jordan's "hot raking shot hit me."[14]

In this confession, Meany accepted Jordan's ideals of higher education. Emphasizing not only character building, but also individual struggle and high goals, he revealed a keen insight into Jordan's conclusions—that the university attained these objectives only when professors accepted them. With that understanding, he pledged his own dedication to Jordan's ideals in these words:

> I have had an up-hill job jumping from the position of registrar to that of professor. Still I am succeeding in the work. No time is wasted and I know how to work. No student in the University learns more than I do every day and I hope to keep up that pace as long as I am permitted to follow this vocation. Help, I seek and obtain from the best men I know. So I crept in under what you said about the young professors and I feel sure that it will never be justifiable to tie me up in one of those cheap bundles.[15]

Meany praised Governor Rogers for his "thoughtful, forceful, and wholesome" address at the inaugural but also revealed more of his hopes and fears by remarking that Rogers' "kind attentions" to him and his family "came like a stream of sunshine from a sky we had thought was buried in clouds." Meany pledged that the governor would "never have occasion to be ashamed of my record in the University of Washington." To regent George H. King he remarked that "it was all a great feast and more than once I felt grateful that I was one of the guests." He noted further that the inauguration reminded him of his graduation day thirteen years earlier, the only event which could equal the inaugural.[16]

Though a "great feast," the inauguration produced a set of contentious remarks when Jordan alluded favorably to Meany's favorite idea that the University served as the capstone to the state's educational system. In so doing, he unhappily aroused Meany's antagonism against the Washington Agricultural College. Saying that the University was starved financially, Jordan pointed to a "great mistake," which was probably irremediable: "You have divided between Pullman and Seattle the strength that should never be divided....You have weakened the force of higher education at the behest of local ambition or it may be sectional jealousy."[17]

Charles V. Piper, the old friend who was professor at the Washington Agricultural College, aroused Meany's ire by objecting to Jordan's reference to the folly of creating two state universities in Washington. Meany accused the Pullman school of illegally offering numerous courses supposedly the exclusive property of the University; Piper and perhaps others at Pullman found Seattle equally guilty of "academic poaching." The arguments continued until June 1899 when Piper invited Meany to attend the Pullman commencement. There is no evidence that he did.[18]

Meany remained ever sensitive to slights given to his university and community, whether offered by friend or foe. For example, when he read the *Post-Intelligencer* one day he roused himself in righteous wrath. His anger stemmed from an article written by John W. Pratt, a legislator from

King County, who praised the agricultural college at the expense of the University. Meany upbraided the author, accusing him of drawing an unfair comparison between the college and the University. It must have been particularly galling to a man with Meany's experience and successes as lobbyist and promoter to belatedly discover disloyalty in the ranks of the King County delegation.[19]

Christmas Day was a time for summing up attitudes and relationships as well as an opportunity for restating aims and objectives. To Dr. J.E. Meany, of Manitowoc, Wisconsin, who had inquired about possible family ties, Meany replied that he had not learned much about his own family before his father's death in 1880 and had had little occasion to discover anything since then. "Of course," he wrote, "I would like to know and love all my kin but I am a great admirer of President David Starr Jordan....In one of his books he says: 'Establish a new dynasty for yourself and teach your son to do the same.'" He did, nevertheless, supply information about his immediate family and asked to be kept in touch with any developments.[20]

On that Christmas Day, Meany felt secure in his personal destiny. He reported to Piper that two of the regents who had opposed him were now supporters. In addition, President Graves was a frequent visitor at his home and often sought his advice and assistance. The president revealed his dependence in early January 1899, asking that Meany prepare several bills to be introduced at the coming legislative session. These included a request for two dormitories, another designating the University's museum as the state's museum, and a third establishing the library as a depository for the state's public documents. It is very likely that Meany had instigated the second and third requests since they fitted both his teaching and research needs. Meany promptly complied with Graves' request, sending the measures to Representative Charles S. Gleason, of Seattle, for introduction. In addition, he asked that Gleason seek a hall of science if the Washington Agricultural College put in such a bid. For himself and the University's library, Meany asked that Gleason collect biennial reports received by the legislature from various state agencies. For good measure, he also asked the state printer and the Secretary of State to supply him with public documents.[21]

The appropriation for two dormitories met little opposition and was granted early in the session. Success continued as the University's museum became that of the state on March 6, with all boards, commissions, and agencies of the state required to regularly deposit there all historical and anthropological documents and materials as well as flora, fauna, and evidence of mineral wealth and natural resources. However, a House bill to supply the University library with all of the state's public documents died in committee. Meany made another contribution to the museum when he persuaded President Graves to hire Edwin C. Starks, a Jordan protégé, as its first curator and as assistant professor of biology.[22]

Meany's next concern was to redeem his vow to President Jordan by seeking advanced training in history. He first thought of attending Harvard's summer session, but changed his plans after learning that Professor A.B. Hart would not be available. He then gained acceptance at the University of Wisconsin, where he went in 1899 for the first of three summer sessions without family but armed with a strong sense of dedication and mission.

Just a few weeks earlier, he had been awarded an honorary Master of Science degree by the University of Washington, a gratifying recognition that he had served his alma mater well since graduation. On his trip to Wisconsin he also carried a letter to a Chicago businessman from James R. Hayden, a Seattle banker and a former regent. Hayden introduced Meany as "a Br: Mason, and a good man, a crank in Educational matters, but his heart is in the right place. Please introduce him to some of your millionaire friends who are interested in Educational matters and he will do the rest."[23]

Meany found the all too brief summer session at the University of Wisconsin a delight and a challenge. He took twenty-one hours of recitation weekly, for which he paid a mere $20 in fees. Frederick Jackson Turner of Madison, the eminent historian of the frontier, was not available, but the assembled faculty would have been envied by students and professors anywhere in the nation. Charles Homer Haskins, the young, already celebrated medievalist of Harvard University, taught him "Historical Method and Criticism." Reuben Gold Thwaites, the eminent director of the State Historical Society of Wisconsin, lectured on "The Struggle of France and England in North America." From Richard T. Ely of Johns Hopkins, a noted political economist, he studied "The Distribution of Wealth," including consideration of those controversial institutions—trusts and monopolies.[24]

It may have been left to Jesse Macy, a visiting professor from Iowa College in Grinnell, to afford Meany the best opportunity to demonstrate his characteristic thinking as a historian. In Macy's seminar on the "History of American Political Parties," Meany wrote a term paper on political party developments between 1845 and the Civil War. "I had the pleasure," he wrote later, "of working on the topic, 'Liberty and Free Soil Parties.'"

The pleasure came partly from discovering a complete file of William Lloyd Garrison's *Liberator* in the library. He also profited greatly from reading the standard authorities in political and constitutional history—Herman Von Holst, James Schouler, and Theodore Clarke Smith.[25]

Meany, who already had accepted John Fiske's rendition of Lewis Henry Morgan's scale of inexorable racial evolution, recognized a moral and historiographical dilemma in his term paper. He wrote that "Every race of people, as it has evolved through the stages of savagery into barbarism and through the stages of barbarism into civilization, has developed and made use of the institution of human slavery." A dilemma arose because "side by side with the ethnic evolution has also invariably developed the ethical and moral sentiment opposed to the idea of property of human beings. These conflicting ideas or sentiments have frequently clashed with violence." From that point, Meany drew a prolix picture of a great tragedy and a final triumph. The American Civil War, one of the most bloody struggles in history, expiated the sin of slavery, for "when the smoke of battle cleared away the most gladsome night the world beheld, next to the Stars and Stripes floating over a strongly forged and welded Nation, was a broken chain and shackle stript forever from the slave."[26]

Outside of his classes that summer, Meany was an active, inquiring person, living up to his self-imposed obligation to the University. Although he failed to interest any midwestern millionaires in philanthropic work, he took every advantage of the unique educational center at Madison, which included the State Historical Society and the University of Wisconsin. Together with Harry C. Coffman, a librarian at the University of Washington, also attending the session, he collected numerous University of Wisconsin publications and duplicate titles from its library. Since his studies took him to the great collections of the State Historical Society, he examined its operation and close relationship with the University. He reported his findings to Seattle's reading public: "Wisconsin seems to realize better than any other American commonwealth that a great library is a source of intellectual strength and development." Here was a university and a society that Washingtonians might well emulate.[27]

It was a difficult if exhilarating summer in which Meany was ill at one point—apparently from overwork. At that time he might have been homesick, for President Graves reported he had seen Lizzie "just before she went camping....She looks as well as ever, albeit a trifle lonesome." Not only did his family miss him, but so did friends and colleagues. When former governor John H. McGraw returned from the Klondike gold fields after making a fortune, Graves reported "almost the first question he asked was 'where and how is Ed Meany?'" Graves, too, certainly missed the presence of his hard-working history professor and confidant. Meany was needed to secure employment for prospective students, as Graves had "at least five dozen" applicants for such work and stated he would hold the list for Meany's return. As an afterthought, perhaps, the president suggested that some of "your millionaire friends" might help the University by providing work for male students. "As you know," he wrote, "they are the real bone and sinew of the university and yet are too often discouraged by running up against a stone wall of expense."[28]

If Meany experienced euphoria while mingling with scholars at Madison, his return to the Seattle campus abruptly brought him down to earth. He remained the only history professor, although the catalog listed courses requiring at least a second full time professor in medieval and modern European history, including the French Revolution and English topics. Meany, of course, continued to teach American and Northwest history and methods classes. That he attempted any European courses is doubtful. He also continued to lecture on forestry.[29]

Meany had carried home from Madison more than inspiration and knowledge for the classroom. The vivid memory of Wisconsin's historical society inspired him to organize a similar society to be associated with his university. He sent invitations to thirty prominent pioneers and business and professional leaders requesting their presence at an organizational meeting on October 13, 1899. Though only a half dozen persons appeared, others signified their interest in writing. The group launched the Columbia Historical Society to collect and preserve pioneer and other historical materials. Meany became the secretary and the group selected a full slate of officers, catering to special interests and sectional sentiments.[30]

The *Seattle Times* approvingly reported the proceedings of the organizational meeting, assuring its readers that the Society had a "sphere of usefulness [which] is practically without limit" and a "timeliness none will deny." Unfortunately, in reality the organization was stillborn. No provisions had been made for popular appeals to join, but perhaps most damaging to productive work was a by-law stating that no membership dues or other fees were to be charged. A year later, when President Stephen B.L. Penrose of Whitman College asked Meany for information on a state historical society, the latter could only suggest the Washington State Historical Society, a Tacoma organization.[31]

Though frustrated in creating a historical society, Meany still found that newspaper and magazine publishers desired his services. H.A. Chadwick employed him to edit a special Christmas 1899 edition of *The Argus*, the Seattle weekly. In it, Meany devoted much space to articles on the material and cultural progress of the city and surrounding area, which were growing rapidly in wealth, business, and population as a result of the Yukon and Alaska gold rushes. Meany also introduced a series of brief historical sketches, headed by his own "History of Puget Sound." A week later in another article on Puget Sound, published this time in the *Post-Intelligencer*, Meany invoked a conventional line of reasoning about the pioneers, stating "if their memories of those days are not already recorded for the benefit of posterity, some one ought to see that it is done now while we are still blessed with their presence among us." The statement perhaps was intended to be rhetorical as Meany had already cast himself as the pioneers' historian.[32]

In January, Meany also became editor for *The Alaskan Magazine and Canadian Yukoner*, one of numerous magazines spawned by the Yukon and Alaska gold rushes. Percival de Wolfe Whitehead of Tacoma started the illustrated journal in which he intended to publish articles devoted to the Northwest—Oregon to Alaska. If Meany had hoped to use it as a vehicle for promoting interest in Northwest history he was soon disillusioned. Whitehead's financing proved inadequate and his interference with Meany's editorial work quickly brought strong protests from the latter. Meany's connection with the magazine lasted perhaps six months. He edited two or three issues before bowing out without having been paid a cent.[33]

When the new University term opened in January 1900, the *Seattle Post-Intelligencer* reported that Meany was teaching six classes averaging twenty-seven students per class. If he felt stress because he handled the burden with little or no help, he rose above it, choosing instead to view developments optimistically. The popularity of his courses and his teaching drew constant inquiries from outsiders interested in enrolling. Meany also delighted in receiving a steady flow of invitations to lecture to civic organizations, fraternal groups, and teachers' gatherings.[34]

Perhaps Meany's most congenial speaking engagement in the spring of 1900 was to an assembly of students at Seattle High School. It afforded him the opportunity to proselytize for the University. He and the high school principal began by congratulating each other on the victories of their athletic teams but Meany then delivered a homily: "Good, clean athletics" were all right, he stated, but only if based on "first-class standing in the classroom." Then, lifting his sights, he recalled words of David Starr

Jordan from his *The Care and Culture of Men*. Humanity would march in ranks undistinguished until a crisis in civilization produced a hero who would rise above the ordinary to fight for mankind. "It is worthwhile for a state to train and educate a man for such an emergency," Meany avowed as he approached his climax: "No state in the Union is doing more for its youth than the state of Washington." The University of Washington, he assured his audience in an argument already familiar, would provide the greatest chance for leadership, for humanity, and as he finally noted, to prepare men to take advantage of material opportunities available in the new century.[35]

In spite of his constant attention to his University tasks and missions, Meany remained a humane and friendly teacher to his students. At examination time in May, nine students in his American history class, presuming upon his good humor, petitioned to be relieved of the requirement to take the final test on the grounds of having been "faithful in attendance and scholarship" and "because they are at present overcrowded with work." Unfortunately Meany's answer has not been preserved. That same season, Meany served as track meet announcer for an event involving the universities of Idaho, Oregon, and Washington. Three hundred and fifty spectators suddenly were treated to the amusing spectacle of the tall professor Meany attempting to stop two small boys from fighting in the bleachers. A reporter noted that "the professor gave chase to one of the combatants, who evaded the onslaught by diving between his assailant's legs, to the great edification of everybody."[36]

Meany was eager to get back to the University of Wisconsin that July, to try out an idea for a Master's thesis which he hoped might be the beginnings of a major work. He wanted to write a history of Chief Joseph and the Nez Perce Indians, narrating their magnificent and tragic struggle with the United States army in 1877. He proposed to begin that study under Frederick Jackson Turner, the great historian of the West, who would be on duty in the summer session. He wrote to Lizzie from Madison that "my plans are so extensive that I don't like to outline them yet." He had not at that point talked them over with Turner, but was confident that the latter would encourage his project. "You are in these plans," he told Lizzie, "and I hope they will materialize as they present themselves to me now. If so it will mean a great summer for you and me next year, and we will be together which is best of all. This being separate for so long a time is a miserable fake."[37]

Meany spent a busy summer at Madison. Turner found him a dedicated worker of ability in his famous "History of the West" course and also possessed of "investigative skill" in seminar and conference work. Otherwise, the Madison session provided Meany with a variety of scholarly studies. He heard lectures on European history from H. Morse Stephens, a scholar of prominence, from Moses Coit Tyler, a pioneer in American intellectual history, and on sociology from Franklin H. Giddings, an eminent authority from Columbia University. Once again, Meany left the University of Wisconsin with a brief but tantalizing immersion in higher education outside of Washington.[38]

Meany must have been impatient to get back to Madison during the academic year 1900-1901. That he needed to finish his program for the degree of Master of Letters was made evident by the University of Washington regent's report dated December 1, 1900. It stated that several "men of ability and broad training have been added to the faculty and all standards of scholarship have been advanced." Among the most illustrious of the recent arrivals was Meany's counterpart in political and social science, Dr. J. Allen Smith, a celebrated advocate of monetary and other reforms. If Meany had not felt misgivings when comparing his training to that of Smith it would have been surprising.[39]

In June 1901, Meany was hard at work interviewing Chief Joseph at his home on the Nez Perce reservation at Nespelem in northeastern Washington. He reported buoyantly that the chief was becoming a good friend. Meany met "with fine success in hunting up facts pertaining to the present day surroundings of Joseph, one of America's greatest Indians." Later that summer he enrolled in several courses at Madison in commerce, history, geography, and international relations. He also completed the thesis, but it represented only a thin report entitled, "Chief Joseph, the Nez Perce."

In addition to interviewing Joseph, Meany had obtained answers to questions posed by mail to generals and other participants in the 1877 war. He had at his command all the standard authorities in the libraries at the University of Wisconsin and at the State Historical Society. Unfortunately for his vaulting ambition, he did not lay the groundwork for a new interpretation of events or a fresh characterization of Joseph. Admirable as his sympathy was for the chief and his people, Meany had not found new information or an interesting theme. Furthermore, the guiding hand of Frederick Jackson Turner cannot be found in this paper.[40]

Meany's graduate studies, which yielded the M.L. degree in the summer of 1901, apparently improved his stature among the University of Washington faculty. The catalog for 1900-1901 carried the announcement that he had joined political scientist J. Allen Smith and Dean John T.

Condon of the Law School to offer an inter-disciplinary "Seminar in the Development of the Pacific States." In addition, Meany introduced two new courses which reflected a growing sophistication. The first course, "Spain in America," occupying one term each year, presented Latin American history from European discoveries to the present. The second, "Development of the Pacific," taught over two terms, treated the international relations and current economic and political problems of the peoples bordering the Pacific Ocean (Pacific Rim). With this course, the University of Washington joined a small group of history departments across the nation that offered work in Oriental history. For good measure, Meany continued to teach forestry and to conduct special seminars for teachers on Saturdays, as did many of his colleagues.[41]

Meany finally prevailed upon the administration, probably in the fall of 1903, to hire a second history professor to teach English and European courses. George H. Alden, a young Ph.D. from the University of Wisconsin, undertook that work. With that matter resolved, Meany could turn to a pressing new task, that of providing a program for the first summer school, scheduled for 1904. Ambitious to begin the program with men of national reputation, Meany first invited Turner to teach. When Turner refused, he sought A.C. McLoughlin, the eminent constitutional historian, and James A. Woodburn, but both declined. Finally realizing that the $350 stipend probably was too small, he took one assignment himself and gave the other to Alden.[42]

As busy as Meany was with curricular matters, he did not neglect extra-curricular activities. Thus, when his mother sent him newspaper clippings from California describing "Labor Day" at the University of California, he quickly adapted it as "Campus Day" in Seattle. Held for the first time on May 6, 1904, the University canceled classes so that students and faculty could clean the grounds. The labor of pulling weeds, removing fallen branches, and carting away winter refuse was lightened by a picnic lunch, singing, speeches, and a dance in the evening. At the 1905 Campus Day Meany, as "Commanding General" received "an ovation wherever he appeared." It seemed the entire campus joined in the ebullient spirit of the popular "new tradition."[43]

Students responded to Meany's devotion to their interests with an affection which was sometimes irreverent. The professor, an inveterate cigar smoker, found himself lampooned in "College Camera," a column of student activities and stories published in *The Pacific Wave.* A contributor offered a playful jibe at Meany, the cigar smoker, while also passing along comment on him as a popular teacher: "'Here, pass those sulphur sticks this way. I'll have to keep that fellow company,' spoke up Doc. 'Cigar? I thought you smoked a pipe last year,' said Ben, as he puffed away at his own little bulldog. 'Oh, I'm majoring with Prof. Meany this year,' was the casual reply."[44]

Two years later, in another column signed "Sourballed," one coed told another how to get along in class without really trying. After remarking briefly that other professors could be "bamboozled," Meany was examined at some length:

> Junior—Of course Prof. Meany is all right. He gave me a B plus last year.
>
> Senior—Prof. Meany is such a brick (I'm not referring to his hair, Lenore) that I honestly don't know what this institution would do without him. He's the rock of refuge for all C-sick mariners on the troubled waters of university life. But its a shame for anyone to get less than an A from him. When he comes to the pathetic parts of his lecture, just wipe away suspicious moisture from the corner of your eye and blow your nose gently a few times and you'll get an A plus.[45]

If Meany sometimes fell victim to sentimentalism regarding appealing characters and tragic events of history, he remained clear-eyed and steadfast in his purpose to elevate regional history and historiography. By connecting the University with a strong local historical society, Meany hoped to emulate the Wisconsin plan he had witnessed in Madison. When on December 15, 1902, Herbert Griggs of Tacoma invited him to speak to a meeting in that city, Meany politely but firmly declined. Griggs had proposed that the meeting support Tacoma's Washington State Historical Society by seeking to couple its budget request to the legislature with that of the University of Washington. Instead, Meany helped lay plans to organize a new society in Seattle which might be tied to the University. Clarence B. Bagley, an indefatigable collector of documents, presided over a meeting held December 23, 1902, at which the Washington University State Historical Society was launched. Joining Meany were civic and business leaders, including Judge Thomas Burke, Thomas Prosch, Samuel Hill, Judge Cornelius Hanford, and E. Ingraham. Of the forty-five persons who signed the charter roll, the majority were active professional people.[46]

Though other men would hold the presidency, Meany assumed leadership from his post as secretary. The articles of incorporation stressed not only collecting and preserving all kinds of historical and archeological records—including those of the Indians—but also emphasized promotion of historical studies at the University. Though the Board of Trustees was empowered to make most of the decisions, the secretary, as executive officer, would be in a unique position to formulate and carry out plans. Meany never managed to obtain the salary permitted in the by-laws but he had charge of all collecting and any publication or other projects which might be developed.[47]

Under Meany's leadership, the Society first sought to fulfill patriotic and other commemorative sentiments by marking sites of early regional historical events. It first commemorated the dramatic meeting in 1792 between Captain George Vancouver, representing Great Britain, and Bodega y Quadra, of Spain, at Nootka Sound on Vancouver Island. Meany accomplished that task in the summer of 1903, as he recalled later, when "a granite obelisk was planted on the summit of a rocky islet in the mouth of the harbor."[48]

That fall, Meany and the Society sought to honor the aged Chief Joseph by bringing him to Seattle for a public meeting at which he might tell his side of Indian-white relations. The Society also used the event to raise funds for historical projects. The affair began badly when Meany took Joseph to a college football game on the afternoon of November 20. A *Post-Intelligencer* reporter covering Joseph's visit adopted a jocular tone to describe the Chief's bewilderment and discomfort upon being "jammed into a seat" on a crowded streetcar on the way to the playing field. The reporter also viewed as incongruous the picture of Meany, referred to as Chief Three Knives—an honorary title bestowed on him by the Nez Perce—"rooting" for the home team with an Indian style war dance which brought a rare smile to Chief Joseph's face.[49]

A public meeting held that evening at a downtown theater proved an unmitigated disaster from the moment students shouted college songs and yells until Chief Joseph appeared on stage, "resplendent in buckskin and in a feather head dress that flapped as he walked, like the feathers on the hats of Floridora [chorus] girls. The hero of the campaign of 1877 was plainly nervous." Indeed, he had grounds for apprehension, for when he stated, through an interpreter, that he longed to return to his home in the Wallowas to die, a wish denied by federal authorities, the crowd laughed callously.

That discourtesy was partially redeemed when Joseph appeared later at a University assembly and was received enthusiastically by 400 students, all of whom tried to shake his hand. Meany, still distressed at the previous meeting's display of racism, described the Nez Perce Indians in favorable terms and concluded with the fervent wish: "if I had the power, I would be glad to go to Wallowa and see if room could not be found for a sufficient home for Joseph and the small remnant of his people, so that he might spend his last days in the home of his fathers, in the land he loves."[50]

Chief Joseph's visit had proven to be expensive, with a deficit resulting, even though admission tickets had sold out at the downtown meeting. Samuel Hill, a Society officer, generously provided a $60 subsidy. A separate campaign to sell $25 life memberships brought in a number of subscribers, enabling Meany to carry out memorial projects. Thus, he then proceeded to commemorate the arbitration of the disputed ownership of the San Juan Islands, a matter settled in favor of the United States in 1872. This undertaking proved to be the most ambitious memorial project Meany carried out for the Washington University State Historical Society. Surprisingly, perhaps, he sought to include the aggrieved British empire, which had lost the San Juans. More than that, Meany invited the German government to send a warship to the festivities in recognition of the arbitration carried out by Emperor William I. Then, becoming apprehensive that he was interfering in governmental affairs, he asked Secretary of State John Hay whether he needed his sanction before foreign warships might enter American waters. For good measure he invited Hay to make the principal address.[51]

The State Department quieted his fears, while refusals to participate from the German Ambassador and British Columbia officials reduced the event to domestic status. Hay, too, sent his regrets. Nevertheless, the ceremonies of October 21, 1904 on San Juan Island were extensive, being supported by three United States naval vessels, military units, patriotic organizations, and civil officials, as well as being graced by the appearance of a few survivors of the boundary dispute. Granite shafts were erected at both the "American Camp," and the "English Camp," which had been established to protect the respective interests of both countries in the San Juans. Pomp and patriotic exercises made the affair a resounding success.[52]

In the spring of 1905, Meany planned to erect a memorial to Chief Joseph, who had died the previous September at Nespelem. It seemed the opportune moment, for Joseph was to be reburied at a plot more suitable than the original grave. Once again, Meany designated the Society as sponsor and persuaded Samuel Hill to underwrite the cost of the monument. Much of Meany's time that spring was taken up in planning the program and ceremonies. Transporting the seven-foot obelisk perhaps was the most difficult problem. It was "lost in transit" once and then had to be freighted from Wilbur's railroad station by wagon for the last thirty-five miles.[53]

Nez Perce chiefs and tribesmen flocked to Nespelem for week-long ceremonies in late June 1905. About 400 Indians from all over the region attended, "grouped in silence, the colors of their blankets standing strikingly forth in the afternoon sunlight," according to an appreciative witness. In addition, approximately 100 whites were present. The ceremonies began with the reburial of Joseph followed by erection of the memorial shaft on the site. Meany spoke of Chief Joseph's greatness, but the day belonged to the Nez Perce. Yellow Bull of Lapwai, Idaho, a veteran of the Nez Perce War and now nearly blind, spoke eloquently about lasting peace between Indians and whites. Later, after feasting, Yellow Bull, wearing Chief Joseph's clothes and astride his horse, orated while he rode three times around the deceased chief's lodge. In a potlatch which followed, among the goods distributed were Joseph's three buffalo robes, one of which Meany received.[54]

Shortly before the Nespelem celebration, Meany became embroiled in controversy with his old nemesis, Ezra Meeker. The spark that touched it off was Meeker's new book, *Pioneer Reminiscences of Puget Sound, the Tragedy of Leshi*, in which he severely criticized Isaac Stevens' treatment of the Indians while he served as Indian Agent and Territorial Governor. Even before reading the book—while perusing a prospectus of it, in fact— Meany warned Meeker that "your proposed assault on the character, motives, and work of Isaac I. Stevens will provoke a controversy in which Ezra Meeker cannot be the victor."

Following that melodramatic pronouncement, Meany read the book and emerged satisfied with most of Meeker's reminiscences, but not with his criticism of Stevens. Though Meeker praised Stevens' railroad surveys and even his philosophy, which he said suggested magnanimity and humanity to the Indians, he severely arraigned Stevens for his haste and dictatorial manner in forcing the Indians to accept treaties which were less than satisfactory. Most damaging, however, at least in Meany's view, was Meeker's insistence that Stevens' unsatisfactory performance in treaty negotiations resulted from bouts of intoxication.[55]

The controversy escalated in intensity when Meany contemplated Meeker's sympathetic treatment of Chief Leschi of the Nisquallys. The latter had not only led much of the fighting on the Sound during the Indian wars of the mid-1850s, but also stood accused by army officers of great cruelty toward the settlers. Once captured, he languished under military arrest until executed. Though Meany and Meeker agreed that Leschi exhibited signs of greatness and that his death was tragic, Meany could not rest content. He found that "Mr. Meeker is stubborn. He is imbued with determination to build Leschi up by tearing Stevens down. That is wholly unnecessary. Leschi's greatness can be shown without throwing mud at Stevens or anyone else."[56]

Meany seized the summer vacation in 1905 as a time to deepen his knowledge of Washington's Indians. He sought to document their current condition and history through visits to eighteen reservations. In order to finance his labors, he agreed to supply editor Erastus Brainerd of the *Post-Intelligencer* with a series of feature stories on the "Native Races of Washington," in return for payment of transportation and standard fees per column. Brainerd praised Meany's reports for providing the first serious study of local tribes. He went so far as to suggest that the Bureau of American Ethnology had encouraged Meany in his undertaking. Meany worked as a good journalist, providing columns of statistics, anecdotes, legends, reports of current social and economic conditions, and photographs. He made Indian friends quickly and developed a sympathetic attitude which often found him remarking on the failure of the federal government to carry out educational provisions of the treaties. When discussing the Lummi tribe, he expressed dismay at the Indians' loss of land to the whites. Meany offered no solution beyond the good will of "well disposed white men" who might "join with the more sensible Indians in an effort to deter the alienation of that land."[57]

The Makahs, he noted in particular, paradoxically seemed to be "the most successful and progressive Indians...because they have clung longest to their old ways." Sometimes there is a note of defeatism and melancholy in these assertions, a sympathy tinged with the feeling that the disappearance of the Indian might be inevitable. More often, however, Meany zestfully depicted his subjects as singular individuals with important stories to relate.[58]

The reports (after the first few) appeared weekly until early November as an addition to the Sunday magazine and pictorial supplement. Meany had experienced no serious problems with the Indians, but he did with editor Brainerd. The latter delayed payment of Meany's expenses and rates for columns. The problem became especially difficult to resolve when Meany asked Brainerd to pay for the historical markers for the next commemorative venture planned by the Washington University State Historical Society—a celebration of the fifty-fourth anniversary of the founding of Seattle. Brainerd erupted in anger at one point in the discussions when Meany argued too aggressively on the matter. Meany withdrew with icy dignity but without the markers and, apparently, without his journalistic fees and expenses. Since he continued to write for the newspaper for many years, payment must have been made sometime later.[59]

Meany persuaded some 200 pioneers and civic leaders to join with the Washington University State Historical Society on November 13, 1905, to celebrate Seattle's fifty-fourth birthday. Recovering quickly from Brainerd's harsh rebuff, Meany induced the *Seattle-Times*, Brainerd's competition, to supply six tablets to mark early Seattle buildings. Miss M.L. Denny also donated a granite shaft to commemorate the landings of her family at Alki Point in 1851 and recognize it as Seattle's first settlement. All went well as speaker after speaker drew contrasts between the early and current conditions of the city as they dedicated the markers. Meany reserved for himself the dedication at Alki Point. To him, Alki Point in West Seattle was the local equivalent of Plymouth Rock. In his remarks he summed up the westward movement of pioneers as representing a straight line from Plymouth to Seattle. The Indians on this occasion were depicted as humble receivers of civilization. "Every American," he concluded, "is proud of the achievement of his race in conquering from the wilderness a continent and winning it from savagery to civilization....Each new settlement was in the nature of a colony encountering the same kinds of danger and hardships."

Meany demonstrated the continued dominance of the Anglo-Saxon interpretation of history and ignored its limitations for explaining life in his day. Reporter John Slattery of the *Seattle Times*, watching the program unfold on Seattle's birthday, perhaps came closer to uncovering the historiographical needs of the new day. He noted not merely the "marked contrast" between the early village and the present city but the fact that "the noise of the city on Monday morning, November 13, 1905, quelled the penetrating voice of the orator where the Indian war whoop rang clear and could be heard for miles fifty-four years ago." How long would people be content to define their history in terms of the contrast which pleased the "sturdy pioneers" but left out everyone else? Would Meany, the leading historian of his community, find the means to develop the modern history of city and region?[60]

CHAPTER SEVEN

Creating the *Quarterly* and Promoting the A-Y-P (1905-1908)

ON NOVEMBER 17, 1905, four days after celebrating Seattle's fifty-fourth anniversary, Meany revealed a larger view of history and patriotism than that concerned with Seattle. At the Founder's Day banquet of the Chamber of Commerce he rose to toast "Early Education" with a charming anecdote:

> When the civilized world was electrified by the crash of Dewey's guns in Manila Bay, princes and potentates came from foreign lands to discover how this nation could leap forward at such [a] surprising pace. One of these princes traversing a prairie state saw a little building with a flag flying in front of it.
>
> "Is that one of your outlying forts?"
>
> "No that is no fort," said his companion with a smile.
>
> "Yes it is too. It's a fort all right. See there is the officer and there are the little soldiers coming out on the field."[1]

With that toast Meany affirmed that America would fulfill its mission for civilization through public education, but he also envisioned an extraordinary melting pot when he said, "Send over your millions from Germany and France, from Italy and Russia, from Japan and the Orient! Send them along! We will cheerfully tax ourselves for more forts [i.e., schools] and we will man them with the greatest captains of these modern days—Yankee school marms—and over their heads will fly the Stars and Stripes—Emblems of the Free."[2]

Meany's statement reflected the strong patriotic sentiment that welled up in Americans in the years preceding World War I. Though he did not blatantly champion racial or Anglo-Saxon supremacy doctrines, he did respond positively to patriotic celebrations honoring the nation's greatness and its heroes by waving the flag, erecting statues, and delivering orations.[3]

Some months before offering his "Early Education" toast, Meany had begun planning a statue of George Washington to be erected on the University campus to inspire both education and patriotism. Seattle's Rainier Chapter of the Daughters of the American Revolution undertook the project and, in a sanguine mood, Meany volunteered to serve as secretary to the finance committee. The DAR accepted his services along with his proposal to invite all chapters of the Daughters' national organization to contribute to the statue.[4]

He soon asked three illustrious sculptors whether they would be interested in the commission: Augustus Saint Gaudens in Paris, Daniel C. French of New York, and Lorado Taft from Chicago. Taft alone replied favorably and, since he was scheduled to lecture in Seattle in early November 1905, Meany seized the opportunity to arrange meetings for him with officials from the DAR and with President Thomas Kane of the University. Taft charmed his audience, but little money came in for the project. There was no possibility of obtaining the statue in time for an unveiling on Washington's birthday, February 22, 1906, as Meany had hoped. He could take heart though, from the recognition by the *Seattle Times* that Washington's birthday should be celebrated vigorously in the city. He could draw comfort, too, from the fact that Mrs. Eliza Ferry Leary, a leader of the Daughters of the American Revolution, paid the bills for continued promotion of the statue.[5]

Three months after Washington's birthday, on May 27, 1906, Meany expressed a devotion deeper than traditional patriotism at a "Service for Peace," sponsored by the University [District] Ministerial Association. University professors joined the local clergy and some 500 other auditors to hear Meany praise the Hague Conference of 1899 by calling it the world's greatest advance toward "a practicable international arbitration."[6]

Meany then affirmed an optimistic view of history and prophecy for world peace in which Anglo-Saxonism, nationalism, and Manifest Destiny were regarded as salutary, progressive doctrines. Mankind's scaling of the higher reaches of civilization in the nineteenth century, he asserted, had destroyed slavery and paved the way for abolishing warfare. He then posed a rhetorical question: "If it be a glory for the century that has passed to have banished this evil [of slavery], how much greater will be the glory of the dawning Twentieth Century when it banishes forever, as I sincerely believe it will, the curse of war itself?"[7]

Though the Hague Conference of 1899 actually had failed to reduce armaments, there was a growing sentiment for American participation in international arbitration. Meany was representative of the movement which Charles DeBenedetti has characterized as the "practical reform movement" of the years before World War I. It was a well-financed, conservative movement of business, educational, religious, and political leaders (including imperialists) whose spokesmen argued that evolution would make war obsolete in the twentieth century.[8]

Meany exhibited an ambivalence not unusual among the proponents of international arbitration. He celebrated his belief that the Monroe Doctrine's militantly nationalistic creed had not been compromised by the peace movement and also expressed his pleasure that the United States unilaterally had concluded the Treaty of Portsmouth in 1905. Meany also accepted the "kings of finance" as allies in the drive to attain permanent peace. The interests of business, he told his audience, required the absence of war. Times were "propitious," he assured the assembly, for Americans to join in building a "goodly fabric for the world."[9]

That "goodly fabric" of peace proved thin and insubstantial, if not already torn—a matter which escaped Meany's immediate attention and probably that of many others who subscribed to the idea of inevitable progress. In concluding his presentation however, Meany struck a new note, citing the need to broaden the concept of heroism in the new century. He advocated that his listeners

> Raise and glorify the standards of peace. Do not withhold your heart from him who offers his life as sacrifice to a good cause in war, but at the same time extend your praise to him who toils and achieves in peace. If you make a hero of him who scales a wall in battle, make him a twin in glory to the man who spans the raging torrent or redeems a garden from the wild.[10]

His mood turned melancholy when Harry Coffman resigned as University librarian and moved to Chehalis. "There are many ways in which your place cannot be filled by another with entire satisfaction," Meany wrote. Coffman responded that "the hardest trial for me in leaving the University will be the severing of my relations with you....I hope the time will never come when the cordial relations and good will that has existed will grow cold. It is simply out of the question to put down on paper or to verbally tell you my appreciation of the many kind things you have done on my behalf. Your enthusiasm and energy has been [*sic*] a great incentive to me and many times, when sore in body and mind, you have tided me over."[11]

Two months later, Meany again expressed his strong sense of loss, writing that "my appetite for a conflab [*sic; i.e.,* chat] with you has been fed on lonely tramps around the familiar campus trails." He had just returned from such an outing and reluctantly "plunged into this awful pile of unanswered letters" on his desk. Loss of companionship has "driven me still more closely to my books and the grind," he confided. Dean John T. Condon of the law school sometimes walked with him but opportunities were few and "somehow they are different," he concluded.[12]

Meany also was caught up in the joys and anxieties arising from living in the fast-growing University District (which included the Brooklyn Addition). The *Post-Intelligencer* reported on November 5, 1905, that in the past year the district had "grown with remarkable rapidity and that the quality of improvements is of the highest." Many faculty joined the Meanys in the district. The entire area enjoyed improved streets (not necessarily paved), sewers, and plank sidewalks. The price of banishing the wilderness and introducing modern conveniences was high. Meany had to mortgage his home to pay for water and sewer lines, street grading, and wooden sidewalk construction, improvements extended to his property between 1903 and 1906.[13]

In addition to the demands posed by numerous assessments for local improvements, Meany sometimes felt besieged by impositions based on kinship. When his Aunt Kate, who lived in San Francisco, telephoned in early March 1906 saying she was in town and would like to visit, he fled from the house. Later, in a strained apology he wrote that he was afraid she might have been another of a group of impostors claiming kinship in order to obtain help. It became obvious that he did not know his Aunt Kate very well when he described himself: "In the first place let me inform you that I am 6 feet 3 inches tall and the mop of red hair has begun to grow white. Now imagine this whole elongated frame bending before you in humble apologetic attitude." He had "no decent excuse" for not being present when she had come to the house. In extenuation, he explained that he tried to use the full weight of his influence to help students work their way through college. A note of contentment tinged with smugness crept into his conclusion: "I have very little time to myself but I enjoy being busy and feel as though I accomplish some good every day I live."[14]

Helping students sometimes extended to their post-graduate careers. Just a few days before he apologized to his Aunt Kate, Meany agreed to assist O.R. Main and Bert Parmalee, two graduates of the University of Washington, in editing their new publication, *The Washington Magazine of Industry and Progress*. With characteristic zeal, Meany asked his friends and acquaintances to prepare articles on their special interests and hobbies for compensation which included only a subscription and off prints.[15]

From E.F. Benson of Prosser he requested an article on "Irrigation in the State of Washington"—2,000 words and photographs to be delivered in a few weeks. To excuse the haste he wrote: "I would not dream of urging you thus but for our old friendship's sake and I want to help these young men get a good start." Within a few days, Meany informed Main of success with Benson and noted that he had approached fourteen other men for contributions.[16]

Though the stated purpose of *The Washington Magazine of Industry and Progress* (soon renamed *Washington Magazine: Alaska–Greater Northwest*) was to publicize commercial and industrial development, the publishers also planned to offer literary, artistic, and scientific essays done in a manner "so wholesome, so beautiful, and so reliable that every copy will be cherished and saved as part of the literary history of the Pacific Northwest." Unfortunately, they had no idea how to accomplish such grandiose objectives. Meany tried to meet the challenge by presenting articles on "Early History of the Northwest: A Series of Studies from the University of Washington." Since his only recourse on the spur of the moment was to publish undergraduate term papers, that project yielded only superficial accounts of events.[17]

Meany made a promising beginning toward offering popular scientific articles when he published Harlan I. Smith's "Archeology of the Yakima Valley," in the June 1906 issue. The author was a curator of the American Museum of Natural History in New York. By August, however, Meany ended his work as "temporary editor" of the *Washington Magazine*. This labor of love had become a source of frustration as he did not control publication policies. He had not heard the last of the magazine, however, as it fell into the hands of new owners who continued to display his name on the masthead, a source of some embarrassment until the magazine died a few months later.[18]

Washington Magazine represented an interlude in Meany's endeavors to establish a University archive and a publication representing the Washington University State Historical Society. At intervals during 1905, officials of the Seattle society and the Washington State Historical Society in Tacoma considered the possibility of merging the two organizations in order to develop a central archive of pioneer history and to publish a high-caliber historical magazine. Clarence B. Bagley and Meany, spokesmen for the Seattle group, failed in their efforts to persuade the Tacomans to move all activities to Seattle.[19]

Meany tried to break the deadlock between the two cities by proposing to make Edwin Eells of Tacoma curator of the combined historical museum and to locate it on the University campus. This plan, of course, followed the model at the University of Wisconsin. By January 1906, however, it was clear that the Tacoma society had rejected the proposal. Meany then turned back to his Seattle society, formulating plans for a journal titled the *Washington Historical Quarterly*. For that purpose he obtained financial backing from Judge Thomas Burke and Samuel Hill and began publication.[20]

An urgent task for Meany, who became editor, was to find enough material to fill the first issue of the *Quarterly*. With no "back log," Meany again called on friends and prominent individuals to supply articles and speeches. As a result the *Quarterly*, upon its inauguration in October 1906, was hardly a model of scholarship. An impressionistic essay by Professor Jacob N. Bowman, of the Bellingham Normal School, on "Washington Nomenclature, A Study," left no clear conception of the accumulated knowledge of that subject. Polished and sophisticated addresses on Pacific Rim history by President Stephen B.L. Penrose, of Whitman College, and on Jason Lee by editor Harvey Scott of Portland's *Oregonian*, provided interesting insights on their subjects but no new interpretations. Other pieces included Clarence B. Bagley's account of the Cayuse War, notable primarily for his admission that "land greed" of white settlers had been the major cause of disturbance between Indians and pioneers.[21]

Meany also began printing "rare or unpublished documents that throw side lights upon the history of the Pacific Northwest." He realized, of course, that an editor should not be content to publish mere "side lights," but must seek large bodies of documents if he was to fulfill his purpose. But, in the young community of Washington no systematic collecting had been undertaken except by a few individuals, such as Bagley. Meany's attention was fixed on the problem when, in the summer of 1906, Governor Albert E. Mead consulted him along with other prominent men on the deplorable condition of state records. To Meany's delight the governor also ventured an opinion that "it is a proper, legitimate and necessary part of the business of government to aid and foster historical work."[22]

Encouraged by Mead's enlightened views, Meany decided to publicize the need for a state archive in the January 1907 issue of the *Washington Historical Quarterly*. He intended to furnish each legislator with a copy of the issue, and also asked the governor to write an article for that number describing his project to collect portraits of all of Washington's territorial and state governors for display in the capitol. He also asked Ashmun Brown, a member of the *Quarterly*'s Board of Editors, to describe the condition of the state's records. Both men complied. Brown's graphic description of the unsystematic filing and poor storage of records also included American Historical Association recommendations for proper archival management. Governor Mead suggested that funds be appropriated for an archive. Legislation passed in 1909, however, failed to provide funding, thus leaving the proposal moribund.[23]

Meany also made editorial statements on the condition of the history profession, stimulated by his attendance at the meeting of the American Historical Association in Providence, Rhode Island, during Christmas season of 1906. He reported in the January 1907 issue of the *Quarterly* that an Association survey revealed "a strong tendency" in the South and West to ally state historical societies with state universities, following the example set in Wisconsin. Since Washington had rival societies in Tacoma and Seattle, Meany seized the opportunity to make a didactic statement:

> At the university town [Seattle], of all communities in the state, exists a body of scholars who can most profitably utilize the collections of the historical society. The scholars need the inspiration of persistent, intelligent collection and publication; the society managers need the academic atmosphere and academic counsel in and with which to broaden and solidify their work, while the historical library finds its excuse in the largest possible circle of users.

Meany had no opportunity to enjoy the prospect of joining his Washington University State Historical Society to the University of Washington, for Governor Mead soon recommended that Tacoma's Washington State Historical Society become the trustee for the state, supported by public funds.[24]

In a happier vein, Meany approved a recommendation made at Providence that historical societies should not only publish scholarly materials but must also guard against removing themselves "too far from the understanding and sympathy of the common people....One of the principal aims of an historical society should be the cultivation among the masses of that civic patriotism which is inevitably the outgrowth of an attractive presentation of local history." He might have felt, with good reason, that the recommendations emanating from Providence validated the historical work he had been engaged in with his classes, the Washington University State Historical Society, and the *Quarterly*.[25]

Meany was still in the East in early January when the *Quarterly's* second number was being prepared for mailing. Clarence B. Bagley read proof while Charles W. Smith, assistant librarian at the University, helped send out 664 copies, meanwhile keeping Meany informed by mail of all developments. Book review policy gave the editor pause. He instructed Smith to ask reviewers to return books with the reviews after overcoming a certain diffidence about withholding that modest compensation. All books were to become the property of the University library.[26]

Launching the historical journal did not exhaust Meany's efforts to promote Seattle and the region. He expressed enthusiasm in 1905 when a group of Alaskans sought to create an Alaska exhibit in Seattle and then assisted in enlarging it into the Alaskan-Yukon-Pacific Exposition. In May 1906, Meany joined forty-nine business and civic leaders to form the board of trustees of a corporation which sought financing for the fair. He wasted little time in asking Governor Mead to recommend the University's tract as the site for the fair, arguing that the buildings erected could later be utilized for college classrooms. Furthermore, he urged the governor to help defeat plans for other sites selected by speculators for personal profit.

Meany also led a delegation of Seattle's prominent leaders to a meeting of the University's Board of Regents on July 16, 1906, to request 250 acres of the unimproved campus be set aside for the fair. Once again he argued that the University, desperately in need of classrooms, might fall heir to the exposition buildings. The regents, quickly impressed, approved the lease for the 250-acre site.[27]

While the exposition obviously was a popular celebration of America's exploitation of the greater Pacific Northwest and an instrument for promoting Seattle's commercial aspirations in Asia, Meany viewed its purposes in broader and deeper contexts. "The expositions of today," he said in an interview on July 2, 1906, "are the milestones that mark the steps in centuries of development in civilization, from the time of barbarism to the intellectual achievements and splendors that distinguish the present race of mankind." He also expressed confidence that the fair would have an important educational value when he stated that "the bringing together in international displays of the fruits of science and invention" would help "to produce betterment in social and national life."[28]

Anxious to insure that educational objectives would be uppermost, he tried to persuade Harlan I. Smith to become curator of a large ethnological exhibit at the fair. If Smith would serve in that capacity, Meany assured him, there was a strong possibility that he might become director of the state museum located at the University. Though Meany's objective was laudable, his plan did not materialize.[29]

Near the end of the summer of 1906, Meany reported to his old friend Harry Coffman that he had been working eighteen hours a day preparing an abridged version of Captain George Vancouver's journal of his famous voyage to the Northwest Coast, covering his movements in 1792 from the time he entered the Straits of Juan de Fuca in April until he departed for California in October. Meany intended the book, entitled *Vancouver's Discovery of Puget Sound*, to be a handy reference work, since the complete journal, though published, was not easily found in the region. Meany submitted the manuscript to the Macmillan Company in New York on October 7, 1906, asking for a quick and favorable decision in order to have it published in time to sell at the Alaska-Yukon-Pacific Exposition. George P. Brett, of Macmillan, however, refused the manuscript, fearing that its sale would be quite limited. But, he also expressed regret, since his readers had assured him that the book contained much valuable material. Meany then proposed to find patrons to guarantee costs of publication for 500 copies. Brett agreed, setting the price at $2.50 per copy and offering a royalty of 10 percent on all copies sold above the first 500.

Meany accepted Brett's offer and before Thanksgiving returned the manuscript with all revisions completed. Within two months, he obtained the "friendly and generous aid" of Judge Thomas Burke, Samuel Hill, former Governor John H. McGraw, and seven other patrons, all local businessmen. About the same time, the Seattle firms of Lowman and Hanford, Macmillan's agent, generously agreed to grant Meany a 10 percent royalty on the first 500 copies.[30]

When Meany boarded the train bound for the East Coast in the Christmas season of 1906, he had two missions in mind. Attending the American Historical Association convention in Rhode Island was merely the prelude to two months of exciting and strenuous activity. Meany had been commissioned to lobby in New York and seven other Northeastern states to gain their participation in the Alaska-Yukon-Pacific Exposition. Until late February, he visited governors and legislators seeking to persuade them to enter exhibits at the fair. He was singularly successful in New York. That state ultimately constructed a building on the exposition grounds, being the only one of two states, in addition to Washington, to do so. He also secured generous appropriations from Pennsylvania and Massachusetts.[31]

Later, at the exposition, state senator Benjamin Wilcox of New York publicly complimented Meany in these words: "He went before our finance committee and he made his little speech and met many a rebuff, but kept at it; and then he tired the finance committee out, he saw every member of the senate and assembly—about two hundred in number—and he visited the Governor; and finally he landed the appropriations." On the same occasion, Judge Thomas Burke praised Meany, saying he was "not only a missionary and an evangelist in the East, but since his return he has taken an industrious and active part in every movement connected with advancement of this exposition."[32]

While he was in the East, Meany lectured at Yale, Vassar, and Union University, but failed to secure a coveted invitation from Harvard. At the latter institution, Albert Bushnell Hart invited him instead to attend a public lecture as a guest in order to meet historians and graduate students socially. He enjoyed at least a minor triumph at Union. The *Seattle Post-Intelligencer* reported a statement from Union's president, Andrew V. Raymond, to Henry E. Reed, an exposition official, "that Prof. Meany of Seattle, has been invited to address the entire university on the Northwest and its resources." It must have occasioned no surprise in Seattle when the report concluded that "Mr. Meany has consented to deliver the address."[33]

Meany also visited Richard E. Brooks, a prominent New York sculptor, to assess his availability to create a statue of William E. Seward for the Seattle Chamber of Commerce. That work was planned as a commemoration of the purchase of Alaska from Russia in 1867, and, more immediately, as a celebration of the Alaska-Yukon-Pacific Exposition. On behalf of the New York Society of Seattle, too, Meany sought support for a statue of John Jacob Astor, the fur entrepreneur responsible for establishing Astoria in 1811. He also visited Lorado Taft in Chicago to obtain ideas for publicizing the George Washington statue, which Taft had recently been commissioned to execute.[34]

After his return to Seattle, Meany reflected that he had too much to do while in the East. "I was simply on the jump and as it was my first trip east of Chicago there was something of cruelty in hurrying me past so many people and places of interest." Writing to a friend in Philadelphia, he explained why he had not visited her: "I was not very sure footed in the large cities when I made my first trip East last winter. With three hours in Philadelphia I spent more than two of them in Old Independence Hall. It was cold weather but I was warm enough to soak up quantities of inspiration for my lectures in American history." He felt equally inspired when visiting Bunker Hill, Concord, Lexington, West Point, Mt. Vernon, Gettysburg, Trenton, and other historic sites.[35]

Lincoln's birthday, February 12, 1907, found Meany confined to his New York City hotel due to bitter cold and the necessity to finish the index for *Vancouver's Discovery of Puget Sound*, which was not finished until three o'clock the next morning. He reported that "after a short sleep I struck out for my busiest day in New York." After meeting many people, he "took dinner with Col. Astor's secretary at the Players" and tried without success to obtain support for a statue of John Jacob Astor. His day had not ended, though, for he then "caught a 9 o'clock ferry and arrived at Trenton at 11 p.m."[36]

Promotion of the Seward statue fared better than did the Astor project. On March 10, Meany, once more in Seattle, informed Richard Brooks that he had been selected as Seward's sculptor and that a subscription goal of $20,000 had been set. Meany immediately launched a strong publicity campaign to raise funds. He also reported to Taft that the first newspaper stories about the statue of Washington had brought poor results. One Seattle newspaper had "scooped" the other (neither being named) by publishing a half-tone cut of the statue's model. Unfortunately, the triumphant editor had little to celebrate as the cut had yielded a blurred picture. Meany seized upon the blunder as an opportunity for obtaining more extensive publicity, "especially," as he wrote to Taft, "if you can furnish a good picture in black and white of the figure and pedestal."[37]

The birth of a son on April 23, 1907, eclipsed all promotional activities. In writing to a former student Meany explained: "I have been exceedingly busy since coming home and to cap the climax the stork brought a fine little red-headed baby boy to my house a week ago last Tuesday." University students had responded by "threatening" to hold an election to select a name for the infant. Suggested names included, "Campus Day," "A-Y-P," "Three Knives," and "Isaac I. Stevens." The father, undoubtedly amused by these undergraduate antics, stated that "they would all lose for the baby's mother and grandmother have agreed on Edmond S., Jr. Even the Supreme Court of the United States would be powerless in such a case as that."[38]

To another correspondent that spring, Meany asserted that his university work (not to mention promotional activities) had prevented him from finishing his biography of Chief Joseph. More than that, he had exciting new plans for the summer of 1907 which would further delay his book. He planned to join Edward S. Curtis, a Seattle photographer and an old friend, in the task of photographing Sioux Indians and recording their recollections at their reservations in South Dakota. Because that summer's field work would comprise an important portion of Curtis' monumental project to depict all of the North American Indians, the photographer did not wait until the end of the University's spring term to put Meany to work. In the first days of June, he sent ethnographical materials for Meany to study and made plans to meet him at Pine Ridge, South Dakota, as soon as possible after June 19.[39]

Meany's principal task was to interview aged Sioux at the Pine Ridge and Rosebud Indian agencies and elsewhere. Most of those interviewed were warriors who recalled the hunt, vigils, and coups or honors they had won in battle, horse stealing, or other confrontations with Indians and whites. Meany's resulting notes were shaped in part by interpreters who relayed his questions to the Indians and their answers to him.[40]

Meany greatly admired Curtis' patience and ability to communicate with the Indians and took the hardships and tribulations of field work in stride. He later reported some of the difficulties: "I have a keen recollection of our first camp among the Ogalalas," he wrote in "Hunting Indians with a Camera," which appeared in *World's Work* for March, 1908. "At dark a terrific storm struck the camp. The tent-poles broke and the tents [were] flattened to the ground. Five Indian ponies in the neighborhood were killed by lightning. At another time the equipment wagon got stuck before it could be got out." In all this there was always the danger to life and limb and the chance that days of hard work might be lost. The latter possibility also existed if the Indians objected to some slight or affront and refused to be photographed. Curtis experienced such threats but always managed to win out.[41]

When the field work was completed early in August, Curtis went on to photograph Indians elsewhere while Meany returned to Seattle where, among myriad activities, he settled down to write a 10,000 word ethnographical sketch of the Sioux to accompany Curtis' photographs. Though its preparation was delayed and Curtis had to remind him of his task several months later, the sketch appeared in 1908 as part of volume three of Curtis' twenty volume work.[42]

Even before Meany began to write the sketch, however, he tried to persuade Curtis to deposit his notes, manuscripts, and photographic negatives at the University of Washington. He also proposed to President Thomas Kane that the University construct a fire-proof vault to house Curtis' materials, thus providing a suitable repository for a great ethnographical collection. Curtis, who was at the Cheyenne Agency, rejected Meany's overtures, in part because some Seattle businessmen had failed to support his work. Indeed, he was so exercised at the attitude of one banker that he was contemplating a move to New York. In particular, he feared that "some local pinhead...might become a regent and trade them [his collection] off for a brass door plate."[43]

Meany, shocked by Curtis' attitude, tried, as a trusted friend, to make him forget the "brainless remark of a youthful banker." Though he acknowledged that "a group of newly rich members of a Seattle club are foolish enough to neglect the chance of aiding one of the greatest literary achievements of the century," he also knew that J. Pierpont Morgan had given Curtis a large subvention to complete his project. Presuming very heavily on their friendship, Meany thundered down at Curtis: "From the pinnacle of my professorship I am going to hurl at you this dictum [regarding your behavior]'You must quit it.'" At the same time, in a mood less Olympian and more characteristically partisan, he contemplated Curtis' threat to leave Seattle: "In regard to your moving to New York—that just gives me the shivers. I will not allow myself to think of it."[44]

In the midst of advising Curtis, Meany digressed for a moment to write that his edition of *Vancouver's Discovery of Puget Sound*, published five months earlier, had received more than a dozen favorable notices. Seattle papers praised Meany for his wisdom and skill in making the record of Vancouver's exploits easily available to the local reading public. *Outlook*, a West Coast magazine, concluded that "it is, indeed, a distinctly original and helpful historical monograph, valuable not only for the information it affords concerning Vancouver's voyage itself and the significance of the names he applied to prominent geographical features of the Oregon Country, but for the light it throws on the operations of Spain in that region and the negotiations which ended in the relinquishment to England of Spanish territorial claims."[45]

A dissenting voice belonged to Porter Garnett, a San Francisco journalist and critic. Writing in the August issue of the *Pacific Monthly*, Garnett judged Meany's book to be serious and valuable but criticized his organization as "rickety." *The Dial*, a Chicago literary journal, found Meany's purpose worthwhile but objected particularly to footnotes which told too much about minor figures at the expense of thorough investigation of important and controversial points.[46]

A note of authority sounded when Professor William R. Manning of George Washington University in Washington, D.C., sharply criticized Meany's style and scholarship in the *American Historical Review*. Meany felt aggrieved and complained to J. Franklin Jameson, the editor, that Manning had embarked on a "mean spirited" fault-finding search. Jameson, though regretful because he thought of Meany as a "fine fellow" (they had met at the Providence meeting), nevertheless fully supported Manning in a letter to Albert B. Hart, which Meany read. Meany's first venture into the realm of eastern scholarship brought him little comfort, though Manning had conceded that the book would "doubtless be very interesting to many, and it will have a large sale, locally."[47]

In the autumn of 1907 Meany had little time to dwell on academic slights, though at one point he admitted being "strongly tempted" to give up scholarly writing. The University regents had acted favorably on his advice that enrollment increases necessitated appointing two additional professors. Thus, the history faculty doubled in size to four in 1907. Joining Meany and George H. Alden were Edward McMahon, an M.A. from Wisconsin, and William A. Morris, a new Ph.D. from Harvard. The regents left Meany in charge of the paperwork and operation of the department, a de facto chairman without the official title.[48]

The history staff, of course, remained too small to permit a high degree of specialization or a particular emphasis on research and publication. Meany's own course offering was diverse, including "Makers of the Nation," "Spain in America," "Northwest History," and the "History of American Diplomacy." He dropped forestry sometime earlier, a matter he confirmed on September 24, 1907, when he donated his forestry books and documents, assiduously collected for two decades, to the University library, with the hope that they would be useful to the recently organized School of Forestry.[49]

Though graduate studies in history were as yet impossible and faculty research extremely limited, Meany alertly gathered source materials for Northwest history when the opportunities could be found. He fell heir, in early December 1907, to "a gift of thirty years of history," when Major General A.W. Greeley donated records from the United States Army's Department of the Columbia, in Vancouver, Washington. Included were General O.O. Howard's account of the Nez Perce campaign of 1877, official reports on the anti-Chinese riots in Seattle, documentation of the 1892 Coeur d'Alene mining troubles, and surveys of Puget Sound defenses. About the same time, Meany also personally sought out and purchased twelve bound volumes of the *San Francisco Herald* (beginning 1853) from a Chicago dealer. This newspaper, in his estimation, was rich in stories on the settlement of the Northwest and Alaska.[50]

That autumn of 1907, Meany became embroiled in a controversy involving the Sigma Nu fraternity which ignited his hostility toward

Washington State College (formerly Washington Agricultural College), and threatened to break up his friendship with Harry Coffman. Both he and Coffman had joined Sigma Nu as faculty members some time after 1896, the year Sigma Nu established its fraternity on the campus. Difficulties first arose when the Ophite Fraternity at Washington State College petitioned for a Sigma Nu charter. Though the majority of the members of the Gamma Chi chapter at the University of Washington endorsed the request, Meany vehemently opposed it. Coffman, tenth district inspector for Sigma Nu, criticized Meany's actions as unwarranted. As he wrote to D.S. Blair of Pullman,

> the whole matter can be sized up in the statements of Bro. Meany which was [*sic*] a review of the competition in the matter of students and legislative appropriation between the University of Washington and the Washington State College from statehood. The argument had no bearing on the advisability of Sigma Nu entering the State College but was simply a recital of...factional fights and petty quarrels that have and do now exist between the faculties of the two institutions and was for the purpose of inciting the enmity of the chapter toward all matters at the State College.[51]

Meany, who had received a carbon copy of the letter, reacted with "painful surprise," and accused Coffman of irresponsibility. He threatened to resign from Sigma Nu on the basis of Coffman's letter to Blair. Though Coffman temporized, in the end he reiterated his claim that Meany and a small group had improperly opposed the petition from Pullman, endangering the welfare of the fraternity. He also expressed the hope that they could continue as friends. Meany rejected Coffman's overtures, pronouncing him unfit to hold office in Sigma Nu for having violated its confidences with his "preposterous" letter to Blair. Relations between the two men broke down completely as Meany insisted that "there are none [Sigma Nu brothers] who have known Washington State College longer or more intimately than I. From that long knowledge I am thoroughly convinced that the institution is unfair, dishonest, and unworthy of Sigma Nu."[52]

Despite his deeply emotional indictment, Meany would not accept Coffman's challenge to fight for his convictions. Instead he vowed to remain aloof, reminding Coffman that "you know as well as anybody living that I have planned a life-work of usefulness that must be kept free from contention, controversy, and rancor." Then, perhaps in a further attempt to rationalize his stiff opposition, he explained that "under my present nervous tension it does not require much to disturb the whole tenor of my programme [*sic*]. The University does not expect me to enter controversies." The upshot regarding Sigma Nu was indecisive. Meany did not resign from the fraternity nor did he accept the new chapter in Pullman. Both he and Coffman subsequently sought to resume their friendship, but failed. For once, his unflinching loyalty to the University of Washington led him down a solitary path: Sigma Nu entered Washington State College in 1910.[53]

The Christmas season of 1907 found Meany once again attending the annual meeting of the American Historical Association, this time in Madison, Wisconsin. He wrote happily that "the meeting was a brilliant success and Madison, 'the city of laws and education,' certainly showed herself a cordial and appreciative host of more than a thousand scholarly men and women." Meany was particularly pleased to have obtained for publication in the *Washington Historical Quarterly* two short papers advocating the teaching of Japanese and Chinese history in the United States in order to improve international relations and the understanding of divergent cultures. Their appearance in the January 1908 issue of the *Quarterly* placed Meany among a small group of editors who recognized the importance of linking Pacific Coast and Oriental history.[54]

Charles W. Smith continued to handle the publication of the *Washington Historical Quarterly* in January 1908, as Meany once again toured the East Coast seeking support for the Alaska-Yukon-Pacific Exposition. He met with legislative finance and appropriations committees in New York, Rhode Island, New Jersey, and Massachusetts. Notably, New York's governor, Charles Evans Hughes, expressed pleasure over the plans Meany submitted for the New York State building. On the other hand, Governor Curtis Guild, Jr., of Massachusetts, told him that Boston was tired of expositions and Meany could expect nothing from that state.[55]

While still in the East, Meany became a trustee of the exposition's corporation for the ensuing year and gained reappointment as chairman of the Committee on Exploitation and Publicity. Canvassing the state legislatures came to a halt after two weeks as Meany suffered an attack of the "grippe." After that he returned home three weeks early.[56]

Meany felt well enough to accept an invitation to speak to the Young Men's Republican Club of Seattle on February 12. His topic was Abraham Lincoln, over whom Meany had developed a passion. His sojourn in the East had, in fact, kindled new patriotic fires.[57]

Meany toasted Abraham Lincoln in pietistic terms. Lincoln's humanity, Meany asserted, made it impossible for anyone to capture his image in "a great statue of bronze or marble. We know too much of his human qualities in all their strength and sweetness." Though some believed that Lincoln would have been greater if he had been better educated, Meany maintained that "there have been few men in the history of this country so well educated. He learned from life itself, and it was the strength he drew from his early training, the sympathy he had for the lowly of station, that made him great." The tragedy of war molded his sublime character: "In his hour of trial he was fair to North and South alike, and North and South alike now honor him."[58]

Later that spring, on April 6, 1908, Charles V. Piper, Meany's college classmate, who had become a noted scientist, sent along to him news that the Kansas Agricultural College was seeking a new president, a man of broad sympathies and training who could diversify the work of the institution. Now a brilliant agrostologist for the U.S. Department of Agriculture, Piper offered to support Meany for the post and confided that he had considerable influence. The position, he further reported, paid $6,000 per year. Though Meany's salary was only $2,250 and he keenly appreciated Piper's confidence, he did not hesitate to reject the suggestion he apply for the post. Indeed, his response was so charged with emotion that he apparently misconstrued Piper's letter, thinking of it as if it were an offer from the institution in question. A bit downcast because of a fever which had caused his doctor to caution against overwork, Meany declared, "This much is certain: I am resolved upon writing my books and upon giving to this institution, our Alma Mater, just as long, as earnest, as faithful, and as useful a service as the years of life permit me to give.....I thank you from the bottom of my heart, but Charles, I do not believe the presidency of Harvard, of Yale, or of the United States would tempt me from the work I am trying to do."[59]

The prospect denied was too exciting not to be shared with others. In the next few days, the Seattle newspapers reported that Meany had refused the presidency of an "Eastern college," at a salary three times that which he earned as a professor. H.A. Chadwick, editor of *The Argus*, was most perceptive in his appreciation of Meany's decision—even if he too interpreted Piper's suggestion as an offer. Chadwick told his readers that Meany had his life's work all planned, that it was focused upon the history of Washington, "and he is the best posted man on the subject in the state." The regents, for that reason, should make certain he was not lost to the University. "He is," concluded Chadwick, "worth more to the University of Washington than he can possibly be to any other college in the United States."

What remained unsaid was that Meany's loyalty made it easy for the regents to keep him without extraordinary inducements, and they offered only a $150 salary increase for the next year.[60]

Piper's letter and the subsequent publicity about a possible college presidency could not soften a psychological blow from an unexpected quarter. He suffered that trauma when a new edition of Arthur A. Denny's memoir, *Pioneer Days on Puget Sound,* appeared, edited and published by Alice Harriman, a rank outsider. She also proposed to write a biography of that patriarch. Meany expostulated with the Denny family, claiming that an understanding existed that he would execute those tasks. He reminded the family that for nearly four years he had spent long hours reading to the elder Denny and making plans to write his biography. The whole enterprise appeared to Meany reduced to a crass "commercial scramble," dishonoring the memory of the old pioneer, as Mrs. Harriman's name was far more prominent on the title page than that of her subject. Though "wounded...deeply," Meany nevertheless reaffirmed friendship for the Denny family and submerged negative thoughts as he uttered a familiar refrain—he would "plunge on and hope for the best."[61]

Hope was bolstered by celebration of loyalty to Alma Mater as well as by plunging into heavy work schedules. In 1907, Meany wrote verses entitled "Washington Beloved" in answer to popular requests for a college anthem. He commissioned Reginald De Koven of New York to write the music, the fee to be paid by the Associated Students. De Koven was "a sound choice," according to Harry C. Bauer in an article published in 1960. De Koven had written the popular *Oh Promise Me* and was "in great vogue following the success of his light opera, *Robin Hood*."[62]

Meany accepted the published sheet music as satisfactory, though he was disappointed that it lacked a solo part. The lyrics proved innocuous with few specific references to Alma Mater, providing instead a nostalgic mood suitable for any college gathering: "Thy name, O Washington renowned,/ We hail, we hail from far and near,/ Thy glories joyfully resound,/ In song of praise and mighty cheer." The only pointed reference to the Seattle institution, mentioning school colors, is found in the lines, "While we through every changing scene,/ Thy purple pennants lift on high."[63]

Meany found a source of comfort and hope in the assurance offered by Charles O. Kimball, the director of music at the University. Kimball stated, after introducing the anthem at a concert on December 17, 1907, that "the song is one that we may well feel proud of and [it] will grow steadily in the appreciation of our students as they gain culture and knowledge of good music."[64]

The first complimentary remarks concerning it gave way to a feeling among the students, according to Bauer, that it was "an inconsequential song." In May 1908, *The Tyee*, a student magazine, published a cartoon depicting De Koven, who had been paid $100 for the music, as having fleeced the student body. Not only was the latter depicted as a lamb being sheared, but the student sketch also showed a cemetery in which the song had been interred. The cartoonist, it turned out, had been too hasty in the death notice, not having reckoned with the actions of Meany's friends in the state legislature.[65]

In the 1909 session a bill to make "Washington Beloved" the state anthem passed the House of Representatives. Meany, who originally had sought only to write verses for a college song book, now was encouraged by senators to lobby for it as the state song. He wrote to friends in the Senate that "it may seem a small matter but such things mean much to one devoted to the work of education and I am frank enough to acknowledge the pride I would have in the success of that resolution." The Senate passed it in the last frantic hours of the session, with little thought concerning the song's merit as a state anthem. On March 18, 1909, Meany happily informed De Koven that Governor Marion Hay had signed the resolution creating the state anthem. Subsequent efforts, however, to persuade the publisher to produce a new edition were without avail. In truth, the legislative action represented the last effort to popularize the song, and it became moribund.[66]

If student critics hesitated in 1908 to accept his anthem, Meany had yet another means of pleasing them. He had landed a superb "catch" for the summer session. Professor Albert Bushnell Hart of Harvard University, whose textbooks Meany had used for several years, agreed to lecture on American history twice a day for three weeks during July and August. Pleasure vanished, though, when Meany learned that Hart planned to speak first at an undisclosed normal school [undoubtedly Cheney] and at Washington State College. The University of Washington depended heavily on Hart to attract students to its summer classes, Meany claimed, and he feared earlier appearances at the other schools might destroy that objective. He was aggrieved too that Hart apparently would place other institutions on the same level as the University.[67]

Hart apologized profusely. His intention had not been to elevate the other schools to the University's rank but merely to give occasional lectures to accommodate old friends and students, including President Enoch A. Bryan of Washington State College. Mollified, Meany renewed cordial relations. He arranged for the largest and best lecture hall and then canceled Hart's class for July 15 in order to conduct him on an excursion to Mt. Rainier. Hart's summer school appearance was a success. One exception arose when Meany was unable to tender Hart a big public reception because, as Meany explained, none of his moneyed friends was available to underwrite it.[68]

In July 1908, Meany closed the second volume of the *Washington Historical Quarterly* with thanks to those subscribers who had paid the $2.00 annual fee, and to Samuel Hill and Judge Thomas Burke "for generous special contributions" which had made publication possible. Delinquents, on the other hand, were told they would get no more issues. The next month, after having bragged a little in a private letter to Bailey Willis about the success of the *Quarterly*, Meany confessed that "this magazine is having the struggle for existence usual among such publications and I used the above word 'big' with the full knowledge that it implied craving on my part and charity on yours."

Undoubtedly, the indulgence he begged so gracefully would have been granted cheerfully by anyone examining the mailing list. The *Quarterly* was sent to 450 persons and institutions, a list which probably included exchanges and gifts as well as paid subscriptions. Most regular readers lived in Washington. Subscribers from western Washington accounted for 63 percent of the list, while an additional 21 percent came from eastern Washington. Many college, university, and public libraries in the West received the publication, along with selected libraries and historical societies in the Midwest and East whose reputation Meany knew.[69]

Indulgence might also have been granted Meany while he sought to achieve the standards set by the *American Historical Review*. He copied many elements of the *Review*'s format and included similar historical materials and notes. Most contributions, of course, were conventional pioneer memoirs, narratives, and documents. But from the start, the *Quarterly* became notable for presenting conflicting interpretations of the Protestant missionary work in civilizing and winning the Oregon Country for the United States.[70]

Much attention centered upon Marcus Whitman's spectacular ride to the East in the winter of 1842-1843 to plead with Boston's missionary authorities to keep open his mission station at Waiilatpu and Henry Spalding's mission at Lapwai. While few questioned Whitman's missionary accomplishments, a major controversy developed around a second objective imputed to Whitman. Certain Protestant clergy and historians insisted that Whitman had traveled to Washington, D.C., where his advice to government officials prevented loss of Oregon to Great Britain. He also, it was claimed, extracted financial aid from the Secret Service fund and used it to raise an immigrant company which he took to Oregon, insuring control of the territory for the United States. That claim collapsed since the Secret Service had not been established during the time of Whitman's journey.[71]

Editor Meany was perplexed and torn between two great loves thrust into conflict by this historiographical battle. The first was his love for truth in history; the second, his vast admiration for the pioneers and missionaries. As a young student and teacher he had accepted the "Whitman saved Oregon" interpretation, with, as he put it, "all the warmth and enthusiasm of my nature." Thus, "It was a rude awakening" when he learned that scholars had created "a doubt" through their research. On March 10, 1906, Meany told the Lewis and Clark Club of Lakeside, Chelan County, that he could no longer support the thesis that the ride "really produced the great result of the treaty between Great Britain and the United States in 1846, fixing the northern boundary of old Oregon at the 49th parallel." On the other hand, he found opposing views equally unsatisfactory. "The other [side] derides all this and claims that the ride was made solely in the interest of the mission and had no political significance or results."[72]

He was becoming prepared for some vexing editorial problems. "I am trying," he reported to the Club, "to follow every blow struck by each side but at the same time, as a historian, I am trying to keep free from bias and prejudice." He expressed confidence that "this ransacking of the records, this prying into the memory of survivors, this study of possibilities will produce a common ground of truth satisfying to all." Bias, however, remained part of his makeup, for he was firmly convinced that "the name and fame of Whitman and his associates will still remain a rich heritage for all who love courage, patriotism, and self-sacrificing devotion to duty."[73]

T.C. Elliott, a Walla Walla banker, severely tested Meany's optimism by offering several articles to the *Quarterly* refuting the claims of the Whitman advocates. Elliott told Clarence B. Bagley he had "in mind to touch up several of the particular forgeries and misstatements" of the Whitman proponents who supported the myth of his political achievements. Elliott also decided to write under a *nom de plume*, "owing to my place of residence and family relations with members of Whitman College."[74]

Meany published the first of Elliott's revisionist articles in the *Quarterly* for July 1907. Writing under the pen name of C.T. Johnson, Elliott refuted charges that the Oregon Country might have been traded to Great Britain in the 1840s by an unsympathetic federal government in order to gain fishing rights in the North Atlantic. Hence, no grounds existed for arguing that Oregon needed to be "saved" from the British. In the October issue, Elliott again maintained that position, exonerating Daniel Webster, the Secretary of State, insisting that he had guarded the claims of the United States south of the 49th parallel.[75]

Edwin Eells, son of pioneer missionary Cushing Eells, spurned Elliott's views. Speaking in a congenial environment at the sixtieth anniversary of the Whitman massacre, in November 1907, Eells supported the "Whitman saved Oregon" myth fervently. He found, first, that Whitman shared a burden with all the Protestant missionaries: "They all saved Oregon. Each in his own place did what he or she could." It was Whitman, though, whose ride to the East had alerted federal authorities to the danger of conquest by Britain, and had enlisted colonists whom he guided over the Oregon Trail to their new home. Then, when murdered by the Indians to whom he was ministering, Whitman became not merely a martyr to his church, but "a martyr to his country."[76]

When Elliott learned Eells had sent the anniversary speech to the *Quarterly* for publication, he cautioned Meany that "as an example of rash and careless statement it was certainly interesting and speaks for itself as such." Then, perhaps emboldened by his own words as well as by Eells' thesis, Elliott remarked sarcastically that he was thinking of writing a paper on "Imaginations in History," which would be appropriate alongside Eells' address.[77]

Elliott's irascible outburst did not deter Meany from publishing Eells' address in January 1908. Meany then reciprocated by publishing one more "T.C. Johnson" piece, "The Evolution of a Lament," which appeared in April. In this article Elliott reviewed the Protestant version of "the lament," a story of certain Nez Perce or Flathead Indians who, it was presumed, had journeyed to St. Louis in the 1830s seeking the Bible and Christianity, but had instead been given only "Popish trappings," or worse. News of "the lament" stirred much interest in supporting missionary activities among eastern Protestants—providing additional credit to the Oregon missionaries for "saving Oregon" for the United States. Unfortunately, the high-level debate Meany sought fell flat as Elliott again waxed sarcastic about Eells, concluding that "in the historical garden of the Pacific Northwest, in the course of years, these rootless flowers will die out and there will yet remain strength and beauty in abundance."[78]

Charles W. Smith came to Meany's assistance and all other editors and writers when he published two articles in the *Quarterly* in 1908 providing aids for research on Whitman and other historical subjects. In January 1908, immediately following Eells' paper, Smith offered an expansion of the Dewey Decimal System, designed to better accommodate cataloging specialized works dealing with Pacific Northwest history. Reflecting the University of Washington's growing history collection, this modification of Dewey also catered to numerous librarians who had asked for its publication.[79]

In the "News department" of the January, 1908, issue, Meany announced that Smith had launched a cooperative program among the larger libraries in "the Old Oregon" country to assemble and publish a bibliography of Pacific Northwest history. The first portion appeared in October. The "Contribution Toward a Bibliography of Marcus Whitman" listed primary and secondary materials dealing with Whitman's missionary activities, "the lament," the ride, the massacre, and all other matters except the controversy over Whitman's political influence.

The sheer bulk of material on the last topic precluded its inclusion, but Smith's strictures against further "undignified criticism upon both sides of the controversy" suggested that political and diplomatic subjects might be included later. In the meantime, Smith instructed readers concerning the location of library and private collections and also expressed his and Meany's hope that the volume of documentation would serve the purpose of truth:

> If it should be the means of causing some few students to suspend judgement until they have had opportunity to carefully examine the sources of information, it will amply justify its compilation....it is refreshing to hope that the time has come when no one will have the temerity to rush into print upon this subject without at least some familiarity with the real sources in the case.[80]

Before any new interpretive works could be published, however, the *Washington Historical Quarterly* suspended publication after Volume 3, Number 1 had been issued for October 1908. Judge Thomas Burke had withdrawn his patronage approximately one year before and no successor had been found to join Samuel Hill as guarantor of publication. Memberships in the Washington University State Historical Society had brought in only $500, hardly a match for the $1,042.50 received from the patrons.

Meany had also silently contributed $150 toward publication in the first two years and Lowman and Hanford, the printers, canceled a $22 debt in order to permit balancing the *Quarterly*'s books. Clearly Meany either had to find new patrons or a new means of publication if the *Quarterly* was to avoid falling into the well-populated graveyard of regional publications.[81]

CHAPTER EIGHT

The Exposition and the *History*, Optimistic Views of the Dawning Twentieth Century World (1909-1914)

WHEN SEATTLE CELEBRATED the centennial of Abraham Lincoln's birth on February 12, 1909, Meany as orator of the day demonstrated the strong influence hero worship had on his view of history. Speaking to a capacity audience at the Seattle Theater, he "indignantly denied" reports of demeaning aspects of Lincoln's lowly beginnings and rumors of marital unhappiness. He also "thrilled his audience with stories of the career of the great president." Meany concluded with the fervent assertion "if Lincoln had lived two years longer, many of the blots that are on the nation's escutcheon because of the evils of the reconstruction period would not be there and many of the horrors of that time would have been averted."[1]

Mayor John F. Miller, who introduced Meany, "found it impossible to control his emotion," according to the reporter. Many in the audience felt as Miller did, including Meany's classmate, Bertha D. Piper Venan, who returned home from the Seattle Theater to describe her strong sentiments. She had attended the patriotic exercises not only to honor Lincoln's memory, but also to measure Meany's progress up his "ladder" of success. Entirely satisfied, she reported to Meany that "Your manner of delivery puts an audience, first, at ease—a vital point, and then I was pleased to note how you carried them with you in your moods and tenses; pathos, power, plausibleness, pleasurable reminiscences and pride—you played on all keys of nature that stir us." Her supreme compliment followed: "your voice rang *true* from your soul today."[2]

Meany also expressed his deep fascination with Lincoln in verse, beginning with "The Elemental Lincoln," a prose poem which appeared in the *Seattle Times* a few days before the patriotic exercises. Those lines transformed the martyred president by metaphor into "a steadfast rock," immune to the baser passions of mankind and, by a strained simile, connected to the power of God.[3]

In three sonnets published in the *Overland Monthly* for March, 1909, Meany sought to further illuminate the martyr's elevated status. In the first sonnet, the youthful Lincoln emerged "as one/ Who bears a manly burden while a child." In the second, "Yet spelled the riven stars his cruel fate:/ To face the avalanche of war and hate/ Till Death entwined the martyr's crown of fame." Finally, in "The Memory," Meany looked beyond the blinding light of martyrdom to find inspiration for all mankind in Lincoln's response to injustice and suffering:

> Ah, such a man empyreal sphere attains,
> Who knows and feels his fellow's hurts and needs,
> Whose heart responds to every wound that bleeds
> And every soul entrapped by cruel pains
> With love that falls like Heaven's fresh'ning rains;
> Uplifts the fallen and all the hungry feeds,
> Ignoring hate of race or jangling creeds,
> Or stains of iron from lately broken chains.
> How strong thy love, yet meek as gentle dove!
> Such perfect bloom from lowly tangled sod!
> While groping mortals, striving upward, plod,
> They'll reach and strain for thy enkindling love—
> Triumphant love vouchsafed from realms above,—
> In human form, the majesty of God.[4]

A week after his Lincoln's birthday address, Meany embarked for Oregon and California with a hundred Seattle and Tacoma civic leaders to publicize the approaching Alaska-Yukon-Pacific Exposition. Right from the first stop in Portland, Meany played a major role when he delivered an "entertaining speech." The group attracted a great deal of attention in San Francisco and adjoining communities. Oakland's leaders in particular reported they had "never entertained a more enthusiastic delegation than that from Seattle and Tacoma. They boosted their cities to everybody and pinned 'A.Y.P.' pins and 'booster' buttons on every lapel they could." The delegation visited more than thirty communities in two weeks, and Meany evidently made speeches at most, if not all, of them. In the end, he was one of three men cited as rendering "signal services" with his powerful appeals to California and Oregon communities to participate in the exposition.[5]

Upon his return, Meany plunged into the installation of the George Washington statue on the exposition grounds. The financial problem was solved when the state's commission for the exposition granted $8,000 to complete the funding. Meany's concerns grew over the height of the pedestal. As planned, he reported to sculptor Lorado Taft, it would elevate the gigantic statue too high above surrounding structures on the exposition grounds.[6]

Two days later, Meany was deeply angered to discover that Mrs. May Thornton Heg, the acting chair of the Daughters of the American Revolution Washington Statue Committee, had written to Taft on the same matter. Meany reproved her for undercutting his authority and declared that he would withdraw from the project except that "the idea behind the Washington statue is greater than any individual. The ceremonies over its successful completion must not be marred in the least by any real or fancied pique." He was, he declared self-righteously, "holding in check my own impulses" in order to carry out the project.[7]

The ladies of the Rainier Chapter of the DAR were appalled at Meany's outburst. Out of friendship, perhaps, but certainly through necessity, they made amends, and insisted that Meany should be the main speaker at the unveiling as had been previously decided. Meany's apologetic letter followed promptly along with a familiar complaint and resolution: "I am simply overwhelmed with work and responsibilities. I am crushing troubles behind me and pushing on the best I know how." Then he added a less familiar note: "I cannot pause for much clear thinking just now."[8]

All strain eased on June 14, 1909, when the statue of Washington was unveiled on a temporary low pedestal near the main entrance to the exposition grounds. The ceremonies were impressive, while Meany, as orator of the day, "was at his best and provoked the greatest enthusiasm by his earnest narration of the heroic deeds of the first president."[9]

The casual observer might have supposed Meany's task finished with the unveiling. Meany, however, felt a growing anxiety that when the fair closed, no money would remain for purchasing a permanent pedestal. His fears were justified. "Heart-sick," in October he reported to Taft the unhappy news that he could not obtain the proper base. Thus, Taft's gigantic brooding figure, designed to gaze across the campus and the centuries, would languish on a temporary concrete foundation at a pedestrian level for an indeterminate period. Nevertheless, Meany and the ladies of the Rainier Chapter inaugurated an annual rite on Washington's birthday in which they laid a wreath of Mt. Vernon ivy at the statue's base.[10]

In the spring of 1909, Seattleites also commemorated William H. Seward's 1867 purchase of Alaska. While sculptor Richard Brooks cast the bronze figure of Seward in his Paris studio, Meany assisted Judge Thomas Burke and the chamber of commerce in collecting funds to pay him. When Meany expressed regret that he could not contribute to the fund, Burke replied that "the work which you have done and which, seeing that one good turn deserves another, we expect you to do, will amount in value to a very substantial subscription, so...the rest of us are satisfied, if you are."

Though gratified by Burke's remarks and by the statue's unveiling on the exposition grounds, Meany reluctantly agreed to Burke's decision to place the statue finally at Volunteer Park. Meany believed that its permanent location at the University along with Taft's Washington would help make that institution the center of artistic activities in the state. Failure in this matter signified for Meany the need for more personal effort before his Alma Mater would become first in the affections of the people.[11]

Meany's confidence in the success of the Alaska-Yukon-Pacific Exposition never faltered though the stakes for him were high. On June 28, about a month after the fair's gates opened, Meany revealed the depth of his commitment to the exposition's success when he confided to Lorado Taft that "as a trustee of the Exposition I have so obligated myself that I will lose my home if it fails. However, there is every indication now of a brilliant success. The pressure on my mind and on my purse is relaxing." As usual, Meany enjoyed his unique position in Seattle's society: "My associates on the [Exposition] Board are all bankers and successful business men. I feel that it is well for an educator in my position to have a place here but it is not easy for me to keep the pace."[12]

Meany did not exaggerate the intrinsic worth of the educator among the exposition's leaders. When scholarly questions arose, his services were invaluable. He frequently found exhibitors calling on him for advice, especially for his well-advertised knowledge of the region's history and Indian lore. In one notable case, L.P. Hornberger, secretary to the state commission, asked him to examine the state museum for artifacts and specimens—especially Indian materials—which might be exhibited. He not only collected items for display, but also borrowed most of the display cases and cabinets in the museum for use at the fair. He also advised the assistant curator of history at the United States National Museum at Washington, D.C., as to the kinds of historical documents to bring to Seattle. Going beyond the obvious Alaskan documents, Meany recommended exhibit of legal papers concerned with the Treaty of 1846, which divided the Oregon Country, and materials illustrating the life of George Washington.[13]

With such recommendations and through his own writings, Meany sought to use the exposition as a means of interpreting the history and predicting the future of Washington and its relation to the nation and to the Pacific Rim countries. Writing about the exposition in *Colliers, The National Weekly*, for September 18, 1909, Meany asserted, "The Pacific slopes are becoming the front terraces of America." In that matter, "the Exposition...is clarifying a recently cloudy atmosphere and is blazing the way to smoother paths for the mighty changes now at their dawn." The spectacularly beautiful setting of the fair on the heavily wooded University campus, with panoramic vistas of water and mountains to both east and west, inspired him to declare, "here, then, are the dynamic forces of the West—mountains and forests, glaciers, lakes and tides."

He recognized that the great beauty and rich resources of the pioneer era, epitomized in the exposition's remarkable Forestry Building of gigantic log construction surrounded by displays of flowers and plants, could not be reproduced in the future. The forests around the Sound were being replaced by towns, cities, and industries. Meany's optimism in the face of this onrush of exploitation remained undiminished. He found conservation in the careful planning of the exposition itself, as its grounds and buildings would become a beautiful and utilitarian addition to the University of Washington campus. On the other hand, he asserted prematurely that conservation of forests, water, and water power sites had been accepted by the general public, loggers, and by other capitalistic interests. In partial defense of his facile argument regarding timber and water conservation exhibits, Meany pointed out that the exposition promoted good roads, a matter closely related to wise resource utilization.

Meany also asserted that a "continental patriotism" would develop in which Canada and the United States would work together "in perfect harmony for the general advancement of Western America." Based upon evidence that was limited and tenuous at best, he saw reassuring signs in the cooperation developing between the two nations at the fair and expressed the hope that the University of Washington and the proposed University of British Columbia would cultivate an "international fraternalism."

Meany alluded to friendly relations with Japan, but only in a perfunctory way, and with little emphasis on material gain. Alaska, in contrast, had first inspired proposals for the fair, and would thus gain the greatest benefits from it, in Meany's estimation. He viewed Alaska's exhibits with great enthusiasm and eagerly sought to lay to rest the myth that Alaska had been "Seward's folly." As a result, Meany boasted of the great pulp and paper resources found in America's northern territory and expressed the optimistic view that it "will yet come to our markets with a surplus of agricultural products. It is as demonstrable as algebra and geometry. The Alaskan pioneers have proven the value of their plow and harrow."

Indeed, Meany expressed the thought that Alaska might become "a new Norway." He borrowed this notion from Charles E. Woodruff, a United States Army surgeon and Nordic supremacist who wrote on "The Destiny of the Northwest," in an article published in the *Post-Intelligencer*. Meany quoted Woodruff as claiming that "The coast of Alaska...is almost identical with northern Scotland and that part of Scandinavia which we now think was the birthplace of the big, brawny, brainy, and blonde race we call the Aryan—the type which by its very superiority, due to the long process of natural selection, has been able to conquer its way all over the world." Meany elaborated on Woodruff's racist theme, stating that "this Exposition of 1909 may be pointing its finger to the place where the finest of the Aryan stock may find its rejuvenation only to evolve a still more robust, vigorous, and brainy type." Meany did not conclude his *Collier's* article on that chauvinistic note, however, but offered advice for all persons who might seek success: "The future beckons on those who are willing to dare and to achieve in fields relatively new but full of promise for the man or woman imbued with the spirit of the true pioneer."[14]

Meany's rhetoric regarding the exposition's meaning may have awakened a latent desire to personally experience the thrill of the unknown and a close relationship with nature. Earlier, in 1907, Meany had been reminded that he had his own mountain to scale—Mount Meany in the Olympics—which had been named for him in 1890 by J.H. Christie of the *Seattle Press* expedition. Asahel Curtis, noted Seattle photographer, had sent him copies of the first photographs ever taken of his mountain. Meany perhaps thought of climbing it, but hesitated because great heights made him dizzy.[15]

Meany certainly was reminded of the challenge presented by his mountain when *World's Work* published Curtis' pictures in the May 1908, issue. In the meantime, Meany had joined The Mountaineers, a Seattle outing club of approximately 400 members. Although he was elected its president, his doubts and fears of climbing lingered. When he joined the 1909 summer outing on 14,000-foot high Mount Rainier, his outlook changed.

Edmond S. Meany. *UW#3366.*

All photographs courtesy of Special Collections Division, University of Washington Libraries.

Above: Meany as the young scholar and orator, University of Washington class of 1885.
Below: Meany in his later years. *UW#3369.*

Meany as a member of the state House of Representatives, 1891-1893.

Lizzie Ward would marry Edmond Meany on May 1, 1889.

The Meany "Home Place," *c.* 1894, before the Meanys' extensive planting brought lush growth to the yard.

The Meanys on a memorial bench on the UW campus, *c.* 1928—perhaps the bench they donated to the University. *UW#534.*

Above: Groundbreaking for the site of the Oregon Building, Alaska-Yukon-Pacific Exposition, March 1908. Meany stands in the front row on the right, next to the young boy. *UW#11744. Below:* Meany heads a procession at the inauguration of Dr. Lee Paul Sieg as UW president, October 1934. *UW#14085.*

Meany and UW President Henry Suzzallo at groundbreaking for University's new stadium, 1920. *UW#2235.*

Meany served as the director of the first Campus Day when founded in 1904. In 1918 President Henry Suzzallo named him "Keeper of Traditions," commissioning him to strengthen Campus Day. *Above:* Meany and Trevor Kincaid prepare for a day of planting on a typical Campus Day. *Curtis#6215. Opposite above:* Meany addresses a Campus Day crowd, 1907. *UW#13549. Opposite below:* Meany bestows an award upon a student at the 1913 Campus Day. *UW#18001.*

The regents broke with tradition in 1914 when they named a UW building after a living person. *Above:* Students greet the Meanys on Campus Day in 1914 after the naming of Meany Hall. *UW#17996. Below:* Meany Hall, the only permanent building constructed for the Alaska-Yukon-Pacific Exposition in 1909. *UW#17993.*

In 1975 the University demolished the original Meany Hall and constructed the "new" Meany Hall. In the foreground is Lorado Taft's statue of George Washington. *UW#4846.* [Photos R, S, T]

Meany was always an outdoorsman and was long one of the most active members of The Mountaineers. *Above:* Meany, center, on a climb with five others. *UW#17997. Opposite above:* Meany camping on a Mountaineers trek, 1911. *UW#17998. Opposite below:* Meany, on horse, on a Mountaineers outing to Mt. Rainier in 1930. *UW#17992.*

Meany championed Native American rights and worked diligently to preserve and recognize Native American cultural sites. *Above:* Meany with Chief Joseph and Red Thunder, December 1903. *NA#610. Opposite above:* Meany delivers oration at the reburial of Chief Joseph at Nespelem in 1905. *NA#620. Opposite below:* Meany with Red Cloud (seated). *UW#17995.*

Meany in a characteristic pose, writing poetry while on a Mountaineers outing in 1911. *UW#17999.*

As he explained later, he "went out with the party to the north side of Rainier expecting to stay but one week. I staid [*sic*] the whole three weeks and succeeded in going to the summit with 61 others on 30 July. My enthusiasm over the experience is boundless."[16]

He did not exaggerate. The next summer he not only scaled Glacier Peak, a 10,000-foot mountain in the northern Cascades, but also played the role of club president to the hilt. A companion on the climb, Dr. Cora Eaton Smith, later praised him for "the unfailing kindness and courtesy you had shown us as our president, always saying the gracious thing, no matter what your own weariness or preoccupation." She was especially gratified that when she reached the top of Glacier Peak breathless and elated, Meany had immediately congratulated her. "That courtliness on your part at once glorified the occasion."[17]

Meany presided over camp fire festivities each evening, leading games, story-telling, and singing. He entertained his audience with poetry written at the end of the day or during the noon stop. In verses entitled "Glacier Peak," Meany celebrated man, nature, and God, the latter as a guarantor that nature was beneficent and, by implication, that progress was divinely ordained:

Thou somber king on throne of granite,
  A pilgrim knocks at rock-strewn gate,
Thy hingeless gate at guarded palace,
  Behold! I climb, I watch, I wait.

Was't weak to fear thy storm-swept kingdom,
  To fear and flee thy ice-chilled roar,
In awe to wave a feeble gesture
  To'rd heights where boldest eagles soar?

I do not boast a heart of valor;
  No upward march of conquest mine;
I slowly creep up storm-carved canyon;—
  Uncovered stand, a child of thine.

Then up thy walls I climb and clamber,
  O'er thy glist'ning snowfields plod;
I come in humble love and yearning
  More truth from thee, new thoughts of God....

Thy garnered streams, man's wheels and spindles,
  A thousand mills in lowlands hold.
Athrob, they turn to solve the riddle:
  From cloud to ice and then to gold.

Thy garnered streams through sagebrush valleys,
Transform coyote's vagrant home
To countless miles of fruit trees laden
With luscious pearls from thy cold dome.

Forever sway thy magic scepter;
Lo, grateful men thy praises sing!
Command thy winds in battle royal
And rule thy realm, Oh, snow-crowned king![18]

Poetic appreciation of the beauties and wonders of nature expressed only part of the avowed purposes of The Mountaineers. Defining the objectives for the members, President Meany wrote "This is a new country. It abounds in a fabulous wealth of scenic beauty. It is possible to conserve parts of that wealth that it may be enjoyed by countless generations through the centuries to come....This club is vigilant for a wise conservation." It did not seek to lock up the economic resources needed by present society, he wrote on another occasion. In practice, The Mountaineers had neither the political influence nor lobbying resources needed to make a significant impact on political developments. Members remained primarily occupied with summer recreation, with none more ardent than Meany.[19]

Of greater interest to Meany than environmental politics were suggestions that booksellers and others had been making for sometime that he write a history of the State of Washington. For a time he hesitated in deference to long-publicized plans to write the life of Chief Joseph and accounts of early exploration and discoveries. The idea of publishing a volume on Washington's history became compelling, however, and he finally tackled the project, telling one correspondent: "My reputation and life-long work here would probably make me an appropriate author of such a book."[20]

He completed the manuscript entitled *History of the State of Washington* sometime in 1908 and submitted it to The Macmillan Company in New York. A few days before Christmas of that year, the publisher reported favorably on Meany's work, and stipulated certain modifications. At the same time, Macmillan offered to pay a 10 percent royalty on all copies sold.

Meany found the terms satisfactory and agreed to modify the manuscript "with an eye to its value a few years hence." In this light, he eliminated all ephemeral or transient data and statistics except in the final chapter. In that chapter on "Federal Activity in the State," he argued persuasively that statistics revealed the federal government's major contribution to

Washington's development. This novel consideration of federal-state relations was accepted by Macmillan on Meany's terms.[21]

The publisher had great concern about Meany's wish to include an extensive array of photographs. His initial list contained eighty-two pictures (eventually reduced to fifty-nine) of pioneers, political leaders, statues, and purely antiquarian subjects such as Sir Francis Drake's chair, which was on display at the Bodleian Library at Oxford. Meany became adamant when demanding a full page portrait of Isaac I. Stevens, arguing that Stevens was "the largest single figure in the book and must have this distinction." Macmillan accepted his argument, and thus Meany's hero worship was once more evident.[22]

When Macmillan proposed a per copy price of $2.50, Meany objected. He wanted the price fixed at $1.50 to make it attractive to school administrators as a textbook. Meany wanted to make it possible for the *History* to "go into every home in the state at that price." In the end, the parties reached a compromise. Macmillan sold the work for $2.25, and Meany obtained ten prominent patrons who guaranteed purchase of the entire first printing.[23]

The book came out in May 1909. Charles W. Smith, Meany's colleague, provided an assessment of the book's place among the state's historical writings. Justifiably ignoring several subscription histories with their "mugbook" biographies, Smith reported in the Seattle *Post-Intelligencer* on June 20 that until Meany's book appeared

> a history of Washington we had not. Hubert Howe Bancroft, it is true, had spoken. His works are seldom history. They are rather transcripts of evidence, sets of printed archives....It is a fact to which the bookstores and libraries of the state can testify that for years a manual of a few dozen pages written in the early nineties by the versatile Prof. Taylor, of Seattle, for use in the elementary schools, was the only readable book that could be put into the hands of a resident of Washington desirous of taking a survey of his state's history.

Then, after sampling numerous passages, Smith concluded with praise for the work which, "starting from the earliest authentic data, and even including the legendary, brings the annals of the state down to events so recent as the death of Gov. [S.G.] Cosgrove [1909]; while its survey of the resources, material progress and possibilities, is the best yet published. It will take its place probably for a long time to come as the most satisfactory history of Washington."[24]

Another friend, Thomas W. Prosch, journalist and president of the Washington Pioneers Association, praised Meany's work in the *Seattle Times*, expressing satisfaction that the author eschewed the "individual puffery" pervading subscription histories which had often been forced upon "a deceived, indignant, nauseated public." The *Oregonian* of Portland, following the same admiring attitude found in the local papers, called the book an "excellent, up-to-date, and scholarly history...singularly free from sectionalism or partisanship, and fashioned along broad, national lines."[25]

On the "Whitman-Saved-Oregon" issue, the *Oregonian*'s critic unaccountably claimed that the subject had been only "briefly but discreetly described." Actually, Meany gave full measure to the controversy, presenting the pros and cons in detail. Following that summary he analyzed Whitman's actions and motives, concluding judiciously that "Whitman did not save Oregon. No one man could have done that. Like all other great events in history, the acquisition of Oregon was an evolution from many smaller events and from the work of many men. But in his own way and in his own time, Dr. Whitman did a full man's share." He urged Whitman partisans to avoid extreme positions, arguing that it was enough that the missionary was a hero for his religious work. In that matter, Whitman "wrought faithfully and well. He died bravely at his post for the cause he loved." Meany, on this issue, so disturbing to scholars and laymen alike at the turn of the century, had substituted empirically grounded fact for patriotic and religious biases.[26]

Meany had not stinted in his praise for the accomplishments of Governor Isaac I. Stevens. Nevertheless, Hazard Stevens, the son, quickly took exception to passages in the *History* not deemed sufficiently laudatory of his father. Meany, who prided himself for his admiration of Isaac, must have been surprised and disappointed when the son cast doubt on his fairness in describing the governor's handling of the 1854 and 1855 Indian treaties and subsequent warfare.

In fact, Meany had quoted Hazard Stevens' filiopietistic evaluations of his father, had consistently praised Governor Stevens' performance, ignored critics hostile to Stevens, and offered his own generous evaluation that Stevens "was governed by a singleness of unselfish purpose and...possessed an unsullied character, the brightest adornment of which was a lofty and steadfast patriotism." Then, to mollify his critical correspondent, Meany even suggested that he might add a paragraph to any subsequent edition calling attention to the tribes that remained friendly to the governor throughout the treaty-making period.[27]

On July 1, 1909, Meany sent a favorable report on his book to editor J. Franklin Jameson of the *American Historical Review*, noting "a desire to let you see how the book is regarded here at home." Jameson's reply, if any, is not known. Another review published in Jameson's journal, written by Professor Joseph Schafer of the University of Oregon, produced a mixed evaluation. Schafer judged the coverage comprehensive and based on the best resources. The result, wrote Schafer, was "a conscientious performance and a useful compendium." He found Meany's "judgement sane, his sympathies admirable," but he disparaged the book's "exclusively episodical form." Schafer then redeemed the author with the hackneyed expression: "He has done so well that we are impatient with him for not taking the trouble to do better."[28]

Indeed, the work is episodic with selection of subjects and information sometimes based on personal experience and interest rather than on a scientific or philosophical scheme. In this matter, both Charles W. Smith and Thomas W. Prosch came closer to understanding Meany the historian than did Schafer. Prosch suggested that the book was to a considerable extent a personal account, written by a man who had grown up in the state and whose accomplishments "added no small measure of the luster which has made and is making it great and glorious." Smith seconded those sentiments and underscored the fact that Meany personally supplied or generated historical data for the pioneer generation and contemporary times.[29]

The *History of the State of Washington* enjoyed a modest sale augmented by an official endorsement. That came in January 1910, when Henry B. Dewey, State Superintendent of Public Instruction, recommended it for the seventh and eighth grade teachers' reading circles. Subsequently, Macmillan issued a less expensive edition ($1.20) for public school use. With these developments, Meany realized his goal, enjoying steady sales for a number of years and making his work a household classic.[30]

While writing the *History* and promoting the exposition, Meany also grappled with problems and challenges arising from academic and professional activities. Heavy enrollments in undergraduate history classes so burdened the small University faculty that they could not seriously undertake research or offer graduate studies. Professor George H. Alden, in charge of European history, resigned in the spring of 1909 to attend full time to business interests. President Kane chose as his successor Oliver H. Richardson, a Doctor of Philosophy from Heidelberg who had taught at Yale since 1897. Richardson soon shouldered the responsibility for organizing the European half of the program, making class assignments, developing schedules, and seeking to enlarge the library holdings needed for advanced studies.[31]

Professor Frederic L. Paxson, of the University of Michigan, recognized Meany's standing as a professional historian by inviting him to read a paper on a Pacific Northwest topic at the December 1909 meeting of the American Historical Association. "I have just received a significant honor," Meany wrote to a friend on the *Post-Intelligencer* staff, "which, like the eastern college presidency I refused last year, is truly appreciated by one working out here so far from educational centers." Nor was that all: he also accepted an invitation to read a paper at the meeting of the Pacific Coast Branch of the American Historical Association at Stanford University.[32]

At the branch meeting on November 20, 1909, Meany read his paper entitled, "The Towns of the Pacific Northwest Were Not Founded on the Fur Trade." In it he offered an early criticism of Frederick Jackson Turner's seminal essay of 1893 on "The Significance of the Frontier in American History." Turner had contended that fur trading posts of the West, located strategically "so as to command the water systems of the country, have grown into such cities as Albany, Pittsburgh, Detroit, Chicago, St. Louis, Council Bluffs, and Kansas City." Though Turner had focused on the Upper Midwest and the Northeast, a plausible inference had been made that fur trading posts in the Pacific Northwest played a similar role in bringing civilization to that area.[33]

Meany denied the pertinence of Turner's fur post thesis to the Old Oregon Country, drawing upon evidence readily available to the historian of the region. He cited Hubert Howe Bancroft to the effect that an 1857 House of Commons report located approximately thirty fur posts still operating in the region. Meany pointed out, however, that subsequently only four had been transformed into towns and cities—Vancouver and Wallula [formerly Ft. Walla Walla,] Washington; Boise, Idaho; and Victoria, British Columbia. Astoria, not on that 1857 report, was another post which might have been counted, he asserted. Meany's critique represented one of the earliest statements narrowing the pertinence of Turner's frontier thesis to the area east of the Missouri and the Mississippi.[34]

Elected vice president of the Pacific Coast Branch at the conclusion of the November meeting, Meany journeyed to New York City a month later to the convention of the parent body, the American Historical Association. There he read "Morton Matthew McCarver, Frontier City Builder." He depicted the subject as a promoter of town building, land speculation, merchandising, and as a man caught up in the trek to Oregon in 1843. His attempts to build Linnton, Oregon, were overshadowed by the rise of Portland. Thereafter, he moved to Commencement Bay on Puget Sound to speculate in building Tacoma. Once again McCarver's plans were shattered when the Northern Pacific Railroad built its terminal elsewhere. Meany did not dwell long on failure, for he found pioneering to be its own reward. Thus, in Meany's eyes, Morton Matthew McCarver joined countless other pioneers who created a great flood of civilization in the Far West, a heroic task.[35]

Though exhilarated by rubbing shoulders with historians at regional and national meetings, Meany never lost sight of the need to find a new publisher for the *Washington Historical Quarterly*. He conferred with President Kane on several occasions in 1908 and 1909 on the proposition that the University of Washington publish it as a state document. A few members sought to revive the Washington University State Historical Society as a means of aiding Meany, but the organization proved moribund.[36]

Rescue came from an unanticipated quarter. The recently established printing department of the University undertook to print the journal in April 1912, issuing number two of volume three. Thomas W. Prosch, member of the board of editors, was one old friend who wrote quickly to express his congratulations: "I had supposed that the publication was gone. I am astonished at your courage and ability in resurrecting it." T.C. Elliott, more restrained, wrote to Charles W. Smith: "I do not see that the publication suffers much by the transition from professional to amateur printers." Then and later, however, he and others occasionally would complain of poor proofreading and of the quality of the editing.[37]

The printing subvention soon became a part of a full-fledged guarantee of the *Quarterly*'s continuation when Charles W. Smith, the University's assistant librarian, became the journal's business manager. He greatly increased the number and regularity of the journal exchanges for scholarly publications of other universities and learned societies. Smith further supported Meany's work with annual reports which, with one exception some years later, showed a favorable balance for the University when the value of scholarly publications received was measured against the *Quarterly*'s printing and distribution costs. Because of Smith's orderly administration, Meany could properly concentrate on editorial tasks and develop his own themes.[38]

T.C. Elliott contributed greatly to the value of the *Quarterly* and to Meany's reputation as editor when he began a serial publication of "The Journal of John Work," in the April 1912 number. Extending through each issue for the next two years, Elliott's presentation covered the travels and fur trading activities of Work, a Hudson's Bay Company agent from 1824-1826. Meany deserved credit for recognizing the value of Elliott's presentation even though the latter added little editorial assistance.

Meany took greater initiative when he introduced the subject of Alaskan history. Frank Golder's "A Survey of Alaska, 1743-1799," appeared in April 1913. A professor of history at Washington State College, Golder provided a sketch of the early Russian fur trade in Alaska, heavily documented from Russian sources. The article significantly broadened the scope of the *Quarterly*. In the following year, Meany displayed a special sensitivity to racial issues when he published sympathetic treatments of the Indians in essays written by Lewis H. St. John and W.J. Trimble.[39]

Meany's proudest achievement for the *Quarterly* in 1914 was probably his presentation of Frederick Jackson Turner's "The West and American Ideals" in the October number. One of Turner's numerous restatements of the frontier thesis, this paper had been delivered as a commencement address at the University of Washington. In spite of Turner's best intentions it had been written hastily. He felt embarrassed after the essay appeared in the *Quarterly*, according to his biographer Ray Allen Billington, because of the grossly exaggerated claims he had made for the West. "His first impulse was to pull out his red pencil to correct factual errors, add marginal qualifications, and scrawl beside one of the most flamboyant statements 'TOO STRONG.'" Nevertheless, in 1920 Turner republished the essay with virtually no changes in his notable collection, the *Frontier in American History*. There, he rationalized that the essay was a true representation of his views in 1914. Thus did Turner in effect exonerate Meany's editorial judgment.[40]

Meany sought to broaden the scope of his textbook writing early in 1910 when he proposed to George Brett of Macmillan that he prepare a United States history for elementary grades. The two men quickly agreed to a contract, suggesting that the publisher now regarded Meany as an established author. A Macmillan reader pronounced the manuscript good, cautioning only that the diction might be a bit too advanced for the upper elementary grades. Taking this criticism to heart, Meany sought advice from three colleagues, including Vernon Louis Parrington of the English department, in an effort to make the text more readable.[41]

Entitled *United States History for Schools*, the book was issued in January 1912, in time to be adopted for September classes. At least two local educational authorities were pleased with the book. C.C. Bras, editor of the *Northwest Journal of Education*, thought "the whole treatment illustrates that ethical revelation of the world which Herbart [Johann Friedrich Herbart, nineteenth century German philosopher and educator] declared to be the chief business of education." Otto L. Luther, principal of Seattle's Queen Anne High School, praised Meany's attempt "to inspire the young citizen with intelligent patriotism."[42]

Shortly after publication, Meany offered thanks to Macmillan for the book's handsome appearance and expressed optimism: "Somehow I feel as though this book will surely lift the mortgage from my house and perhaps bring some comfort beyond even that," a matter over which he was to be disappointed. Brett believed that if Meany could capture the Oregon and Washington markets, they might realize a financial success. But Macmillan sold only modest numbers of the book during the First World War period, netting Meany no more than $50 in royalties in any one year.[43]

That Meany's reputation as a writer did not depend on royalties was made abundantly clear when the prestigious Author's Club of London elected him to membership in 1911. H.A. Chadwick, writing as "The Stroller" in *The Argus*, characterized the election as a "real success." Chadwick then eulogized Meany for turning his back on money-making. "If Ed Meany should die today," he wrote, "a hundred years hence—yes, five hundred—his name would be known to every man of education in the State of Washington. If some of his old school mates, who have amassed dollars to his cents, were to drop out, they would be forgotten before the grass was green over their graves." Chadwick ended by expressing the hope that Meany might some day be elected president of the University.[44]

Frank P. Graves, former president of the University of Washington, and now a dean at Ohio State University, wrote on May 16, 1911, that he had read *The Argus*' comment with pleasure. "It is fully deserved and I congratulate you on it." In his response, Meany reverted to nostalgia, regretting no longer being able to learn the names of all students, but repeating his commitment to teaching and writing. He assured Graves, too, that he was loyal to President Thomas F. Kane and had no desire to succeed him. He and Kane "understood each other perfectly." As if to corroborate Meany's testimony to their close relationship, Kane spoke extravagantly of Meany's worth, as reported in an unidentified newspaper clipping: "the University had turned out three men who were worth to the state, each one of them, more than the total amount expended on the institution since its foundation in 1861....Professor Meany was one of the three."[45]

Later in 1911 Meany's public image took on a new dimension when Eugene Lorton, a Walla Walla newspaper publisher and editor, loosed a trial balloon for Meany as a Republican nominee for the governorship. Writing in the *Vancouver Spokesman*, he pronounced the gubernatorial race as unsettled, with Republican Governor Marion E. Hay by no means certain of gaining nomination. Recalling Meany's experience as a legislator in the 1890s, Lorton stressed his familiarity with "the practical as well as the purely ethical side of the history of the state." Meany, he found, was a "good mixer," who possessed "a fine and unimpeachable private character and a wide acquaintance" around the state. Though Meany would have a particularly popular following among the so-called "moral element," Lorton guessed that he would receive approximately the same loyalty from "the liberal-minded voters, owing to his previous fair and liberal attitude." Lorton's trial balloon for Meany did not fully inflate before it fell to earth. Meany quickly denied any interest in the governorship, accepting Lorton's proposal as one of "flattering kindness."[46]

To Myrtle Crowley, city editor of the *Vancouver Spokesman*, and a former student, Meany explained his refusal to run for office in familiar terms: "A year or so ago I received an offer of the presidency of an eastern university at a salary three times as great as that paid me here. Before the day had ended I sent my reply, expressing gratitude for the honor but declining the offer." That apparent self-denial induced someone—perhaps Crowley—to make the following warm response: "As professor at the University of Washington, he is loved and revered by every student and every member of the Faculty, and it is a common sight to see his tall figure hurrying over the campus with half a dozen 'coeds' and 'eds' endeavoring to keep up with him, and get a few words with the best loved professor on campus."[47]

The political canvass of 1912 disturbed Meany's comfortable world when he noted that regents, faculty, and students campaigning in the 1912 state elections questioned President Kane's competence as an administrator. When Democratic candidate Ernest Lister became governor, Kane and sympathetic faculty believed they had grounds for apprehension. Meany and colleagues in the Men's Faculty Club watched nervously for signs of political interference in October 1913, when Lister appointed a new regent. Their fears proved groundless. In consequence, Meany wrote happily to Lister that he and fellow club members "especially gloried in your statement that the University is an 'educational and not a political institution.'"[48]

Celebration proved to be premature, however, for the Board of Regents was determined to find a new president more fitting for a great future than Kane. The regents, reconstituted by the new governor, dismissed Kane as of January 1, 1914, and began its search. Quite unexpectedly, the board asked the faculty to set up its own committee to assist the regents. The faculty chose Meany as a member, along with political scientist J. Allen Smith and Engineer E.J. McCaustland. Meany was overjoyed. The turn of events seemed, in his estimation, to give the faculty a real voice in running the University, a significant step toward converting a "monarchical" institution to one democratically governed.[49]

Meany's optimistic remarks disturbed newly appointed regents Otto A. Fechter, Charles E. Gaches, and Winlock W. Miller. They felt that Meany had misunderstood the faculty committee's assignment, which in their view was merely to compile information. Their dismay mounted when they learned Meany intended to submit an article to *Harper's Weekly* praising recent developments as representing "an Evolution of Educational Independence." In his mind, a journalistic report of those events would counteract the bad publicity received by the University over the Kane incident, and would provide evidence of an increased stature for the faculty. When reminded that the regents had the legal authority to make appointments, Meany was not discomfited. He simply acknowledged the board's legal control in his article, which appeared in *Harper's Weekly* for April 25, 1914.[50]

The faculty trio worked more closely with the regents than the latter had first anticipated. Henry Suzzallo, who would be appointed president in 1915, did not at first find favor with the faculty. When John Dewey, Columbia University's noted philosopher, endorsed his colleague Suzzallo, the tide turned. Meany successfully urged regent Fechter to visit Suzzallo while he was in the East. Meany, of course, had been too sanguine in his prediction of an academic revolution putting the faculty at least on equal terms with the administrators. Nevertheless, as Charles Gates acknowledged in *The First Century at the University of Washington*, "It was significant...that they [the faculty] were consulted, for even that measure of participation was practically without precedent."[51]

The regents broke another tradition that spring of 1914—they named the University auditorium Meany Hall. The student body had agitated for the name ever since that structure—the only permanent building from the Alaska-Yukon-Pacific Exposition—had become University property in 1909. The Board of Regents, in succeeding years, had been reluctant to violate its own rule against naming buildings after living persons. It finally relented and the naming ceremony was held on Campus Day, May 1, 1914, before some 2,000 interested students, faculty, alumni, and state officials. The ceremony, a grand party, once again provided Meany an opportunity to extol loyalty and service to the University.[52]

Meany's standing in the coterie of professional historians of the Far West continued to rise when, in November 1913, the Pacific Coast Branch of the American Historical Association elected him president for the ensuing year. He was not present at its Los Angeles meeting in December, having chosen instead to travel to the convention of the parent body at Charleston, South Carolina, a gathering held soon after the branch meeting. Meany's office was largely honorific and did not present onerous tasks. The secretary-treasurer, William A. Morris of the University of California, easily managed the 276 members while the small budget indicated little activity other than the annual meeting. Stimulated by Meany's election to the branch presidency, the Seattle members decided to hold a special spring meeting in their city on May 21-23, 1914. Meany appointed colleague Edward McMahon as program chairman and the latter responded by filling six sessions with participants from five western states and the province of British Columbia.[53]

President Meany addressed the Seattle meeting on "Three Diplomats Prominent in the Oregon Question," praising the work of John Quincy Adams, Albert Gallatin, and Henry Clay in the making of the Treaty of Ghent. A handsome tribute, it was designed to "show something of the debt of gratitude which the Oregon country owes to the diplomatic triumphs achieved by the brains and hands of these three great men." He suggested that the people of the Pacific Northwest "should join in such a celebration, for it was at Ghent that the Oregon Question first entered the realm of diplomacy." Meany had more in mind, though, for he also told his audience that "English-speaking people throughout the world are preparing to celebrate the century of peace which was begun on Christmas Eve, 1814, by the signing the Treaty of Ghent."[54]

The outbreak of World War I in June 1914, and President Woodrow Wilson's neutrality declaration caused Meany concern that his celebration plans might not be supported. His fears proved groundless as a number of eastern historians joined in his project to lay wreaths on the graves of the three honored diplomats.

In a simple ceremony at Quincy, Massachusetts, Worthington C. Ford, director of the Massachusetts Historical Society, laid Meany's wreath on John Quincy Adams' grave, while Brooks Adams, a distinguished descendent, looked on. William A. Dunning, the noted historian of the Reconstruction period, along with several prominent colleagues, bestowed a wreath at Albert Gallatin's grave in New York City. He expressed delight to Meany: "There is something that to me is very impressive in the project that you have devised." Henry Clay's memory was similarly commemorated at his tomb in Lexington, Kentucky, by Professor James E. Tuthill of the University of Kentucky, whose eulogy covered several full columns in a local newspaper.[55]

Meany persisted in the hope that he was not merely speaking for himself but that he was acting in the name of the people of his community, which on some occasions extended to the scholars of the whole Pacific Coast. When Worthington C. Ford reported the ceremonies at Quincy, he admitted that he had not known at first to whom he should attribute the wreath and the tribute which came from the Northwest, whether to some institution or other, but had decided it was a personal gesture from Meany. A clipping Ford sent from the *Boston Herald* simply stated that it was from private sources. Meany responded gratefully, assuring Ford that it had been planned as "a tribute from the Northwest, and I was, therefore, much gratified to observe that my own initiative in the matter was in no way obtrusive."[56]

Subsequently, when the Seattle Ministerial Association asked the churches to hold prayer meetings on Sunday, February 14, 1915, commemorating the century of peace, Meany joined a minority of speakers who went beyond prayer to examine the political aspects of the centennial celebration. Speaking in two Seattle churches, after recounting the moments during the past century when threats to the peace between the United States and Great Britain arose and were vanquished, Meany called on the parishioners to contemplate the special role he envisioned for the Pacific Northwest in the contemporary crisis in Europe: "From these fair terraces of the Pacific slope...on the mountains and the plains, to the shores of the Atlantic, there stretches a boundary between two English-speaking nations. We who live on either side of that line are proud of the fact that it is the longest undefended boundary on the planet. Though many crises have threatened in the past, and though a crisis seems to threaten in the present, we are confident that the peace will continue unbroken."[57]

From the depth of his faith in history as determinant of the future, Meany assured his hearers of a glorious destiny carved out at Ghent. In 1915, he faced a world at war with unquestioning belief in progress and goodness.

CHAPTER NINE

"To Fight in Behalf of the Democracy and the Civilization of the World" (1915-1919)

"MEANY WILL TRUST WOODROW WILSON," ran the headline of a brief front-page story in the *University of Washington Daily* on February 15, 1915, reporting a speech he made to the Seattle Ministerial Association. It was another rendition of his earlier address on the hundred years of peace with Great Britain. "We have passed through many crises in the past," he reportedly declared. "Another now looms upon the horizon. Republican as I have always been, I am willing to trust the patriotism of our president in the present crisis." Trust in that case required Meany to be neutral in both thought and action toward the war in Europe, as President Wilson had asked in his "Appeal to the American people," made on August 18, 1914.[1]

If Meany thought his colleagues would maintain the rigorous neutrality Wilson urged, he was soon disillusioned. Numerous students reported that Professor Bowman was introducing war topics into the "Teaching of History," a methodology course. Later, Professor Richardson complained that Bowman had unilaterally inserted numerous war topics into the course on contemporary history. In both instances, Meany, backed by Acting President Henry Landes, required elimination of the new topics.[2]

Meany persisted in his support of Wilson as the war expanded. Evidence came on October 6, 1915, when Charles Rohwer, a former student, asked Meany whether the Monroe Doctrine and neutrality had been breached when American bankers had loaned huge sums of money to carry on the war. After an uncharacteristic delay, Meany merely replied "I do not wish to discuss the war at present." Then, while celebrating George Washington's birthday in February 1916, Meany demonstrated his faith in the Monroe Doctrine and tied its strength to Washington's "Farewell Address." According to a reporter, Meany asserted that "The Monroe Doctrine, which is all that prevents this country from being torn to shreds by such contests as are now being waged in Europe...has its origin in Washington's neutrality proclamation."[3]

The aloofness from Europe implicit in Meany's view of the Monroe Doctrine was consistent with his customary patriotic teaching in the classroom. J. Orin Oliphant, who later became an authority on Pacific Northwest history, heard Meany speak at a Lincoln County Teacher's Institute in 1913 and was "so greatly impressed by Meany's eloquence and by his appearance" that he decided to major in history when he enrolled in the University of Washington in September 1914. One of the courses Oliphant recalled vividly a half century later was Meany's "Makers of the Nation." He reminisced that "this course was intended to be inspirational rather than profound." It included a large number of heroes from both North and South, ranging from George Washington to Jefferson Davis and featured the celebrated Adams family. Meany was, in the words of Oliphant, "to a considerable extent a worshipper of heroes."[4]

Another impressionable student, Miss A.E. Strong, encountered Meany for the first time in the 1916 summer session. She offered the following evaluation of the fifty-three year old professor:

> As he looked down at us, from his great height, with his quiet dignity and genial smile, he won instantly that involuntary homage due a leader. His tawny gray beard and hair seemed not so much a feature in themselves as a setting for the great brow, beak-like nose and keen blue eyes. His light gray suit fell loosely from his erect shoulders and was worn carelessly. By its very unimportance it seemed to emphasize the man.
>
> Despite his years he was still the debonair spirit of youth, with something of the courtliness of the old-fashioned gentlemen.
>
> When he finished we felt we had met a man of broad view, kindly in nature, a fair man, one who had lived many years worthily and was content with the sheaves he had gathered.[5]

Though perhaps flattered, Meany could not have agreed entirely with this summation of his career. That spring he had published a declaration in *The Tyee*, the student yearbook, that the real University had begun in 1895 upon removal to the new campus. Though he and his classmates were "growing gray," he vowed that he "must not acknowledge that we are growing old, for I have so much to do. Anyway, the university is still young and earnestly striving toward the highest ideal."[6]

Acting President Henry Landes had revealed his personal support for Meany's historical projects by appointing Victor J. Farrar, a graduate student at the University of Wisconsin, as his research assistant. Farrar was to "furnish an additional arm or an additional lobe of brain tissue to Professor Meany" for collecting records of pioneers before they passed away. Meany was also partially gratified in his desire to offer a regular appointment to Frank Golder, a professor at Washington State College and a pioneering specialist in Russian history. The University hired Golder to teach Russian and Far Eastern history during the summer session of 1915, but no regular appointment was forthcoming.[7]

On May 18, 1915, the Board of Regents appointed Henry Suzzallo, a professor of education at Columbia University, as the new president of the University of Washington. He, they hoped, would become the brilliant leader able to convert the Seattle institution into a major university. Meany's customary close personal relations with the occupant of the presidential office were soon tested. On November 2, 1915, Suzzallo appointed Meany to a committee to revise the University seal, a minor function. Thereafter, that body transformed into a more prestigious Committee on Plans. A month passed without communication between the president and the professor. Meany voiced his disappointment that the president had ignored his pledge to hold an interview with Meany before the Committee on Plans met. Suzzallo immediately apologized, explaining that when he had learned that Meany was satisfied to remain on the committee with the alumni member as chairman, "I naturally assumed that everything was settled in your mind. I had merely meant to hold things up long enough to get what would be absolutely satisfactory to you....I had no intention of violating the spirit of our agreement whatever, and hope you understand it."

Since Meany had sent sketches to Suzzallo from his "Living Pioneers" series, published in the *Post-Intelligencer*, the new president seized upon that courtesy as a further opportunity to mollify his correspondent. He was reading the biographies, Suzzallo wrote, and found them to be "bully work." He exhorted Meany to "get everything you can down before some of those good citizens die and put themselves beyond your scholarly reach."[8]

Meany's family was a greater source of concern in 1915 than was the new and largely unknown University president. Meany was greatly troubled to discover that his son Mercer, enrolled at Lincoln High School, could not complete his academic studies satisfactorily, a matter attributed to deficient eyesight. When Samuel Hill asked Meany to write a poem that spring the latter uncharacteristically refused his patron, explaining that he could only compose when in "tune" with the world. In addition to Mercer's troubles, Meany was very worried over the condition of his mother who was gravely ill and at one point had been near death.[9]

In June, however, Meany had the pleasure of giving his daughter Margaret in marriage to J. Arthur Younger, a University student whom he greatly admired. The two young people graduated early in June from the University of Washington and then on the last day of that month celebrated their marriage before 200 guests at the University Congregational Church. The *Post-Intelligencer* reported the wedding in detail, emphasizing the prominence not only of Margaret and Arthur as students, but also the role of the elder Meanys in the life of the community.[10]

Shortly after, when old friends Mr. and Mrs. Thomas W. Prosch died in an automobile accident, Meany took the opportunity to aid the surviving members of the family by promoting the purchase of Prosch's valuable collection of newspaper files for the University library. He turned once again to Samuel Hill and the latter responded by contributing $200 to purchase eighteen bound volumes of newspapers. Hill then generously added $50 as a wedding gift for Margaret. In his note with the money, Hill warmed Meany's heart with a profession of faith: "I always come through, because I believe in you and believe in your work, but remember, dear boy, that money just now is a very scarce article. Everything is going badly in a business way, and has been for over a year." Meany, responding, found it "painful" to learn that Hill had felt the "pinch" of "tight money" and expressed the fervent hope that it would not be for long.[11]

In the fall of 1915, Meany introduced the biographical series on "Living Pioneers of Washington" to the editorial page of the *Post-Intelligencer*. These sketches first appeared on October 28, 1915, and ran through June 3, 1916, by which time the paper had published 189 short biographies. Although Meany had help from Farrar, his research assistant, he also asked his readers' aid in discovering worthy pioneers and in gathering information about them. In this he pursued disparate objectives. On the one hand, he described the sketches as "flowers of our appreciation while the handclasp of friendship is still possible," a sentimental goal. On the other hand, he promised the pieces would be "priceless" documents, a permanent historical file which would be preserved at the University for "further study, even by remote generations." Sentimentality easily prevailed. Concerning prominent pioneers, such as Edwin Eells, the statements were too short to yield much information or serious judgments, and equal treatment of obscure pioneers did not elevate them above obscurity.[12]

Near the completion of the series, Meany responded negatively to the suggestion that he collect the sketches into a book. He acknowledged that his research had not yielded serious history but "just a handclasp sort of greeting for the pioneers." However, the enthusiasm of the *Post-Intelligencer*'s editor, Scott C. Bone, had not been dampened. Bone thanked Meany for his work and stated that "the feature is a good one and I am sure it made friends for the *Post-Intelligencer*."[13]

That same autumn of 1915, Meany began a series of articles for the *Post-Intelligencer* on Washington's territorial and state chief executives. Shortly after its newspaper run, this series was published in book form as *Governors of Washington: Territorial and State*. Meany wrote in the preface that this effort had a dual purpose. He wished, first, to illuminate the "greatly accelerated" speed with which Washington passed from raw frontier to "the present cosmopolitan generation" by portraying the governors as "living witnesses" of that evolution. Second, he hoped his sketches would inspire youth, since "nearly every one of the governors achieved the high station from a humble beginning." Furthermore, he wrote that the qualities of "industry, perseverance, honesty and courage" which had made the leaders successful were still available to youth.[14]

Predictably, Meany's depiction of Isaac I. Stevens resulted in a version of the "great man" theory of history. The first governor emerged as a paragon in motives and works, not in any way responsible for the Indian wars which followed his treaty negotiations. Hero worship toward governors gave way to sheer parochialism when Meany prophesied that Miles C. Moore, the last territorial governor, "would always be remembered" simply because he had held that office during the last few months before Washington's admission to the Union.[15]

On the other hand, Meany displayed broad historical sympathies when portraying John R. Rogers, the Populist governor who had threatened to destroy Meany's University career. Meany recognized that in twice electing Rogers to office the voters had exhibited a "wholesome independence." The governor, he also noted, had given the legislature "common-sense advice about further economies in government." Probably an equally severe test for Meany was his favorable treatment of Governor Ernest Lister, the Democratic incumbent. Though Lister was heavily embroiled with the Republican majority in the legislature, Meany did not dwell on partisan matters but praised him for his statesman-like qualities and discussed the increased role of state government in society. Lister had a constructive attitude, he concluded: "He desired and urged economy, but he also requested that care be used in applying the economies so that no real need [would] be jeopardized."[16]

The didactic mood pervading Meany's recounting of the governors' virtues found additional outlets in the wartime atmosphere of 1916. While engaged in patriotic exercises at Lorado Taft's statue on Washington's birthday, Meany once again extolled the peerless character of the first president. Speaking before the Daughters of the American Revolution and nearly a thousand other people, Meany praised Washington's sense of justice and duty to others, finding that those qualities had raised him above ordinary criticism:

> Whereas in thinking of others of his time we must bear in mind the difference of standards [between that day and this], yet in the life of Washington were mingled such qualities that not a day has passed from his death to the present moment when his life would suffer in comparison with and in judgement by any of modern standards. He lived and wrought for all time.

Mindful perhaps of the setting of the public exercises on the University of Washington campus, Meany recalled the admonition in Washington's Farewell Address to "promote, then, as an object of primary importance, institutions for the general diffusion of knowledge. In proportion as the structure of a government gives force to public opinion, it is essential that public opinion should be enlightened." Progress of civilization and the safety of the Republic, Meany reminded his audience, depended upon an enlightened citizenry exercising its prerogatives.[17]

Nine days later in Olympia, while speaking on "The First American Settlers on Puget Sound" before 150 members and guests of the Pioneer and Historical Society of Thurston County, Meany made the most of another opportunity to evaluate the role of heroes and citizens in America's development. With Hazard Stevens presiding, Meany praised the local pioneers' courage and achievements as equal to that of all frontiersmen since the first landing at Plymouth Rock. In terms familiar to readers of his *History of the State of Washington*, he declaimed that on the shores of Puget Sound "there are the same kind of log cabins for the first sheltering homes. There are very similar dangers from wild beasts and wild men, the same general series of hard knocks."[18]

The pioneers, however, were not the sole determiners of progress, Meany asserted. Remaining true to earlier statements, he gave full credit to diplomats in settling the Canadian-American international boundary at the 49th parallel. But when that task was finished, the settlers on the Sound had shaped their future—and that of the nation—when they created their government and society. Citing Isaac I. Stevens' prophecies that Washington would become a center of American enterprise in the Far East as well as an ideal home and bulwark of strength in the nation, Meany urged his audience in profound gratitude to "clasp the hands of the white haired remnants of that noble band of men and women, but above all let us press forward, carrying the torch of enlightened progress given us by the pioneers."[19]

In an extended, unpublished paper entitled "The Attempt to Appraise the Present as an Epoch in Human History," Meany reaffirmed his faith that civilization was marked by inexorable progress which in his day took the form of increasing democracy and efficiency, or science. The European war then raging he regarded as an interlude. Science had so united the world, he believed, that no nation—not even Germany—could gain military domination. Science, together with accumulated wealth (by which he meant industry and philanthropy) had worked miracles in achieving well being for men everywhere. In the end, Meany stated confidently that "greater democracy, aroused by the evolution of efficiency and lured or driven to its practice, will usher in the new revolution of civilization by a route different from the older ways of invasion of lands and mixture of peoples." Science, democratic society, and the wise use of wealth enabled men "to think in planetary terms, with the dawning concept that the truest national dignity lies in international honor." Movements in that direction he found in America's Progressive reforms, the new laws promulgated under Lloyd George's government in Great Britain, and in such ambiguous examples of democracy as the Russian Duma, the Portuguese Republic, and the unrest in Spain. "We are now," Meany concluded, "at the dawn of a new epoch in history."[20]

Meany's intended use of that unpublished paper is not clear, but the ideas in it formed part of his address on "The Limits of Nationalism and the Dawn of a New Internationalism," delivered July 8, 1916, to a religious assembly at Seabeck on Hood Canal. Speaking from a platform containing Protestant clergymen from twelve denominations as well as Governor Ernest Lister and James A. Duncan, a prominent Seattle labor leader, Meany defined nationality as "unity of spirit," rejecting culture or language as its basis. He then referred to the state as the "hands and feet" of the people while the nation he saw as its soul. Americans practiced nationalism in its most exalted form when they placed "duties" above "rights." The presence of imperialism did not contradict that sense of duty, he maintained, since imperialism was a European phenomenon which the United States had practiced only once when it conquered The Philippines. The

Monroe Doctrine, on the other hand, was a benign instrument which in the early nineteenth century had established the principle of duty toward mankind, still the prime motivation for American foreign policy.

International accord, Meany told his Seabeck audience, would be the outcome of the fulfillment of the new ideals of nationalism. Indeed, he believed that Americans had been ready to adopt the "new internationalism" for many years, a matter recently attested by statements of both Charles Evans Hughes and Woodrow Wilson in their campaign for the presidency in 1916. Each supported peaceful settlement of international disputes.

Meany predicted that the European people also would want a new internationalism. He told his audience that "We surely will see a new and stronger internationalism [in Europe] after the torn fields are once again smoothed with the farmer's ploughs and harrows." Toward that end, Meany advanced the idea that the "new education" should be directed toward making the peoples of the world appreciate and practice the new duties of men to "hearken back to the old dignity of labor and brotherhood of man." When that task was completed, and Wilson's hope for a new, open diplomacy had been achieved, the "new internationalism will then come as blooms the rose when the snow has gone."[21]

In the summer of 1915, while leading one hundred members of the Mountaineers who were encircling Mount Rainier at the snow line, Meany decided to edit and publish a collection of narratives of the discovery and exploration of the mountain, as well as to provide information on its geology, geography, and botany. Entitling the volume *Mount Rainier: A Record of Exploration*, he hoped to see the book published in time to capture the tourist trade the following summer. Houghton Mifflin declined to consider publication, citing limited and local interest in the subject. Macmillan agreed to publish it after Meany had assembled twenty-four prominent citizens as guarantors of sales. Thereafter, Macmillan published a special edition, offered before the regular edition appeared, which Seattle's Bon Marché department store undertook to sell at $2.00 with a 10 percent royalty to Meany.[22]

The Dial of Chicago, a magazine devoted to literary criticism, described Meany's publication as "a handy and inviting collection of historical and descriptive and scientific material much to the taste of mountain-climbers and other lovers of the great out-of-doors." The Bon Marché's campaign, delayed until the Christmas season of 1916 and prominently, if briefly, advertised in both the *Post-Intelligencer* and the *Times*, yielded a sale of only 468 of the 1,200 copies consigned. On March 15,

1917, R. Nordhoff of the Bon Marché informed each sponsor that he must purchase thirty copies at $2.00 each to complete the contract. At that point, sponsor Robert Moran, a prominent Seattle ship builder, proposed to Samuel Hill that they assist Meany's commendable historical labors by donating their copies to public libraries around the nation. Hill and at least eight other guarantors agreed to that plan.[23]

Although a few sponsors may have defaulted, the Bon Marché shouldered any deficits and even increased the royalty paid to Meany. The latter wrapped, addressed, and mailed more than 200 copies of the guarantors' volumes to public, state, and university libraries, happily paying the postage himself. Privately, he felt he had failed the trust placed in him by the sponsors and, as he wrote to Nordhoff, "all I can do now is to seek to recover in some other way my standing with those twenty-four men."[24]

Meany worried little—perhaps not at all—about his scholarly reputation or the scientific value of the work. Editing selections such as those from George Vancouver's journal on the discovery and naming of Mount Rainier and Hazard Stevens' report on his ascent of the mountain, the first on record, was a labor of love. Indeed, Meany's chapter on "Place Names and Elevations in Mount Rainier National Park" broke new ground by rationalizing the need for more systematic naming of places. He wrote at the head of the chapter:

> The ranger who discovers from a look-out peak a distant fire near some unnamed lake or cliff hastens to a telephone, but finds his work of sending fire fighters to the place of danger much more difficult than if he could use some definite place name. Trail builders and patrols continually find a similar need for names. For their own use they proceed to invent names which often stick.[25]

Then, as if to underscore the need to cooperate with the United States Geographic Board in its task of providing appropriate and universally accepted names, Meany related an anecdote: "The Mountaineers in 1915 found that a trail builder had supplied such a need by giving a beautiful waterfall near his trail the name of his favorite brand of canned peaches." Following that, Meany offered a compilation of place names in the National Park—omitting the canned peaches—and inviting readers to send him facts in their possession regarding place names.[26]

When the United States declared war against Germany on April 7, 1917, Meany responded as a journalist, expressing militant patriotism in a series of twelve editorials published in the *Post-Intelligencer*. In "Pacifists of Other Days," which appeared on April 8, he commended the "unexampled patience" of Americans in maintaining neutrality. Now, however, he declared his own opposition to the "noise we call pacifism." The nation, by fighting the German Empire, would reach "the loftier idea of nationalism." In agreement with President Wilson's pronouncements, Meany concluded that embracing the "nobler aspirations of nationalism" would lead its people "to fight in behalf of the democracy and civilization of the world."[27]

A few days later, in another editorial, Meany applauded the suspension of intercollegiate athletics at the University of Washington as admirable "restraint" in the war crisis. The gravity of the times suggested to Meany that a deep and thoroughgoing sense of duty must prevail. "Do not permit hysteria to become ascendant," he wrote. "The colleges and universities must go on soberly and earnestly with their important work. A feverish or panic stricken nation would be greater calamity than war." To fulfill his moral obligations, Meany felt that each person must find a constructive role in war activities, either as a producer, soldier, student, or cultivator of a home garden, for everyone would be needed to win the war.[28]

In a subsequent editorial, Meany expressed surprise that the military had found a considerable number of young men physically unfit for service. Perhaps more shocked and fearful than he would admit, Meany insisted that the rejections would not affect patriotism or the cause America upheld in the conflict. If catastrophe threatened, he was certain that all youth would be pressed into service, each becoming more intensely patriotic than before the war. In a crisis, the "people...will be quick to resent any disrespect of deed or word against the flag or the government....True Americanism is being reborn. The whole citizenship is being lifted to a higher level. This may well be called subjective patriotism." Then, without a hint of doubt, Meany cited President Wilson's high-minded claim that the nation was fighting for humanity, not for conquest, and forecast that success in that endeavor would mean "the world will salute the man or woman who can rightfully declare 'I am an American citizen! Hail the day!'"[29]

In another editorial, Meany proclaimed the United States had a "Glowing Chance" to quickly realize Wilson's objective of spreading democracy around the globe by sending an army to the aid of the liberal provisional government of the Russian revolution. Terming it "the youngest of the democratic governments," he wondered "who can measure the enthusiasm, the electric uplift, of the people of Russia if an army from democratic America would rush across Siberia to her assistance!" Deeper in that lead editorial, Meany noted that the defeat of Russia by Germany might well constitute a threat to America's possession of Alaska. At that point he did not recognize the possibility of the Bolshevik triumph—an ignorance shared with the State Department and President Wilson, among others.[30]

Aside from America's entry into the war, Meany's chief concerns in the spring of 1917 were for his relations with President Henry Suzzallo of the University and the condition of the Department of History. The president asked Meany to evaluate his departmental faculty in late March, but the latter procrastinated until almost the end of April. He admitted that Professors Oliver H. Richardson and Jacob N. Bowman had not worked well together for some time but that relations recently had improved, with Bowman promising to cooperate with Richardson. Meany's detailed report on the faculty concerned five professors in addition to himself. Richardson and Bowman taught European history, along with Ralph H. Lutz. By coincidence, all three held doctor of philosophy degrees from Heidelberg. Charles W. David, a junior member and doctoral candidate at Harvard, taught ancient and medieval history.

Edward McMahon, who joined Meany in teaching American history, possessed a Master of Arts degree from the University of Wisconsin. Often protective of McMahon, Meany wrote, "He says he uses rough and hammering methods compared to those of Dr. Richardson." Nonetheless, Meany concluded that McMahon obtained good results. In fact, the two men were supportive of each other, as a mutual friend reported to Meany after meeting McMahon in Chicago. "Seeing him made me see you (in imagination) and we discussed your many fine qualities. Mac is very loyal to you, as you know." Richardson, on the other hand, according to Meany, was a refined scholar and thorough in class preparation but also subject to physical weakness. Meany would have to rely on those two and Bowman to develop any special wartime programs, as David would soon resign and Lutz would join the army. President Suzzallo could hardly escape the conclusion that the department was really quite limited in scope and not productive of much scholarship, though Meany had put the best face he could on the matter.[31]

Meany's anxieties about his own future came to the surface on June 2, 1917, when he congratulated Suzzallo for his address before a Red Cross assembly, and then got to the point: "For the last six months I have been growing ever more hungry for a chance to light a cigar with you to visit as colleagues or as mere friends." Suzzallo, however, kept Meany at arm's length, stating "these are strenuous days. It is very difficult indeed to have any social or friendly life. Those opportunities have been so long delayed that I wonder if they will ever come. Still I am keeping up hope."[32]

It was, of course, perfectly evident to Meany that ordinary campus life had given way to frenetic wartime activity. He wrote to Professor Franklin H. Giddings of Columbia University that "Here on the Pacific Coast we are squaring our shoulders for the burdens [of war]. About 700 of our young men students have withdrawn for [the] 'Military Emergency.' The people are drilling, planting potatoes, building ships and buying Liberty Bonds. Democracy with a conscience must prevail." To another correspondent he wrote that enrollment at the University had dropped sharply, so that he had lost 109 of his 367 students to military service and war-related jobs. When it became apparent that he could not talk to Suzzallo, Meany reported by mail that he had given seventy public lectures or talks during the past academic year. He stated quite frankly that he was trying to emulate the president's performance, and concluded with an extravagant compliment: "With abundant pride in the splendid service you are rendering for the high purposes of the University and the State, I am Yours Faithfully, Edmond S. Meany."[33]

To Waldo G. Leland, secretary of the newly organized National Board of Historical Services, Meany provided more details regarding his support for the war. He reported that he had prepared an address on "Our State in National Crisis," which had been delivered to all sorts of audiences—lodges, churches, high schools, and others. Meany quickly became interested in the National Board when urged by Leland to develop curricula and programs explaining America's position in the world to students and the public. No doubt Meany, like many other history department chairmen, was impressed that the self-constituted board had been formed by a score of professional historians headed by the highly esteemed J. Franklin Jameson and Frederick Jackson Turner.[34]

War programs at the University developed slowly. The Department of History offered no special war courses in the summer session of 1917, while Meany contented himself with delivering popular lectures on standard western and Pacific Northwestern topics. In the fall term, however, the University made plans to instruct army recruits at Camp Lewis, south of Tacoma. On October 26, Meany and his departmental colleagues voted to offer war-related lectures in the Camp Lewis program.[35]

Soon thereafter, Meany began teaching Pacific Coast history at the army post on Monday and Thursday evenings. Bowman and Richardson joined him, as did nine other colleagues, mostly science and engineering professors. They had to leave the campus at 4 p.m. on a round-trip train ride of approximately 100 miles and did not finish their weary trek until well after midnight. Though gratified by the response to his lectures, Meany soon found the work exhausting and begged to be excused from delivering other outside addresses. Upon hearing of Meany's late returns to Seattle, Suzzallo cautioned him to guard his health and to remember that he was needed elsewhere for more important work.[36]

The National Board of Historical Services provided Meany with another task in the autumn of 1917, when Leland asked the Washington State Council of Defense to establish a project to collect records of the war on a county by county basis. The state council then called upon Meany to promote the work of county history committees by providing encouragement, advice, and instruction. Meany readily accepted the responsibility. Since none of the members of the county committees were conversant with archival work and because the materials would be housed locally, he first circulated a letter of information filled with suggestions of ways and means of collecting and preserving newspaper clippings, photographs, posters, programs, letters, documentary records of enlistments, opinions about the war, and other items. He assured his readers, too, that preserving war records at the grassroots level would make "more accurate and more vital the national history."[37]

Though encouraged by the quick organization of several county history committees, Meany soon found that the obstacles to collecting materials were great. He was not free to appoint his own committees but had to wait upon procrastinating county defense councils, whose members undoubtedly believed that they had more important work to undertake. Once appointed, the county history committees received Meany's letter but no additional direction nor any funds with which to operate. Hence, Meany could neither direct them nor call them to accountability. Nevertheless, putting the best face on the matter, Meany reported to Suzzallo, who was chairman of the State Defense Council, that he had received a cordial response in the counties and that he believed "a good measure of success will be achieved."[38]

Results across the nation were very poor with no far western state singled out as having produced an extensive or useful archive of domestic war documentation. Meany's report for Washington that "most of the 39 counties were successful in accumulating materials for deposit in the most central library of each" yielded no evaluation of content. Furthermore, few county libraries had the means of utilizing or preserving such materials. In any event, the short-lived American participation in the war, followed quickly by a return to peace-time life, cut off thoughts of preserving local records.[39]

Meanwhile, when Suzzallo, about to leave on an eastern trip, gave Meany seven tasks to complete, the latter responded with alacrity and eagerness. When Suzzallo returned he found seven reports from Meany lying on his desk. The president was particularly pleased with Meany's introduction of a special pledge of honorable conduct—the Ephebic Oath—which he had administered to the freshman class. The president found the ceremony "inspiring" and expressed the hope that it would be "only a matter of time...[until] this will be one of the great ceremonies of the University."[40]

At a conference a few days later, Suzzallo gave Meany some "painful information" of Professor Bowman's eccentric teaching practices. Mindful of earlier difficulties with Bowman, Meany now concluded that he should be discharged. Meany strongly recommended that Professor Richard Scholz of the University of California be employed as Bowman's successor and urged that Suzzallo interview Scholz while on a trip to California. Scholz, he told Suzzallo, would be able to strengthen the offerings in ancient history, leaving Charles David to concentrate on medieval history. Though decisive in the matter of Bowman, the next day Meany must have tried his president's patience when he complained that "Richardson has now become part of my unhappiness" and requested another meeting to deal with that matter.[41]

If Bowman and Richardson were troublesome, Ralph H. Lutz, who had joined the army, pleased Meany very much. Stationed at Camp Kearney in California, Lutz wrote ironically that on a bright and clear Thanksgiving Day he was preparing for war. He added a note which Meany might have found wryly amusing: "I think of you all often and of the calm and intellectual life of the university." Then, as if recognizing the true character of his department chairman, Lutz remarked: "Knowing your views on the war I am sure that you are a tireless worker and are making your influence felt throughout the state."[42]

In early 1918, Suzzallo named Meany "Keeper of Traditions," commissioning him to strengthen Campus Day (founded in 1904 with Meany as director) and to develop ceremonial tree planting on campus. In addition, Meany collaborated with Suzzallo in developing a permanent setting for the classical columns saved from the demolished downtown University building. The columns were erected at the Sylvan Theater as a symbol of the continuity of campus life. Suzzallo looked with enthusiasm upon the various projects, assuring Meany that he was eager to "build up a rich and characteristic tradition in this place."[43]

The two men participated in ceremonies of the Daughters of the American Revolution on Washington's birthday in 1918. At this happy event, Meany heard Suzzallo compliment him in public. Even more satisfying, Meany orchestrated a ritual at the celebration in which local consuls of seventeen nations laid wreaths at the base of Lorado Taft's statue of Washington in a show of solidarity with the United States. While reporting this success to Waldo G. Leland, he urged that America's teachers be supplied with patriotic propaganda to "imbue them with the wisdom of holding up England once more as the 'Mother Country.' This is certainly to be one of the beautiful results of this awful war." For Leland this suggestion must have been satisfying—Meany's Anglophile sentiments repeated those which the National Board of Historical Services had held from the first day of organization.[44]

But only a few days after Suzzallo had complimented him, Meany drafted a letter to J. Franklin Jameson complaining that "after long years of service here in my Alma Mater, under seven presidents, I am encountering an uncomfortable circumstance. Our new president, Henry Suzzallo, has given some friends the impression that he holds my worth too low." He went on to express his puzzlement over Suzzallo's attitude. Meany did not believe he was in "real danger," but nevertheless asked Jameson to commend his work to Suzzallo, using information already filed with the National Board of Historical Services. Whether he sent the letter to Jameson is not known, but he had added reason to do so the next day when Suzzallo responded to him tartly for differing on a matter of policy. Meany then, perhaps in an effort to parry Suzzallo's acerbic thrust, described his work as "Keeper of Traditions" and noted that by commencement he would have delivered eighty outside addresses during the academic year, a measure of achievement that the dynamic president might appreciate.[45]

Meany continued in the early months of 1918 to teach his regular courses, which had not changed for some time. In the spring, for example, he taught "Makers of the Nation," "American Diplomacy," "Northwestern History," and a seminar in Washington state history. In addition, he delivered five lectures to the military cadets on the history of the United States army, offered on days when rain made outdoor drills impossible. He continued to teach at Camp Lewis until February 12, slogging through the mud at the training base and suffering from laryngitis.[46]

Meany did not lecture at a new program sponsored by the National Board of Historical Services at Camp Lewis, but devoted considerable time assigning other historians to the classes and to finding money to purchase needed lantern slides. He remained excited about his patriotic work and also reported with satisfaction to Secretary Leland that dissension and criticism of the war in the community were very limited: "The only off-side group that I hear about is the so-called 'I.W.W.' and the authorities are continually after them."[47]

Release from lecturing to troops enabled Meany to resume his accustomed heavy schedule of off-campus speeches. In answering a young correspondent's request for advice on what he should do upon graduation from high school, Meany replied that he had delivered a dozen commencement addresses in which he inserted advice from Secretary of War Newton D. Baker to young men about to graduate. Baker had urged them to attend colleges which offered military science. They might then be inducted into the army but would be enrolled in classes until needed for active duty. "That is by all means the best thing for you to do," Meany concluded.[48]

The University's curriculum had to be greatly modified due to the decline in civilian enrollment and heavy, war-inspired emphasis on practical studies. Nevertheless, in the spring of 1918 Meany had reason to be satisfied with his department and his position within the University. He received a substantial increase in salary and enjoyed good relations with Richardson and David, although the latter soon departed for Bryn Mawr College in Pennsylvania with no effort having been made to keep him. Meany also defended McMahon against accusations of radicalism. Affirming that "at one time he was deemed too radical by some critics," Meany insisted that "as times have changed during the last year his attitude is that of perfect loyalty." Furthermore, McMahon had just the right training for his teaching, Meany argued, although he possessed only the Master of Arts degree. To underscore his conviction, Meany recommended that McMahon be promoted to full professor.[49]

During the summer of 1918 Meany enjoyed his usual three weeks of vacation with the Mountaineers, hiking in the Monte Cristo region of the Cascades. When he returned to Seattle for the fall term, he found the transformation of the campus complete. Women overwhelmingly predominated in regular classes as virtually all civilian male students had disappeared. The latter, however, had been replaced by 2,000 army recruits who formed a Student Army Training Corps (SATC). For them, intensive military drill and special technological and academic classes replaced the regular curriculum. Everything else seemed trifling, Meany wrote to Victor Farrar, his research assistant, now on duty in the army in France, except for the news of the "glorious American drive toward Metz." He went on to state, "I cannot see clearly through it all but, like the others, I am straining to prepare for my share of the work."[50]

As one of his new tasks, Meany supervised introduction of a "War Aims" course required in all units of the SATC across the nation. He chose professors Richardson and Scholz to present "Issues and Origins of the War" in the fall term. The instructors prepared their own syllabi but Meany obtained additional scholarly publications, maps, and textbooks for their classes. Each student also received numerous pro-ally propaganda pamphlets supplied by the federal government's Committee on Public Information.[51]

While expressing his jubilation to Farrar on the progress of the war, Meany also had depicted his own role as modest and far removed from the war's dire consequences. "As soon as I finish in the office," he wrote, "I plunge into our war garden [at home] each day. It has been a success." By October 1918, however, the dreaded influenza pandemic posed a threat to campus and to Meany's comfortable world. The "Spanish Influenza" had closed down all schools in Seattle, including the University of Washington. The high incidence of the disease and death made it necessary that Meany and all other faculty and students obtain special passes to enter the campus. But not all of Meany's contacts with war were threatening or deleterious. On October 23, Meany reported to a correspondent that just that morning a cable from France announced that Captain Arthur Younger, his son-in-law, had entered the war zone, a step which they saw as intensely patriotic and noble.[52]

Meany's interest in the progress of the war lost none of its fervor as he anticipated Germany's defeat. Adopting an attitude much like that which he and Suzzallo earlier had agreed to, Meany wrote to George W. Soliday, an old friend: "Many times I have been hungry for an old fashioned visit and powwow with you. But the war has absorbed you and me and all of us. It is best so for the present and up to the successful termination of America's wonderful programme." These sentiments were bolstered by colleague Ralph H. Lutz, now an army officer in France, who reminded Meany of the many conversations they had about the "ultimate triumph of the democracies of the world over German imperialism." That distant date now seemed imminent. "Victory now seems to follow victory and I am sure," Lutz wrote, that the "glorious deeds of American and allied armies have thrilled all America. The final collapse of Germany can not be far distant." The armistice came just eight days later, on November 11, 1918.[53]

Meany channeled some of his joy over the end of the war, as he had years earlier at the conclusion of the Spanish-American War, into soliciting more than two dozen inspirational messages from prominent leaders for use in the classroom. He asked President Woodrow Wilson for thoughts on the impending peace conference. He congratulated King Albert of Belgium for the "love poured out" by his "wonderful" subjects and asked for his thoughts as he resumed the throne. From Marshal Foch of France, as well as from several other French, British, and Belgian political, military, and religious leaders, he requested letters describing some significant event of the war which might inspire generations of students. In his remarks to Foch he stated his own conviction that American educators were proud of the recent achievements on "behalf of civilization." Before his avid search for inspirational messages abated, Meany had solicited letters from a corresponding number of American leaders as well.[54]

As the Christmas season of 1918 approached, Meany focused attention on the human interest aspects of demobilization and peace. Readers of the *Post-Intelligencer* opened the paper on December 6 to find Meany's letter to the editor in which he lectured the community on its responsibilities to returning soldiers. He reported that faculty colleagues were teaching courses in business law, economics, and civics and providing vocational training to ease the transition to civilian life for the soldiers at Camp Lewis. In addition, he urged the public to help the fighting men returning from France find jobs or to resume positions lost when they went off to war.[55]

Among the events marking the end of the war for the University of Washington was the last big drill of the Student Army Training Corps in mid-December. Meany reported to a friend in the American Expeditionary Force that more than half of the members of the Corps planned to resume regular University studies in the winter term. The University was to abandon the "War Aims" course and related war preparatory offerings. At Christmas he sent greetings to Lieutenant Lutz in France, writing "We thrill daily with news of the crisis through which the world is passing. Americans are taking noble parts. I hope we may not be too proud or boastful. As I see it, we now have the gratitude of the world. May we continue to deserve it."[56]

Meany's greetings to Sergeant Victor J. Farrar gave a glimpse of family life at the Christmas season when he wrote that "Ned [Edmond S. Meany, Jr.] has distributed the gifts from our little tree and I have come to the same long table [in Denny Hall on campus] where you and I have spent so many long hours together. It is strewn with items clamoring for attention."[57]

Ned was eleven years old, the youngest and most excited member of the family gathered around the Christmas tree. Many years later, after a distinguished career as an educator, he recalled the customary Christmas activities. Celebrations at home were relatively unexciting since the gifts generally were utilitarian. However, after opening those packages, the family usually went to the home of Dillis B. Ward, Ned's grandparents, on fashionable Queen Anne Hill. There "Grandpa Ward," a patriarch with "a flowing mustache and mustache cup," presided at a large table seating numerous relatives, with side tables for the children. On the wall behind the patriarch was an immense family portrait. "These celebrations were great," Ned recalled, "because I always got the presents that were different, not presents that were useful." His father, Ned recalled, felt he could not shop in stores because he was so often recognized, so he gave sums of money or copies of his books, duly autographed.[58]

At other seasons, the family's entertaining was quite limited. Dinner parties were rare but Ned recalled "a Valentine's party...[when] there were red hearts all over the place." His father and mother, however, enjoyed social events at the University, including student dances. His mother was "as the pictures show, a very beautiful woman. She was short, about five feet," a contrast to her husband at six feet, three inches. "They would always waltz, they loved to dance together."[59]

Ned recalled that his father sometimes stopped at a favorite shop in the evenings to buy cigars and to bring him candy. The youngster eagerly sought these "rattles," a name derived from his habit of jiggling his father's pockets "to see if there was candy inside." One of Ned's earliest memories was of his father taking him on Sunday walks along the shore of Lake Union to see the houseboats, birds, and plants. He also remembered that they once were among a throng greeted by Sarah Bernhardt from a train platform at University Station and recalled his father telling him that she was "one of the greatest actresses of all time."[60]

Meany's faith in the progress and survival of his comfortable world seemed justified when the armistice halted the war. Amid affirmations of the steady advance of civilization, however, he began to read historian Henry Adams' recently published *Education* and found a very disturbing note. He wrote to Frederick Jackson Turner that although he was fascinated, he found that Adams' denigration of his own historical work and those of others had given him "an attack of melancholia which I have not been able to throw-off. Such an intellect, on reaching the Biblical span of years, pronounces the work to which we are giving our lives a failure!"[61] Meany confessed to Turner that "this book has shaken me up as has no other that I remember. It would be a great joy to have our two backs against a driftwood log on the shore of Hood Canal to talk this all over." Lacking that opportunity, Meany wrote to Brooks Adams for enlightenment regarding his deceased brother. Adams agreed with Meany that *Education* was a great work but did not resolve Meany's puzzlement over Henry Adams' professions of failure. To another question on the meaning and outcome of the war, one that Meany had posed to celebrities at home and abroad, Brooks Adams provided a pessimistic and disillusioning answer. Far from bolstering Meany's view of a peaceful post-war world, he stated that "Wilson appears to me to be clean out of his depth. So do all the men in Europe. They do not know what to say or do. A League of Nations...would mean war-war-war and war in short order."[62]

Neither Brooks Adams' thorough pessimism—his literary trademark—nor the outcome of the war affected Meany's writing, editing, and promoting of local and regional history. In March 1918, a new series of pioneer sketches from Meany's pen began to appear in the *Post-Intelligencer*, an indication that the war had not destroyed his interest in a personal, romantic view of the past. The editorial policy of the *Washington Historical Quarterly*, still under his devoted attention, had remained uncompromisingly historical and detached from war propaganda, no matter that he had been willing to promote the use of patriotic pamphlets provided by the National Board of Historical service at his Camp Lewis classes. The only number of the *Quarterly* devoted to the war, published in October 1918, was characterized by Meany's essay on the use of Pacific Northwest spruce in the war effort.[63]

When the summer session of 1919 opened, Meany's life seemed back to normal. He taught American diplomatic history to fifty-three students, interpreting recent international politics. His students' response and a very large summer school enrollment were gratifying but he looked forward to climbing Mt. Rainier on his annual outing. When he left Seattle on that vacation he took with him a signed testimonial from all fifty-three students in his class, expressing their gratitude for his teaching in the following words: "We greatly appreciate the abundance of historic content and minute personal touches in your lectures, and we thank you especially for the sympathy, zeal, enthusiasm, and love of country enkindled by you as a teacher."[64]

CHAPTER TEN

"Keeper of Traditions" and Promoter of New History (1919-1929)

"AFTER THE ARMISTICE," Meany wrote to Bernard Pelly, the British consul in Seattle, "a young American Captain, still in his uniform, came to my room here at the University of Washington and, saluting, said: 'While in London, I had some spare time and went to Petersham to stand by the grave of your hero, Captain George Vancouver, and while there I thought of my old professor in Seattle.'" Meany then remarked to Pelly, "I hardly need tell you that Captain Ray Dumett, a former student, had brought me compensation greater in value than any money." On this occasion, as in countless others throughout his career, the high esteem of a close-knit community in the University and Seattle reinforced Meany in his function as historian and, especially in his later years, as "Keeper of Traditions."[1]

At the time Captain Dumett knocked on his door in Denny Hall, Meany's colleagues in history were preparing to move out of that venerable structure to the new Philosophy Hall, no doubt anticipating with pleasure the use of its modern facilities. Meany, their chairman, refused to move. His quarters in Denny were comfortable and spacious, and more importantly, had the vault needed to house his collection of documents and relics. Philosophy Hall lacked such a facility. Of Meany's decision to remain in Denny, the *University of Washington Daily* declared on October 11, 1920: "And everybody's glad! Denny Hall without Professor Meany! Impossible! Twenty-five years ago he 'moved in,' bringing a few of the scrap books and tomahawks with him. Since then the vault has been added, and the papoose pictures hung on the walls." Then, in notes of affection for the man and awe, mixed with a hazy understanding of the nature of his collection, the reporter concluded, "the ghosts of old relics would come back and haunt the corridors if he moved away."[2]

The reporter overlooked the breadth of Meany's vision of history and current events. Meany retained his keen, if somewhat romanticized, interest in world affairs. He made that plain in "Vigor," a poem dedicated on May 30, 1920, to the graduating class at the University. In it, Meany justified America's participation in the war by celebrating the "Resplendent vigor in our men,/ Who rose from hill, from plain or sea." They were peace loving free men who responded reluctantly to the German challenge "Till crime on crime and every hell-born deed/ Were piled to glowering skies!"

Once entered into conflict, with "sad, reluctant eyes," the Americans had fought for freedom idealistically and honorably:

A people's sword was drawn
In pledge of power. Each valiant lad,
With scorn for fear of scars,
Would front red flood or flame;
With soul among the stars,
Would fight in Freedom's name
With strong, unsullied hands![3]

Frederick Padelford, his colleague in the English Department, congratulated Meany for some of the best lines he had ever written, urging him to "work in this line." Other comment was more critical. E.D. Adams, of Stanford's History Department, thought the poem "charming," but doubted the survival of idealism. Acknowledging that "we all felt it [idealism] somewhat at the time, at least we who were in the teaching profession," he disclosed that military experience and the peace conference made him pessimistic. Mrs. Fanny Garrison Villard, a well-known suffragist and peace advocate, sternly challenged Meany's optimism, causing him to respond that he hated war as much as she. He protested: "I tried to show in my poem that all Americans love peace...but I wish to uphold the right purpose and bearing of our young men if a crisis comes." Meany remained confident, however, as he told Mrs. Villard, that "as soon as these reconstruction clouds of selfishness are lifted or dispersed I feel that our Nation will be seen to be looking upward and forward in the truest sense."[4]

Another opportunity to express Meany's sanguine hope for America's future came on December 21, 1920, when he addressed the children at the Tulalip Indian agency on Puget Sound. Meany participated in a celebration of the tercentenary of the Pilgrims' landing at Plymouth. Speaking on "A Prophecy Fulfilled," he called attention to the fact that "A cycle has been completed; a continent has been spanned; and two races of men have learned the meaning of clasped hands as together they turn hopeful eyes toward the future."

Perhaps he misunderstood the apparent eagerness of the Indian children to celebrate Plymouth, for all Indian agencies had been directed to offer appropriate ceremonies. Nevertheless, Meany's sympathy for the Indians had led him—perhaps quixotically—to hold out a hope that contradicted his earlier conviction that the aborigines might die out. On this occasion, he assumed the Indians would share time-honored American ideals "of good government, civil and religious freedom, improved education [and] equality of opportunities for all." The first step would be to bind up the war wounds and establish permanent peace. That accomplished, domestic goals could be realized.

Though the remaining Indians might be absorbed into white society by the end of another century, Meany prophesied that there would remain an appreciation of Indian traditions, shared by all, especially the love of nature: "They will love the same great mountain peaks cleaving the sky, the same great rivers running toward the sea, the same wide shores of 'Whulge' [an Indian name for Puget Sound] at ebb and flow of tide. They will cherish faint echoes of the forests and your fathers' legends of eagle, of beaver and bluejay. They will know that we met here to remember the past and to greet the future."[5]

When Worthington C. Ford of the Massachusetts Historical Society read a copy of the speech he expressed surprise: "Who would have thought that such a celebration could be had in an Indian School? You were fortunate in your occasion and the opportunity you made of it." After reading the reports of other local celebrations in the *Seattle Times* and the *Post-Intelligencer*, Meany might have agreed with Ford. Neither paper reported any but the most conventional celebrations with the most stereotyped views of the Plymouth landing, and the consequent dominance of Anglo-Saxon attitudes and values in America.[6]

Confident utterances such as those in "A Prophecy Fulfilled" did not assuage Meany's daily fears of the decline of moral values in American society. Youthful challenges of the "Flapper Age" had appeared on the University of Washington campus, to the consternation of the older generation. In early February 1921, on the authority of President Suzzallo, Meany directed the Junior Prom Committee to put a stop to "cheek to cheek" dancing. He then wrote to Suzzallo, who was lobbying at Olympia, regarding "social evils" on the campus: "such impacts have me stirred up for days, but I really felt that the good name of Washington was imperiled."

He hoped, he told Suzzallo, that policing student dances might help the president defend the University against its critics in the legislature.[7]

Another blow to Meany's sense of well-being and optimism came when he broke his close ties with the *Post-Intelligencer* in November 1921. The preceding May he had reviewed his association with the newspaper in the most friendly terms: "Somehow I always feel myself to be a part of the *Seattle Post-Intelligencer.* Three years of my young manhood were filled with experiences on that paper, which were to me of great importance." But when the editor decided to report the lurid details of the "Fatty" Arbuckle trial in San Francisco, involving a Hollywood movie star in a wild party in which a young woman lost her life, Meany broke his connection of forty years. In a furious mood, he canceled his subscription with the words, "I am unwilling that any more Arbuckle slime shall be sent into my home."[8]

When Judge Everett Smith of Seattle wrote to criticize behavior on the campus, Meany replied with a broader indictment of society: "These days of jazz music, cheek-to-cheek dancing and 'vodvil' extremities are hard to endure." He found consolation, however, in his work with the Boy Scouts and the Mountaineers, and in the majority of the students who "retain their sanity." Further consolation came from his confidence that the faculty supported his position on the current social ills and from his stubbornly hopeful view that "the miserable wave we are passing through is a part of the general disturbance wrought by the war. If so, we can hope for a cure."[9]

Meany scarcely permitted campus tribulations or social disturbances to affect his teaching, according to Miss Cecil Dryden, his student from 1919-1921. Years later she recalled that she had been attracted by his close acquaintance with historical scenes and actors, and by his inspiring presentation. Unlike many observers, however, she thought his use of dramatic devices unnecessary to his audiences—"the theatrical pose, the sentimental patriotic fervor, the studied moments of silence when he gazed dreamily at Mt. Rainier or counted the wind jammers waiting at the Strait." Dryden, who served for many years as a history professor at Cheney Normal School regarded Meany as old, but acknowledged that "he was a 'presence' at any assembly."[10]

If Dryden found Meany "so dignified, so absorbed, so remote" as to be difficult to approach, Gilbert B. Foster, another former student, thought otherwise. Writing in *Sunset Magazine* for April 1922, Foster stated that "As head of the history department at the University of Washington Professor

Meany is serving as 'Keeper of Traditions' for his flock of five thousand students." Foster further claimed that Meany's course, "Makers of the Nation," was unrivaled in popularity on the campus and "his lectures on Lincoln are carried for years in the memories of the university's alumni." Meany also had close contact with students, according to Foster, because to every new freshman class he administered the Ephebic Oath, "charging the new generation to uphold the dignity and honor of the Washington whose name has been given [to] a state and a university." Meany was, preeminently, "'the bond between the trail blazer and the citizen.'"[11]

Classroom census figures confirm Dryden's and Foster's judgments of Meany as an educator, as the latter continued to attract large numbers of students to his courses. In the fall term of 1919, for example, some 279 students registered for his "Makers of the Nation" course. He taught 700 students the following spring. The student burden was so heavy that in April 1920, he declined two invitations to deliver commencement addresses, a task he relished.[12]

Though Meany's class schedule was almost overwhelming, he gave no thought to relinquishing his position as chairman of the department. His office in Denny Hall, as one student recalled, "was a pleasant office [with] a friendly...atmosphere." But, since Meany's colleagues were in Philosophy Hall, consideration of personnel and other departmental concerns sometimes became difficult. Meany remained the departmental representative to the administration but Edward McMahon became the informal spokesman of the Philosophy Hall group. Robust, forceful, and an excellent teacher, McMahon was respected for his knowledge and dedication to learning. When, years later, his widow, Theresa Schmid McMahon, a faculty member perhaps more distinguished than her husband, claimed that he had guided Meany on many matters, Edmond S. Meany, Jr. agreed with her that it was true "as the years went on."[13]

Though the History Department enjoyed large enrollments in undergraduate courses and offered good teaching by popular professors, it had not developed the foundation for a strong graduate program. Nevertheless, in November 1919, Graduate Dean J. Allen Smith asked Meany to consult his colleagues and draw up a list of requirements for offering a doctoral program. The historians asked for several graduate seminars to cover advanced studies in European and American history, the only fields in which they had expertise. They also requested $5,000 to purchase needed library materials and gave details suggesting that grave weaknesses existed in several subject areas. Meany felt, correctly, that his own field of Pacific

Northwest history was best equipped, but insisted it too needed additional resources. He did not ask for more faculty, being aware that funds were stretched to the limit simply to cover undergraduate instruction. He did, however, seek several graduate student assistants.[14]

Paradoxically, the administration approved the program for the Ph.D. degree in 1921—the sixth granted in the University—without providing the funds requested. When J. Orin Oliphant, earlier an undergraduate, returned in 1923 to study for a Master of Arts degree, he found few other graduate students in history and an inadequate library. Nevertheless, Meany closely supervised Oliphant's studies, involving him in producing the *Washington Historical Quarterly,* as he did other students from time to time. Oliphant responded by publishing the first of numerous offerings in the July 1924 issue, editing reminiscences of an 1843 pioneer. He also read proof and criticized style and content of manuscripts submitted to the *Quarterly.* Before the completion of his studies, Meany gave Oliphant a complete set of the *Quarterly* and put him on the editorial board, matters designed to inspire further studies. Years later, near the end of a long and distinguished scholarly career at Bucknell University, Oliphant stated that "More than any other person, Meany 'pushed' me into historical writing."[15]

Indeed, the *Washington Historical Quarterly* became Meany's most important medium for influencing regional and local historiography in the years after the armistice. His editing reached a new professional plane in 1921 when he collaborated with the Massachusetts Historical Society in publishing the 1792 log kept by John Boit during Robert Gray's voyage of discovery of the Columbia River. Since Gray's log had been lost, Boit's full report confirming the captain's discovery held great significance. Meany provided editorial notes on West Coast navigation for the highly esteemed and venerable Massachusetts Historical Society. In gratitude, editor Worthington C. Ford of that society permitted Meany to publish the portion of Boit's log concerning the Northwest Coast. It appeared in the *Quarterly*'s January 1921 issue.[16]

The *Oregonian* described Meany's extensive introduction to Boit's log as "illuminating" and predicted that "almost as much interest will be felt in the story of the document itself as in the confirmations which it contains of details previously obtained from fragments of the lost log of Captain Gray, the journals of Haswell, Haskins, Ingraham and others." Superintendent Joseph Schafer of the State Historical Society of Wisconsin recognized the importance of Boit's journal and commended Meany: "You have done an excellent service, through your magazine, by printing the north-western portion of the journal before it is brought out by Massachusetts people." Indeed, the Council of the Massachusetts Historical Society noted that Meany's publication "attracted much attention in the Far West and in Canada as a valuable and highly interesting record." Meany, boldly asserting that the Boit journal was one of the best things he had done, sent a copy of the issue to President Suzzallo in Olympia, suggesting that it might help his lobbying for the University's budget with Columbia River legislators.[17]

Not all of Meany's editing was free of faults. When a correspondent asked him if the claim were true that the United States Secret Service had partially funded the Rev. Jason Lee's recruiting of fifty workers in 1838 for his Oregon Mission, Meany began an inquiry which led him to a dubious conclusion. He asked J. Franklin Jameson, the prestigious director of the department of Historical Research of the Carnegie Institution, to investigate the Secret Service records on the matter. The latter found no such records before 1865 and cast serious doubt on the idea that such a fund had existed in Jason Lee's time.

Ignoring the negative result, Meany succumbed to an old temptation to exaggerate missionary achievement. In a July 1924 article in the *Quarterly* entitled "Secret Aid for Oregon Missions," he wrote: "It is significant, if true, that part of the money for chartering his [Lee's] vessel [*The Lausanne*] was supplied from the secret service fund of the United States Government." Later, in the same article, he concluded that:

> Students of Northwestern history have never been sure that such secret aid was actually extended. However, they have not been particularly disturbed as the cause for such an expenditure could hardly have been a better one. Future researches may disclose an account book with a record of as much as $3,000 expended on behalf of the *Lausanne*'s passengers from New York to Oregon. Such a record would be definite and authoritative. No one will be able to compute in dollars and cents the good those passengers did in helping to redeem Oregon from a wilderness and to retain it as a part of the United States.

The most recent scholarship does not sustain Meany's hope.[18]

Meany was on firmer ground when he edited material which did not touch his biases. A study of Washington place names, begun in the *Quarterly* in 1917, was continued in post-war issues. To an inquiry about his method, Meany replied that he and his assistants looked for evidence in old maps, diaries, travel books, newspapers, government reports, and records of exploration. Meany also questioned pioneers and other knowledgeable persons, usually by mail. He then edited the accumulated material, publishing the result in a 1923 volume entitled, *Origin of Washington Geographic Names*. It quickly became a standard reference work, recognized as such by the Smithsonian Institution. Reprinted in 1968, the work has retained its place as an invaluable reference tool.[19]

In July 1922, Meany offered in the *Quarterly* the first installment of "Newspapers of Washington Territory," a series of sketches describing the birth, life, and death of all the newspapers he could find. He ended with a plea that readers send him additional information so that a book version might be as complete as possible. "Diogenes," who conducted the "Literary Guide Post" in the *Tacoma Daily Ledger*, applauded Meany's "noteworthy contribution to Washington history." He especially approved of Meany's statement that "In an expanding democracy, such as the United States in the latter half of the 19th Century, the frontier newspaper rendered various kinds of service, many of them essential to the peculiar genius of the American form of government." "Diogenes" also commented favorably on Clarence Bagley's memoir in that issue of the *Quarterly*, on "Crossing the Plains" to Oregon in 1852. He concluded that the magazine ought to be read by the public on a regular basis.[20]

In 1923, Meany began revising his *History of the State of Washington*. The San Francisco office of Macmillan had encouraged headquarters in New York to publish another edition, as it clearly had demand. Charles H. Seaver of the New York office approached Meany with a plan to issue the new edition at $2.50 per copy, a price which would not yield a profit to the publisher, but would accommodate the author's wish that the volume be accessible to the maximum number of people. Meany agreed to compose an additional chapter bringing Washington's history down to the post-war period, but otherwise would revise only statistics. He readily accepted a reduced royalty in order to retain a low price.

The new chapter, "Evidences of Recent Advance," provided a summary of political events, economic data, and notes on wartime activity within the state. Meany augmented his first-hand accounts of experiences and observations—which enlivened the first edition—with only a reference to President Warren G. Harding's visit to Seattle in 1923.[21]

A certain unhappiness with his publisher, which had disturbed Meany earlier, continued to trouble him after publication of the revised edition. When George Brett, with whom Meany had dealt many times, made a tactful inquiry as to Meany's complaint, Meany opened flood gates of frustration—if not resentment—in a remarkable letter on June 22,

1925. There had been irksome delays in publishing the second edition, he wrote, which had been compounded with disappointment when the contract mailed to him stipulated that royalties would not be paid until Macmillan had sold 1,000 copies. The proposal to which Meany had agreed had called for the author's royalties to be paid after the sale of 500 copies.

There were other grievances. Brett had earlier expressed confidence that the *United States History for Schools*, on which Meany had worked for two years, would be profitable. Unfortunately, the work had not sold well and Meany professed not to know why. The small amount paid in royalties embarrassed Meany. Then too, Macmillan had withdrawn *Mount Rainier: A Record of Exploration* without explanation, even though Meany believed firmly that some copies could be sold on the mountain every summer. In addition, he feared that his *Vancouver's Discovery of Puget Sound* would be withdrawn without transfer of copyright and return of plates to him, in accordance with his contract.

Meany also confessed a nostalgia for the "old days" when the Macmillan Company had treated him with considerable deference. He recalled that Brett had entertained him at a delightful dinner with Sir Frederick Macmillan and his lady, Gertrude Atherton, Hamilton Wright Mabie, and other literary and publishing figures. His complaints about book withdrawals and poor royalties related to his status in the community. Denying that monetary figures were the chief complaint, Meany spoke of a deeper concern:

> I confess to much pride in authorship. Before many audiences each year I am introduced as the author of such and such books. Pageants and plays, paintings and sculpture, and songs are being produced, based on the researches recorded in my books. The only definite knowledge available as to the sale or distribution of the books comes from your royalty statements. *The present situation as to those statements would indicate that the author is almost, if not quite, dead. This hard inference the author resents as he feels that he is very much alive.*[22]

In response, Brett expressed regret at the "deplorable" sales of Meany's books but also made some candid remarks. Sales of *Vancouver's Discovery of Puget Sound* had been few in spite of extensive advertising. *The United States History for Schools* was a good book, Brett patiently explained, but was not teachable in the upper elementary grades for which it had been prepared. Such statements did not console Meany, who recalled several school superintendents who praised the book.

Mount Rainier: A Record of Exploration was another matter. Brett reminded Meany that 1,200 copies of a special edition had been sold by the Bon Marché department store in Seattle before Macmillan's regular edition had been published. The special edition had saturated the local market, but in spite of that Meany had received $46.88 in royalties on 193 copies of the regular edition sold in 1916-1917. Thereafter the royalties were insignificant and the book went out of print in 1922.

Fortunately, the story of the second edition of *History of the State of Washington* had a more satisfactory conclusion. An underling at Macmillan had mistakenly sent the contract asking Meany to waive royalties on the first 1,000 copies instead of the agreed upon 500. Brett now invoked the original contract but cautioned that no royalties would be forthcoming immediately since only 294 copies had been sold. In subsequent years Meany's faith in this work and presumably in himself were bolstered by steady, if modest sales. In 1928, for example, he received a check for $50.16 and in 1929, for $37.18. Three hundred ninety-seven copies were sold in those two years. The book remained in print until after World War II, testimony to Meany's strong influence on the teaching of Washington's history.[23]

With publication of the second edition of the state history, Meany stopped writing serious books and devoted his scholarly interests largely to editing and publishing the *Washington Historical Quarterly*. Business manager Charles W. Smith proudly stated in his annual report for April 1, 1926, that messages of appreciation for the journal's value, accuracy, and human interest had come not only from Washington "but from distant and wholly unexpected sources," from reputable scholars as well as from local subscribers. The basis for congratulation, in the view of this loyal coworker, was not hard to find: "a comparison with other similar publications makes evident the editorial skill of Professor Meany in conducting a magazine that is human as well as historical."[24]

Meany's successes, however, resulted more from finding and publishing new scholarly authors and subjects (as well as continuing to cultivate older contributors) than from editorial skill and human interest features. A focus on Alaska, though begun earlier, now became a major theme for the *Quarterly*, producing a score of articles, including eleven groundbreaking pieces by Alaskan resident Clarence Andrews. T.C. Elliott, long a zealous critic of editorial slips, continued to be one of the most significant contributors, especially his editing of documents on the fur trade and the discoveries of David Thompson. Meany's student, J. Orin Oliphant, by now an instructor at the State Normal School at Cheney, introduced new topics, including a contemporary controversy over legislative reapportionment in Washington and a pioneering study on Oregon's cattle industry. His colleague at Cheney, C.S. Kingston, offered authoritative discussions of Idaho's political history and of "The Walla Walla Separation Movement," among other political topics.[25]

Meany seized an opportunity to enlarge the scope of the *Quarterly* to include the Pacific Rim countries while serving on the program committee for the November 1925 Seattle meeting of the Pacific Coast Branch of the American Historical Association. Having first helped arrange a symposium on the Pacific Rim, Meany then published the four papers growing out of it in the April 1926 issue of the *Quarterly*.

Taken together, the papers demonstrate the very limited nature of American scholarship on the Rim as a historical, economic, or political entity. Nevertheless, the historians offered some insights needed to improve research and teaching. Payson J. Treat, of Stanford University, discussed illusions and misconceptions about oriental history and thereby made clear some of the difficulties of teaching a course on the Pacific Rim. Walter N. Sage, of the University of British Columbia, contributed a thoughtful treatise on British Columbia's relations both with the United States and Canada, and suggested that future studies should include Canada as a Pacific nation. Rev. Herbert Gowen, who taught oriental languages at the University of Washington, indicated the current status of Pacific Rim scholarship most accurately. Gowen presented a chapter from his forthcoming textbook, *Outline of Asia*, in which he reiterated the conventional wisdom that the Pacific was important as an "American Lake."[26]

Meany's faith that progress was inevitable and that scientific discoveries constituted the chief means to that end inspired his most ambitious editorial project—a symposium on "History and Science." Charles A. Beard, the noted American historian, had aroused Meany's interest in the subject when he reviewed Vernon L. Parrington's *Main Currents in American Thought* in the May 1927 issue of *The Nation*. In the midst of praising this pathbreaking intellectual and literary history, Beard had paused to comment in a magisterial way that "Mr. Parrington's chief sin of omission is his neglect of natural science and its influence on theology, politics, and letters."[27]

Meany asked his colleague Parrington about Beard's criticism and received the reply, "Yes, I know about that. I intend to treat the influence of science in my third volume. I feel that science had but little effect on

American thought prior to 1860." Parrington's explanation was not entirely convincing. Rather, it recalled to Meany the image of Horace Greely Byers, a chemist and former colleague, who "in one of his pugnacious intervals about twenty years ago...blurted out: 'You historians neglect science. You all deal in politics, in economic and social development, but none of you pay any attention to the influence of science on civilization.'"[28]

In April 1928, Meany began publishing the lengthy symposium which ran in the *Quarterly* until July 1929. He had asked scientists at the University of Washington to present summaries of progress in their fields so "that students and writers may realize how history has been enriched by science in at least one of the commonwealths of the nation."[29]

Before turning the field over to the scientists, however, Meany pondered the possibility of creating a true science of history. Assuming the mantle of a philosopher, Meany informed his readers that E.A. Freeman's dictum, "history is past politics," no longer defined the scope of the discipline. In fact, he reminded his readers that "nearly every generation has insisted on re-writing history for itself." Meany then reported that George Sarton, in his *Introduction to the History of Science*, published in 1927, had impressed him with the assertion that "the acquisition and systematization of positive knowledge [i.e. science] is the only human activity which is truly cumulative and progressive." He also persuaded Meany of the importance of science by stating that modern civilization differed from earlier cultures "because we have gradually learned to disentangle the forces of nature, and because we have contrived, by strict obedience to their laws, to capture them and to divert them to the gratification of our own needs."[30]

Meany drew inspiration, too, from a paper read by historian Frederick J. Teggart of the University of California at the 1927 meeting of the American Historical Association. Teggart placed an "enormous burden of responsibility upon his colleagues," Meany wrote, "by insisting that the historian alone is in a position to create what is, in our day, the greatest of all desiderata, 'historical science.'" In that view, history must be the product of a staggering task—the eliciting of fundamental human experiences from a comparative study of the histories of all peoples, at a given time, and, indeed, throughout all history.[31]

The eight essays which followed, written by Meany's colleagues, yielded competent surveys of geologic history, and fisheries and botanical research, but only John Weinzirl's report on progress in bacteriology and public health consciously touched on possibilities that science might illuminate general history. Meany maintained his own enthusiasm for science by joining the prestigious History of Science Society in 1928, but neither he nor other writers were inspired by the symposium to publish additional articles in the *Quarterly*. Historian Arthur M. Schlesinger, Sr., two decades later, in another journal, pointed to inadequacies in scholarship which had frustrated many editors such as Meany. First, historians had continued to write primarily political and military history. Second, neither America's historians nor her scientists had seriously considered the fundamental relationships between science and history.[32]

Meany's role as "Keeper of Traditions" brought him much satisfaction in the aftermath of World War I—satisfaction based on a sense of community solidarity. Celebration of Washington's birthday did not merely continue year after year, but gained added stature. In 1921, in a gesture of international good will, Meany broadened the scope and meaning of the ceremonies. He invited nearly thirty consuls of foreign governments resident in Seattle and a number of businessmen to participate. The gathering was, he announced, "intended as the beginning of an annual patriotic festival which will help make Seattle more conscious of international opportunities and more appreciative of the representatives of other powers within our midst."[33]

The *Post-Intelligencer*, in a generous editorial, gave its support to the approaching celebration, and recognized Meany's proposal as representing the increased commercial importance of the city. Twenty-four consuls responded to Meany's invitation by graciously placing wreaths and small flags of their nations at the base of Lorado Taft's statue of Washington. At the luncheon which followed, Ernest B. Hussey, state president of the Sons of the American Revolution, praised George Washington in conventional terms. The French consul responded with an affirmation of good will between France and the United States, evoking memories of LaFayette. Appropriately, the businessmen present contributed to international amity by paying for the luncheon.[34]

In the next few years, Meany was gratified by increasing attendance at the event but also suffered more complex organizational problems as a result. More than seventy consuls, businessmen, and others sat down to the luncheon in 1924 and again in 1926. At least once, not having found a sponsor, Meany reached into his own pocket to pay the bill. He vowed, however, to continue the annual luncheons even though he might have to pay for them out of his small income.[35]

Armistice Day presented another opportunity for patriotic exercises. On November 11, 1920, Meany participated in planting fifty-seven

Sycamores along Memorial Way on campus in honor of the fifty-six University men and one woman who had died in service during the World War. In 1921, Meany and a few friends "kept tradition alive" by planting elms and sycamores. In 1923, in more formal ceremonies, Meany helped unveil a "Roll of Honor" tablet on the campus. The following year, Ned and his father kept memories green by planting a single hard rock maple. Meany's own listing shows ceremonies in 1925 and 1926, but none thereafter.[36]

Campus Day flourished in the 1920s, much to Meany's satisfaction and to that of President Suzzallo. The latter, in fact, asked Meany in March 1924 to begin early preparations for the May event since the lower campus needed a thorough cleaning. Former students, not surprisingly, remembered Campus Day with great favor. Mitchell V. Charnley of Detroit, Michigan, testified after an alumni meeting in his state that Campus Day was "the thing that we alumni cherish most vividly and fondly of all our memories." He then linked Suzzallo with Meany in developing the University's sentimental life: "This one alumnus remembers best that day when you and Dr. Suzzallo dedicated the Columns in their new home; he remembers the camaraderie of that day, of the luncheon on campus and the speeches and the fun. And he has just a little lump in his throat....It's Washington—that's what Campus Day is."[37]

In 1924, as he did every year, Meany presided over the luncheon which followed the working portion of Campus Day. As usual, he took great pleasure in introducing students pledged to honor societies and in bestowing other marks of recognition which came near the end of the school year. Suddenly, to his great surprise, a new Buick sedan appeared around the corner, with Mrs. Meany seated as a passenger. The automobile was a gift to the Meanys from friends, alumni, and students.

Mathew W. Hill, who had directed the gathering of contributions by the Alumni Association, presented the vehicle with a "glowing tribute" to Meany for his "service as the ideal alumnus." Two years later, on another Campus Day, the Meanys reciprocated for both the naming of Meany Hall on Campus Day 1914 and for the gift of the Buick by dedicating a bench near Denny Hall on behalf of the class of 1885.[38]

In the 1920s, Meany found new outlets for his creative energy in patriotic pageantry—both as performer and author. In a sense, it was surprising that he had not earlier occupied himself with this art form which involved the whole community. It had been popular since the world's fairs in Philadelphia (1876) and Chicago (1893). The first exposition had called attention to the nation's centennial, a source of much patriotic celebration. The second, of course, had given Meany an intimate understanding of patriotic symbols and drama.[39]

In 1921 and 1922, Meany served as "prolocutor," or commentator in front of the curtain between scenes, for "The Wayfarer," a gigantic religious pageant written by a local minister, the Rev. James E. Crowther. Previously staged in Columbus, Ohio, and in New York's Madison Square Garden, the pageant portrayed the eventual fulfillment of Christian salvation despite the horrors of the World War and other catastrophes. Clearly inspired by "The Wayfarer," Meany took up the pen to write "Americanus," a historical pageant depicting the rise of the American nation.[40]

"Americanus," produced in the University of Washington stadium in the summer of 1923, was hardly a one-man venture. In fact, it became a major community enterprise underwritten by eighty-one professional and business men and firms of the city. Ten thousand local singers, musicians, and actors were required to stage the huge tableaux. Meany also publicized the pageant by delivering twenty-seven promotional speeches, the last delivered in Everett just before the opening on July 23. Entranced with their production and mindful of the popularity of "The Wayfarer," the proud promoters claimed Seattle had established a reputation as "The Pageant City."[41]

In the six episodes of "Americanus," Meany traced American history in familiar patriotic terms. Clio, the muse of history, narrates important events from the birth of the nation to the post-war world of the 1920s. Americanus, a character representing the fundamental spirit of the nation, appears at critical times to instill nationalistic and Christian values into historical figures who sense his unseen presence.[42]

The spirit of the pageant is most graphically delineated through Meany's greatest heroes, Washington and Lincoln. Scene one opens with General Washington praying on his knees in the snow at Valley Forge. The buckskin-clad Americanus approaches behind the kneeling figure and utters the promise that "the Great Spirit will hear your prayer." Bewildered, Washington rises in wonder at the words he has heard. Then, Americanus is clearly established as the national spirit for George Washington as well as for the audience when he says, "I am Americanus, a spirit from the people and the soil of the new world, come to help those who would seek the way to freedom and to peace." In the following scene, after President Washington refuses to bow to Citizen Genet's demand that the United States enter war on the side of France, Americanus "utters impressively" the words,

"Freedom and Peace!" Washington's resolve to follow those goals is visibly strengthened as he vows to grant freedom to his own slaves in his will and to maintain neutrality in foreign matters.[43]

In episode IV, entitled "Father Abraham," Americanus appears according to Meany's stage directions "as a spirit or as a part of Lincoln's silent thought." Americanus instructs Lincoln, then President-elect, to "be true to the spirit of America. Through all the darkness find the way of broader freedom, seek the light of more enduring peace." Lincoln, indeed, seems almost indistinguishable from Americanus. Upon his departure from Springfield to take up his presidential duties, in the dark days before the Civil War, Meany has Lincoln say "I now leave, not knowing when or whether I ever may return, with a task before me greater than that which rested upon Washington. Without the assistance of that Divine Being who ever attended him, I cannot succeed. With that assistance, I cannot fail."[44]

Meany recounted the nineteenth century's proud advance in civilization in episode VI, "Sword or Law." Here Meany treats the Spanish-American War as no exception to the march of progress. It permitted America to become a world power and brought, in Meany's view, the nation's benign influence upon world affairs. Forced to deal with the World War, Meany, through Americanus, acknowledged that progress had been threatened by the "terrible scourge in Europe."[45]

As he approached the finale, Meany turned to the spirit of America represented by Lincoln, offering verses he had written for the pageant. Speaking through Euterpe, muse of music and lyrical poetry, Meany saw Lincoln as possessing the true character of humanity:

> If soldier's plea to soldier be in vain,
> Or memory of wars, let one implore,
> Whose humble heart knew every mortal pain—
> A manly man, who mighty burdens bore,
> Who held aloft a nation's flick'ring light.
> O Europe, raise a Lincoln for thy need!
> Behold, O Kings, a modern prophet's call!
> A tender hand where wounds of foemen bleed—
> "No malice here" but "charity for all."
> Divinely human! O men, arise and heed!
> "Achieve, as God gives us to see the right."[46]

The finale conveyed Meany's belief that the end of the World War meant resumption of progress through science and the peaceful arts. "A new era has dawned," Clio declares. "The air is conquered and the depths beneath the sea. Service of man to man is the slogan...humanity has made its greatest stride forward." If men did not deliberately destroy progress, "Old Glory, emblem of freedom, peace and progress," would stand high among the flags of the nation. Americanus, dressed all in white, needed only to close the pageant shouting: "Land of the Free, and Home of the Brave," while the multitude sang the "Star Spangled Banner."[47]

The press reported large and enthusiastic audiences. The *Seattle Times* praised "Americanus" as a "great pageant" and "a striking lesson in lofty patriotism." Its editor also approved of it as a countervailing force against unrest and radicalism. Meany complimented Montgomery Lynch, the producer, and others in charge, in a signed article published in the *Seattle Post-Intelligencer*. There was good reason to be pleased with the production for the crowds had ranged from 6,700 on July 23, to a high of 16,000 before it closed on July 28. Fortunately, receipts matched expenses.[48]

Meany, however, suffered the tortures of an author who feels his work is slighted. After opening night, he complained with some heat to Darwin Meisnest, the business manager, of several minor slips in the production and of one major change in the "wonderful finale." There, someone had introduced a cheap and tawdry sign about the "melting pot." In Meany's opinion, it misrepresented the finale, which was designed to show that America's progress had carried it beyond the workings of the melting pot to a new culture and society.

Four days later, Meany again complained to Meisnest, claiming that he had failed to furnish a promised complimentary box in which Meany might entertain friends. Instead, Meisnest had offered inferior seats in the audience. Equally troubling was the fact that Montgomery Lynch had claimed co-authorship, though he had written nothing. Indignantly, Meany refused all gratuities, paying his own way into performances. Meisnest, a friend of long standing, was greatly disconcerted, although Meany had expressed his personal regard for the young business manager. He also predicted that his annual mountain vacation would take away the sting he felt. He was right. Upon his return from vacation in mid-August, Meany found a check for the promised $500 honorarium and a cordial letter from Meisnest which he very much appreciated.[49]

Although pageantry was well suited to Meany's skills and philosophy, he did not repeat the experience of "Americanus." On the other hand, he did appear on radio a number of times in his role as "Keeper of Traditions." As early as March 10, 1925, he helped celebrate the forty-ninth anniversary of the invention of the telephone by speaking over Seattle's KFOA on the subject "Puget Sound and Washington Before and Since the

Telephone." In May, he gave a short talk at the same radio station during a "Pioneer Day" program sponsored by the Seattle Women's Club.[50]

In the spring of 1929, University of Washington faculty inaugurated extramural radio programming on station KOMO. Meany served on a committee which arranged a series of popular lectures on "The Puget Sound Country." Among the subjects, in addition to history, were geology, botany, zoology, and industrial and social conditions. Meany began the series with a familiar talk on the "Early History of the Puget Sound Country." Later, he discussed the Wilkes Expedition's survey of the Sound. Then on July 22, when Meany announced his topic as "The First Pioneer Homes on Puget Sound," the *Seattle Times* commented that he would

> thereby assure himself of a vast audience among Washingtonians whose hair grew white before radio was even known....This gentleman, who is affectionately called "The Grand Old Man of Washington" on the University campus, does well to choose the radio for his medium. The aggregation of people who will be interested in his message couldn't be crowded into any existing building; neither the civic auditorium nor the University stadium.[51]

Meany did not use the novel medium of radio to present new research or fresh interpretations. Not surprisingly then, when he concluded the series with "When the Early Settlers Built Blockhouse Forts," a familiar account of warfare with the Indians in the Puget Sound country, he faced an ideological dilemma. He had the task of reconciling his current friendships with Indians and his abiding loyalty to Governor Isaac I. Stevens, despite his stern Indian policies. Meany drew careful distinctions. "There are probably many Indian friends listening to these words," he said. "It is far from my purpose, now or at any other time, to take advantage of them by recording the deeds of their fathers in an unfair or partial manner."

The audience then heard him repeat Stevens' "perfectly sincere" belief that the treaties concluded with the tribes had nothing to do with the resulting hostilities. Nevertheless, a new note appeared in Meany's customary defense of Stevens, for he acknowledged that the governor might have protested too much: "the need of his denial points to the conclusion that the treaties were involved in the war." That departure from convention aside, Meany then repeated Stevens' claim that the war arose from "the native intelligence of restless Indians," who by their values were rightly defending their land. Meany agreed with Stevens, quoting his statement that "We may sympathize with such a manly feeling, but in view of it, we have high duties." Those duties, of course, were to protect white society. In conclusion, Meany turned to the more congenial task of exhorting his listeners to honor the pioneers by respecting the blockhouses as relics of warfare and as "evidences of supreme struggles by brave men and women who built and protected the foundations of our homes of this brighter day."[52]

A month later, on September 30, 1929, Meany revealed the depth and breadth of his devotion to preservation of historical materials when he gave his thirty-five-year accumulation of documents to the University of Washington. Writing to librarian Charles W. Smith, his collaborator in this and other enterprises, Meany disclosed that although his son Ned was preparing to become a professional historian, they had decided to relinquish the collection. The materials, they realized, would be of greater value if made easily available to other scholars. Nevertheless, he must have felt considerable emotion when he wrote, "Although in one sense it is like parting with old friends we are convinced that they will be better housed in the Library."[53]

Actually, Meany had delivered important acquisitions earlier. In December 1926, for example, he sent to the library the voluminous papers of James G. Swan, inveterate diarist of frontier life, author of *The Northwest Coast; or, Three Years' Residence in Washington Territory* (1857) and an amateur ethnographer. He also transmitted "two precious [Arthur A.] Denny books," in November of 1928, instructing Smith to acknowledge their receipt to the donor, a resident of Los Angeles, California.[54]

The collection which Meany donated on September 30, 1929, reflected many aspects of pioneer history and also provided valuable information on his collecting experiences. One group of "hundreds of papers in twenty packets tied into one combined bundle," dealt with public events, early institutions, and politics for the period 1853-1876. They had been rescued from the attic of the old capital building in 1897 as a result of encouragement from Governor John R. Rogers. Quite dramatically, Meany reported the papers had been found "scattered between the unfloored joists," of the old building. "Many of the papers show tobacco stains and footmarks where workmen had evidently trampled them while repairing the building's roof." The documents, he hardly needed to add, were "of prime value as source material in local history, politics, economics and sociology."[55]

Other sub-groups in that inventory included Winfield Scott Ebey's diaries describing his crossing of the plains in 1854 and events down to 1863, together with letters, biographies, and photographs of other members of the Ebey family. The donation included business records from Port

Gamble lumber operations and numerous pioneer collections. Meany presented these papers with an appraisal of their usefulness in depicting regional history.[56]

Meany's hectic life dramatically slowed on the evening of October 1, 1929, after his involvement in a four-car collision on a smoke-shrouded stretch of the Seattle-Tacoma highway. Meany sustained a broken knee and his wife suffered severe bruises and shock. They were returning from a meeting in Tacoma as passengers in a vehicle driven by a Japanese businessman. By the next day, news of the accident had spread over the city. Governor Roland H. Hartley and other dignitaries as well as many friends and acquaintances showered Meany with condolences.[57]

Lizzie Meany recovered quickly at home but Edmond remained in the Seattle General Hospital for seven weeks and then was confined to his home for seven more before hobbling back to his classes. Son Ned, newly enrolled as a graduate student in history, took charge of his father's classes. That teaching assignment lasted the entire fall term, long enough to prevent Ned from completing a Master of Arts degree before embarking upon graduate studies at Harvard.[58]

Meany did not lose all contact with normal campus activities during his confinement. Charles W. Smith shouldered many of Meany's editorial tasks and also carried materials to him for decisions on publication in the *Quarterly*. Even the Ephebic Oath for freshmen was attended to: radio KOMO broadcast Meany's administration of the oath to 1,500 students from his hospital bed. Then, on October 21, the KOMO production crew returned to the hospital to broadcast his initiation of a new University lecture series.[59]

Meany's confinement was alleviated when willing hands helped with his tasks, postponing the time when the sixty-six-year-old professor might be forced to accept retirement. His wife Lizzie had not been so fortunate. When her mother-in-law, Margaret Meany, had become an invalid in 1916, much of the time suffering greatly, Lizzie had nursed her without assistance until her death in 1920.[60]

Shortly before Margaret's funeral, the Meanys' older son, Mercer, had contracted tuberculosis and remained bedridden at home for several months. After that he was a patient at Firlands Sanitorium from October 1921 to April 1923. Thereafter he was again at home, most of the time confined to bed. His death on July 13, 1928, ended a sad existence for the whole family and finally freed Lizzie from crushing burdens.[61]

Edmond's great consolation came from companionship with Ned. The Boy Scouts drew them together. Edmond Senior became so interested in the movement that he became a Scout commissioner in 1920. Ned, no doubt already a fledgling member, found in his father a parent who eagerly encouraged and directed him until he became an Eagle Scout. Of great solace, too, was Ned's interest in mountain climbing. He became a member of The Mountaineers in 1924 and accompanied his father on the outing to Mount Rainier that summer.[62]

The following summer, father and son enjoyed the club's trek to the Wenatchee range, climbing 9,400-foot Mount Stuart and several smaller peaks. Father Edmond always cherished the release from his demanding professional life which came from the outings, but in 1925 he seemed ecstatic. The reporter of the expedition published his opinion that "never was a camp-fire program more absorbing than on the first night at Snow Lake when Professor Meany interpreted...the spirit of the camp." Later, "he launched into the romantic history of pioneer days in the Snoqualmie region," including praise for Chief Patkanim and his warriors who fought side by side with the pioneers against hostile Indians in the "Blockhouse War." The reporter recalled in *The Mountaineer* some months later that Meany's audience was "thoroughly imbued with the spirit of those rugged days of 1855."[63]

Meany expressed his joy in a poem entitled "Ned," written in quiet moments in camp:

When mountain mornings waken
 And the trumpet bids us rise,
Like a tree by clean winds shaken,
 I thrill with a new surprise.

Away from the burden and bother,
 At the end of a long forest tramp,
I know the joy of a father
 With a son for a chum in camp.

Each mountain bird and flower,
 Old friends yet ever rare,
Again weave mystic power;
 We live a tender prayer.

The camp-fire embers glowing,
 Our hearts obeisance make,
Ned's boy scout trumpet blowing
 Plaintive taps across the lake.

In far-away December,
When winter tempests break,
I think I may remember
Echoed taps across the lake.

In subsequent years, through the 1931 outing, after which Ned took his bride Dorothy Grace Adjutant east with him to engage in graduate studies at Harvard, father and son were always together on the outings.[64]

Lizzie Meany stayed at home, but she wrote in motherly fashion in 1925 to "Boys of Mine" in camp, describing with satisfaction the condition of the garden, particularly the Golden Bantam corn which her husband relished. The following summer, when Ned and his father went to the Olympics, she again wrote of the garden and other domestic news. Ned later recalled that although his mother made only one trip to the mountains, she took other vacations and had many absorbing activities in Seattle.[65]

Ned also remembered life at the "home place," located on several city lots purchased in 1894. The property located in the Brooklyn District near the University extended from a line of Poplars along 40th Street (between 9th and 10th Avenues) to a point only a short distance north of Portage Bay. The modest home faced 10th Avenue and had a lawn and two beautiful maple trees in front, one of which held a hammock. A clump of madronos added to the shade while a lilac hedge along 9th Avenue contributed to privacy and to a forest-like appearance. The Meanys maintained numerous fruit trees, roses, a grape arbor, and vegetable garden. A large raspberry patch provided the fruit for berry parties given for friends, faculty, and visiting professors at summer school. Grandmother Meany had chickens at one time but their coop later served as a woodshed.[66]

A clay tennis court completed the formal installations, though whether it was used is not known. Ned seems not to have played tennis. Instead, as a young boy during the World War he and his friends played soldier, digging "dugouts" in a high bank along the street. Ned also delighted in breaking rocks from a huge pile deposited on the outskirts of the "home place," looking for mica and even finding a few garnets. In the "wild place," remote from the house, he and the family often enjoyed bonfires. Late in the fall of 1920, the family had the trees along 40th Street cut down. They had become a nuisance because of their cottony seeds. The thirteen year old Ned did not witness the excitement. He was in the hospital recovering from an appendectomy.[67]

The heart of the faculty community lay several blocks to the north of the campus, across 45th Street and near Ravenna Boulevard, but the Meanys did not feel socially isolated. Ned recalled that the McMahons lived across the street and were good neighbors, especially at Christmas. The two professors sometimes walked to campus together or home from classes, enjoying the opportunities for conversation made rare by differing schedules and locations on campus.[68]

The "home place" became potentially valuable commercial property when the University Bridge, spanning the northern reach of Portage Bay, opened on July 1, 1919. The bridge, which connected the University District to downtown Seattle via Eastlake Avenue, abutted on 10th Avenue. Meany, as keynote speaker at the dedication ceremonies, predicted before 5,000 people that the bridge would carry heavy automobile traffic, although he urged the use of the new trolley line which had carried dignitaries across the bridge to the proceedings.[69]

To take advantage of the increased traffic, in 1924 Meany built a large garage on 10th Avenue to lease to automotive businesses. The garage displaced the house, which was enlarged, refurbished, and turned around to face 9th Avenue. Sometime before 1928, a second commercial garage was erected adjacent to the first. Unfortunately, anticipated revenues were not fully realized. In June 1928, for example, both garages were occupied—one by a Chevrolet agency. However, in September one became vacant and the lease for the second remained under long and unsatisfactory negotiation. When son-in-law J. Arthur Younger, now a Seattle businessman, recommended capital improvements worth $10,000, Meany refused further indebtedness.[70]

Though newly interested in rents as a source of income, Meany lost none of his zeal to hold onto his professorship. News received in 1923 that Frederick Jackson Turner planned to retire he found "rather disconcerting," probably because he was only a year younger than the man he regarded as his mentor. Instead of accepting the noted historian's retirement as normal, Meany imagined an accident or other unfortunate happening. Turner's cheerful reply that retirement would be "a flood of sunshine" might have reassured Meany about his friend but did nothing to assuage his own personal anxieties.[71]

In June 1926, at its commencement exercises, the College of Puget Sound reinforced Meany's self-image by making him an honorary Doctor of Letters. The Tacoma Mountaineers added to his esteem by presenting him with a gift of the full doctoral regalia. Old anxieties did not die, however, for they were based on serious considerations of livelihood and a sense of duty which he never forgot. Thus, when talk of fixing a precise retirement age for the University became widespread in 1927, Meany's anxieties came to the surface again. He opposed such a policy, but discussed it in purely personal terms in a letter to an old friend at Stanford University. Referring to University of Washington authorities, Meany defiantly wrote, "I am disposed to fight them all off as long as I can, preferring to go as well as possible to the end." But in the next sentence he conceded that his superiors "seem perfectly willing to keep my load up to the maximum and so my days are filled with the joy of work."[72]

Actually, he must have known that as a "star" performer in the classroom, he had little cause to fear that he would be forced to retire. Both Suzzallo's administration (which ended October 4, 1926, with his dismissal by the Board of Regents), and M. Lyle Spencer's which followed, warmly regarded high student-to-faculty ratios. Meany qualified as outstanding. Indeed, his "Makers of the Nation" course was one of the most popular on campus.[73]

Meany's salary for 1928-1929 was $5,250; for 1930-1931, it was $5,500. Both figures placed him well above the average for faculty of his rank. But Meany and his colleagues worried about the steady decline of their purchasing power. An added concern, one which loomed larger to Meany with each passing year, was the lack of a retirement benefits system. Thus, like many senior colleagues, Meany feared he might find himself without a competence if forced to retire.[74]

The 1929 Washington birthday celebration once again helped exorcise mundane concerns. In ceremonies held on the steps of Meany Hall, the French Consul Marcel Daley reciprocated for the annual invitations extended him by bestowing upon Meany the title of Chevalier of the French Legion of Honor. The surprised and visibly moved recipient heard himself praised for his "international viewpoint and his work as an historian." More than a year later much of his emotional response lingered as he declared to another Chevalier, Professor Gilbert Chinard of John Hopkins University, that the occasion was "one of the great days of my life."[75]

A full appreciation of the community's regard for Meany encouraged reporter Floyd A. Fessler to describe him in a series of informal, human interest, articles for the *Seattle Star* during February of 1930. "The Chevalier of the Legion of Honor lay in bed, fully clothed, and smoked a cigar," Fessler described to his readers. Meany, still recovering from the broken knee, was resting after a day at the University. Then, in staccato style, Fessler completed his portrait: "Smoke from the cigar drifted slowly thru [*sic*] his white Van Dyke. And he smiled, for he was once a reporter himself. The Chevalier has lived. A full life, active, given to service. Remuneration for service not always in money; peace, contentment and honor are sometimes its legal tender."[76]

EPILOGUE

Last Days and a Summing Up (1930-1935)

ON FEBRUARY 9, 1930, a feature story entitled "The 'Fountain of Youth' is in Seattle, Says Prof. E.S. Meany," appeared in the *National Weekly*, Sunday supplement to the *Seattle Times*. Harold P. Burdick, the author, reported that his subject, "One of the state's foremost sons and the 'grand old man' of the University of Washington Faculty," praised the salutary effect of the geography and climate of the Puget Sound country upon the creativity, morality, and perpetuation of youthful attitudes of its people. "One cannot live in the presence of our mountains, our forests and our sea," Meany stated, "without experiencing the desire to keep forever young, *and the desire is father to the deed.*" Then, tacitly recognizing that flights of rhetoric had to be tempered, the sixty-seven-year-old Meany concluded that "my only rule is: keep moving; keep interested in the progress of life about you; keep working."[1]

Walking, however, presented some difficulties. At Commencement on May 27, 1930, Meany as usual led the procession as grand marshal, but used two canes and showed a slight limp. Indeed, he told a friend nine months later that "my broken knee still requires the aid of a cane and automobile or street car for trips formerly made on foot with ease." He was happy, however, that he could lecture unimpaired and that, except for the lameness, he was well. Adding to his pleasure, daughter Margaret often acted as his chauffeur. Nevertheless, travel difficulties caused him on several occasions to refuse out-of-town speaking engagements, pleading that he had to conserve his strength.[2]

The fires of creativity, too, burned fitfully. Years before, in 1920, Meany had begun editing the proceedings of the state's constitutional convention of 1889—an ambitious project because the original shorthand minutes had been destroyed before they could be transcribed. Newspapers comprised his primary source. He finally completed the laborious editing in

1934. Mounting costs prevented publication despite the fact that the sum needed was only $1,500. Meany appealed personally for aid from his former student, Governor Clarence Martin, but was unsuccessful.[3]

Meany edited three souvenir books, two depicting statues and life masks of George Washington, and the third presenting Abraham Lincoln's views on Washington. Though costly in time and money, none was the product of serious scholarship. At the request of President Suzzallo, though, he undertook to write a history of the University. Meany only completed 107 manuscript pages of this work, and they reveal a heavily annalistic chronicle and anecdotal account of the institution down to 1904. The fragment was never published.[4]

Meany's innovations of earlier years as editor of the *Washington Historical Quarterly* were not repeated during this period. The journal, however, continued to serve the region well. Meany and Charles W. Smith took satisfaction from the record of unbroken publication since 1912 and from the *Quarterly*'s healthy financial condition despite the national depression. In 1934, the journal was mailed to approximately 400 addresses in 45 states and 13 foreign nations. It enjoyed prominent representation in major university, historical society, and other research libraries, signifying its long-range usefulness. When Meany died in 1935, he had accumulated a large backlog of material awaiting publication—a significant measure of the editor's success.[5]

Meany's accomplishments as department chairman, and to a considerable extent as scholar, depended at least in his last years upon the efficient and tireless efforts of his secretary, Mrs. Margaret P. Smith. The editor of the *University of Washington Daily* "discovered" Mrs. Smith in the spring of 1932 and sent a reporter to interview her. That journalist came away with illuminating stories and data. He learned that the secretary handled Meany's correspondence—much of which she termed "fan mail"—registered all history majors and minors and kept the grade records for the 400-500 students enrolled in Meany's classes. She also read proof for the *Quarterly* and maintained numerous documentary files, including scrapbooks on historical subjects and on the professor himself. Somehow finding the time, Mrs. Smith regularly clipped pioneer biographies from newspapers to add to Meany's collection.[6]

No secretary could ease the chairman's burdens which arose from the reduction of faculty salaries in the midst of the depression. Receipts for University operations decreased by about $300,000 during 1931-1932. The regents responded by denying promised salary increases, and finally by cutting salaries 10 percent effective October 1932. After the state's voters passed an initiative measure in the November general election reducing the millage for higher education by slightly more than one-half, salaries were cut 32 percent. The severe reduction forced the firing of one out of every eleven teachers and heaped a higher student burden on those faculty remaining. Conditions did not significantly improve until the 1935-1936 biennium when salaries returned, almost, to the 1931-1932 level.

Meany, of course, suffered the cuts along with his colleagues. Thus, when he learned that Ned, now a graduate student at Harvard, had been awarded an assistantship for the next year, he rejoiced for two reasons—because Ned had been "deemed worthy" and because of his own diminished income. He soon suffered another of the pangs of a chairman when his staff was reduced. Librarian Beardsley had taught English constitutional history, but the University withheld funds for that assignment. Meany was forced to add that course to the teaching load of professor Donald G. Barnes.[7]

The latter, indeed, became chairman Meany's greatest concern. A highly valued member of the faculty since 1930, Barnes disturbed Meany by sharply criticizing the prevailing low salaries and large classes and by calling for establishment of sabbatical leaves and retirement insurance. When the regents obtained emergency funds from Governor Clarence Martin for bargaining to keep Barnes and a dozen other dissidents from leaving for higher paying positions elsewhere, he spurned negotiations. Barnes declared the University's offer to be $700 less than he had been paid when first hired. In the fall of 1934, he departed for Western Reserve University in Cleveland, Ohio, telling newspaper reporters that he would receive a much higher salary there. He would also enjoy generous sabbatical leaves and a retirement allowance, all unavailable at the University of Washington.[8]

Meany suffered sleepless nights as he took to heart Barnes' criticism and departure. He believed Barnes had been treated justly and, hence, that his criticism was unjustified. Meany's other colleagues felt the same tensions and also directed their unhappiness at him. Meany felt a growing sense of isolation, evidenced by his failure to respond immediately to the presentation of a loving cup tendered to him on his seventieth birthday at a party in Barnes' home. He had hesitated in responding, he rationalized later, because the McMahons had often spoken of such gifts as foolish. His colleagues had been so dismayed that they considered not inviting the Meanys to a similar celebration of Edward McMahon's sixtieth birthday. Only Mrs. McMahon's intercession, apparently, prevented that studied insult from being carried out.[9]

As Keeper of Traditions, Meany continued to enjoy promoting customs, interpreting patriotic sentiment, and heralding progress. One satisfying occasion involved the dedication of the Hotel Edmond Meany, a seventeen-story building opened in the University District on November 12, 1931. Built by a corporation formed by businessmen of the district, the hotel was planned as a means of promoting general commercial enterprise near the University. Meany's name had been a widely popular choice in a local contest where the naming of the hotel constituted the only prize. Meany had no investment in the corporation.

One reporter compared the formal opening of the hotel to a Hollywood premier. Some 475 civic and state dignitaries and leading citizens attended the event, complete with "clicking movie cameras, flashlights, [and] limousines rolling up in a stream to the new black and white chromium doorway." Speaking before that glittering assembly, Meany accepted the honor of name tearfully and recalled early days in the district. To professor Walter N. Sage, who wrote from Vancouver, British Columbia, that he had listened to the ceremonies on the radio, Meany responded that the wonder of the instrument was great "but a bigger one is the measure of affection pouring out to one poor fellow who cannot believe that he deserves it." President M. Lyle Spencer of the University had to set the record straight. He pointed out to the audience at the dedication that instead of the community having honored "one of its most distinguished citizens, it was Professor Meany who paid the tribute in allowing his name to be used."[10]

The 1932 bicentennial of George Washington's birth provided the nation an opportunity to carry out patriotic exercises such as those Meany directed every year. His own planning for the event had been stimulated by the death in 1923 of the so-called "Washington Elm," in Cambridge, Massachusetts. Legend, whose truth few patriots questioned, held that General Washington had taken command of the Continental Army under that tree on the Cambridge Common, July 3, 1775. In Meany's view, the "Washington Elm" lived on in a scion which had been planted on the University of Washington campus in about 1896. Subsequently, the Sons of the American Revolution placed a bronze tablet at the foot of the tree, thus giving the legend legitimacy. Formal exercises before the tree in November 1927, by that group reinforced the credibility of the "Washington Elm" story.[11]

In 1930 Meany began a campaign to link plantings of another generation of "Washington Elm" scions with the celebration of Washington's bicentennial. Supported by President Spencer, he campaigned successfully to plant Elms on the White House grounds and on the Cambridge Common. For Meany's services to Cambridge, he received a medal presented by the Grand Army of the Republic. His task was complete when, in mid-September of 1931, he reported with satisfaction that the Daughters of the American Revolution would plant a scion on the capitol grounds in Olympia as a "rallying point for future patriotic occasions."[12]

The bicentennial celebrations on February 22, 1932, in Seattle and elsewhere across the nation were rallying points for oratory treating George Washington's character as impeccable and his Farewell Address as if it were holy writ in support of isolationism and other aspects of narrowly defined nationalism. Meany played his customary role, conducting the celebration at Lorado Taft's statue with a mixed display of international amity and patriotism. Later in the afternoon, foreign consuls and local dignitaries planted trees in an international grove. In the luncheon address, federal judge Jeremiah Neterer praised Washington's advice against entangling alliances.[13]

The patriotic and collegial events which Meany promoted were so firmly rooted they were accepted with little question as part of every University of Washington student's campus experience. Thus, when in early October 1930, the student editor discovered no plans had been made to administer the Ephebic Oath to the freshmen, he was shocked into action. Declaring that the Oath was one of the most significant and sacred University traditions, the student spurred the leaders into action. After extraordinary efforts, Meany finally delivered the pledge and a homily on "Fairness." Unfortunately, only one-third of the freshmen were present, weakening the sense of high purpose and suggesting that a fracturing of student solidarity might be developing. Nevertheless, the Oath ceremony continued in the following years.[14]

The fate of Campus Day was also in question. Highways and automobiles drew students away to other places and activities on that work day. Furthermore, janitors and gardeners performed most of the maintenance on the campus. Little remained for the students to do. Thus, the original purpose of sprucing up the grounds for spring activities had been lost. When the administration abolished the work day in 1931, the Oval Club, undoubtedly under Meany's counsel, successfully appealed for a reprieve. Campus Day shifted from Friday to Wednesday to lessen the temptation for students to slip away from campus, but only a small percentage of students participated during the years 1932 through 1934. Reluctantly, Meany agreed with a faculty resolution that Campus Day be stricken from the University Calendar.[15]

Burdens of office vanished, as usual, for a few weeks each summer while Meany vacationed with The Mountaineers. But, since he continued to serve as the club's president, his role in alpine recreation recapitulated, on a small scale, his career on the campus and in the community. Thus, he presided over an organization whose membership reached 836 in 1927. He had to deal primarily with decisions on recreational programming, but also faced occasional debates and resolutions regarding national park development and protection of the environment. Though a gracious, skilled, and diplomatic presiding officer, vigilant to protect the club's welfare, he never became a vociferous or aggressive advocate for national parks or conservation measures.

Although he was chosen as Western vice president of the American Alpine Club in 1926, the office proved to be honorary. In making the appointment, the national officers cited his long service to The Mountaineers, itself a club of considerable prestige, and complimented his mountain climbing exploits. Though respectable, his climbing accomplishments were neither innovative nor especially daring. Yet, less than 10 percent of the Seattle membership could match his status as a "Six Peaker"—one who had climbed six major peaks in Washington.[16]

The automobile accident in 1929 in which Meany's knee was broken terminated serious mountain climbing. A few weeks before the mishap, he scaled his last peak, the 8,834 foot Mount Shafer in the Canadian Rockies. It is unlikely that he required much commiseration on succeeding outings. Camp activities, comradeship, and enjoyment of the flora and scenery along meadow trails and clearings always occupied more of his attention than did "peak grabbing." The 1934 outing to Glacier National Park in Montana, his last trip, brought other diversions, such as ordinary tourist sightseeing. Meany undoubtedly found that occasion most enjoyable because Lizzie was with him for the first time on an outing.[17]

Often in the later years he traveled by car or on horseback to mountain camps, with Ned always attentive. But his companions never gave him reason to feel out of place. Quite the contrary, in the green memories of his friends of the trail, recorded in published recollections two decades after his death, the strong conviction prevailed that he had shaped the club's ideals and its destiny.[18]

As a relatively young Mountaineer, he "was tall and trim of figure and carried his red head proudly," according to Lydia L. Forsyth, who then recalled the costume and bearing associated with Meany's alpine activities. "On the trail he wore a corduroy suit, high boots and broad brimmed ranger style felt hat. At campfires he stood erect; the straight trees behind him; the light of the fire upon him—a symbol of the best in mountaineering."[19]

By precept and example, he taught exemplary conduct and ethics in the woods. As Forsyth remembered, "He set high standards and we felt it a privilege to maintain them. 'Leave a campsite better than you found it' was always the rule of the day." While appreciative of the satisfactions found in scaling peaks, Meany enjoyed studying nature and contemplating its salutary effect on character, taking as much interest in small things as in great. "To Professor Meany," Forsyth also observed, "the little hairbell was as important as the glacier beyond." His daily observation often found expression in verse he shared at camp fires, along with recounting local history and legends.[20]

When an interest in skiing developed among The Mountaineers in the mid-twenties, President Meany used his personal funds and moneys from the Everett and Tacoma branches to purchase sixty-four acres of prime recreational land on which a ski lodge to accommodate fifty skiers was built. Located near Stampede Pass, the structure was dedicated as the Meany Ski Lodge on November 11, 1928. It quickly became a busy center for winter recreation, contributing materially to the growth and welfare of the club and the sport. Two years later, in August of 1930, members seized another opportunity to express their gratitude for Meany's leadership. While hiking in the vicinity of Summerland, a park in the shadow of Mount Rainier, the group came upon a "rugged dome" which they promptly and unanimously named "Meany Crest," a title which subsequently became official.[21]

In the 1930s, mountaineering in Washington ceased to be the prerogative of the middle class professional and business people who had formed the club. Great numbers of new climbers flocked to Mount Rainier and other peaks, following roads and trails recently constructed by workers from New Deal federal relief agencies. In the case of Mount Rainier, in effect the home base of The Mountaineers, National Park rangers and club leaders found it necessary about the time of Meany's death to introduce safety standards, new equipment, and training in climbing techniques. The amateur era of climbing was over, its history lodged in records of climbs, dutifully recorded in the club's journal and in group consciousness. Many of these journal entries became fixed in the form of tributes to Meany and to the carefree joys of the trail.[22]

Son-in-law J. Arthur Younger maintained his persistent efforts to improve the Meany family's fortunes, but to no avail. Younger's last extant financial report (April 11, 1932) on the Meany properties reveals three mortgages—on the house and the two commercial garages—with a balance due of $13,950. Unfortunately, only one of the two commercial garages was rented, and that at a modest rate of $200 per month. Taxes due in June, 1932, on all ten lots were $956.37 (half the year's taxes), whereas the bank balance was less than $400. In spite of the financial burdens, Meany sent his "usual check" to the National Republican Campaign for Hoover's run against Franklin D. Roosevelt. Then, in December, during severe salary reductions, he contributed to the *Post-Intelligencer*'s Christmas fund for the needy.[23]

Edmond Stephen Meany died of a stroke at age seventy-two on Monday, April 22, 1935, a few minutes before the start of his 10 a.m. class on the history of Canada. The day before, Meany had attended Easter services at the University Congregational Church, where he had worshipped for many years. He had spent the remainder of the day in the company of family and friends. On Monday, he arrived at Denny Hall as usual at 9:30, cheerful and apparently in good health.[24]

The body lay in state at the University Congregational Church and then, just before the funeral, on Friday, April 26, in the foyer of Meany Hall. Afternoon classes at the University were canceled on the day of the funeral. Twenty-five hundred students, faculty, and townspeople crowded Meany Hall for the services. After that, the St. John's Lodge of the Masonic Order held graveside services for Meany, who was the past Master of the lodge. Meany was buried at Lake View cemetery on Seattle's Capitol Hill, appropriately in full view of both the Cascade and Olympic Ranges which he had celebrated so often.[25]

In the period of mourning, much sentiment welled up on campus, in Seattle, and throughout the Pacific Northwest. The *University of Washington Daily* called Meany the "Greatest Friend" of students, praising his work of inaugurating and guarding traditions. The article affirmed that he had become an institution—one could not consider his education complete without taking a course from Professor Meany. Newspapers from Alaska to California—including at least twenty from Washington—echoed the campus sentiments as they printed the Associated Press dispatch reporting his death.[26]

Editorials in some of the papers offered personal insights which strongly suggested that the editors and their associates had been Meany's students and friends. The *Cathlamet Eagle* asserted that it had been axiomatic that the poorer students received B's while the remainder obtained A's in Meany's classes. But, the *Eagle* continued, grades had not reflected the most valuable lessons offered, for "more than any other man he has symbolized that part of a great university which cannot be measured in dollars and set down in black and white."[27]

Even more boldly, the editor of the *Yakima Republic* asserted that "the death of Prof. Edmond S. Meany entails a feeling of personal loss to more people than would have been the case in the death of almost any other man in the Pacific Northwest." The reason had more to do with the fact that he had experienced much of history at first hand, rather than through scholarly attainment, the editor continued. Primarily, though, Meany's fame would rest on large numbers of students over the course of forty years who had responded sympathetically to his humanity and who would now "join in tribute to one...who taught because he liked to teach, and who claimed and held their attention through his personality as much as through his knowledge of the subject."[28]

Resolutions by the student government and the faculty repeated the idea that Meany's teaching had been inspirational. His presence, as a faculty memorial put it, had been "a benediction to the University and to all connected with it, and his memory will be an inspiration!" Even the *Argus*, a critical Seattle weekly which had closely followed Meany's career from his newspaper days, concluded that his memory would live not only through his scholarship but that "down through the lives of his students the example, the precepts and the purposes of Prof. Meany will ever be a guiding influence and a blessed benefaction."[29]

It remained for voices from Oregon to appraise Meany's scholarship. Perceptively, the *Oregonian* noted that his death signified that the pioneer stage in the region's history was rapidly passing away. As one of the "most distinguished members" of the second generation of the region's historians, Meany had saved the stories of the pioneers:

> With a love for the dramatic combined with a love for the accurate, he did much to fix forever the picture which people of Washington will carry of the founding of their state. His *History of the State of Washington*...remains the standard in spirit, and in conception of the early years.[30]

Charles H. Carey, an Oregon historian, recognized the *Washington Historical Quarterly* as a great monument Meany had left to posterity. It "has occupied a field of its own," he wrote. "It has been privileged to represent and to speak for the pioneers of Washington, and with a full understanding and sound scholarship, it has done this." The magazine had been a success in large measure, Carey stated, because Meany's spirit pervaded its pages—"his cheerful optimism, his never failing gift of humor, and his genuine interest in people." Thus, his editorial gifts—though sometimes failing in technical matters—were sustained by the human interest found in the pioneer narratives. His deeply felt optimism, Carey concluded, led him to believe "that the teachings of the past help solve current problems." Thus, at an age when contemporaries of his conservative bent were content to relive the past uncritically, editor Meany kept the *Quarterly* exploring new topics and themes.[31]

Official mourning soon ended but various roles Meany had played in preserving customs and traditions and in public service produced additional tributes. When classes resumed in the fall of 1935, with a new group of freshmen to be indoctrinated, the *Daily* sounded an alarm. What would happen to the Ephebic Oath? The editorial writer confessed to having mixed feelings about the ritual, probably felt by many students and faculty:

> Traditions are shadowy things, easily scorned in these days of New Deals and hi-de-ho's and cigarette advertisements. And perhaps to 3,000 eager entering students the solemn oath of loyalty would bring but slight entertainment in between hours of Joe E. Brown movies and sneak dances. If so, the Ephebic Oath is best forgotten.

But, Professor Meany had carried out the ritual successfully, making believable, as the *Daily* writer admitted, the vague idealism of the oath which freshmen repeated after him:

> I will strive both alone and with the many to honor the name of Washington above all private and selfish interests....As I revere the God of my fathers, I call him to witness my intent.

Would anyone try to follow Meany's path? The student editor thought it unlikely. However, President Lee Paul Sieg stood firm in his conviction, voiced at Meany's death, that the latter and other great teachers excelled in building character. Sieg administered the oath to some 3,000 freshmen crowded into Meany Hall, and thus carried on the idealism which Meany had so greatly valued.[32]

Numerous tributes to Meany included commemoration of his role in welcoming alumni at homecoming, and his contribution to Boy Scout activities and mountaineering. In the meantime, the Department of History and Meany's family had to resume a normal life. Edward McMahon became the executive officer of the department, while Meany's courses were spread among three faculty members and one student assistant. These shifts signified no immediate changes in policy.[33]

Merrill Jensen, who joined the history faculty in the fall of 1935, became editor of the *Washington Historical Quarterly*, which he retitled the *Pacific Northwest Quarterly*, beginning with the next volume. Readers soon discovered that Jensen would employ an impersonal, indeed, at first an anonymous, editorial policy and would adopt a completely scholarly tone. He eliminated the pioneer narrative in favor of a broader social science scope with much attention to anthropology. At one stroke of the pen, then, the new editor transformed the journal into a purely scholarly publication.[34]

Edmond Stephen Meany's death precipitated a sharp change in the life of his family. He left a modest, but heavily mortgaged estate valued at $25,000. His widow, Sarah Elizabeth Meany, had no means of maintaining the "home place" or the two commercial garages and no particular incentive to stay in Seattle. In early October 1935, she joined daughter Margaret and son-in-law Arthur Younger in Washington, D.C., where Arthur was employed by a federal agency. Son Ned and his wife Dorothy were also residing in Washington, D.C., at that time. Thus ended the saga of the Meanys in the Pacific Northwest.[35]

Meany's memory remained alive with the passing years as evidenced when the University demolished the antiquated Meany Hall in 1975 and then constructed a magnificent new Meany Hall as a center for musical arts. Though the arts were not Meany's professional concern, the new structure remains appropriate in its location at the center of campus and in its identification with Meany. The latter would have been proud to have this temple to the arts associated with his name, if only because it represented progress in the evolution of collegiate life and the culture of the community. Progress in life and history was the hallmark of his ventures and, he always believed, of his city and his state.[36]

ENDNOTES

Papers of all members of the Meany family are found in the Meany Papers, University of Washington Special Collections, unless otherwise noted.

Notes for Prologue

1. A good discussion of Seattle's business leaders is found in Norbert MacDonald, *Distant Neighbors: A Comparative History of Seattle and Vancouver* (Lincoln: University of Nebraska Press, 1987), 14-20, 36-39, 56, 75, 100, 101.
2. Will L. Visscher and W.H. McEwen, *A Souvenir of Washington's Third Legislature* (Olympia, 1893), 80 (quotation "simple story") and 81 (quotation "foremost in the councils"); Lewis O. Saum, "William Lightfoot Visscher and the 'Eden of the West,'" *Pacific Northwest Quarterly* 71(January, 1980):2 (note 13).
3. Robert E. Burke, "The Role of the Editor: Watchful Waiting and/or Purposeful Searching," in *The Changing Pacific Northwest: Interpreting its Past*, eds. David H. Stratton and George A. Frykman (Pullman: Washington State University Press, 1988), 145.

Notes for Chapter One

1. Edmond S. Meany to Mrs. Margaret D. Gregg, 6 March 1920, Meany Letterpress Book (1918-1920); Meany to William Barry Meany, 5 April 1912, Meany Letterpress Book (1909-1912); T.C. Elliott to Meany, 20 January 1915; Meany to Elliott, 6 April 1915, Meany Letterpress Book (1915-1916); and Floyd A. Fessler, *Seattle Star*, 4 February 1930 (quotation), clipping in *Edmond Stephen Meany, 1862-1935, Tributes, II*, a scrapbook located in Northwest Collection, University of Washington Library.
2. Penciled notes on Meany family history, in Edmond S. Meany's hand, n.d., Meany Papers.
3. *Ibid.*
4. *Ibid.*; the Baltic Medal awarded Edmond Meany's father is engraved "Stephen Meaney [*sic*], Cap. M. Top, *H.M.S. Majestic*," and is located in folder 31-10; R.D. Awdry, Admiralty [London] to E.S. Meany, 6 June 1900; for discussion of the terms of the award of the Baltic Medal, see *Encyclopedia Britannica*, 1911 edition, XVIII: 13. For explanation of technical terms, see *The Oxford English Dictionary* (1933), II, 100; VI, 54, 556.
5. Penciled notes on Meany family history in Edmond S. Meany's hand, n.d.; *Seattle Times*, 15 September 1920, and *Seattle Post-Intelligencer*, 16 September 1920; Certificate of Naturalization for Stephen Meany, 21 January 1867, Meany Papers. The position of Alexander English as a local entrepreneur in shipping and lime kilns is established by Edmond S. Meany's penciled notes, and by Gladys F. Blakely, Hoyt Public Library, Saginaw, Michigan, to George A. Frykman, 24 March 1966, describing contents of

city directories (letter in possession of the author). Information on Saginaw Valley is contained in Willis F. Dunbar, *Michigan: A History of the Wolverine State*, 2nd ed. (Grand Rapids, Mich.: Eerdman's Publishing Company, 1970), 353, 358-359, 377, 471-472, 483-484.

6. Certificate of Membership, Stephen Meany in the Independent Order of Odd Fellows; B.J. Brown to Captain S. Meany, 16 July 1866 (quote); A. English to Margaret [Meany], 29 August 1870, Meany Papers.
7. Penciled notes on Meany family history in Edmond S. Meany's hand, n.d.; Certification of Naturalization for Stephen Meany, 21 January, 1867 (information on back indicates he was in San Francisco as late as 4 September 1871); A. English to Captain S. Meany, 6 August 1870.
8. Penciled notes on Meany family history in Edmond S. Meany's hand, n.d.; Blakely to Frykman, 24 March 1966; Stephen Meany's presence in San Francisco during 1875 is established by grocery bills dated 20 November 1875, and 1 April 1876, from McAuliffe and Freeman, Grocers, San Francisco; Meany to Mrs. Mary Wager-Fisher, 28 April 1892, Meany Letterpress Book (1891-1893) contains his "vivid recollections of my boyhood in Iowa, Illinois, and my native Michigan."
9. Benedict and Smith [to whom it may concern], San Francisco, 10 July 1877, is a letter of recommendation for Edmond Meany in possession of E.S. Meany, Jr.; S. Bonnifield to S. Meany, 25 May 1876, and R.W. Wood to Captain Meany, 27 June 1876.
10. *The Daily Intelligencer* (Seattle), 19 and 27 (quotation) February 1877. The description of Seattle is from Alexander Norbert MacDonald, "Seattle's Economic Development, 1880-1910" (Ph.D. diss., University of Washington, 1959), *passim*, and from Robert C. Nesbit, *"He Built Seattle," A Biography of Judge Thomas Burke* (Seattle: University of Washington Press, 1961), x, xi. In 1880, Seattle's population was 3,553. See Roger Sale, *Seattle Past to Present* (Seattle: University of Washington Press, 1976), 35; "United States Inspector's Certificate to Masters," (1877) contains the quotation on his privileges as a master of steam vessels.
11. [Edmond S. Meany] Untitled identification slip (on biography); Cornelius H. Hanford, "Professor Edmond S. Meany," *Washington Historical Quarterly* 1(April 1907):165; Fessler, *Seattle Star*, 4 February 1930, clipping in *Edmond Stephen Meany, 1862-1935, Tributes, II*, contains a characterization of the house. The Stephen Meany family ultimately included a son, Jay, who was born in 1878 and lived to adulthood. Three children died in infancy or early childhood, all before arrival of the family in Seattle. See penciled notes on Meany family history in Edmond S. Meany's hand, n.d.
12. MacDonald's "Seattle's Economic Development, 1880-1910," pp. 1-2 presents a description which is corroborated by inspection of the photographs published in Clarence B. Bagley, *History of Seattle from the Earliest Settlement to the Present Time*, 3 vols. (Chicago: S.J. Clarke Publishing Company, 1916), vol. 1: photographs opposite pp. 60, 88, 100, 130; vol. 2: text on pp. 673, 682; Norman H. Clark's *Washington, A Bicentennial History* (New York: W.W. Norton and Co., Inc., and Nashville: American Association for State and Local History, 1976), 10, offers a dismal picture of Seattle; Janice Krenmayr, *Foot-loose in Seattle*, vol. 1(Midway, Wash: Osborn-Warne, Inc., 1961), 26, mentions the cow at Denny's residence, First Avenue (formerly Front Street) and Union Street. Seattle's *Evening Dispatch* for 23 July 1877, puts the residence at Front and Spring Streets; Sale, *Seattle Past to Present*, 16-26.
13. Fessler, *Seattle Star*, 5 February 1930, clipping in *Edmond S. Meany, 1862-1935, Tributes, II*; E.S. Meany, Jr., Commentary on Floyd Fessler's articles pertaining to E.S. Meany published in the *Seattle Star*, 3-15 February 1930 (in the possession of the

author); R.C. Pitt (Comp), *Directory of the City of Seattle and Vicinity, 1879* (Seattle: Hanford and McClaire, Printers, 1879), 58.

14. Kenneth E. Selby, Assistant Superintendent of Seattle Public Schools, to Frykman, 26 March 1963, establishes Meany's presence at Central School (letter in possession of the author); Joseph T. Hazard cites Ingraham's education and makes it clear that he was Meany's teacher at Central School. See Hazard's *Pioneer Teachers of Washington* (Seattle: Seattle Retired Teacher's Association, 1955), 63-67; E.S. Meany, Jr., Commentary on Fessler corroborates a lifelong association and friendship between Ingraham and Meany; Frederick E. Bolton and Thomas W. Bibb, *History of Education in Washington*,(U.S. Department of the Interior, Office of Education, Bulletin no. 9, 1934), 155-156; Charles M. Gates, *The First Century at the University of Washington, 1861-1961* (Seattle: University of Washington Press, 1961), 30-42; *Daily Intelligencer*, 6 November 1877; Fessler, *Seattle Star*, 4 February 1930, clipping in *Edmond S. Meany, 1862-1935, Tributes, II*, contains quotes characterizing Captain Meany's mood regarding his son's education; G. Thomas Edwards, "Pioneer President Alexander Jay Johnson and the Formative Years of the University of Washington and Whitman College," *Pacific Northwest Quarterly* 79 (April 1988): 65-73.
15. Meany described himself to William B. Meany, 5 April 1912, Meany Letterpress Book (1909-1912). See also "The Stroller" in *The Argus*, undated clipping in Meany Papers; Gates, *First Century*, 30-42.
16. University of Washington Territory, *Annual Announcement*, June 1878, unpaged.
17. University of Washington Territory, Catalogue for 1878-1879 [missing title pages], 5-9; *Daily Intelligencer*, 14 June 1879.
18. Bagley, *History of Seattle*, I, 178, 180 (quotation on Sunday School); Brown Church, Seattle, *Record Book, 1878-79*, Meany Papers; Methodist Protestant Sunday School [Brown Church], Seattle, *Record Book* [1 April 1883-5 July 1885], Dillis B. Ward papers, University of Washington; Meany to C.B. Bagley, 7 April 1910, contains the quote on "upbuilding and strengthening the University," Bagley Papers, University of Washington.
19. Meany is incorrectly named "Edward" S. Meany and is also incorrectly listed as a student in the scientific collegiate course, second year, in University of Washington Territory, *Annual Register for 1879-80* (Seattle: Steward and Ebersold, 1880), 5; *Daily Intelligencer*, 20 March 1880.
20. Seattle *Fin-Back*, 5 April 1880; Gates, *First Century*, 40-45; *Daily Intelligencer*, 19 June 1880.
21. Thomas Prosch, "Chronological History of Seattle," (undated MSS, Prosch Papers, University of Washington), 214; *Daily Intelligencer*, 16 September 1878; 12 October and 7 December 1879, *ibid.*, 29 April 1880, reports the drowning and contains the quotation. See also *ibid.*, 13 May 1880.
22. Hanford, "Professor Edmond S. Meany," p.165; *Daily Intelligencer*, 7 and 21 October 1880; "Edmond S. Meany Reviews His Newspaper Work," *Seattle Post-Intelligencer*, 30 May 1921, indicated he lived on an uncle's farm while in California; letters were addressed to Edmond Meany at Los Gatos by W.B. Whittenmyer on 6 March and 29 May 1881, and by E.C. Cheasty on 24 March, 18 May, and 15 June 1881(in possession of Edmond S. Meany, Jr.); and by Louis F. Anderson, 7 May 1881. Whittenmyer also sent a letter to Meany at San Jose on 19 July 1881 (in possession of Edmond S. Meany, Jr.). These letters and the following item confirm his rural and social activities: The hunting reference is found in his memoir, "Madrona," part of a series entitled *Western Miniatures* (undated MSS., Meany papers); Anthony J. Meany to "My Dear Sister," 8 April 1881; *Seattle Daily Times*, 22 April 1935.

23. Fessler, *Seattle Star*, 5 February 1930, clipping in *Edmond S. Meany, 1862-1935, Tributes, II*, and E.S. Meany, Jr., Commentary on Floyd Fessler's articles in the *Seattle Star*, 3-15 February 1930.
24. *University of Washington Territory, Annual Register, 1881-82* (Seattle: Steward and Ebersold, 1882), 7; Ed. Meany, "The Bear," 20 January 1882, an essay found in Young Naturalists, *Essays on Natural History by Members, and Minutes of the Young Naturalists' [Society]*, 27 January, 31 March, 7 April 1882 (Young Naturalists' Papers, University of Washington).
25. *Catalogue of the University of Washington Territory for the Scholastic Year 1882-3* (Seattle: C. Hanford, printer, n.d.), not paged. The undergraduate academic record for Edmond S. Meany was compiled by members of the registrar's staff and supplied through the courtesy of Mrs. Ethelyn Toner, registrar, University of Washington, 24 April 1959 (in possession of the author); Gates, *First Century*, 42-43.
26. Gates, *First Century*, 42-43 (quotation is on p.43). The relationship between Meany and Miss Hansee will be discussed in chapter two. See the *Seattle Post-Intelligencer*, 12 June 1884, for information on O.B. Johnson.
27. Mrs. Ethelyn Toner to Frykman, 24 April 1959; Melville H. Hatch, "The Young Naturalists' Society (1879-1905)," in *Studies in Honor of Trevor Kincaid*, ed. Melville H. Hatch (Seattle: University of Washington Press, 1950), 30-34; articles in the *Seattle Post-Intelligencer*, for 24 and 29 July, and 15 September 1883, 18 March 1884, and 17 March 1885, give evidence of field trips. For the contribution to Villard celebration, see, *ibid.*, 15 September 1883.
28. "Departments of Instruction," [catalog], University of Washington Territory, 1888 (Seattle: B.B. Dearborn, 1888), 17, 24, 25 (quotations on p. 24). The library had 2,500 bound volumes and 800 pamphlets and periodicals in 1884-1885. Apparently no regular budget was available, but $140 was raised for the library by public lectures. See "General Information," *Catalogue of Officers and Students of the University of Washington Territory for 1884-5* (Seattle: Lowman and Hanford, n.d.).
29. Wilson Smith, *Professors and Public Ethics: Studies of Northern Moral Philosophers Before the Civil War* (Ithaca: Cornell University Press, 1956); Francis Wayland, *Elements of Moral Philosophy*, ed. Joseph Blau (Cambridge, Mass.: Harvard University Press, reprinted in 1963); Bolton and Bibb, *History of Education in Washington*, 217-18; Seattle *Post-Intelligencer*, 23 October 1883, 22 March (quotation by Rev. D.J. Pierce) and 24 March 1885. See Meany to David Starr Jordan, 25 June 1895, Meany Letterpress Book (1894-1895), for quotation on "natural religion."
30. Minutes of the Young Naturalists' Society, 6 October 1882 (Young Naturalists' Papers, University of Washington Library); *Seattle Post-Intelligencer*, 4 September, 13 and 30 October 1883.
31. Fessler, *Seattle Star*, 5 February 1930, clipping in *Edmond S. Meany, 1862-1935, Tributes, II*, and E.S. Meany, Jr., Commentary on Floyd Fessler's articles in the *Seattle Star*, 3-15 February 1930; Nesbit, *He Built Seattle*, 362-365; Meany's activity may be traced in the newspapers. See *Seattle Post-Intelligencer*, 13 June, 6, 12, 15 July, 21 August, 23-25 October 1884; 27 June and 8 December 1885; Meany served as Third Vice President of the club for 1884-1885, according to a notice of the Young Men's Independent Political Club, 10 December 1884 (Meany papers); Agnes M. Greene to Meany, 16 November 1886.
32. Meany, "Reminiscences," *The Washington Alumnus* 3 (2 November 1909): 6; "Edmond S. Meany Reviews Work as a Newspaper Man," *Seattle Post-Intelligencer*, 30 May 1921; on Crawford, see *ibid.*, 3 and 9 October 1883.
33. "Edmond S. Meany Reviews Work as Newspaper Man," *ibid.*, 30 May 1921; Meany, "Reminiscences," p.6; *Seattle Post-Intelligencer*, 7 March 1884; Edmond S. Meany, Jr.,

Commentary on Floyd Fessler's articles in the *Seattle Star*, 3-15 February 1930. The estimated population of Seattle is from the Seattle *Post-Intelligencer*, 13 April, and 31 July 1883, as modified and cited in Norbert MacDonald, *Distant Neighbors: A Comparative History of Seattle and Vancouver* (Lincoln: University of Nebraska Press, 1987), p. 19; Meany's Account Book of Newspaper Subscribers, 1 January 1884 - 1 June 1884, Collection Ledger, 20 August 1884 - 14 July 1885, and his Collection Day Book, 20 August 1884 - 14 July 1885, are found in the Meany Papers. The latter book has records which run to 13 March 1886; Edmond S. Meany, "Diary from 1 January 1885, to _____," entry for 10 January 1885; James Gordon Bennett to Meany, 12 February 1884.

34. See entries from 3-10 January 1885 in his "Diary from 1 January 1885 to _____". All quotations are from diary entries.
35. *Seattle Post-Intelligencer*, 23 May 1885 (quotation); *University of Washington Territory, 1888* [Catalog], 34.

Notes for Chapter Two

1. Ollie [Miss Olive Snyder] to Meany, 1 July 1885.
2. Carlos A. Schwantes, *Radical Heritage: Labor, Socialism, and Reform in Washington and British Columbia, 1885-1917* (Seattle: University of Washington Press, 1979), 22-25 (quotation on p. 24).
3. Robert C. Nesbit, *"He Built Seattle": A Biography of Judge Thomas Burke* (Seattle: University of Washington Press, 1961),166-207, presents a detailed account of the anti-Chinese agitation in Seattle; Jules A. Karlin, "The Anti-Chinese Outbreaks in Seattle, 1885-1886," *Pacific Northwest Quarterly* 39 (April 1948):103-130; *Seattle Post-Intelligencer*, 7 March 1886; George Kinnear, "Anti-Chinese Riots at Seattle, Wn., 8 February 1886: Twenty-Fifth Anniversary of Riots," pamphlet (Seattle: 8 February 1911), 3-10, 16, 17; Schwantes, *Radical Heritage*, 24-25, discusses the effect of the riots on labor organization; Meany to C. Marcus Wienand, 9 January 1929.
4. Nesbit, *He Built Seattle*, 166-212; Roger Sale, *Seattle Past to Present* (Seattle: University of Washington Press, 1976), 45-49. I have accepted Sale's estimate that 350 Chinese were marched to the docks, 200 of whom were shipped out; *ibid.*, 45-46; *The Official History of the Washington National Guard*, vol. 4, *The National Guard in the Philippine Insurrection*, (Headquarters, Military Department, State of Washington. Office of the Adjutant General, Tacoma), 333; *Oregonian* (Portland), 11 February 1886.
5. Edmond S. Meany, *History of the State of Washington* (New York: The Macmillan Company, 1909), 276-277 (quotations).
6. *The Official History of the Washington National Guard*, vol. 4: 340-341, 358-363; "U.W. Celebrity Active Up to Time of Death," *Seattle Post-Intelligencer*, 23 April 1935, clipping in *Edmond Stephen Meany 1862-1935, Tributes, I* (Northwest Collection, University of Washington Libraries); *Seattle Post-Intelligencer*, 23 May 1886; R.J. Fisken to Meany, 22 October 1888; Seattle's fire is well described in Clarence B. Bagley, *History of Seattle from the Earliest Settlement to the Present Time*, vol. I (Chicago: S.J. Clarke Publishing Company, 1916, pp. 419-426; Fessler, *Seattle Star*, 13 February 1930, clipping in *Edmond Stephen Meany, 1862-1935, Tributes, II*, and Edmond S. Meany Jr., Commentary on Floyd Fessler's articles in the *Seattle Star*, 3-15 February 1930; Meany, *History of the State of Washington*, 278, 279 (quotation from Moore).
7. *Seattle Post-Intelligencer*, 6 August 1886, and 11 January 1887; Bagley, *History of Seattle*, I, 192-194; Meany to Agnes M. Green, 25 February 1887; note from Edmond S. Meany, Jr., shows that Mildred Meany loaned her brother a pocket Bible inscribed

"Seattle, January 27, 1887," on the occasion of his being appointed Telegraph Editor of the *Post-Intelligencer;* "Edmond S. Meany Reviews Work as a Newspaper Man," *Seattle Post-Intelligencer,* 30 May 1921 (quotation "carrying too heavy a load"); Fessler, *Seattle Star,* 6 February 1930, clipping in *Edmond Stephen Meany, 1862-1935, Tributes, II;* Meany's experience in collecting lumber production data is contained in letters such as one from Meany to W.J. Adams and Co., Port Hadlock, 28 October 1887. Replies include the following: from Washington Mill Company, 1 December 1887; and from Mr. E.E. Adams of Puget Mill Company, 9 January 1888, which contains the quotation on "Braggadocio."

8. Bagley, *History of Seattle,* I, 203-204; Frederick James Grant, *History of Seattle, with Illustrations of Some of its Prominent Men and Pioneers* (New York: American Publishing and Engraving Company, 1891), 370; Meany, "Newspapers of Washington Territory," *Washington Historical Quarterly* 14 (July 1923): 105; *The Trade Journal* (Seattle), 13 August 1888; Winnie A. Freeman to Meany, 11 September 1888; Frederick James Grant to Meany, 17 September 1888, as found in *The Puget Sound Magazine* II (September 1888): 33; "The Editor's Desk," *ibid.,* (October 1888):67-68; "The Naval Station," *Seattle Morning Journal,* 9 February 1889.
9. *Seattle Daily Press,* 26 March and 6 April 1889; Alexander Begg to Meany, 27 March 1889 (quotation), and 24 December 1891.
10. *Seattle Daily Press,* 6 April 1889; the story of the marriage of Meany and Sarah Elizabeth Ward reveals that the firm of Meany and Ward was already developing its nursery and flower garden in North Seattle. *Seattle Post-Intelligencer,* 5 May 1889; *Seattle City Directory for 1890* (Polk's Seattle Directory Company, Publishers, 1890), II, 495, in the Seattle Public Library. Traces of business may be seen in: a delivery list found in 1889 files, Meany Papers; C.H. Van Sant to Messers Meany and Ward, 6 May 1890, and Bessie E. Hastings to Meany, 7 November 1890. See also *State of Washington: Barton's Legislative Handbook and Manual, 1891-1892* (Olympia: State Printing and Publishing Company, 1891), 327; Emmons and Emmons to Meany, 28 November 1891; Dillis B. Ward to Meany, 20 October 1890. Meany briefly ventured into the real estate business, first being urged to do so by his father-in-law, but joined instead with Charles A. Briggs for a short time. See the Seattle Public Library for *Corbett and Company's Second Annual Seattle City Directory, 1891-1892,* 658, 960.
11. Meany, "Newspapers of Washington Territory," 189, 190 (quotation "enterprise"); Fessler, *Seattle Star,* 7 February 1930, clipping in *Edmond Stephen Meany, 1862-1935, Tributes, II.* For collecting statistics, see Abram Barker to _____, 1890; F.A. Macrum to Abram Barker, 24 June 1890, and A.F. Eastmen to *Seattle Press,* 1 August 1890, Meany Papers.
12. Fessler, *Seattle Star,* 7 February 1930, clipping in *Edmond Stephen Meany, 1862-1935, Tributes, II* (quotation "The engineer put on steam"); Edmond S. Meany Jr., Commentary on Floyd Fessler's articles in the *Seattle Star,* 3-15 February 1930; Meany, "Newspapers of Washington Territory," 189, 190 (quotation "That's what I call enterprise").
13. Robert L. Wood, *Across the Olympic Mountains: The Press Expedition, 1889-90* (Seattle: The Mountaineers and the University of Washington Press, 1967), provides the most authoritative account of the expedition. See especially pages 4, 5, 10-18 (quotation "poetic and striking description" on p. 10); Ruby El Hult, *The Untamed Olympics: The Story of a Peninsula* (Portland: Binfords and Mort, 1954), 150-152.
14. Wood, *Across Olympic Mountains,* 13-18, 27, 28. Wood incorrectly referred to Meany's place as a ranch rather than a greenhouse; Murray Morgan, *The Last Wilderness* (New York: Viking Press, 1955), 220-223.

15. Fessler, *Seattle Star*, 7 February 1930, clipping in *Edmond Stephen Meany, 1862-1935, Tributes II;* Wood, *Across Olympic Mountains,* 22-26; Morgan, *Last Wilderness,* 220-223.
16. Wood, *Across Olympic Mountains,* 33, 34, 197; Telegram: Christie to Meany, 21 May 1890.
17. Wood, *Across Olympic Mountains,* 201-206.
18. *Ibid.*, 217-219; Fessler, *Seattle Star*, 7 February 1930, clipping in *Edmond Stephen Meany, 1862-1935, Tributes, II* (quotation).
19. A mimeographed letter from the *Seattle Press* dated 16 July 1890, was sent out to many editors, along with copies of the July 16 edition of the *Press*, and an offer to loan any cuts and the report for publication, without charge. Many editors took advantage of the offer, as seen in the Meany file for July and August 1890, but not the *Tacoma Record* (see Albert B. Bailey to *Seattle Press*, 21 July 1890, Meany Papers). The fact that Meany traveled by rail, rather than by coast-wise vessel, is made clear in the telegrams: S.R. Frazier, editor of the *Seattle Press*, to Meany, San Francisco, 23 and 30 June 1890.
20. Meany, Diary from 1 January 1885 to _____, entry for 21 September; Fessler, *Seattle Star*, 13 February 1930, clipping in *Edmond Stephen Meany, 1862-1935, Tributes, II.* Edmond S. Meany, Jr., corroborates the story, reporting that his father found it correct (see his Commentary on Floyd Fessler's articles in the *Seattle Star*, 3-15 February 1930). For statement on Hanlan, see *Encyclopedia Americana*, 1964 edition, vol. 23: 730.
21. The close bond with professor Johnson is revealed in the gift of a prize three-volume set of the *Works* of Charles Lamb, which Johnson gave to Meany on 28 December 1886, inscribed, "Dear Ed.—May these volumes inspire you to active thought and noble deed—and incidently recall our *old* relation of teacher and pupil."; E.S. Meany, Jr., to Frykman, 10 February 1975; *Seattle Post-Intelligencer*, 8 (quotation) and 11 August 1885. For evidence of his collecting and soliciting aid and advice, see: Thomas Howell to Meany, 10 September 1885; H.O. Chipman to Meany, 29 September 1885; Mrs. G.H. Collier to Meany, 6 January 1886; Henry S. Durden to Meany, 14 October 1886.
22. *Seattle Post-Intelligencer*, 29 July 1886; 26 July 1887 (quotation).
23. *Ibid.*, 27 June 1888.
24. *Ibid.*, 29 April, 1 September, and 3 and 19 December 1885; 3 March, 3 June, and 22 October 1886; Mrs. W.A. Jennings to Meany, 14 August 1885.
25. *Seattle Post-Intelligencer*, 13 November 1885; postcard, Committee of the Avon Club to Meany, 15 December 1885; editor of Shakespeariana to Meany, 8 October 1886; George O. Curme to Meany, 14 February and 4 April 1886.
26. E.S. Meany, Jr., Commentary on Floyd Fessler's articles on E.S. Meany in the *Seattle Star*, 3-15 February 1930. See commentary for February 9 quoting anecdote about serenading; *Seattle Post-Intelligencer*, 22 January 1884, establishes Meany's presence in Miss Hansee's Latin class, and Hansee's letter to Meany, 7 November 1887, establishes the age differential; Meany, Diary from 1 January 1885 to _____: entry for 1 January 1885 (quotation on Miss Hansee).
27. *Ibid.*, entries for 2, 4, 7, and 9 (quotation) January, and 21-27 September 1885.
28. Meany to Agnes M. Greene ["My Dear Friend Agnes"], 28 June 1886 (quotation "dearest friend"); Greene to Meany, 24 October 1886.
29. Meany to Greene, 7 December 1886 (possibly 9 December).
30. Meany to Greene, 21 March 1888 (quotation); Greene to Meany, 21 May 1888.
31. Hansee to Meany, 26 May, and 10 September 1887; and 17 September 1888 (quotation).

32. Hansee to Meany, 10 September 1887 (quotation "so fond of society"), and 26 May 1887 (quotations "the many pleasurable incidents," and "delightful recollections").
33. Hansee to Meany, 7 December 1888; *Seattle Post-Intelligencer*, 5 May 1889; interview with Edmond S. Meany, Jr., 6 March 1975, in possession of author; "Guest Book," Golden Wedding Anniversary, Mr. and Mrs. Dillis B. Ward, Seattle, Washington, 24 September 1913, in Dillis B. Ward Papers, University of Washington; Joseph T. Hazard, *Pioneer Teachers of Washington* (Seattle: Seattle Retired Teacher's Association, 1955), 71 (quotation), 72.
34. *Seattle Post-Intelligencer*, 5 May 1889; Fessler, *Seattle Star*, 13 February 1930, clipping in *Edmond Stephen Meany, 1862-1935, Tributes, II.* See map showing T. Mercer's land claim, as found in Norbert MacDonald, *Distant Neighbors: A Comparative History of Seattle and Vancouver* (Lincoln: University of Nebraska Press, 1987), 5.
35. Summons no. 9100, *L.H. Griffith Realty and Banking Company v. Alexander Begg and Edmond S. Meany*, 25 August 1890, Superior Court of King County, State of Washington, Meany Papers; *Seattle Post-Intelligencer*, 26 August 1890; N.H. Latimer to Meany, 24 October 1890, in which the writer hopes Meany "will keep punching Begg until something is done [about his debt]"; *Seattle City Directory for 1890*, II, 495.
36. Hazard, *Pioneer Teachers,* 71 (quotation); on Lizzie's mother-in-law, see Meany to Mrs. M.C. Jones, 21 June 1892, Meany Letterpress Book (1891-1893); on Birdie, see: Hansee to Meany, 30 November 1887; Walter V.L. Sur, Monterey County, California, to Ed [Meany], 3 August 1890; Eva, San Francisco, to "Dear Sister Maggie," [Margaret Meany, Edmond's mother], 5 August 1890; "Piggie" [Mable Ward] to "Dear old *country* folks" [Clarence C. Ward], 4 March 1891, William Dickey Papers, University of Washington; "Your Papa" [Dillis B. Ward] to Lizzie, 19 February 1892, Dickey Papers.
37. John C. Sundborg to Meany, 22 September 1890; Dillis B. Ward to Meany, 20 October 1890; *Who's Who in America*, vol. 18 (1934- 35), 1640, lists the name of the child as Elizabeth Lois.
38. Meany's public relations activities at the Northwestern Industrial Exposition and later events are discussed in chapter three; Lizzie Ward Meany to Clarence Ward, 17 February 1891, Dickey Papers; Dillis B. Ward, "From Salem, Oregon, to Seattle, Washington, in 1859," *Washington Historical Quarterly* 6 (April 1915): 100-106; Hazard, *Pioneer Teachers,* 71-72; *Brown Church Record Book, Seattle, 1885-1886*, Meany Papers; *Seattle Times*, 7 September 1889; Ward, "Private Journal," MSS. in Dillis B. Ward Papers. See especially entries for 1 January 1894 and 3 January 1896; *Seattle Post-Intelligencer*, 19 August 1881, 9 March 1883, 27 April 1884, 29 September 1886, 13 September 1887, and 3 May 1888; for the summation of Ward's career, see: Ward, "Private Journal," entries for 16 August, 8 and 30 November 1878.

Notes for Chapter Three

1. State of Washington, *Journal of the House*, first legislature, extra session (September 1890), 902. [Journals of the House and Senate hereafter will be cited as: *House Journal* or *Senate Journal*, with sessions and year]; N.G. Blalock to Meany, 16 September 1890, and Meany to "the Editor" 23 September 1890.
2. *Seattle Post-Intelligencer*, 26 September 1890; *Spokane Falls Spokesman*, 27 September 1890; *Proceedings of the Washington World's Fair Association, Mapping out the Work for the Great Chicago Exposition*, 10 October 1890, in World's Fair scrapbook, Meany Papers.
3. Blalock to Meany, 16 September 1890 (quotation); Meany to "the Editor," 23 September 1890; the World's Fair scrapbook contains numerous clippings of Meany's news releases; "Nelson Gales Blalock," *Dictionary of American Biography*, 2:349, 350.

4. The *Spokane Falls Chronicle*, 18-19 August 1890, and the Spokane Falls *Spokesman*, 25 and 27 September 1890, have relevant items; C.W. Robinson to Meany, 20 August 1890; Thomas W. Prosch to Meany, 6 September 1890 (quotation).
5. Newspaper clipping, unidentified paper, 16 September 1890, in World's Fair scrapbook; Prosch to Meany, 25 September 1890; On 10 October, Meany's estimate that the fair was successful and the King County exhibit well located appeared in the *Seattle Post-Intelligencer*. For frustrations, see *Kent Journal*, 30 September 1890, clippings in World's Fair scrapbook; Spokane *Spokesman*, 1 October 1890, in *ibid.*, and the *Spokane Globe*, 2 October 1890, *ibid.*
6. Spokane Falls *Spokesman*, 12 October 1890; Prosch to Meany, 25 September 1890 (quotation); *Seattle Telegraph*, 10 October 1890, clipping in World's Fair scrapbook; D.T. Denny to Meany, 18 October 1890.
7. *Seattle Post-Intelligencer*, 11 October 1890. Evidence of his work is summed up in Meany to Executive Committee of the Washington World's Fair Association, 14 October 1890.
8. *Seattle Post-Intelligencer*, 21 September, and 28 October 1890 (quotation).
9. Grant to Meany, 4 October 1890; J.R. Kinnear to Meany, 8 and 17 October 1890; G.E. DeSteiguer to Meany, 18 October 1890 (quotation).
10. Grant to Meany, 17 October 1890; Prosch to Meany, 18 October 1890; Clark Davis to Meany 22 October 1890 (quotation).
11. *Seattle Post-Intelligencer*, 30 October and 5 November 1890; *State of Washington: Barton's Legislative Hand-Book and Manual, 1891-1892*, 370-374; J.R. Kinnear to Meany, 8 November 1890.
12. Itinerary and expenses for his extensive travels October-December, are listed in Meany to Dr. N.G. Blalock, 30 March 1891; R.J. Neergaard to Meany, 5 December 1890. The *Seattle Post-Intelligencer*, 2 December 1890, contains a news item signed E.S.M. in which Meany reported creation of a board of trade and publicized the fair.
13. Meany to _____, 25 November 1890 is the circular letter asking legislators about the fair. Twenty-eight replies are found in the Meany Papers; Frank R. Spinning to Meany, 28 November 1890 (quotation). The Seattle politician Clarence B. Bagley expressed strong disapproval of a joint Washington-Oregon exhibit on the grounds that Oregon had already taken credit for many of Washington's products, see *Seattle Post-Intelligencer*, 25 October 1890.
14. *Seattle Post-Intelligencer*, 6 January 1891.
15. Telegram: the *Seattle Press* to Meany, 9 January 1891; Erastus Brainerd to Meany, 10 January, 1891.
16. The *Seattle Press*, 12, 13, 15, 16 January 1891, provided examples of Meany's reporting; Brainerd to Meany, 14 January (quotations), and 10 February 1891.
17. *Seattle Post-Intelligencer*, 20 January 1891 (quotations); *House Journal*, second legislature (1891), 80-81.
18. *Seattle Post-Intelligencer*, 5 February 1891 (quotation, "The Hero of the Staircase"); Charles A. Briggs to Meany, 20 January 1891 (quotation, "I see by the Mornings Post").
19. *Seattle Press*, 15 January 1891 (quotation); *House Journal*, second legislature (1891), 38, 49, 98; *Session Laws of the State of Washington, 1891*, 444-445; *Seattle Post-Intelligencer*, 7, 13, 18, and 19 January 1891; *Barton's Legislative Handbook and Manual, 1891-1892*, 304-305.
20. *Seattle Post-Intelligencer*, 7 and 15 January, 14 February 1891.
21. At least nine petitions from organized groups and mass meetings reflecting criticism of the proposed tax and appropriation are found in the Meany Papers for December 1890 and January and February 1891; *Seattle Post-Intelligencer*, 22 January 1891.

22. *Ibid.*, 14 February 1891.
23. *Ibid.*, 28 February 1891 (quotation); *Barton's Legislative Hand-Book and Manual, 1891-1892*, 373.
24. *Seattle Post-Intelligencer*, 28 February 1891 (quotation); *House Journal*, second legislature (1891), 451-452; *Barton's Legislative Hand-Book and Manual, 1891-1892*, 338, 374.
25. *House Journal*, second legislature (1891), 451-452, 657; *Seattle Post-Intelligencer*, 7 March 1891; *Session Laws of the State of Washington, Session of 1891*, 203-207.
26. Neal O. Hines, *Denny's Knoll: A History of the Metropolitan Tract of the University of Washington* (Seattle: University of Washington Press, 1980), chapters 1 and 2; Charles M. Gates, *The First Century at the University of Washington, 1861-1961* (Seattle: University of Washington Press, 1961), 49-50.
27. See letter quoted in Gates, *First Century*, 50-51; *Seattle Post-Intelligencer*, 23 and 28 January 1891. For establishing Meany's membership, see *House Journal*, second legislature (1891), 101, 105, and *Session Laws*, 1891, 436; *Senate Journal*, second legislature (1891), 104.
28. *Seattle Post-Intelligencer*, 28 January, 6 and 7 February 1891 (quotation).
29. *Ibid.*, 8 February 1891; Gates, *First Century*, 50-51.
30. *Seattle Press*, 9 February 1891.
31. *Seattle Post-Intelligencer*, 24 February 1891, (editorial quoting Meany); *House Journal*, second legislature (1891), 372, 549; *Barton's Legislative Hand-Book and Manual, 1891-1892*, 310-311; *Senate Journal*, second legislature (1891), 358, 460, 469- 471; *Seattle Post-Intelligencer*, 4 March 1891; *Session Laws of the State of Washington, Session of 1891*, 229-235.
32. Robert C. Nesbit, *"He Built Seattle," A Biography of Judge Thomas Burke* (Seattle: University of Washington Press, 1961), 343-346.
33. *Seattle Post-Intelligencer*, 7 January and 18(quotation), 19, 27 February 1891.
34. *Ibid.*, 9, 14, 17, 18, 20 (quotation) March 1891.
35. *Seattle Press-Times*, 10 March 1891 (quotation); Meany's political relationship with Grant is shown in letters from Grant to Meany 27 and 28 January 1891; *Seattle Post-Intelligencer* 28 January 1891. The legislative history of the bill is found in the *House Journal*, second legislature (1891), 115, 210, and 653, and in *Session Laws of the State of Washington, 1891*, 364-365.
36. *Seattle Post-Intelligencer*, 12 April 1888; F.J. Splitstone, *Orcas-Gem of the San Juans* (Bellingham: Cox Brothers, 1954), 41, 43, 53, 77-78; S.R.S. Gray to Meany, 21 October 1890; *Seattle Post-Intelligencer*, 19 March 1891.
37. "Waterville, Washington," *West Shore* 16 (28 June 1890): 818; "The Metropolis of the Big Bend," *ibid.*, (12 July 1890): 873.
38. Charles Liftchild to Meany, 23 November (quotation, "the outfit"), 4 and 30 December 1890, and 19 March 1891; *Big Bend Empire* (Waterville), 27 November 1890, 30 April 1891 (quotation "The Coming City"), 14 May 1891; Meany discussed both the World's Fair and the "Waterville Land and Improvement Company" and its promotion in the *Spokesman* (Spokane Falls), 16 and 20 December 1890, 1 January 1891.
39. Fred Ward to Meany, 5 and 8 December 1890; A.H. Foote to P.E. Berry, 5 December 1890, Meany Papers; J.D. Bassett to Meany, 26 March 1891.
40. Liftchild to Meany, 19 and 23 March 1891; Charles A. Briggs to Meany, 19 March 1891; Meany to Briggs, 15 May 1891 (quotations).
41. *Big Bend Empire* (Waterville), 9 and 23 July 1891; C.T. Conover to Meany, 9 December 1891, 27 January 1892 (quotation); Meany to Conover, 30 January 1892, Meany Letterpress Book (1891-1893).

42. *Seattle Post-Intelligencer*, 28 March 1891; notes by E.S. Meany in Meany Letterpress Book (1890-1892) on letters written to Ezra Meeker, E.C. Ferguson, and N.G. Blalock, 30 March 1891, asking their views on the nature of Washington's participation in the exposition. Also found in *ibid.*, are Meany to George Bethune, George Pfunder, and C.H. Ballard, 31 March 1891; press release, May [1891] featuring an interview with Geo. R. Davis in Edmond S. Meany, "Washington's Fair Commission" (Press releases, Washington World's fair Commission Scrapbook, 1893), Northwest Collection, University of Washington Library; *Seattle Post-Intelligencer*, 29 May 1891.
43. *Seattle Press-Times*, 19 May 1891; *Seattle Post-Intelligencer*, 26 May 1891; "Ezra Meeker," *Dictionary of American Biography*, 12: 495, 496; *Session Laws of the State of Washington, Session of 1891*, 203, 204; Meany, "Many Willing to Work," press release, 15 June 1891, in Washington World's Fair Commission Scrapbook; Meany, "Will Carry Exhibit Free," press release, 3 July 1891, in *ibid.*; Ezra Meeker to N.G. Blalock, 30 May 1891; Meeker to C.G. Austin, 4 June 1891; Meeker to G.A. Snowden, 11 June 1891; Meeker to W.H. Gilstrap, 12 June 1891; all are found in Ezra Meeker's World's Fair Letterpress Book, Meany Papers.
44. Meeker to Blalock, 30 May, 27 and 30 June 1891, *ibid.*
45. Meany to J.C. Fisher, 21 July 1891, Meany Letterpress Book (1890-1892); Blalock to Meany, 26 July 1891; Meeker to Blalock, 27 July 1891, Meeker's World's Fair Letterpress Book; *Seattle Press-Times*, 10 August 1891; F.G. Grant to Meany, 11 August 1891.
46. *Seattle Post-Intelligencer*, 23 August 1891.
47. *Ibid.*, 6 September 1891.
48. The *Seattle Press-Times*, 9 September 1891, stated that Meany and his family would move to Walla Walla shortly, but he did not move the family until 26 October as reported in *The Daily Statesman* (Walla Walla), 27 October 1891; quotation in Meany to J.W. Dodge, 11 September 1891, Meany Letterpress Book (1891-1893).
49. Meany to F.J. Grant, 12 September 1891, *ibid.* Grant, replying to an earlier letter from Meany on the same subject, assured Meany that the attacks were the result of vindictiveness, that Meany had a perfect right to his position, and that he and publisher L.S.J. Hunt supported Meany (Grant to Meany, 11 August 1891); Meany later wrote another anxious letter to E.B. Piper, 1 October 1891, Meany Letterpress Book (1891-1893), which contains the quote.
50. *The Daily Statesman* (Walla Walla), 21 October 1891; Blalock to Meany, 22 October 1891 (quotations).
51. *The Daily Statesman*, 27 October 1891; Blalock to Meany, 22 October 1891. For publicity releases see Meany's Washington World's Fair Commission Scrapbook. For evidence on articles and speeches see William E. Smythe to Meany, 17 December 1891; Meany "The Washington Fair Building," *Frank Leslie's* (magazine), 26 December 1891, in World's Fair scrapbook, Meany Papers; and Meany to George R. Davis, 15 July 1892, Meany Letterpress Book, Assistant to Executive Commissioner (1892). On the state board of trade: W.T. Clark to Meany, 11 November 1891; Meany to Clark, 14 November 1891, Meany Letterpress Book (1890-1892); Clark to Meany, 13 January 1892; Meany to J.W. Dodge, 12 January 1892, Meany Letterpress Book (1890-1892). On the building: W.A. Ritchie to Meany, 30 November 1891, and Bullard Haywood to Meany, 11 December 1891; Warren P. Skillings to Meany, 25 January 1892. On exhibits, examples include Meany to E.W. Hilgard, 16 March 1892, Meany Letterpress Book (1890-1892), and Meany to A.L. Rogers, 19 May 1892, Meany Letterpress Book, Assistant to Executive Commissioner (1892). On relations with Chicago, see Meany to Major M.P. Handy, 25 April 1892, Meany Letterpress Book (1890-1892).

52. The souvenir book will be discussed in more detail in chapter four; Meany to D.K. McDonald, Lincoln County Assessor, 18 March 1892, Meany Letterpress Book (1890-1892); Meany wrote to fourteen commissioners on 19 March 1892, asking them to inquire whether their county officials had gathered the statistics (see these letters in *ibid.*); W.L. LaFollette to N.G. Blalock, 22 September 1892; Meany to Percy W. Rochester, 24 September 1892; Meany to Blalock, 6 October 1892; Meany to M.A. Rush, 7 October 1892; Meany to editor of *The Courier* (Dayton, Washington), 13 October 1892 (example of the form letter mailed to every newspaper in the state); and Meany to Rush, 26 October 1892, all found in Meany Letterpress Book, Assistant to Executive Commissioner (1892).
53. The formal title of the institution was Agricultural College, Experiment Station, and School of Science; Meany, speech at Pullman, Washington, 4 July 1892, MSS, pp. 1-2, Meany papers. Festivities are described in *The Spokesman* (Spokane), 5 July 1892.
54. Meany speech at Pullman, 4 July 1892, p.3.
55. *Ibid.*, p.4.
56. *Ibid.*, pp. 5-11 (quotation p. 10).
57. Meany to Blalock, 12, 15, and 26 September 1892, Meany Letterpress Book, Assistant to Executive Commissioner (1892); Meany to Blalock, 5 November, 5 December 1892, *ibid.* (1892-1894); Meany to John R. Reavis, 31 October 1892, *ibid.*; Meany feared that Dr. Blalock would not call a commission meeting so he quietly started a movement among members to call a meeting. See Meany to C.B. Hopkins, 5 December 1892, and several identical letters sent to other commissioners that same day, Meany Letterpress Book (1891-1892).
58. Meany to Charles V. Piper, 14 December 1892, Meany Letterpress Book (1891-1893); Meany to W.C. Jones, 8 December 1892, *ibid.*; Meany to William LaFollette, 5 and 6 (quotation) December 1892, *ibid.*; Meany to Warren I. Hastings, 14 December 1892, *ibid.*
59. *Seattle Press-Times*, 15 December 1892 (quotation "docked"); *The Spokesman*, 16 December 1892; *Seattle Post-Intelligencer*, 16 December 1892; Meany to William LaFollette, 6 December 1892 (quotation), Meany Letterpress Book (1891-1893).
60. Meany, notes on Thomas Mercer Meany, 15 July 1928; *Seattle Press-Times*, 15 December 1892 (quotation "superior officer"); *Seattle Post-Intelligencer*, 16 and 17 December 1892; *Seattle Press*, 12 January 1891 (quotation on Dr. Calhoun).

Notes for Chapter Four

1. Meany to Fred J. Grant, 11 September 1891, Meany Letterpress Book (1891-1893); Meany to John B. Allen, 29 January 1892(quotation), *ibid.*
2. Meany to Allen, 27 February 1892, *ibid.*
3. Meany to Allen, 7 April 1892, *ibid.*
4. Meany to Mrs. Mary Wager-Fisher, 28 April 1892, *ibid.*
5. *Seattle Post-Intelligencer*, 10, 13, 20 March 1892; Meany to McGraw, 16 March 1892 (quotation), Meany Letterpress Book (1891-1893).
6. Meany to S.L. Maxwell, 2 April 1892, *ibid.*; Meany to Allen, 7 April 1892 (quotation), *ibid.*; Allen to Meany, 25 July 1892.
7. Meany to S.B. Conover, 29 February 1892, Meany Letterpress Book (1891-1893); Meany to Trustees of the Seattle Chamber of Commerce, 7 March 1892, *ibid.*; Enoch A. Bryan, *Historical Sketch of the State College of Washington, 1890-1925* (Pullman: Alumni and Associated Students, 1928), 75, 517-519; George A. Frykman, *Creating the People's University: Washington State University, 1890-1990* (Pullman: Washington State University Press, 1990), 44.

8. Meany to Trustees of the Seattle Chamber of Commerce, 7 March 1892, Meany Letterpress Book (1891-1893).
9. Meany to Thomas W. Prosch, 5 October 1892, *ibid.*; *First Biennial Report of the State Board of Horticulture of the State of Washington for the Years 1891-2* (Olympia: O.C. White, State Printer, 1893), *passim; Second Biennial Report . . . 1893-4, passim: Third Biennial Report . . . 1895-6, passim.*
10. *Seattle Post-Intelligencer*, 7, 10, 12, 21 August and 25, 26 October 1892; *Seattle Press-Times*, 25 October 1892.
11. Meany to Will H. Perry, 25 October 1892, Meany Letterpress Book (1891-1893); Meany expressed gratitude to the following for their praise of McGraw in the *Post-Intelligencer*, 25 October 1892: W.P. Boyd, Henry Yesler, and Fred Grant, see Meany Letterpress Book (1891-1893). His own statement in praise of McGraw, including the quotations, is found in the *Post-Intelligencer*, 25 October 1892.
12. *Ibid.*, 11 and 16 November 1892; *Barton's Legislative Handbook and Manual, 1893-1894*, 358.
13. Meany to Charles V. Piper, 7 November 1892 (quotation), Meany Letterpress Book (1891-1893); Bryan, *Historical Sketch,* 4 (quotation on patronage).
14. Meany to O.B. Johnson, 11 November 1892, Meany Letterpress Book, (1891-1893); on 11 November Meany addressed requests to eight public figures, including McGraw and Gilman, in support of Piper, *ibid.;* Meany to E.P. Heliker, 11 November 1892, *ibid.*, (quotation "a loyal young man."); Meany to Board of Regents, Washington Agricultural College, 11 November 1892, *ibid.*; Meany to Piper, 14 December 1892 (quotation, "abundance" and "true friends"), *ibid.*
15. Bryan, *Historical Sketch,* 94 (quotation), 240-241; Meany to Board of Regents, Washington Agricultural College, 11 November 1892, Meany Letterpress Book (1891-1893); John W. Heston to Meany, 21 February 1893.
16. Ernest L. Newell to Meany, 25 November 1892; Meany to Newell, 14 December 1892 (quotation), Meany Letterpress Book (1891-1893); *Spokane Spokesman*, 17 December 1892; on Johnson's tenure as editor and his editorial practices, see Robert Allen Henderson, "The *Spokesman-Review*, 1883-1900: A Mirror to the History of Spokane" (Ph.D. diss., Washington State University, 1967), 17-24, 205; John W. Heston to Meany, 21 February 1893; Meany to Heston, 24 March 1893 (quotation on desiring a fair trial for Newell), Meany Letterpress Book (1891-1893); Jonathan Edwards, *An Illustrated History of Spokane County, State of Washington* (W.H. Lever, publisher, 1900), 205.
17. Spokane *Spokesman*, 4 (quotation on "Pullman college"), 17, 19, and 22 December 1892; Meany to Joseph French Johnson, 6 December 1892, Meany Letterpress Book (1891-1893).
18. The following Meany letters establish his role as chairman: to C.F. Kellar, 7 December 1892, and to J.G. Megler, 8 December 1892 (quotation "nice compliment"), Meany Letterpress Book (1891-1893); Assistant to Executive Commissioner (1892-1894); to J.M. Frink, 26 December 1892, and to J.S. Sallee, 26 December 1892, Meany Letterpress Book (1891-1893); *Seattle Press-Times*, 5 December 1892; Spokane *Spokesman*, 22 December 1892 (quotation on aiming to be controlling power).
19. *Ibid.*
20. *Ibid.*, 27 (quotations on the press), 30 December 1892.
21. Robert C. Nesbit, *"He Built Seattle," A Biography of Judge Thomas Burke* (Seattle: University of Washington Press, 1961), 345-347; Claudius O. Johnson, "George Turner: Part I," *Pacific Northwest Quarterly* 34 (July 1943):252; *Seattle Post-Intelligencer*, 17 January 1893; Edmond S. Meany, *History of the State of Washington* (New York: The Macmillan Company, 1909), 307-308; *Seattle Post-Intelligencer*, 20 and 27 January,

5 February 1893. The 101st ballot is found in *Barton's Legislative Handbook and Manual, 1893-1894*, 379.

22. Spokane *Spokesman*, 17, 20 (quotation), and 22 January 1893; Bryan, *Historical Sketch*, 75-104.
23. Spokane *Spokesman*, 28 January 1893; *Seattle Post-Intelligencer*, 2 March 1893; *Senate Journal, Third Legislature, 1893*, 473, 474 (quotation). The full report may be found in Bryan, *Historical Sketch*, Appendix C.
24. *Seattle Post-Intelligencer*, 5 January 1893.
25. *Seattle Press-Times*, 2 February 1893; *Yakima Herald*, 2 February 1893; *Seattle Post-Intelligencer*, 4 February 1893.
26. *Senate Journal, Third Legislature, 1893*, 217; *House Journal, Third Legislature, 1893*, 321.
27. *Seattle Press-Times*, 9 February 1893; Spokane *Spokesman*, 10 February 1893; *Seattle Post-Intelligencer*, 3 February 1893.
28. *Ibid.*, 4, 5 (quotation) February 1891.
29. *Tacoma Sunday Ledger*, 12 February 1891.
30. Progress of the hearings can be traced in the *Seattle Post-Intelligencer*, 12, 14, 16, 22, and 26 February 1893; *Senate Journal,. . . 1893*, 399 (quotation).
31. *Ibid.*, 395, 396, and 413; *House Journal,. . . 1893*, 573, 591, 592; *Seattle Post-Intelligencer*, 2 March 1893 (quotations); *Session Laws of the State of Washington, Session of 1893*, 70-72.
32. *Seattle Post-Intelligencer*, 12 March 1893; Spokane *Spokesman*, 4 January 1893 (quotation on "Washington Needs a University"). The statement from the *Tacoma Ledger* is reprinted in the *Seattle Post-Intelligencer*, 1 March 1893 (quotation).
33. Charles M. Gates, *The First Century at the University of Washington, 1861-1961* (Seattle: University of Washington Press, 1961), 50-55.
34. *Seattle Post-Intelligencer*, 9 and 19 February, 7 March 1893.
35. E.S. Meany, Jr., Commentary on Floyd Fessler's articles in the *Seattle Star*, 3-15 February, 1930; *House Journal, . . . 1893*, 552; State of Washington, Third Legislature, 3rd Regular Sess., *House Bill 470* (quotation), Washington State University Library. That the campus held 350 acres is corroborated in Gates, *First Century*, 46-47.
36. *House Journal,. . . 1893*, 552; *Seattle Post-Intelligencer*, 7 March 1893. Discussion of the modifications in Meany's bill is based on a comparison of the original bill, *House Bill 470*, and the text of the law as found in *Session Laws, . . . 1893*, 293-300.
37. *House Journal, . . . 1893*, 765-766; *Senate Journal, . . . 1893*, 628; *Seattle Post-Intelligencer*, 5 and 12 March 1893; *House Journal, . . . 1893*, 709; *Session Laws,. . . 1893*, 456-459.
38. *Seattle Post-Intelligencer*, 12 March (quotation on "the most substantial manner") and 16 March 1893 (Meany's "delight").
39. Meany, *History of the State of Washington*, 291.
40. *Ibid.*; *House Journal, . . .1893*, 237, 262; *Session Laws,. . .1893*, 50-51.
41. *House Journal, . . .1893*, 504, 703, 774; *Session Laws, . . .1893*, 254-263; *Tacoma Daily Ledger*, 12 March 1893; *Session Laws, . . .1893*, 456-457; Frederick E. Bolton and Thomas W. Bibb, *History of Education in Washington*, Bulletin No. 9 (U.S. Department of the Interior, Office of Education, 1934), 279-280, 313-314; J. Orin Oliphant, *History of the State Normal School at Cheney, Washington* (Spokane: Inland-American Printing Company, 1924), 35-46.
42. References to "pruning" and "pruning knife" are found, respectively, in *Tacoma Sunday Ledger*, 12 March 1893, and *Seattle Press-Times*, 18 March 1893, and in Meany, *History of the State of Washington*, 292 (quotation); Oliphant, *Cheney*, 36 (quotation from the *Post-Intelligencer*).

43. Spokane *Spokesman*, 10 February 1893 (quotation on "versatile Mr. Meany"); Carlos A. Schwantes, *Radical Heritage: Labor, Socialism, and Reform in Washington and British Columbia, 1885-1917* (Seattle: University of Washington Press, 1979), 135-136; *House Journal, . . .1893*, 315- 321; Spokane *Spokesman*, 10 February 1893 (quotation "Representative Meany"); *Seattle Post-Intelligencer*, 10 February 1893; *Tacoma Daily Ledger*, 10 February 1893 (quotation "sat down . . . on Mr. Meany," and "a tool of corrupt capitalists and corporations").
44. Schwantes, 49-50; *Seattle Post-Intelligencer*, 14 February 1893 (quotation); *House Journal, . . . 1893*, 358; W.H. Middleton to Meany, 6 March 1893.
45. Spokane *Review*, 11 March 1893 (quotation "the most important work"); Meany to J.H. St. Lawrence, 22 March 1893 (quotations "placed under," "in coming out," and "satisfactorily proven"), Meany Letterpress Book (1891-1893).
46. *Seattle Post-Intelligencer*, 20, 22, March 1893; Percy W. Rochester to Meany, 1 April 1893, in G.V. Calhoun Letterpress Book (9 March-24 April 1893), vol. 5 of Executive Commissioner's World's Fair Commission Letterpress Books, University of Washington.
47. Meany to Calhoun, 5 and 22 April 1893, Meany Letterpress Book, Assistant to Executive Commissioner (1892-1894); *The State of Washington: A Brief History of the Discovery, Settlement, and Organization of Washington, "The Evergreen State," as well as a Compilation of Official Statistics Showing the Material Development of the State of Washington up to Date* (Tacoma: Washington World's Fair Commission, 1893), 4 (although both Elwood Evans and Meany were listed as editors, Meany actually performed all the editorial work); Meany to William L. LaFollette, 10 April 1893 (quotation), Meany Letterpress Book (1891-1893).
48. *Tacoma Daily Ledger*, 25 (first three quotes) and 27 (final two quotes) April 1893.
49. *The State of Washington*, *passim*; Meany also wrote G.V. Calhoun's *Final report of the Washington World's Fair Commission, 1894* (Olympia: O.C. White, State Printer, 1894); Meany to Alfred Dickey, 2 April 1894, Meany Letterpress Book, Assistant to the Executive Commissioner (1892-1894).
50. *Tacoma Daily Ledger*, 3 May 1893; Meany to P.C. Kaufman, 7 May 1893, Meany Letterpress Book (1891-1893); Meany to L.R. Grimes, 13 May 1893, *ibid.*; The *New York World's* statement was reprinted in the *Tacoma Daily Ledger*, 12 April 1893 (quotations).
51. *Tacoma Daily Ledger*, 26 May 1893; Meany to C.A. Hughes, 23 May 1893, Meany Letterpress Book (1891-1893); Meany to Manager, *Daily Dispatch* (Chicago), 19 May 1893, *ibid.*, Assistant to Executive Commissioner (1892-1894). E.S. Meany, Jr., Commentary on Floyd Fessler's articles in the *Seattle Star*, 3-15 February 1930 describes the information booth, the newspaper room, and the work of his mother at the *Post-Intelligencer* booth. The number of people registered by 21 October was 13,760, according to Meany to Mrs. Martha A. Griggs, 21 October 1894, Meany Letterpress Book, Assistant to the Executive Commissioner (1892-1894).
52. Meany, "Washington at the Fair," 8 May 1893 (quotation), found in Meany, Washington's World's Fair Commission Scrapbook (34 mounted Commission press releases), Northwest Collection, University of Washington Library.
53. Meany to Joseph Wheelock, 1 June 1893, Meany Letterpress Book (1891-1893); Meany, "Snapshots in the New Northwest," *The Graphic* (Chicago, 15 July 1893), clipping in untitled scrapbook on the World's Fair, Meany Papers; Meany, "The Home of this New State at the World's Fair," *The National Builder* (Chicago, August 1893), clipping in *ibid.*; [J. Ronald Todd], "Bibliography of Edmond Stephen Meany," (1935 Mimeograph, University of Washington Library), page 24 contains a long list of press releases, "all of which were published in one or more papers."

54. Meany, "Beating the Whole World," 21 October 1893, in Meany, Washington World's Fair Commission Scrapbook; "Bibliography of Edmond Stephen Meany," lists Meany as author of "Washington, the New Evergreen State at the World's Fair," *American Tid-Bits*, (Chicago, September 1893); Meany to P.C. Kaufman, 3 April 1894, Meany Letterpress Book, Assistant to the Executive Commissioner (1892-1894). A comparison of the press releases in Meany's Washington World's Fair Commission Scrapbook with material Meany cited in "Beating the Whole World," as taken from the *American Tid-Bits* article confirms his coup.
55. Meany, "Beating the Whole World," Washington World's Fair Commission Scrapbook (quotations); Meany to Mrs. Martha A. Griggs, 21 October 1894, Meany Letterpress Book, Assistant to the Executive Commissioner (1892-1894); the effect of the gold rushes on Seattle and, hence, Washington, may be studied in Alexander Norbert MacDonald, "Seattle's Economic Development, 1880-1910" (Ph.D. diss., University of Washington, 1959) and in Dorothy Johansen, *Empire of the Columbia*, 2nd edition (New York: Harper and Row, 1967), 370-371.
56. E.S. Meany, Jr., Commentary on Floyd Fessler's articles in the *Seattle Star*, 3-15 February 1930 reveals that Governor McGraw commissioned Meany to close the Washington exhibits and return them to the state; Meany to Joseph Painter, 27 January 1894, Meeker World's Fair Letterpress Book (1891)(quotation "one single dollar"), Meany Letters, 1893-1894 ; Meany to Alfred Dicky, 2 April 1894 (quotation "frightful Democratic times"), Meany Letterpress Book, Assistant to the Executive Commissioner (1892-1894); Meany to P.B. Groat, 20 January 1894, Meeker World's Fair Letterpress Book (1891), Meany Letters, 1893-1894.
57. Meany to L.R. Grimes, 27 January 1894, Meany Letterpress Book, Assistant to the Executive Commissioner (1892-1894); Meany to Marshall Field, 20 January 1894, Meeker World's Fair Letterpress Book (1891), Meany Letters, 1893-1894; Meany to E.C. Ayer, 23 January 1894, *ibid.*; Meany to Messrs. Lester, Lawrence, and Miller, 25 January 1894, *ibid.*; Meany to Charles V. Piper, 2 April 1894 (quotations), *ibid.*
58. Meany to the Honorable Board of University Regents, 12 February 1894, Meeker World's Fair Letterpress Book (1891), Meany Letters, 1893-1894; Meany to F.J. Grant, 13 and 15 April 1894, *ibid.*; eulogy to Margaret Meany in Rev. Sidney H. Buchham, "A Triumphant Life," pamphlet (n.d., circa 1945-1946), Northwest Collection, University of Washington Library; Meany to L.R. Grimes, 24 April 1894, Meeker World's Fair Letterpress Book (1891), Meany Letters (1893-1894); Meany to W.B. McAuley, 27 May 1894, *ibid.*; Meany to William D. Wood, 28 June 1894, University of Washington Regents Letterpress Book (1893-1894), University of Washington Special Collections.
59. Frederick E. Bolton, "A History of the University of Washington, 1855-1953," 2 vols.(unpublished MSS): I, 4 of preface (quotation), University of Washington Special Collections; Gates, *First Century*, 57.
60. *Seattle Post-Intelligencer*, 18 May, 18 June, 19 and 23 August 1894; Meany to Board of Regents, 13 June 1894, University of Washington Regents inter-office correspondence (1880-1939), University of Washington Special Collections; Meany to William D. Wood, 28 June 1894, University of Washington Regents Letterpress Book (1893-1894): Meany, "The University of Washington in A.D. 1900," *The Pacific Wave* IV (August 1894), 3-5 (quotation).
61. Meany to Thomas M. Gatch, 23 October 1894, University of Washington Regents Letterpress Book (1894-1895); Meany, "Report to the Honorable Board of Regents of the University of Washington, 14 November 1894," University of Washington Board of Regents inter-office correspondence (1880-1939).

62. *Seattle Post-Intelligencer*, 19 August 1894.
63. "Secure a Home in Brooklyn," *ibid.* (advertisement), 23 December 1900; Meany to John Hudson, 18 October 1894, Meany Letterpress Book (1894-1895); Clarence B. Bagley, *History of Seattle from the Earliest Settlement to the Present Time),* 3 vols. (Chicago: S.J. Clarke Publishing Company, 1916), II: 564, 570; Meany to William L. LaFollette, 10 December 1894, Meany Letterpress Book (1894-1895); additional letters to John T. Blackburn and Amos T. Shawn, 8 December 1894, *ibid.*, and D.E. Lesh, 12 and 18 December 1894, *ibid.*; Meany to R.H. Thompson, 14 December 1906, *ibid.*; Meany's property indebtedness is found in Meany Papers, file 106.

Notes for Chapter Five

1. *Seattle Post-Intelligencer*, 6 January 1895.
2. Meany to J.R. Hayden, 25 January 1895, Interoffice Correspondence (1880-1939), Regents Papers, University of Washington Records Center.
3. Meany to Hayden, 21,24 February and 4 March 1895, *ibid.*; *House Journal, Fourth Legislature, 1895*, 283-284, 624; Charles M. Gates, *The First Century at the University of Washington* (Seattle: University of Washington Press, 1961), 56- 57.
4. Meany to Hayden, 21 February 1895, Interoffice Correspondence (1880-1939), Regents Papers; telegram, Meany to Hayden, 27 February 1895 (quotation "euchered"), *ibid.*; *Seattle Post-Intelligencer*, 28 February, 1 and 6 March, 1 April 1895; Meany to Hayden, 4 March 1895 (quotation "good strong report"), Interoffice Correspondence (1880-1939), Regents Papers. A synopsis of the report was published in the *Seattle Post-Intelligencer*, 6 March 1895.
5. Norman H. Clark, *The Dry Years: Prohibition and Social Change in Washington* (Seattle: University of Washington Press, 1965), 56; *Seattle Post-Intelligencer*, 1 April 1895; *Session Laws, 1895*, 134.
6. Meany to Hayden, 2, 4, 6, 12 (quotation), and 13 March 1895, Interoffice Correspondence (1880-1939), Regents Papers.
7. Hayden to Meany, 12 March 1895, *ibid.*; Meany to Hayden, 12 March 1895 (quotation), *ibid.*
8. Gates, *First Century*, 56-57 (quotation of Gowey; quotation from Meany about King County delegation); *Seattle Post-Intelligencer* 1 April 1895; Meany to Hayden, 4 March 1895, Interoffice Correspondence (1880-1939), Regents Papers.
9. *Seattle Post-Intelligencer*, 2 April 1895; Meany to George K. Hazlitt and Company, 4 April 1895 (quotation "the tedious game" and "the new district"), in Meany Letterpress Book (1894-1895); Meany to Watson C. Squire, 9 August 1895, *ibid.*
10. Meany, "The Student's Alma Mater," *The Pacific Wave* 5 (May 1895): 30, 31.
11. Meany to J.B. Allen, 29 January 1892 (quotation), Meany Letterpress Book (1891-1893); Meany to W.H. Doolittle, 29 December 1894, *ibid.*(1894-1895); Meany to B.E. Fernow, 16 August 1894, University of Washington Regents Letterpress Book (1894-1895); Meany to C.S. Sargent, 17 April 1893, Meany Letterpress Book (1891-1893).
12. Meany to Hazard Stevens, 27 November 1894, Meany Letterpress Book (1894-1895); Meany to Henry H. Kitson, 27 November 1894 (quotation), *ibid.*; Meany to A.R. Spofford, 6 December 1894, *ibid.*
13. Meany states that Hazard Stevens had agreed to assist the statue project but the evidence is missing. See Meany to Kitson, 30 December 1894, *ibid.*; Meany to Stevens, 26 July 1895, *ibid.*, provides negative evidence; Meany to Stevens, 18 July 1895 (quotation), *ibid.* On collecting see: Meany to Commissioner of Indian Affairs, 18 July

1895, *ibid.*, and Meany to A.S. Clark, 3 August 1895, *ibid.* On prospects for the statue after the depression, see Meany to Kitson, 3 August 1895, *ibid.* For a characterization of Hazard Stevens as his father's biographer, see Kent D. Richards, *Isaac I. Stevens, Young Man in a Hurry*, (Provo: Brigham Young University Press, 1979), xii.

14. Meany to A.R. Spofford, 6 December 1894, Meany Letterpress Book (1894-1895); Meany to H.H. Spalding (son of the missionary), 15 December 1894, *ibid.*; Meany to Kitson, 30 December 1894 (quotation), *ibid.*; Meany to W.D. Lyman, 10 December 1894, *ibid.*; Meany used Nixon's "portrait" of Whitman in his *History of the State of Washington* (New York: The Macmillan Company, 1909), opposite p. 127, and included Nixon's footnoted rationalization on pp. 127, 128.
15. Meany to John F. Gowey, 18 March 1895, University of Washington Regents Letterpress Book (1895-1897); Meany to Gowey, 13 July 1895, Meany Letterpress Book (1894-1895), quotation.
16. Meany to David Starr Jordan, 25 June 1895, *ibid.*
17. Meany to Jordan, 25 June (quotation), 23 July, and 9 October 1895, *ibid.*
18. Meany to O.L. Elliott, 18 July 1895, *ibid.*
19. Meany to Mary Sheldon Barnes, 16 July 1895, Meany Letterpress Book (1894-1895); Meany to Jordan, 23 July 1895, *ibid.*; Meany to Herbert Baxter Adams, 16 July, 1 August 1895, *ibid.*; Meany to William Carey Jones, 1 August 1895, *ibid.*; Meany to A.R. Spofford, 26 July 1895, *ibid.*; Meany to James G. Swan, 26 July 1895, *ibid.*
20. Meany to W.K. Ealing, 13 July 1895, Meany Letterpress Book (1894-1895); Meany to James Wickersham, 26 July and 5 August 1895, *ibid.*; Meany to Elwood Evans, 26 July 1895, *ibid.*; Meany to Clarence L. Andrews, 26 July 1895, *ibid.*; Meany to W.C. Squire, 26 July and 9 August 1895 (quotation), *ibid.*
21. Meany to A.A. Lindsley, 11 August 1895, *ibid.*; Meany to James R. Hayden, 18 August 1895, Interoffice Correspondence, 1880-1939, Regents' Papers; Meany to Hazard Stevens, 24 August 1895 (quotation "earliest territorial period"), Meany Letterpress Book (1894-1895).
22. Meany to Watson C. Squire, 7 September 1895, *ibid.*
23. Frederick James Grant Memorial Association, Minute Book (1895-1896), 1-10, University of Washington Special Collections; Meany to Mary Sheldon Barnes, 10 and 12 August 1895, Meany Letterpress Book (1894-1895), and 7 June 1896, *ibid.*,(1896-1899); Meany to W.C. Squire, 9 August 1895, *ibid.*; Meany to Herbert Baxter Adams, 11 October 1895, *ibid.*, (1894-1895).
24. Meany to Mary Sheldon Barnes, 10 and 12 August 1895, *ibid.*; [Barnes] "General Syllabus for Course in History of the Pacific Slope, 1894," Meany Papers; Meany to Barnes, 11 October 1895, Meany Letterpress Book (1894-1895); Meany to C.W. Bowen, 11 October 1895, *ibid.*; Meany to H.B. Adams, 11 October 1895, *ibid.*; Meany repeated the familiar story of family obligations to David Starr Jordan, 7 June 1896, Meany Letterpress Book (1896-1899).
25. Classbooks of Edmond Stephen Meany for "Forestry" course of 1896, and "Development of Washington" course of 1896, Meany Papers; Meany to B.E. Fernow, 8 June 1896, Meany Letterpress Book (1896-1899). The lecturer title is recorded in the *Fourth Biennial Report of the Board of Regents of the University of Washington to the Governor of Washington*, 1896 (Olympia: O.C. White, State Printer, 1896), 5.
26. Classbook of Edmond Stephen Meany, for "Development of Washington" course of 1896. He sent syllabi for both courses to David Starr Jordan on 7 June 1896, Meany Letterpress Book (1896-1899); earlier on 18 March 1896 he had sent them to several regents. See Meany to David Kellogg, 18 March 1896, University of Washington Regents Letterpress Book (1895-1897); Meany to Barnes, 8 February 1896 (quotation), Meany Letterpress Book (1896-1899).

27. *Ibid.*, (Meany quotation); *The Pacific Wave* I (23 April 1896): 8 (quotation).
28. Classbook of Edmond Stephen Meany [1896], "Books Loaned,"; F.E.B. Smith, "The Library," *The Pacific Wave* I (May 1896):77; *Fourth Biennial Report of the Board of Regents. . .1896*, 18, 30, 31; Meany to Mark W. Harrington, 22 June 1896 (quotation), University of Washington Regents Letterpress Book (1896-1899).
29. Meany to J.M. Hitt, 8 May 18[96], Meany Letterpress Book (1896-1899); Meany to David Starr Jordan, 7 June 1896, *ibid.*; Meany, "History of our own State in the Schools," speech delivered to the Washington State Teacher's Association, Spokane, 5 July 1896 (quotation from p.1), Meany Papers.
30. *Ibid.*, quotation p.5.
31. Meany to H.R. Cox, 6 July 1896, Meany Letterpress Book (1896-1899); Meany to H.J. Langfitt, 31 July 1896 (quotation), *ibid.*; Meany to Susan Lord Currier, 12 October 1896, *ibid.*
32. Classbooks of Edmond Stephen Meany, "Development of Washington," 1896-1897, and "Forestry," 1896-1897.
33. Meany to H.H. Kitson, 8 February, 12 May, 12 October 1896, Meany Letterpress Book (1896-1899); Meany to General [Hazard Stevens], 9 October 1896, *ibid.*
34. *Seattle Post-Intelligencer*, 27 January 1897.
35. *Seattle Post-Intelligencer*, 4 July (on Hazard Stevens) and 11 July 1897 ("constrained"); Richards, *Isaac I. Stevens,* xi, xii, 273, and 274 shows conclusively that Stevens' career was controversial during his lifetime and after because of his treatment of the Indians.
36. Gates, *First Century,* 61-64.
37. Meany to Hazard Stevens, 21 January 1897, Meany Letterpress Book (1896-1899).
38. Meany to George H. Preston, 16 February 1897. Meany to Neal Cheetham, 27 February 1897, University of Washington Regents Letterpress Book (1895-1897); Meany to W.B. Hawley, 3 April 1897, Meany Letterpress Book (1896-1899).
39. Marion Edwards to Meany, 27 February, 8 March 1897, *ibid.*; Gates, *First Century,* 62 (quotation).
40. Classbooks of Edmond Stephen Meany, 1896-1897; Gates, *First Century,* 62-63; *Seattle Post-Intelligencer*, 22 April 1897; Meany to David Starr Jordan, 27 April 1897, Meany Letterpress Book (1896-1899); Meany to George K. Hazlitt, 27 April 1897, *ibid.* That the appointment was only for one year is stated in Meany to Edmund P. Dole, 19 February 1898, *ibid.* That it began 1 May 1897 is recorded in the *Seattle Post-Intelligencer*, 22 April 1897.
41. Meany to Jordan, 27 April 1897 (quotation on the long, hard struggle), Meany Letterpress Book (1896-1899); Meany to Edwin C. Starks, 15 May 1897, *ibid.*; Meany to A.B. Hart, 27 April 1897, *ibid.*; Meany to William Righter Fischer, 22 May 1897, *ibid.*; Meany to John Hoge, 6 May 1897, *ibid.*; Meany to Jordan, 14 June 1897, *ibid.* Meany to Fischer, 1 October 1897, *ibid.*, provides evidence that Fischer had advised home study and Meany's statement he had followed that advice.
42. Meany to John R. Rogers, 6 July 1897, *ibid.*; Rogers to Meany, 9 July 1897 (quotation).
43. Meany to Board of Trustees of the Frederick James Grant Memorial Association, 10 July 1897 (a draft written on scratch paper). The H.H. Bancroft collection was reported on 11 April 1897 in the *Seattle Post-Intelligencer;* Isaac S. Bradley to Meany, 11 October 1897.
44. Classbook of Edmond Stephen Meany, 1897-1898.
45. E.S. Meany, "Scientific Forestry," *Seattle Times*, 30 November 1897 (quotation); Meany to B.E. Fernow, 26 and 27 November 1897, and 12 February 1898, Meany Letterpress Book (1896-1899); Meany to William Trelease, 11 December 1897, *ibid.*; Meany to Charles S. Sargent, 15 January 1898, *ibid.*; Meany to J.M. Thorburn and Com-

pany, 26 November 1897, *ibid.*; Meany to W.B. Judson, 25 November 1897, *ibid.*; Meany to John Gifford, 26 November 1897, *ibid.*

46. Meany to editor of the *Oregonian*, 3 January 1898, Meany Letterpress Book (1896-1899); Meany to B.W. Everman, 25 March 1898, *ibid.*; Meany to E.C. Starks, 27 November 1897 and 12 February 1898, *ibid.* For full list of articles in both series, see [J. Ronald Todd], "Bibliography of Edmond Stephen Meany" (1935), 23 (University of Washington Library).
47. Clifford M. Drury, *Marcus and Narcissa Whitman and the Opening of Old Oregon*, 2 vols., (Glendale, Calif.: The Arthur H. Clark Company, 1973), II: 341-343; E.S. Meany, "In Memory of Marcus Whitman and Narcissa, His Wife," *Seattle Post-Intelligencer*, 21 November 1897.
48. *Ibid.* Also see G. Thomas Edwards, *The Triumph of Tradition: The Emergence of Whitman College, 1859-1924* (Walla Walla: Whitman College, 1992).
49. *Ibid.*
50. Drury, *Marcus and Narcissa Whitman,* II, 375-385 (quotation of Bourne, p. 383); Meany to Mrs. Wegner [*sic*], 9 November 1897, Meany Letterpress Book (1896-1899), reports regarding Nixon's book that he must "glean some more notes from it" and hence, could not loan it to her.
51. Classbook of Edmond Stephen Meany, 1897-1898; Meany to George K. Hazlitt, 8 January 1898 (quotation on "red Republican head"), Meany Letterpress Book (1896-1899); Meany to Mark W. Harrington, 14 February 1898 (quotation "much has happened"), *ibid.*; Meany to A.A. Lindsley, 25 February 1898, *ibid.*
52. Meany to E.C. Starks, 22 May 1898, *ibid.*
53. John R. Rogers to L.D. Godshall, 23 May 1898 (quotation), John R. Rogers Papers, Outgoing File, State Archives, Olympia (called to my attention by Dr. Thomas Riddle); Meany to Stanton Warburton, 21 May 1898, Meany Letterpress Book (1896-1899); Meany to James Z. Moore, 14 June 1898, *ibid.*; Meany to E.C. Starks, 28 August 1898, *ibid.*
54. Meany to W.B. Judson, 27 July 1898, Meany Letterpress Book (1896-1899); Meany to W.L. LaFollette, 31 July 1898, *ibid.*; Meany to James Z. Moore, 14 June and 31 July 1898, *ibid.*; Meany to R.E.M. Strickland, 31 July 1898, *ibid.*; Meany to Jerome L. Drumheller, 31 July 1898, *ibid.*; Meany to L.D. Godshall, 2 August 1898, and to John P. Hoyt, 2 August 1898, *ibid.*; Meany to Clark Davis, 3 August 1898, *ibid.*; John R. Rogers to John J. McGilvra, 3 September 1898, Meany Papers; J.T. Ronald to John R. Rogers, 16 August 1898, *ibid.*, a penciled draft (in Meany's hand).
55. John R. Rogers to Frank R. Graves, 11 August 1898, an enclosure in Graves to Meany, 18 August 1898, Meany Papers (quotations); Rogers to Graves, 22 August 1898, Outgoing File, Rogers Papers, State Archives, Olympia (courtesy of Dr. Thomas Riddle).
56. *Ibid.*, (quotation on Meany's visit).; Rogers to Graves, 11 August 1898 (quotation "hundreds of people"), Meany Papers; Graves to _____, 11 August 1898, *ibid.*
57. See Gates, *First Century,* 70-71, on the Board of Regents' decision and for a general discussion on the meaning of the struggle and its outcome. See also an editorial in the *Seattle Post-Intelligencer*, 16 September 1898, claiming that Meany's reappointment had a wider significance for higher education than simply restoring the professor to his post.

Notes for Chapter Six

1. *Seattle Post-Intelligencer*, 9 June 1898 (quotations); *Seattle Times*, 9 June 1898. Meany stated that he utilized Lewis Henry Morgan as found in John Fiske's *Discovery of*

America, Vol. I. See Meany to S.L. Crawford, 23 December 1897, Meany Letterpress Book (1896-1899). That letter also indicates his familiarity with H.H. Bancroft, the journals of Lewis and Clark, the publications of the American Museum of Natural History, and the reports of the U.S. Bureau of Ethnology.

2. *Seattle Post-Intelligencer*, 9 June 1898 (quotations). The speech was also published as "The Passing of the Red Man," in the *Whitman College Quarterly* II (June, 1898): 3-13. Reference to arms and ammunition provided to American forces by the Hudson's Bay Company in the 1855 Indian wars was probably Meany's. See Meany, *History of the State of Washington* (New York: The Macmillan Company, 1909), 183-184. The reference to 1898 is unclear but probably pointed to South Africa and to the Spanish-American War.
3. *Seattle Times*, 11 June 1898.
4. Meany, *History of the State of Washington*, 296.
5. Meany to Admiral Beardslee, 6 June 1898, Meany Letterpress Book (1896-1899); Meany to Rev. W.H.G. Temple, 22 May 1898 (quotation, "Old Glory"), *ibid.*; Edmond S. Meany to Jay Meany, 14 June 1898 (quotations, fatherly advice; mutual helpfulness), *ibid.*; F.N. Killam to Meany, 23 June 1899; Meany to Frank W. Smith, 13 June 1898 (quotation on pride in their service), Meany Letterpress Book (1896-1899).
6. Walter Millis, *The Martial Spirit* (The Literary Guild, 1931), 340 (quoting John Hay). In his *History of the State of Washington*, Meany quotes the official historian on page 298.
7. Meany to John H. Wholley, 8 October 1898, Meany Letterpress Book (1896-1899).
8. Meany to William McKinley, 8 October 1898, *ibid.* For other letters see also *ibid.*
9. Meany to Her Majesty, Queen Victoria, 10 October 1898, *ibid.* Other letters similar to this are also found in *ibid.*
10. Meany to Lieutenant Winslow, 31 October 1898, *ibid.*
11. Meany, "For College Correspondence," follows a letter from Meany to W.B. Wells (probably an enclosure), 22 October 1898, Meany Letterpress Book (1896-1899); Meany to Dr. F.H. Coe, 21 and 29 October 1898, *ibid.*; Meany to Charles V. Piper, 13 February 1899, *ibid.*
12. Meany to Macmillan Company, 21 October 1898, *ibid.*; Samuel E. Morrison, "Albert Bushnell Hart," *Dictionary of American Biography*, Supplement Three (1941-1945), 335-338.
13. Enclosure in letter: Meany to Mrs. Richard Winsor, 6 November 1898, Meany Letterpress Book (1896-1899).
14. *Seattle Post-Intelligencer*, 1 December 1898 (quotation on "formation of character"); Meany to Jordan, 6 December 1898 (quotations on "professors tied in bundles" and "hot raking shot"), Meany Letterpress Book (1896-1899); Charles M. Gates, *The First Century at the University of Washington* (Seattle: University of Washington Press, 1961), 72-73.
15. Meany to Jordan, 6 December 1898, Meany Letterpress Book (1896-1899).
16. Meany to John R. Rogers, 6 December 1898 (quotations: Meany's avowals to the governor), *ibid.*; Meany to George H. King, 6 December 1898 (quotation "great feast"), *ibid.*
17. *Seattle Post-Intelligencer*, 1 December 1898.
18. Meany to Charles V. Piper, 25 December 1898, Meany Letterpress Book (1896-1899); Piper to Meany, 12 June 1899.
19. John W. Pratt, "Issues on the East Side," *Seattle Post-Intelligencer*, 25 December 1898; Meany to Pratt, 25 December 1898, Meany Letterpress Book (1896-1899).
20. Meany to Dr. J.E. Meany (Manitowac, Wisconsin), 25 December 1898, *ibid.*

21. Meany to Piper, 25 December 1898, *ibid.*; Meany to Charles S. Gleason, 9 and 10 January 1899, *ibid.*; Meany to Gwin Hicks, 9 January 1899, *ibid.*; Meany to Will D. Jenkins, 27 March 1899, Meany Letterpress Book (1899; 1904-1906).
22. *Session Laws,. . . 1899*, 30, 40-41, 1023; Meany to Edwin C. Starks, 10 March and 22 April 1899, Meany Letterpress Book (1899; 1904-1906); Starks to Meany, 21 and 29 April 1899.
23. Albert Bushnell Hart to Meany, 1 May 1899; Meany to R.T. Ely, 10 May 1899, Meany Letterpress Book (1899; 1904-1906). The degree of Master of Science was conferred 1 June 1899, according to the records of the Registrar, University of Washington, and it was awarded as honorary, i.e. no course work required. James R. Hayden to John Summerfield (Chicago), 30 June 1899, Meany Papers (quotation).
24. E.A. Birge to Meany, 20 July 1899; Meany, "The Professor Abroad During His Vacation, Part I," *Seattle Post-Intelligencer*, 10 September 1899.
25. *Ibid.* (quotations).; Meany, "The Liberty and Free Soil Parties," draft of term paper [thesis] written for Prof. Jesse Macy, University of Wisconsin Summer Session, 1899.
26. Meany, "The Liberty and Free Soil Parties," (for quotations, "every race" and "side by side," see p.1, and for "when the smoke of battle cleared," see p.2). General discussion is found in pp. 1-8, 32.
27. Meany, "The Professor Abroad During His Vacation, Part II," *Seattle Post-Intelligencer*, 17 September 1899.
28. Frank P. Graves to Meany, 21 July 1899.
29. *Catalogue for 1898-1899 and Announcements for 1899-1900 of the University of Washington* (Olympia: Gwin Hicks, State Printer, 1899), 77-78, 108-109. That he taught forestry each year may be deduced from the *Catalogue for 1903-1904 and Announcements for 1904-1905 of the University of Washington* (Seattle: The Graham-Hickman Co., n.d.), 116.
30. Meany to _____, 10 October 1899, Washington University State Historical Society Papers [hereafter cited as WUSHS], folder II, University of Washington Special Collections; Undated memo: "Notice of the Columbia Historical Society Meeting," *ibid.*; unsigned memo with rough notes on the meeting of the Columbia Historical Society, *ibid.* The formation of the Columbia Historical Society has been presented in another context in George Frykman, "Development of the *Washington Historical Quarterly*, 1906-1935: The Work of Edmond S. Meany and Charles W. Smith," *Pacific Northwest Quarterly* 70 (July 1979): 122.
31. *Seattle Times*, 24 October 1899 (quotations); *Seattle Post-Intelligencer*, 25 November 1899; Stephen B.L. Penrose to Meany, 11 December 1900; William F. Prosser to Meany, 7 February 1901, contains an acknowledgment that the Columbia Historical Society was dead.
32. Susan Lord Currier to Meany, 25 October 1899, and Myron Eells to Meany, 27 October 1899, both in WUSHS Papers, Folder II. A copy of *The Argus*, 23 December 1899, may be examined at the Northwest Collection, University of Washington Library. The quotation is found in Meany, "History of Puget Sound," *The Argus*, 23 December 1899, p. 31. Meany also edited the Christmas editions of *The Argus* for 22 December 1900, and 21 December 1901.
33. Whitehead published perhaps eight issues before the enterprise collapsed. See Frank Luther Mott, *A History of American Magazines, IV: 1885-1905* (Cambridge: Belknap Press of Harvard University Press, 1957), 109; P.D. Whitehead to Meany, 31 January [1900], 12 and 16 February, 24, 28, and 31 March, 10 April, 9 May 1900 and 15 June [1900]; Meany to James Wickersham, 3 July 1916, Meany Letterpress Book (1915-1916).

34. *Seattle Post-Intelligencer*, 17 February 1900. Typical of these invitations to speak is Emma S. Yule to Meany, 20 February 1900. See also, A. Melvin Cole to Meany, 18 April 1900, and Charles W. Smith to Meany, 21 March 1900.
35. *Seattle Post-Intelligencer*, 5 June 1900.
36. H.A. Hanson to Meany, 14 May 1900 (quotations from petition); *Seattle Post-Intelligencer*, 20 May 1900 (Meany anecdote).
37. Ed [Meany] to Mrs. E.S. Meany, 30 July 1900.
38. F.J. Turner to Meany, 7 August 1900; H. Morse Stephens to Meany, 6 August 1900; Franklin H. Giddings to _____, 8 August 1900; W.D. Hiestand to Meany, 15 August 1900.
39. *Sixth Biennial report of the Board of Regents of the University of Washington to the Governor of Washington, 1900* (Olympia: Gwin Hicks State Printer, 1900), 5,6,7-9,18 (quotation on pp. 5-6). For Smith's career, see Cushing Strout's "Introduction" to J. Allen Smith, *The Spirit of American Government* (Cambridge: The Belknap Press of Harvard University Press, 1965).
40. *The Argus* (Seattle), 6 July 1901, contains a letter written by Meany at Nespelem, 24 June 1901 (quotation). Meany's preface in "Chief Joseph, The Nez Perce," (M.L. thesis, University of Wisconsin, 1901) contains a description of his work and sources. (A microfilm copy of the thesis is available in the Washington State University Library). Several letters of recommendation written by Meany's professors indicate his schedule and achievements. Meany's academic performance, summer of 1901, is found in letters to Meany from F.J. Turner and other Wisconsin faculty, sent in August.
41. *Catalogue for 1900-1901 and Announcements for 1901-1902 of the University of Washington* (Olympia: Gwin Hicks, State Printer, 1901), 113-114, 133-135; *Catalogue for 1901-1902 and Announcements for 1902-1903 of the University of Washington*(Seattle: The Metropolitan Press, 1902), 125-127, 132. Miss Birdie S. Beals, who had served as principal at Sedro Wooley High School and had done graduate work at Yale University, was appointed instructor of English and history in May, 1901, but there was no evidence that she taught above the preparatory department. See *Seattle Post-Intelligencer*, 19 May and 16 August 1901. On the status of collegiate teaching of the Pacific Rim and Oriental [Asian] history, see Archibald Carey Coolidge, "Report of the Conference on Oriental History and Politics," *Annual Report of the American Historical Association for the Year 1907*, 2 vols.(Washington, D.C.: Government Printing Office, 1908)I: 71-78.
42. As late as January 1903, the regents reported that Meany was the lone professor of history. See *Seventh Biennial Report of the Board of Regents of the University of Washington to the Governor of Washington, 1903* (Seattle: Denny-Coryell Co., Printers, 1903), 22-23; Assistant Professor George H. Alden taught in the 1903-1904 academic year, see *Catalogue for 1903-1904 and Announcements...*, 104-107; Meany to Frederick Jackson Turner, 2 April 1904, Meany Letterpress Book (1899; 1904-1906); Meany to A.C. McLoughlin, 2 April 1904, *ibid.*, and Meany to James A. Woodburn, 2 April 1904, *ibid.*; *Bulletin of the University of Washington: Announcement, First Summer Session*, June 20-July 30, 1904, 11-12.
43. *Seattle Times*, 15 September 1920, credits Mrs. Margaret Meany with inspiring Campus Day. Meany, "The Rise and Fall of Campus Day," Meany Papers. "General Orders Numbers 1 and 2, Second Annual Campus Day, May 12, 1905," *ibid.; Seattle Times*, 12 May 1905 (quotation).
44. *The Pacific Wave* XI (18 November 1903): 2.
45. *Ibid.*, XIII (22 December 1905): 4.
46. Herbert S. Griggs to Meany, 15 December 1902, WUSHS Papers, Folder II; Meany to Griggs, 23 December 1902, *ibid.*; Seattle *Post-Intelligencer*, 24 December 1902;

C.B. Bagley to Meany, n.d., Washington Historical Quarterly Papers, Box 1 (University of Washington Special Collections); list of signers at organization of the Washington University State Historical Society, 23 December 1902, WUSHS Papers, Folder I.

47. Articles of Incorporation, WUSHS, 1 January 1903, WUSHS Papers, Folder I; by-laws, particularly Article VIII, WUSHS, in *ibid.*; minutes, WUSHS, 1 January 1903, *ibid.*
48. Meany to W.R. Thompson, 22 July 1903, WUSHS Papers, Folder II; *The Pacific Wave* XI (30 September 1903): 3; Meany, *History of the State of Washington*, 44 (quotation).
49. *Seattle Post-Intelligencer*, 21 November 1903 (quotation). Meany was adopted into the Nez Perce tribe in 1900 as "Three Knives," by Vancouver Island Indians as "The Sun Warming in the Morning," while placing the marker at Nootka Sound in 1903, and as "Two Arrows," by the Sioux in 1907, while making notes about them on their South Dakota reservation. See, Gilbert B. Foster, "Keeper of the Traditions," *Sunset Magazine* 48 (April 1922): 26- 27; Ticket of Admission to Chief Joseph Meeting, Seattle Theater, 20 November 1903, in WUSHS Papers, Folder II.
50. *Seattle Post-Intelligencer*, 21 November 1903 (quotation "resplendent in buckskin"); Ticket of Admission to Chief Joseph Meeting, 20 November 1903, WUSHS Papers, Folder II; *Seattle Post- Intelligencer*, 24 November 1903 (quotation "if I had the power").
51. Memo: Financial Account of Chief Joseph and Red Thunder visiting Seattle on 20 November 1903 as guests of the WUSHS, in WUSHS Papers, Folder II. A draft of an invitation to join WUSHS with life membership was drawn by Meany to _____, 1904, WUSHS Papers, Folder I; list of life members, WUSHS, *ibid.*; Minutes of Trustees Meeting, WUSHS, 12 September 1904, *ibid.* On the San Juan ceremonies see the following: *Seattle Times*, 1 September 1904; *Seattle Post-Intelligencer*, 2 September 1904; Meany to Theodore Roosevelt, 27 June 1904, WUSHS Letterpress Book (1904-1914); Meany to William II, Emperor of Germany, 27 June 1904, *ibid.*; Meany to Edward VII, 27 June 1904, *ibid.*; Meany to Clarence W. Ide, 3 September 1904, *ibid.*; Meany to John Hay, 3 September 1904, *ibid.*; Meany to Hay, 8 September 1904, *ibid.*; Meany to Imperial German Ambassador, 3 September 1904, *ibid.*
52. Alvey A. Adee to Meany, 15 September 1904; John Hay to Meany, 16 September 1904; Starnburg to Meany, 16 September 1904; R.E. Gosnell to Meany, 19 September 1904; *Seattle Post-Intelligencer*, 23 October 1904, contains a full report of the ceremonies.
53. Meany to Samuel Hill, 8 May 1905, WUSHS Letterpress Book (1904-1914); Meany to Henry Steele, 27 May 1905, *ibid.*; Meany to Steele, 11 June 1905, *ibid.*; *Seattle Post-Intelligencer*, 18 June 1905 (quotation).
54. *Ibid.*, 20, 23, and 25 June 1905; *Spokesman Review* (Spokane), 23 June 1905 (quotation).
55. Ezra Meeker, *Pioneer Reminiscences of Puget Sound: The Tragedy of Leschi* (Seattle: Lowman and Hanford Stationary and Printing Co., 1905), 1-3, 252-262, 409-414, 457; Meany to Meeker, 18 February 1905 (quotation), Meany Letterpress Book (1899; 1904-1906). The controversy may be followed in the *Seattle Times* for 29 and 30 March, 15, 17, 25, and 29 April, and 1 May 1905.
56. *Ibid.*, 15 April 1905; Meany to W.C. King, 17 April 1905 (quotation), Meany Letterpress Book (1899; 1904-1906).
57. *Seattle Times*, 15 April, and 1 May 1905 (quotation); Hazard Stevens recognized Meany's devotion to the memory of his father in, Stevens to Meany, 18 May 1905; Kent D. Richards, *Isaac I. Stevens, Young Man in a Hurry* (Provo: Brigham Young University Press, 1979), xiii, 289, 316-317, 359.

58. Meany to Erastus Brainerd, 23 September 1905, Meany Letterpress Book (1899; 1904-1906); Meany to A.P. Sawyer, 1 December 1905, *ibid.*; *The Ellensburg Localizer*, 8 July 1905. The following newspaper stories are representative of his "Native Races of Washington," *Seattle Post-Intelligencer*, 20 June, 16 and 30 July, 13 and 27 August, 3, 10, and 24 September (quotation "The Makahs"), 1 (quotation "well disposed white men"), 8, 15, and 22 October 1905. See editorials supporting Meany's work in *ibid.*, 30 July 1905.
59. Meany to Brainerd, 23 September 1905, Meany Letterpress Book (1899; 1904-1906); Meany to A.P. Sawyer, 1 and 3 December 1905, *ibid.*
60. Meany to Mrs. Mary Sinclair, 1 November 1905, *ibid.*; Meany to Samuel Hill, 6 November 1905, WUSHS Letterpress Book (1904-1914); Meany to J.R. Williamson, 6 November 1905, *ibid.*; receipted bill, New England Granite and Marble Co., Inc., 13 November 1905, WUSHS Papers, Folder II; *Seattle Times*, 13 November 1905 (all quotations).

Notes for Chapter Seven

1. Meany, "Early Education, Toast at Founder's Day Banquet of the Chamber of Commerce, Hotel Washington, 17 November 1905," unpaged, penciled manuscript, Meany Papers.
2. *Ibid.*
3. Merle Curti, *The Roots of American Loyalty* (New York: Columbia University Press, 1946), 173-178, 180-191; Wallace E. Davies, *Patriotism on Parade: The Story of Veterans' and Hereditary Organizations in America, 1783-1900* (Cambridge: Harvard University Press, 1955), 44-47, 76, 77, 215-219, 222-228.
4. Meany to Mrs. John Leary [Eliza Ferry Leary], 27 March 1905 and 6 January 1906, Meany Letterpress Book (1899; 1904-1906); Meany to Mrs. Angie Burt Bowden, 12 December 1905, *ibid.*; Meany to Mrs. Justin V.R. Townsend, 3 January 1906, *ibid.*
5. Meany wrote to the three sculptors on 11 April 1905, *ibid.*; Meany to Lorado Taft, 9 October 1905, *ibid.*; *Seattle Times*, 1 and 2 November 1905; *Seattle Post-Intelligencer*, 4 November 1905, and *Pacific Wave* XIII (10 November 1905): 1-4; Meany to W.T. Walton, 8 January 1906, Meany Letterpress Book (1899; 1904-1906); Walton to Meany, 27 January 1906; *Seattle Times*, 23 February 1906; Meany to Mrs. Eliza Ferry Leary, 6 January 1906, Meany Letterpress Book (1899; 1904-1906).
6. Meany, *Address on the History of International Arbitration*. Service of Peace at Denny Hall, 27 May 1906 (Seattle: University Ministerial Association, 1906), 13 (quotation), Northwest Collection, University of Washington Library. The *Seattle Post-Intelligencer*, 28 May 1906, estimated the audience to be about 500.
7. Meany, *Address on the History of International Arbitration*, 5-7 (quotation p. 7).
8. Charles De Benedetti, *The Peace Reform in American History* (Bloomington: Indiana University Press, 1980), 79; Arthur A. Ekirch, Jr., *Progressivism in America: A Study of the Era from Theodore Roosevelt to Woodrow Wilson* (New York: New Viewpoints, 1974), 212-217.
9. *Ibid.*, 212-214; Meany, *Address on the History of International Arbitration*, 11-14, (quotation p. 14).
10. *Ibid.*, 15. Meany to Trevor Kincaid, 7 January 1906, Meany Letterpress Book (1899, 1904-1906).
11. Meany to H.C. Coffman, 21 January 1906, *ibid.*; H.C. Coffman to Meany, 22 January 1906.
12. Meany to H.C. Coffman, 4 April 1906, Meany Letterpress Book (1899; 1904-1906).

13. *Seattle Post-Intelligencer*, 5 November 1905. The Meany Papers contain receipts and statements, dated 1903-1906, showing installation of water and sewer, grading streets, and construction of wooden sidewalks (box 12-19, and 13-2); Meany to J.G. Megler, 19 January 1906, Meany Letterpress Book (1899; 1904-1906); Meany to R.H. Thompson, 14 December 1906, *ibid.*, (1906-1908).
14. Meany to Mrs. P. Roche, 11 March 1906, Meany Letterpress Book (1899; 1904-1906).
15. The names of the publishers are confirmed by the following: Meany to O.R. Main, 10 March and 15 May 1906, and O.R. Main to Meany, 8 May 1907; Meany to W.J. Colbert, 22 February 1906, Meany Letterpress Book (1899; 1904-1906).
16. Meany to E.F. Benson, 2 March 1906, *ibid.*; Meany to Main, 10 March 1906, *ibid.*
17. *Washington Magazine of Industry and Progress*, 1 (March 1906): 41. Meany introduced the history series in, *ibid.*, 1 (March 1906): 23. A typical paper is Mabel C. Griffith, "Spanish Names in Washington Geography," 23-25, *ibid.*
18. *Washington Magazine, Alaska-Greater Northwest*, 1 (June 1906), 282-286; Meany to Harlan I. Smith, 2 July 1906, Meany Letterpress Book (1906-1908); Meany to John Fleming Wilson, 29 August 1906 (quotation "temporary editor"), *ibid.*; Meany to James F. Stickles, 28 April 1907, *ibid.*; O.R. Main to Meany, 8 May 1907. Meany was listed as president by the new owners though he was neither a director nor a stockholder. See *Washington Magazine, Alaska-Greater Northwest*, 1 (June 1906), prefatory page, unnumbered and *ibid.*, Vol. 2, (September 1906). Data on articles he was responsible for is extensive. See, Meany to Main, 15 May 1906, Meany Letterpress Book (1899;1904-1906) and Edwin E. Elliott, "The New Agriculture," *Washington Magazine, Alaska-Greater Northwest*, 1 (June 1906): 266-267.
19. R.L. McCormick to Meany, 2 May 1905, Washington University State Historical Society Papers [WUSHS], folder II, University of Washington Archives; Meany to Samuel Hill, 15 May and 5 June 1905, WUSHS Letterpress Book (1904-1914). Bagley's role is best seen in his letter to W.H. Bonney, 27 October 1905, Box 13, Bagley Papers, University of Washington; Edwin Eells, "History of the Washington State Historical Society," in Charles Miles and O.B. Sperlin (eds.), *Building a State: Washington, 1899-1939* (Tacoma: Washington State Historical Society, 1940), 352-355.
20. Meany to Edwin Eells, 18 November 1905, WSUHS Letterpress Book (1904-1914). Meany to Samuel Hill, 15 May 1905, *ibid.*, has Meany's version of the proposed compromise whereby Eells would be made curator of the combined historical museum located in Seattle; Meany to Mrs. A. Denny Lindsley, 7 January 1906, Meany Letterpress Book (1899; 1904-1906); Meany to Eells, 29 March 1906, WUSHS Letterpress Book (1904-1914); Meany to Thomas Burke, 14 December 1906, *ibid.*
21. For a general discussion of the *Washington Historical Quarterly*, see Frykman, "Development of the *Washington Historical Quarterly*, 1906-1935: The Work of Edmond S. Meany and Charles W. Smith," *Pacific Northwest Quarterly* 70 (July 1979): 121-130; *Washington Historical Quarterly*, 1, Number 1 (October 1906), *passim* [pagination is not consecutive for numbers 1 and 2 of Volume 1, making use of the issue number necessary].
22. "Documents," *Washington Historical Quarterly*, 1, No. 1 (October 1906): 71 (quote on "rare or unpublished documents"); "Documents," *ibid.*, 1, No. 2 (January 1907): 51; A.N. Brown to Meany, 13 August (quotation) and 19 September 1906; *Session Laws, State of Washington, 1909*, 57-59.
23. Meany to Brown, 1 December 1906, WUSHS Letterpress Book (1904-1914); Brown, "Preserving Our Public Records," *Washington Historical Quarterly*, 1, No. 2 (January 1907): 10-15; Albert E. Mead, "Collecting Portraits of Washington's Governors,"

ibid., 5-9; *Second Message of Governor Albert E. Mead to the Legislature of 1907* (Olympia: C.W. Gorham, Public Printer, 1907), 4-5; *Session Laws, 1909*, 57-59.

24. "News Department," *Washington Historical Quarterly*, 1, No. 2 (January 1907): 84-89.
25. *Ibid.*, 87.
26. Charles W. Smith to Meany, 5 January 1907, *Washington Historical Quarterly* Papers; Meany to Smith, 13 January 1907, Meany Papers; [Smith] to Meany, 22 January 1907, *Washington Historical Quarterly* Papers; Meany to Smith, 27 January 1907, Meany Papers.
27. Barry J. McMahon, "Seattle's Commercial Aspirations as Expressed in the Alaska-Yukon-Pacific Exposition" (M.A. thesis, Washington State University, 1960), 12-16; Meany to Albert E. Mead, 11 June 1906, Meany Letterpress Book (1899; 1904-1906); "Greater Washington Day," *The Washington Alumnus* III (25 October 1909), 13-14. For a full account of Meany's participation in promotion of the Exposition, see George Frykman, "The Alaska-Yukon-Pacific Exposition, 1909," *Pacific Northwest Quarterly* 53 (July 1962): 89-99; Charles M. Gates, *The First Century at the University of Washington* (Seattle: University of Washington Press, 1961), 124.
28. *Seattle Post-Intelligencer*, 2 July 1906.
29. Meany to Harlan I. Smith, 2 July 1906, Meany Letterpress Book (1906-1908); *Eleventh Biennial Report of the Board of Regents of the University of Washington to the Governor of Washington, 1911* (Bulletin of the University of Washington, series 1, No. 56, January 1911): 30, 53.
30. Meany to H.C. Coffman, 27 August 1906, Meany Letterpress Book (1906-1908); Meany, *Vancouver's Discovery of Puget Sound: Portraits and Biographies of the Men Honored in the Naming of Geographical Features of Northwestern America* (New York: The Macmillan Company, 1907); Meany to the Macmillan Company, 7 October 1906, Meany Letterpress Book (1906-1908); Meany, *Vancouver's Discovery of Puget Sound*, x (quotation); George P. Brett to Meany, 22 October 1906; Meany to Macmillan Company, 31 October 1906, Meany Letterpress Book (1906-1908); Brett to Meany, 8 November 1906; Meany to Brett, 21 November 1906, Meany Letterpress Book (1906-1908); John N. Jackson to Meany, 20 November 1906.
31. Meany to J.N. Bowman, 11 December 1906, WUSHS Letterpress Book (1904-1914), and Meany to Samuel Hill, 14 December 1906, Meany Letterpress Book (1906-1908); *Seattle Post-Intelligencer*, 19 December 1906, 4 January, 14, and 27 February 1907; *Seattle Times*, 26 February 1907; Watson C. Squire to Meany, 11 and 15 January 1907; R.S. Woodruff to George Boole, 23 February 1907, reveals that Meany arrived in Connecticut too late for business to be taken up in the current session.
32. Report of the Legislative Committee from the State of New York to the Alaska-Yukon-Pacific Exposition (1910), 177 (quotation from Wilcox, p.177; from Burke, p. 163).
33. *Seattle Post-Intelligencer*, 3 January (quotation), and 25 February 1907; Albert B. Hart to Meany, 23 January 1907.
34. Before he left Seattle for the East, Meany summarized the plans for these statues in his letters to Lorado Taft, 7 October and 22 November 1906, Meany Letterpress Book (1906-1908); Judge Thomas Burke to Meany, 28 December 1906, and 17 January 1907; *Seattle Post-Intelligencer*, 25 February 1907. *Seattle Times*, 26 February 1907; Meany to Taft, 10 March 1907, Meany Letterpress Book (1906-1908).
35. Meany to Rev. E. Victor Bigelow, 7 April 1907 (quotation, "I was simply on the jump"), *ibid.*; Meany to Mary Wager-Fisher, 19 August 1907 (quotation, "I was not very sure footed"), *ibid.* The list of historic sites visited by Meany was compiled from above and, Meany to W. Edward Starr, 4 March 1907, *ibid.*, and Meany to John D. Rockefeller, Jr., 7 April 1907, *ibid.*

36. Meany to Arthur B. Carle, 7 April 1907, *ibid.*; Colonel John Jacob Astor expressed interest in a statue of his famous ancestor but promised no financial aid, *ibid. Seattle Post-Intelligencer*, 25 February 1907, 10 March 1907.
37. Meany to Richard E. Brooks, 10 March 1907, Meany Letterpress Book (1906-1908); *Seattle Times*, 10 March 1907; *Seattle Post-Intelligencer*, 3 April 1907; Meany to Cass Gilbert, 10 March 1907, Meany Letterpress Book (1906-1908); Meany to Charles Hopkins Church, 12 May 1907, *ibid.*; Meany to Lorado Taft, 10 March 1907 (quotation), *ibid.*
38. Meany to Stanley Griffiths, 6 May 1907 (quotations), *ibid. Who's Who in America*, 1978-79, II, p. 2208, reported the birth date of Edmond S. Meany, Jr., as 23 April 1907.
39. Meany to Camille Williams, 28 April 1907, Meany Letterpress Book (1906-1908); E.S. Curtis to Meany, 3 June 1907.
40. Meany (recorder), Field Notes on Sioux Indians [1907], Box 13, Folders 6-64, Meany Papers.
41. Meany, "Hunting Indians With a Camera: Adventures of Mr. Edward S. Curtis Who is Devoting a Large Part of a Working Lifetime to Making Permanent Records of Our Vanishing Red-Men," *World's Work* 15 (March 1908): 10004-10011 (quotation on p. 10010).
42. Meany to Curtis, 25 August 1907, and 26 January 1908, Meany Letterpress Book (1906-1908); Curtis to Meany, 17 January 1908; Edward S. Curtis, *The North American Indian, Being a Series of Volumes Picturing and Describing the Indians of the United States and Alaska* III (1908; reprint edition by Johnson Reprint Corporation, New York, 1970).
43. Meany to Curtis, 11 August 1907, Meany Letterpress Book (1906-1908); Curtis to Meany, 20 August 1907 (quotation).
44. Meany to Curtis, 25 August 1907 (quotations), Meany Letterpress Book (1906-1908). Morgan's patronage is stated in the title page of each volume.
45. Meany to Curtis, 25 August 1907, Meany Letterpress Book (1906-1908); *Seattle Times*, 10 February 1907, and *Seattle Post- Intelligencer*, 20 April 1907; *Outlook* LXXXVI (20 July 1907): 610 (quotation).
46. *The Pacific Monthly* (August 1907), 262; "Porter Garnett," *Who Was Who in America*, Vol. 3 (1951-1960), 313-314; review by Lawrence J. Burpee, *The Dial* XLIII (1 August 1907): 60-61.
47. William R. Manning, review in *American Historical Review* XIII (October 1907): 160 (quotation), 161; *Who Was Who in America*, Vol. 2, 1950, p. 344; "The Meeting of the American Historical Association in Chicago," *American Historical Review* X (April 1905): 507. Meany to Albert Bushnell Hart, 16 October 1907 (quotations from Meany), Meany Letterpress Book (1906-1908); J.F. Jameson to Hart, 28 October 1907 (quotation "a good fellow"), Meany Papers.
48. Meany to Hart, 10 November 1907, Meany Letterpress Book (1906-1908); *Ninth Biennial Report of the Board of Regents of the University of Washington to the Governor of Washington, 1907* (Bulletin of the University of Washington, Series 1, No. 32, January 1907): 22-23; *Catalogue for 1907-8 and Announcements for 1908-09 of the University of Washington* (Olympia: C.W. Gorman, Public Printer, 1908), 5-25, 119-122. No designation of chairman was used by the regents for any academic unit, but Meany's tasks obviously were those of chairman; McMahon actually joined the staff earlier, teaching summer school in 1907, as shown in *Announcement: Fourth Summer Session: June 24-August 2, 1907* (Bulletin of the University of Washington, series 1, No. 33, 1907), 3, 16, 17; *Who's Who in America*, 1950, Vol. 3, 384.

49. Meany's courses are those listed for 1908-1909; none was new. See *Catalogue for 1908-9 and Announcements for 1909-10 of the University of Washington* (Olympia: E.L. Boardman, Public Printer, 1909) 129-133; Meany to Thomas F. Kane, 24 September 1907, Meany Letterpress Book (1906-1908).
50. *Seattle Post-Intelligencer*, 7 December 1907.
51. Gates, *First Century*, 102-103; H.C. Coffman to D.S. Blair, 7 November 1907 (quotation), Meany Papers.
52. Meany to H.C. Coffman, 9 November 1907 (quotation, "painful surprise"), Meany Letterpress Book (1906-1908); Meany to Coffman, 14 November 1907, *ibid.* Coffman to Meany, 17 November 1907. Meany to Coffman, 26 November 1907 (quotations, "preposterous" and "there are none"), Meany Letterpress Book (1906-1908).
53. Coffman to Meany, 17 November 1907; Meany to Coffman, 26 November 1907 (quotations), Meany Letterpress Book (1906-1908); Clarence E. Woods to Meany, 18 December 1907; Meany to Woods, 14 March 1908, Meany Letterpress Book (1908-1909); Meany to F.V. Keesling, 24 August 1908, *ibid.*, (1908-1909); Meany to Coffman, 12 June 1909, *ibid.*, and Coffman to Meany, 3 November 1909. Sigma Nu entered Washington State College on 10 March 1910, according to Enoch A. Bryan, *Historical Sketch of the State College of Washington, 1890-1925* (Pullman: Alumni and Associated Students, 1928), 409.
54. "News Department," *Washington Historical Quarterly* 2 (January 1908): 177 (quotation). The articles in question are Charles D. Tenny, "Chinese History," 99-104, *ibid.*, and K. Asakawa, "Why and How Japanese History May be Studied with Profit in America," 127-131, *ibid.*; Kenneth S. LaTourette, "Far Eastern Studies in the United States: Retrospect and Prospect," *The Far Eastern Quarterly* 15 (November 1955): 3.
55. *Seattle Times*, 23 January 1908; Curtis Guild, Jr., to Meany, 26 February 1908.
56. W.M. Sheffield to Meany, 7 and 18 January 1908; *The Pacific Wave* XV (24 January 1908): 4.
57. Meany to D.B. Trefethen, 26 January 1908, Meany Letterpress Book (1906-1908); *Seattle Times*, 13 February 1908.
58. Reported in the *Seattle Times*, 13 February 1908.
59. C.V. Piper to Meany, 6 April 1908. Meany to Piper, 12 April 1908 (quotation), Meany Letterpress Book (1906-1908); William Markham to Meany, 12 June 1907; Bryan, *Historical Sketch of the State College of Washington*, 1890-1925, 94, 240, 241.
60. *Seattle Times*, 16 April 1908; *Seattle Post-Intelligencer*, 17 April 1908; *The Argus*, 18 April 1908 (quotations); William Markham to Meany, 12 June 1907. Meany induced further misunderstandings about the offer: see Edward McMahon to Meany, 27 April 1908, and Meany to McMahon, 1 May 1908, Meany Letterpress Book (1906-1908).
61. Meany to Miss Nora Denny, 5, 8 (quotation), and 14 April 1908, *ibid.*
62. Meany to Henry Louis Reginald De Koven, 10 May 1907, *ibid.*; Harry C. Bauer, "Requiem for an Anthem," *Pacific Northwest Quarterly* 51(April 1960): 81-85 (quote on p. 81).
63. Meany to De Koven, 24 and 27 August 1907, Meany Letterpress Book (1906-1908). The verses are taken from Bauer, "Requiem for an Anthem," p. 83.
64. *Ibid.*, 82.
65. *Ibid.*, 82, 83 (quotation).
66. Meany to Robert F. Booth, 9 March 1909 (quotation), Meany Letterpress Book (1908-1909); Meany to Loren D. Grinstead, 14 March 1909, *ibid.*; Bauer, "Requiem for an Anthem," 80-85.
67. Meany to Albert B. Hart, 25 August 1907, Meany Letterpress Book (1906-1908); Meany to Hart, 29 May 1908, *ibid.*; Hart to Meany, 6 June 1908.

68. *Ibid.*; Meany to Hart, 21 June, 12 July, and 21 August, 1908, Meany Letterpress Book (1908-1909).
69. *Washington Historical Quarterly* 2 (July 1908), inside front cover (quotation, "for generous special contributions"); Meany to Bailey Willis, 21 August 1908 (quotation "this magazine"), Meany Letterpress Book (1908-1909); Frykman, "Development of the *Washington Historical Quarterly*," 125.
70. Meany to Clinton A. Snowden, 18 July 1906, WUSHS Letterpress Book (1904-1914).
71. For a convenient summary of the "Whitman Saved Oregon" controversy, see Clifford M. Drury, *Marcus and Narcissa Whitman and the Opening of Old Oregon*, 2 volumes (Glendale, Calif.: The Arthur H. Clark Company, 1973), II: 375-386.
72. Meany to Mrs. Katherine P. Nims, 10 March 1906, Meany Letterpress Book (1899; 1904-1906).
73. *Ibid.*
74. T.C. Elliott to Clarence B. Bagley, 25 February 1907, Bagley Papers, University of Washington.
75. C.T. Johnson [T.C. Elliott], "Daniel Webster, Lord Ashburton, and Old Oregon," *Washington Historical Quarterly* 1 (July 1907): 209-216; Johnson [T.C. Elliott], "Daniel Webster and Old Oregon," *ibid.*, 2 (October 1907): 6-11.
76. "News Department," *Washington Historical Quarterly* 2 (January 1908): 178-179. The published version of Edwin Eells' paper is cited: "Heroes and Heroines of the Long Ago," *ibid.*, 132-145.
77. T.C. Elliott to Meany, 14 December 1907.
78. C.T. Johnson [T.C. Elliott], "The Evolution of a Lament," *Washington Historical Quarterly* 2 (April 1908): 195-208.
79. Charles W. Smith, "Expansion of the Dewey Decimal System of Classification for the History of the Pacific Northwest," *ibid.*, (January 1908): 146-160. "News Department," *ibid.*, 179.
80. *Ibid.*, 179. Smith, "A Contribution Toward a Bibliography of Marcus Whitman," *ibid.*, 3 (October 1908): 3-62 (quotations are found on pp. 3, 4, 6, 7).
81. Frykman, "Development of the *Washington Historical Quarterly*," 125.

Notes for Chapter Eight

1. *Seattle Times*, 12 February 1909 (quoting a reporter).
2. *Ibid.*, (quotation on Miller); Bertha D. Piper Venan to Meany, 12 February 1909.
3. Joseph Blethen to Meany, 27 January 1909; Meany to Blethen, 28 January 1909, Meany Letterpress Book (1908-1909); *Seattle Times*, 7 February 1909 (quotation from "The Elemental Lincoln").
4. Meany, "Abraham Lincoln," *Overland Monthly*, 53 (March 1909): 226-227.
5. *Seattle Post-Intelligencer*, 19 and 21 (quotation on Meany) February, 6 March 1909; *San Francisco Chronicle*, 23 February 1909 (quotation on "enthusiastic delegation"); *San Francisco Examiner*, 24 February 1909; I.A. Nadeau and C.B. Yandell to the Seattle Chamber of Commerce, 8 March 1909 (quotation on "signal services"), Meany Papers; Meany to J.A. Wood, 8 March 1909, Meany Letterpress Book (1908-1909).
6. Meany to J.W. Slayden, 7 March 1909, *ibid.*; Report of the Alaska-Yukon-Pacific Exposition Commission to the State of Washington [n.d., Seattle], 29; Meany to Lorado Taft, 16 May 1909, Meany Letterpress Book (1908-1909).
7. Meany to Mrs. May Thornton Heg, 18 May 1909 (quotations), *ibid.*; Meany to Lorado Taft, 18 May 1909, *ibid.*
8. Mrs. Elinor Ingersoll Thorne to Meany, 15 and 24 May 1909; Meany to Mrs. Thorne, 25 May 1909 (quotations), Meany Letterpress Book (1908-1909).

9. *Seattle Times*, 14 June 1909 (quotation); *Seattle Post- Intelligencer*, 15 June 1909.
10. *Seattle Times*, 14 and 15 June 1909; Meany to Taft, 18 October 1909 (quotation), Meany Letterpress Book (1908-1909); Meany to Taft, 5 February 1910, Meany Letterpress Book (1909-1912). Meany vainly sought new state appropriations in succeeding years. See especially, Meany to Mrs. Eliza Ferry Leary, 18 November 1912, Meany Letterpress Book (1912-1915); minutes of the Rainier Chapter, 30 November 1909, and January 1910, as copied for Meany, 27 February 1921, by Mrs. Bowden, found in Meany scrapbook, 1921-1922, Meany Papers; Meany to Anna Rollins Johnson, 13 February 1913, Meany Letterpress Book (1912-1915).
11. Celebrating began with civic exercises and ceremonies at the new exposition auditorium, and was reported in the *Seattle Post-Intelligencer*, 18 May and 11 September 1909; Edmond S. Meany, *History of the State of Washington* (New York: The Macmillan Company, 1909), 319; Meany to Thomas Burke, 25 January 1909, Meany Letterpress Book (1908-1909); Burke to Meany, 25 January 1909 (quotation); Meany to Burke, 30 March 1909, Meany Letterpress Book (1908-1909); Burke to Meany, 11 November 1909; Meany to Burke, 12 November 1909, Meany Letterpress Book (1908-1909); Meany to Richard E. Brooks, 25 April 1909, *ibid.*
12. Meany to Lorado Taft, 28 June 1909, *ibid.*
13. Meany to L.P. Hornberger, 11 April 1909, *ibid.*; Meany to E.L. Reber, 26 April 1909, *ibid.*; Meany to Theodore T. Belote, 26 April 1909, *ibid.*
14. Meany, "What it all Means," *Collier's The National Weekly* 43 (18 September 1909): 14, 15 (quotations both pages). The author of "The Destiny of the Northwest" was Major Charles E. Woodruff, an Army surgeon who had been stationed in the Philippines. See, *Who Was Who in America*, Vol. 1 (1897-1942), 1377.
15. Meany to Ashahel Curtis, 19 August 1907, Meany Letterpress Book (1906-1908); Meany to Albert B. Hart, 3 October 1907, *ibid.*; Meany to Walter H. Page, 27 May 1908, Meany Letterpress Book (1908-1909). As late as 12 May 1909, he confessed in a letter to E.R. Butterworth (*ibid.*) that he could not climb mountains because of dizziness.
16. Meany to Henry L. Pittock, 30 August 1909 (quotation), *ibid.*; Meany to Walter Hines Page, 27 May 1908, *ibid.* Total membership is found in Meany, "Objects of our club," *The Mountaineer* 3 (November 1910): 5-7.
17. *The Mountaineer*, the Club's annual, lists Meany as having climbed Glacier Peak in the Summer of 1910 (see Vol. 3, November 1910, p. 39); Cora Eaton Smith to Meany, 2 September 1910 (quotation).
18. "Glacier Peak" was first published in *The Mountaineer* 3 (November 1910): 24-25. The version published here is from Meany, *Mountain Camp Fires* (Seattle: Lowman and Hanford Co., 1911), 34-35; Julie Nettleton, "Mountaineers' Outing on Glacier Peak," *The Mountaineer* 3 (November 1910): 29-38.
19. Meany, "Objects of Our Club," *ibid.*, pp. 5-7 (quotations p. 5); Meany, "The Olympic National Monument," *ibid.*, vol. 4 (1911): 54-59.
20. Meany to H.C. Coffman, 14 September 1905, Meany Letterpress Book (1899; 1904-1906).
21. Edward C. Marsh to Meany, 22 December 1908; Meany to the Macmillan Company, 2 January 1909 (quotation), Meany Letterpress Book (1908-1909).
22. Meany to George P. Brett, 26 January 1909, *ibid.*; Brett to Meany 2 February 1909; Meany to Brett, 7 February 1909, Meany Letterpress Book (1908-1909); Meany to Macmillan Company, 18 April 1909 (quotation), *ibid.*
23. Meany to Brett, 7 May 1909 (quotation), *ibid.*; Meany to Brett, 20 May 1909, *ibid.*; Meany proudly reported the names of his ten guarantors to Brett on 23 May, 1909, *ibid.*, stating that "Five of them are millionaires. The other five men are of substance

and prominence," including University of Washington President Kane and former Governor McGraw.

24. C.W. Smith, "Some of the Newest Books," *Seattle Post-Intelligencer*, 20 June 1909.
25. *Seattle Times*, 27 June 1909; *Oregonian* (Portland), 30 May 1909.
26. *Ibid.*, (quotation "briefly but discreetly described"); Prosch stated in the *Seattle Times* (27 June 1909) that Meany had handled the Whitman controversy with fairness, as did the *Wenatchee Daily World* on 3 June 1909; Meany, *History of the State of Washington*, 127 (quotations on Whitman), see pp. 122-127 for full discussion.
27. Meany to Hazard Stevens, 21 June 1909, Meany Letterpress Book (1908-1909); Meany, *History of the State of Washington*, 188 (quotation).
28. Meany to J. Franklin Jameson, 1 July 1909, Meany Letterpress Book (1908-1909); *Who's Who in America* Vol. 21 (1940-1941), 2277. Joseph Schafer's review is found in the *American Historical Review* 15 (October 1909): 167-169.
29. *Seattle Times*, 27 June 1909 (Prosch's quotation); *Seattle Post-Intelligencer*, 20 June 1909. Other favorable reviews include the statement in *The Dial* XLVI (16 June 1909): 405, that Meany's work "is a distinct advance on the usual state history, being well-balanced, well-written, and well-printed," and a favorable report in *The Nation* (29 July 1909): 103-104.
30. Henry B. Dewey, "Department of Public Instruction: This Year's Teachers' Reading Circle," *Northwest Journal of Education* 21 (January 1910): 19-20. For information on sales see Macmillan Company, Annual Statement of Royalty Account [1912, 1913, 1916, 1917, 1918, 1922], Meany Papers; Meany to Samuel Hill, 24 August 1910, Meany Letterpress Book (1909-1912); The Macmillan Company to Meany, 25 September 1912.
31. Meany, "Graduate Work at the University of Washington," a statement written 12 or 13 April 1909 and impressed in Meany Letterpress Book (1908-1909), 574. It may have been attached to Meany to J.N. Bowman, 12 April 1909, *ibid.* "Faculty Matters," the Washington *Alumnus* 2 (April 1909): 12; "New Members of the Faculty," *ibid.*, 3 (18 October 1909), 8; *Who Was Who in America*, 1 (1897-1942): 1031; Meany to Thomas Kane, 22 July 1910, Meany Letterpress Book (1909-1912); O.H.R. [Oliver H. Richardson] to Meany, 6 August 1912.
32. Frederic L. Paxson to Meany, 21 May 1909; Meany to Paxson, 26 May 1909, Meany Letterpress Book (1908-1909); Meany to Ashmun N. Brown, 26 May 1909 (quotation), *ibid.*; Meany to J.N. Bowman, 9 October 1909, *ibid.*
33. Jacob N. Bowman, "Proceedings of the Sixth Annual Meeting of the Pacific Coast Branch of the American Historical Association," *Annual Report of the American Historical Association, 1909* (Washington, D.C., 1911), 81-89; Frederick Jackson Turner, "The Significance of the Frontier in American History," in *The Frontier in American History* (New York: Henry Holt and Company, 1920), 14 (quotation).
34. Meany, "The Towns of the Pacific Northwest Were Not Founded on the Fur Trade," *Annual Report of the American Historical Association, 1909*, 165-172. Hubert Howe Bancroft, *Works*, XXVII, p. 448.
35. On Meany's election as vice president, see Jacob N. Bowman, "Proceedings of the Sixth Annual Meeting of the Pacific Coast Branch of the American Historical Association," *Annual Report of the American Historical Association, 1909*, 89; Waldo G. Leland, "Report of the Proceedings of the Twenty-Fifth Annual Meeting of the American Historical Association, New York City, December 27-31, 1909," *ibid.*, 33. Meany's paper was published in *ibid.*, pp. 173-179.
36. Meany to Thomas Kane, 21 December 1908, WUSHS Letterpress Book (1904-1914); Meany to Kane, 24 April 1909, Meany Letterpress Book (1908-1909); Thomas W.

Prosch to Charles W. Smith, 26 June 1909, Library Director's Office Records, University of Washington; [Charles W. Smith] to Prosch, 1 July 1909, *ibid.*; T.C. Elliott to C.B. Bagley, 12 November 1910, Bagley Papers; Meany to Samuel Hill, 28 June 1909, WUSHS Letterpress Book (1904-1914).

37. The resumption of publishing is discussed more fully in George Frykman, "Development of the *Washington Historical Quarterly*, 1906-1935: The Work of Edmond S. Meany and Charles W. Smith," 125-126; Thomas Prosch to Meany, 14 April 1912 (quotation on his astonishment); T.C. Elliott to Charles W. Smith, 19 April 1912 (quotation "publication suffers"), Smith Papers, University of Washington Archives; Elliott to Smith, 13 July 1914, *ibid.*; Meany to Joseph Schafer, 14 April 1912, Meany Letterpress Book (1909-1912). The nature of the new press and its relation to the *Washington Historical Quarterly* are described in Willis Armstrong Katz, "A Historical Survey of Washington Publishers and Printers from 1842-1956" (Master of Librarianship thesis, University of Washington, 1956).
38. Frykman, "Development of the *Washington Historical Quarterly*," 25.
39. *Ibid.*, 128-129; Lewis H. St. John, "The Present Status and Probable Future of the Indians of Puget Sound," *Washington Historical Quarterly* 5 (January 1914): 12-21; W.J. Trimble, "American and British Treatment of the Indians in the Pacific Northwest," *ibid.*, 32-54.
40. Ray Allen Billington, *Frederick Jackson Turner: Historian, Scholar, Teacher* (New York: Oxford University Press, 1973), 448-449 (quotation p. 449). Two presentations of the essay may be compared as follows: *Washington Historical Quarterly* 5 (October 1914): 243-257, with *The Frontier in American History*, 290-310. The terms "stark and strong" and "full of life" referring to the influence of the forest (or the frontier) in creating democracy were removed from the 1920 revision.
41. George P. Brett to Meany, 29 January 1910; Meany to Brett, 5 February 1910, Meany Letterpress Book (1909-1912); Brett to Meany, 15 February 1910, and 19 May 1911; Edward C. Marsh to Meany, 19 May 1911, to which is attached an anonymous "Reader's Report" on Meany's "U.S. History for Schools." In the Preface to the complete work Meany thanked the following colleagues for assistance: Edward O. Sisson, Edward McMahon, and Vernon Louis Parrington.
42. *Northwest Journal of Education* 23 (April 1912): 344. For information on Bras and his journal, see Mrs. Josephine Corliss Preston, *Twenty-Third Biennial Report of the Superintendent of Public Instruction for the Biennium ending June 30, 1916* (Olympia: Frank M. Lamborn, Public Printer, 1917), 154; Otto L. Luther's review appeared in the *Northwest Journal of Education* 23 (June 1912): 464. Information on Luther is in *ibid.*, 25 (May 1914): 409.
43. Meany to Brett, 2 February 1912 (quotation "Somehow I feel"), Meany Letterpress Book (1909-1912); Brett to Meany, 9 February 1912; Meany to Brett, 27 June 1912; Meany to James C. Strong, [August] 1915, Meany Letterpress Book (1912-1915). On royalties see Macmillan Company, Annual Statement of Royalty Account, Meany Papers.
44. *The Argus* (Seattle), 29 April 1911 (quotation), clipping in Box 17-5, Meany Papers (106-2-75-10); Meany to H.A. Chadwick, 13 May 1911, Meany Letterpress Book (1909-1912).
45. Frank P. Graves to Meany, 16 May 1911 (quotation "fully deserved"); Meany to Graves, 23 May 1911 (quotation "understood"), Meany Letterpress Book (1909-1912); "Professor Meany Will Stay with the University," unidentified clipping, not dated but after 27 September [1911], Box 17-1, Meany Papers (106-2-75-10), has Kane's statement to Meany.

46. Unidentified newspaper clipping on Meany's possible candidacy for governor [1911], Box 17-1, Meany Papers (106-2-75-10); "Meany Nips the Boom to Make Him Head of the State of Washington," *Seattle Times*, 22 October 1911, reveals details of Lorton's trial balloon and quoted Lorton's statement from the *Vancouver Spokesman*. On Lorton, see *Who Was Who in America*, vol. 2 (1950), 330, the quote "flattering kindness" appeared in the *Seattle Times*, 22 October 1911.
47. Meany to Myrtle Crowley, 4 October 1911, Meany Letterpress Book (1909-1912). The version quoted in the text is from the *Seattle Times*, 22 October 1911. Quotation "As professor at the University of Washington," is from an unidentified clipping "Professor Meany Will Stay With the University," Meany Papers, Box 17-1.
48. The issues leading to President Kane's dismissal are discussed in Charles M. Gates, *The First Century at the University of Washington, 1861-1961* (Seattle: University of Washington Press, 1961), 135-142; Neal O. Hines, *Denny's Knoll, A History of the Metropolitan Tract of the University of Washington* (Seattle: University of Washington Press, 1980), 117-119, adds valuable information, especially on the personnel of the Board of Regents; Meany to Ernest Lister, 29 October 1913 (quotation), Meany Letterpress Book (1912-1915).
49. William Markham To J. Allen Smith, Edmond S. Meany, and E.J. McCaustland, 27 April 1914, Meany Papers; Meany to Norman Hapgood, 21 February 1914, Meany Letterpress Book (1912-1915); Meany to Lister, 21 February 1914, *ibid.* Meany used the term "monarchical" in his "Electing a College President," *Harper's Weekly* (25 April 1914), 13.
50. Winlock W. Miller to Meany, 27 February 1914; Charles E. Gaches to Meany, 3 and 7 March 1914; O.A. Fechter to Meany, 7 March [1914]; Meany to Fechter, 17 March 1914; Meany's draft of an article "An Evolution of Educational Independence," is found in Meany to Norman Hapgood, 6 March 1914. Meany to Hapgood, 23 March 1914, provides a penciled draft of Meany's added statement acknowledging the authority of the regents under state law; Meany, "Electing a College President," *Harper's Weekly* (25 April 1914), 13.
51. J. Allen Smith, E.J. McCaustland, and Edmond S. Meany to the Regents' Committee on the Selection of a President, [12 May 1914], Meany Papers; John Dewey to Meany, 18 May 1914; Meany to Fechter, 31 May 1914, Meany Letterpress Book (1912-1915); Fechter to Meany, 3 June 1914; Gates, *First Century,* 142 (quotation).
52. *University of Washington Daily*, 9 and 17 November, and 22 December 1909, 26 January 1910; *Seattle Post-Intelligencer*, 2 May 1914; *Seattle Times*, 1 and 3 May 1914.
53. Meany to J. Franklin Jameson, 13 January 1914, Meany Letterpress Book (1912-1915); William A. Morris to Meany, 3 and 13 December 1913, and 25 January 1914; Meany to Morris, 10 February 1914, Meany Letterpress Book (1912-1915); "Report of the Proceedings of the Thirtieth Annual Meeting of the American Historical Association, Chicago, December 29-31, 1914," *Annual Report of the American Historical Association, 1914*, 2 volumes (Washington, D.C., 1916) I: 47, gives statistics on the Pacific Coast Branch; Meany to Edward McMahon, 25 December 1914, Meany Letterpress Book (1912-1915).
54. The Seattle address delivered on 22 May 1914, was published as "Three Diplomats Prominent in the Oregon Question," *Washington Historical Quarterly* 5 (July 1914): 207-214; see *ibid.*, pp. 213- 214 for quotation "to show something of the debt," and p. 207 for quotations "English-speaking people," and "should join in such a celebration."
55. He disclosed his fear that Wilson's neutrality policy would defeat attempts to celebrate a century of peace since Ghent, in a statement in the "News Department" of

the *Washington Historical Quarterly* 6 (January 1915): 75. Evidence of the celebration is found in the following items, all of which are clippings found in the Meany Papers: Worthington C. Ford, editorial, *Boston Herald*, 24 December 1914; Brooks Adams to Meany, 1 January 1915; W.A. Dunning to Meany, 8 December 1914 (quotation), and 25 December 1914. The *Lexington* (Kentucky) *Herald*, 25 December 1914; Meany to James E. Tuthill, 19 January 1915.

56. W.C. Ford to Meany, 31 December 1914; Meany to Ford, 19 January 1915.
57. *Seattle Times*, 15 February 1915; *Seattle Post-Intelligence*r, 15 February 1915 (quotation).

Notes for Chapter Nine

1. *University of Washington Daily*, 15 February 1915; Woodrow Wilson, "An Appeal to the American People," in Arthur S. Link, ed., *The Papers of Woodrow Wilson*, vol. 30 (6 May-30 September, 1914), 393-394.
2. Meany to J.N. Bowman, 14 November 1914, Meany Letterpress Book (1912-1915); O.H.R.[Richardson] to Meany, January 1915; Meany to Bowman, 19 January 1915.
3. Chris J. Rohwer to Meany, 6 October 1915; Meany to Rohwer, 16 November 1915 (quotation "I do not wish"), Meany Letterpress Book (1915-1916). Meany's remarks regarding the Monroe Doctrine were recorded in the *Tacoma Daily News*, 16 February 1916.
4. Quotations and reminiscences are found in J. Orin Oliphant to G.A. Frykman, 10 April 1970 (in the author's possession). See also Oliphant's notes for Meany's lectures on "Makers of the Nation," 2 vols., MSS, Oliphant Papers, Washington State University Libraries—Manuscript Archives, Special Collections (MASC); *Directory of American Scholars*, 6th Edition, I, History, p. 417.
5. An enclosure on Meany by Miss A.E. Strong in Frank Kane to Meany, 17 June 1916. She described Meany for a journalism class assignment.
6. "Students May Obtain Tyees at Bookstore." The clipping quoted here is found in J. Orin Oliphant's scrapbook, "Editorials and Correspondence, Sept. 1915 - May 1917," Oliphant Papers, Washington State University Libraries—MASC.
7. Meany reported the appointment of Farrar and quoted Henry Landes as to the purpose in a letter to Max Farrand, 1 February 1915. Landes to Meany, 29 April 1915, contains notification of Farrar's reappointment for 1915-1916; Meany to F.A. Golder, 1 February 1915; Golder to Meany, 11 February 1915; Meany to Golder, 18 April 1915, Meany Letterpress Book (1915-1916).
8. Charles M. Gates, *The First Century at the University of Washington, 1861-1961* (Seattle: University of Washington Press, 1961), 143-146; Suzzallo to Meany, 2 November 1915; Meany to Suzzallo, 4 December 1915, Meany Letterpress Book (1915-1916); Suzzallo to Meany, 4 December 1915 (quotation). Since alumnus James E. Gould was chairman of the committee in both communications from Suzzallo to Meany, it is assumed the original committee remained after being given additional functions.
9. Meany to V.K. Froula, 14 February 1915, Meany Letterpress Book (1912-1915); Meany to Samuel Hill, 30 May 1915, *ibid.*, (1915-1916); Meany to Mrs. Eva E. Bruce, 24 July and 28 November, 1915, *ibid.*
10. *Seattle Post-Intelligencer*, 1 July 1915 describes the wedding and the young couple. See also the *Seattle Times*, 1 July 1915 for additional details.
11. Meany to Samuel Hill, 30 July 1915, Meany Letterpress Book (1915-1916); Hill to Meany, 3 August, 1915 (quotation); Meany to Hill, 23 August 1915 (quotation), Meany Letterpress Book (1915-1916).

12. Meany, "Living Pioneers of Washington," *Seattle Post-Intelligencer*, 27 October (quotations), 28 October, and 1 November, 1915; Meany to Henry B. McElroy, 25 November 1915, Meany Letterpress Book (1915-1916); C.H. Hanford to Meany, 13 December 1915.
13. Meany to Allen Weir, 1 January 1916, Meany Letterpress Book (1915-1916), contains his "handclasp" statement; Scott C. Bone to Meany, 27 May 1916 contains Bone's statement.
14. *Seattle Post-Intelligencer*, 27 September 1915; E.S. Meany, *Governors of Washington: Territorial and State* (Seattle: Department of Printing, University of Washington, 1915), v.
15. *Ibid.*, 5-7, 71 (quotation on Moore).
16. *Ibid.*, 85-87, for quotations on Rogers see p. 86; *ibid.*, 111-114, for quotations on Lister see p. 112.
17. *Seattle Post-Intelligencer*, 23 February 1916 (quotations); Mrs. Elinor I. Thorne to Meany, 3 February 1916.
18. Meany, "First American Settlement on Puget Sound," *Washington Historical Quarterly* 7 (April 1916): 136-143 (quotation p. 136). The passage to be compared in the Meany, *History of the State of Washington* (New York: The Macmillan Company, 1909) is on pp. 221-222.
19. Meany, "First American Settlement on Puget Sound," 141-143 (quotation p. 143).
20. [Meany], "The Attempt to Appraise the Present as an Epoch in Human History," MS, 24 pp., Meany Papers. Though undated and unsigned, it is written in Meany's hand and expresses sentiments clearly attributable to Meany. A close study of this paper and "The Limits of Nationalism," endnote 21, which Meany signed, indicates the same authorship for both papers. Internal evidence dates the manuscript between late 1915 and early 1916. The paper reviews Meany's knowledge of Lewis Henry Morgan's ideas as interpreted by John Fiske, first published by Meany in "Passing of the Red Man," *Whitman College Quarterly* 2 (June 1898): 3-13. Quotations are found on pp. 23-24 of "The Attempt to Appraise the Present as an Epoch in Human History."
21. *Seattle Times*, 7, 8, and 9 July 1916; Meany, "The Limitations of Nationalism and the Dawn of a New Internationalism," 8 July 1916, MS, 14 pp., Meany Papers. For quotations see p. 4 ("unity of spirit," "hands and feet," and "soul"), p. 9 ("duties" and "rights"), p. 13 ("we surely will see"), and p. 14 ("the new education," "hearken back," and "the new internationalism").
22. Meany to Houghten Mifflin Company, 19 April 1916, penciled draft, Meany Papers; Houghton Mifflin Company to Meany, 6 May 1916; Meany to the Macmillan Company, 13 May 1916; the Macmillan Company to Meany 23 May 1916; Meany to the Macmillan Company, 14 July 1916, Meany Letterpress Book (1915-1916). The preface (p. vii) of his *Mount Rainier: A Record of Exploration* (New York: Macmillan Company, 1916) makes Meany's writing purposes clear.
23. *The Dial, a Fortnightly Journal of Literary Criticism, Discussion and Information* 62 (17 May 1917): 447. The advertisement appeared in the *Seattle Times* on 19 December 1916, and in the *Post-Intelligencer* on 20 December 1916; Meany to the Macmillan Company, 29 December 1916, Meany Letterpress Book (1916-1917); R. Nordhoff to Meany, 13 February and 14 March 1917; Robert Moran to Samuel Hill, 20 March 1917, Meany Papers; Meany to Moran, 1 April 1917, Meany Letterpress Book (1916-1917).
24. Meany to Samuel Hill, 8 April 1917, *ibid.*; R. Nordhoff to Meany, 10 April 1917; Meany to Nordhoff, 15 April 1917, Meany Letterpress Book (1916-1917); Meany to Moran, 1 May 1917, *ibid.*; Meany to Nordhoff, 8 April 1917 (quotation), and 11 April 1917, *ibid.*

25. Meany, *Mount Rainier, A Record of Exploration*, 302.
26. *Ibid.*
27. The editorials appeared during the period 8 April - 1 May 1917. Although they were unsigned, Meany's authorship is established in Scott C. Bone to Meany, 7 April 1917, found in clippings pasted in Meany's scrapbook for 1917.
28. "Duties of the Home," *Seattle Post-Intelligencer*, 11 April 1917.
29. "Subjective Patriotism," *ibid.*, 17 April 1917.
30. "America's Glowing Chance," *ibid.*, 12 April 1917. On the ignorance of the United States government regarding Bolsheviks, see George Kennan, *Soviet-American Relations, 1917-1920*, 2 vols. (Princeton: Princeton University Press, 1956), I: 8-19.
31. Henry Suzzallo to the Heads of Departments, 22 March 1917, Meany Papers. Meany to Suzzallo, 26 April 1917, Meany Letterpress Book (1916-1917) contains his detailed report and quotation on McMahon's methods. Albert H. Yoder to Meany, 2 January 1915 contains the quotation on Meany and McMahon by the third party.
32. Meany to Henry Suzzallo, 2 June 1917, Meany Letterpress Book (1916-1917); Suzzallo to Meany, 5 June 1917.
33. Meany to Franklin H. Giddings, 4 June 1917, Meany Letterpress Book (1916-1917); Meany to Waldo G. Leland, 20 May 1917, *ibid.*; Meany to Suzzallo, 17 June 1917, *ibid.*
34. Meany to Waldo G. Leland, 12 and 20 May 1917, *ibid.* On the history of the National Board of Historical Services see Carol S. Gruber, *Mars and Minerva, World War I and the Uses of Higher Learning in America* (Baton Rouge: Louisiana State University Press, 1975), 120-130.
35. "History in Summer Schools, 1917" *The History Teacher's Magazine* 8 (May 1917): 166; Meany to Dean A.R. Priest, 26 October 1917, Meany Letterpress Book (1916-1917).
36. *Seattle Post-Intelligencer*, 23 November 1917; Meany to J. Franklin Jameson, 8 December 1917, Meany Letterpress Book (1917-1918); Henry Suzzallo to Meany, 20 November 1917; Meany to Rev. P.H. Raymond, 24 November 1917, Meany Letterpress Book (1917-1918).
37. Meany to State Council of Defense, 29 August 1917, Meany Letterpress Book (1916-1917); Henry Suzzallo, "Washington War History Committees," *Washington Historical Quarterly* 9 (January 1918): 23-25; Meany to state Council of Defense, 14 October 1917, Meany Letterpress Book (1916-1917); longhand draft of Meany's circular letter: "Historical Service During the War," 16 October 1917, *ibid.* The letter was mailed 24 October 1917 to the thirty-nine county councils of defense as a primer on collecting and preserving historical materials; Waldo G. Leland regarded it as a model and published it in "The Archives of the War," *Annual Report of the American Historical Association for 1917* (Washington, D.C., 1920), 117-123 (quotation "More accurate" is on p. 121).
38. For committees organized almost immediately, see Meany to C.M. Riddell, 28 October 1917, Meany Letterpress Book (1916-1917); Meany to Judge William C. Brown, 30 October 1917, Meany Letterpress Book (1917-1918). The next records found are for early December: for example, Meany to J.A. Perkins, 2 December 1917, *ibid.* Lack of funds is stated in Meany to A.J. Craven, 14 November 1917, *ibid.*, and Meany to Suzzallo, 30 October 1917 (quotation), *ibid.*
39. *Annual Report of the American Historical Association for 1920* (Washington, D.C.: Government Printing Office, 1925), I, 135-137, 285 (quotation from Meany).
40. Meany to Suzzallo, [1 November 1917], Meany Letterpress Book (1917-1918), indicates separate reports on the tasks were enclosed. Suzzallo to Meany, 13 November 1917, acknowledged receipt of reports (quotation on Ephebic Oath).

41. Meany to Suzzallo, 20 November 1917 (quotation "painful information"), Meany Letterpress Book (1917-1918); Meany to Suzzallo, undated [*c.* November 1917], a penciled draft found in the Meany Papers, presents the information on Scholz and his possible role in the department. Meany to Suzzallo, 21 November 1917 (quotation "Richardson"), Meany Letterpress Book (1917-1918).
42. Ralph J. Lutz to Meany, 29 November 1917.
43. Suzzallo to Meany, 22 February 1918, and 13 March 1919 (quotation). Meany to Suzzallo, 10 February 1918, Meany Letterpress Book (1918-1919). Further contemporary testimony of the serious intent behind the title "Keeper of Traditions" is found in an unpublished history by Edwin B. Stevens entitled "Henry Suzzallo, President, University of Washington, 1915 to 1926," chapter 2, revised (University of Washington Archives).
44. Meany to Mrs. Eliza Ferry Leary, 13 February 1918, Meany Letterpress Book (1918-1919); *Seattle Post-Intelligencer*, 22 February 1918; Meany to Suzzallo, 23 February 1918, Meany Letterpress Book (1918-1919); Meany to Waldo G. Leland, 24 February 1918 (quotation "imbue them"), *ibid.*; Gruber, *Mars and Minerva,* 135.
45. [Meany] to [J.F.] Jameson, 24 February 1918, a penciled draft (quotations "After long years" and "real danger"), Meany Papers; Suzzallo to Meany, 25 February 1918; Meany to Suzzallo, 4 March and 20 May 1918, Meany Letterpress Book (1918-1919).
46. Meany to professor George S. Wilson, 18 February 1918, *ibid.*; Meany to President's Office, 18 February 1918, *ibid.*; Meany to A.R. Priest, 6 January 1918, Meany Letterpress Book (1917-1918).
47. Meany was coordinator of Camp Lewis lectures as he reported in a letter to the National Board of Historical Services, 18 April 1918, *ibid.* Meany guaranteed the cost of the lantern slides: Meany to Jameson, 17 January 1918 (penciled copy of telegram); J.F. Jameson to Meany, 14 February and 4 March 1918. Meany to Norman F. Coleman, 10 March 1918 indicates that the syllabi came from the National Board of Historical Services, Meany Letterpress Book (1917-1918); Meany to Waldo G. Leland, 24 February 1918 (quotation), *ibid.* (1918-1919).
48. Meany to Albert J. Whitney, 17 July 1918, Meany Letterpress Book (1917-1918); Meany to Recorder Stone, University of Washington [14 July 1918], *ibid.*
49. Meany to Suzzallo, 1 June 1918, *ibid.*; Meany to Dean David Thomson, 15 April 1918, *ibid.*; memo from Meany [Annual Review of Faculty] 27 April 1918, with quotation; C.W. David to Meany, 22 April and 8 May 1918; Suzzallo to David, 24 April 1918, Meany Papers.
50. Meany to Victor Farrar, 15 September 1918, Meany Letterpress Book (1917-1918).
51. Meany, "War Aims Course: Outline of the Work at the University of Washington," 6 October 1918, *ibid.*; Meany to Edward C. Elliott, 6 October 1918, *ibid.*; N.D. Mereness (ed.), "American Historical Activities During the World War, IV," American Historical Association, *Annual Report*, 1919, Vol. I: 285.
52. Meany to Farrar, 15 September 1918 (quotation), Meany Letterpress Book (1917-1918); Meany to Farrar, 23 October 1918, *ibid.*; *Seattle Post-Intelligencer*, 9, 10, and 17 October 1918.
53. Meany to George W. Soliday, 27 October 1918 (quotation "many times"), Meany Letterpress Book (1917-1918); Ralph H. Lutz to Meany, 3 November 1918 (quotations "ultimate triumph" and "victory").
54. Meany to Albert, King of the Belgians, 26 November 1918 (quotations "love poured out" and "wonderful"), Meany Letterpress Book (1917-1918); Meany to Marshal Ferdinand Foch, 29 November 1918 (quotation "behalf of civilization."), *ibid.* Other pertinent letters were sent to Woodrow Wilson, Raymond Poincaré, Georges

Clemenceau, King George V, and numerous American leaders, see *ibid.*, 26 November to 24 December 1918.

55. Meany, "Remember Men at the Front," *Seattle Post-Intelligencer*, 6 December 1918.
56. Meany to Capt. Harold O. Sexsmith, 12 December 1918, Meany Letterpress Book (1918-1920); Meany to Lutz, 25 December 1918 (quotation "We thrill daily"), *ibid.*; Gruber, *Mars and Minerva,* 238-252; Meany to Houghton Mifflin Company, 28 December 1918, Meany Letterpress Book (1918-1920) indicates the war aims course would not be continued.
57. Meany to Farrar, 25 December 1918, *ibid.*
58. Interview with Edmond S. Meany, Jr., 7 March 1975, by the author.
59. *Ibid.*, 6 March 1975.
60. *Ibid.*
61. Meany to Frederick Jackson Turner, 29 December 1918 (quotation "an attack of melancholia"), Meany Letterpress Book (1918-1920); Meany to Turner, 3 January 1919, *ibid.*
62. *Ibid.*, (quotation "this book has shaken me up"); Brooks Adams to Meany, 7 January 1919 (quotation "Wilson").
63. Meany to Frank Fitts, 2 March 1919, Meany Letterpress Book (1918-1920); Meany, "Western Spruce and the War," *Washington Historical Quarterly* 9 (October 1918): 255-258.
64. "Summer Quarter, 1919," *Bulletin of the University of Washington*, general series, No. 128 (May 1919), 23-24; Meany to Ensign Phil J. Weiss, 19 July 1919, Meany Letterpress Book (1918-1920). "Testimonial to Prof. Edmond S. Meany," July 1919 (quotation), Meany Papers.

Notes for Chapter Ten

1. Meany to Bernard Pelly, 20 September 1923, Meany Letterpress Book (1922-1923).
2. *University of Washington Daily*, 11 October 1920.
3. Meany, "Vigor," a poem dedicated to the class of 1920, University of Washington, Junior day, 30 May 1920, Meany Papers. Special thanks to University of Washington archivist, Gary A. Lundall, for making this poem available to the author.
4. Frederick M. Padelford to Meany, 1 July 1920; E.D. Adams to Meany, 2 July 1920; Meany to Mrs. Fanny Garrison Villard, 14 July 1920, Meany Letterpress Book (1920-1921). For Mrs. Garrison's biography, see the *Dictionary of American Biography* (New York: Charles Scribners' Sons, 1936), XIX, 272-273.
5. Meany, "A Prophecy Fulfilled; Address Before the Tulalip Indian School, Tulalip, Washington, 21 December 1920," pamphlet, unpaged.
6. Worthington C. Ford to Meany, 28 January 1921; *Seattle Times*, 21 December 1920 (editorial); *Seattle Post-Intelligencer*, 22 December 1920.
7. Meany to Henry Suzzallo, 6 February 1921, Meany Letterpress Book (1920-1921).
8. Meany, "Edmond S. Meany Reviews Work as a Newspaper Man," *Seattle Post-Intelligencer*, 30 May 1921 (quotation "Somehow"), 13 November 1921; Meany to *Post-Intelligencer*, 9 November 1921, Meany Letterpress Book (1921-1922).
9. Meany to Judge Everett Smith, 4 March 1922, *ibid.*
10. Cecil Dryden to Frykman, 14 April 1970 (letter in author's possession).
11. *Ibid.*; Gilbert B. Foster, "A Keeper of Traditions," *Sunset Magazine* 48 (April 1922): 27 (quotation); Foster to Meany, 6 June [1921].
12. Meany reported an enrollment of 279 students in his "Makers of the Nation" course to Brooks Adams, 5 October 1919, Meany Letterpress Book (1918-1920); Meany to L.E. Robinson, 16 April 1920, *ibid.*; Meany to J.A. Mitchell, 16 April 1920, *ibid.*

13. Interview with Joseph T. Bradley, 16 December 1969 (quotation "a pleasant office"); Theresa Schmid McMahon, "My Story" (mimeographed, n.d.), 57; interviews with Edmond S. Meany, Jr., 6 and 7 March 1975; J. Orin Oliphant to Frykman, 10 April 1970. On Theresa McMahon's faculty status in economics see her "My Story," *passim.*
14. Statement of the Department of History in support of the proposal to establish a doctoral degree program is found in a letter from Edmond S. Meany to Dr. J. Allen Smith, Dean of the Graduate School, 22 November 1919; Charles M. Gates, *The First Century at the University of Washington, 1861-1961* (Seattle: University of Washington Press, 1961), 156-157; Oliphant to Frykman, 10 April 1970.
15. "News Department," *Washington Historical Quarterly* 12 (April 1921): 160; Oliphant to Frykman, 10 April 1970. For Oliphant's biography, see *Directory of American Scholars*, 6th edition, I, History, p. 471.
16. John Boit, "New Log of the Columbia," *Washington Historical Quarterly* 12 (January 1921): 3-50; Worthington C. Ford to Meany, 28 January 1921.
17. *The Oregonian* (Portland), 30 January 1921 (quotations "illuminating" and "almost as much interest"); Joseph Schafer to Meany, 24 January 1921 (quotation "you have done an excellent service"); "Report of the Council," *Proceedings of the Massachusetts Historical Society* 54 (October, 1920-June 1921): 248 (quotation "'attracted much attention'"); Meany to Henry Suzzallo, 2 February 1921, Meany Letterpress Book (1920-1921).
18. Meany to Dr. Minnie F. Howard, 22 July 1923, Meany Letterpress Book (1922-1923); J.F. Jameson to Meany, 7 August 1923; a carbon copy to Meany of Jameson to Howard, 13 August 1923; Meany, "Secret Aid for Oregon Missions," *Washington Historical Quarterly* 15 (July 1924): 211-214 (quotation "It is significant, if true" on p. 211; "Students of Northwestern History," on p. 214). In 1932 Cornelius J. Brosnan denied the Secret Service story for lack of evidence in his *Jason Lee: Prophet of the New Oregon* (New York: Macmillan Company, 1932). See also, Robert J. Loewenberg, Review of *Marcus and Narcissa Whitman and the Opening of Old Oregon*, by Clifford M. Drury, in *Journal of American History* 61 (September 1974): 482-483.
19. See, for example, "Origin of Washington Geographic Names," in *Washington Historical Quarterly* 8 (October 1917) and 12 (October 1922); Meany to George W. Fuller, 9 March 1921, Meany Letterpress Book (1920-1921). Meany's volume, *Origin of Washington Geographic Names*, was published in 1923 by the University of Washington Press. A reprinting was issued in 1968 by Gale Research Corporation of Detroit, Michigan. Robert Hitchman's *Place Names of Washington*, published in 1985 by the Washington State Historical Society, supplements Meany's *Origin of Washington Geographic Names*. See "Washington Centennial Bookshelf" pamphlet (Olympia and Pullman: Washington Centennial Commission, 1989), 14.
20. Meany, "Newspapers of Washington Territory," *Washington Historical Quarterly* 13 (July 1922): 181-195. The volume was published by the University of Washington Press in 1923. "The Literary Guide Post by Diogenes," *The Tacoma Daily Ledger*, 2 September 1922 (quotations); Clarence B. Bagley, "Crossing the Plains," *Washington Historical Quarterly* 13 (July 1922): 163-180.
21. Charles H. Seaver to Meany, 20 August 1923; Meany to Seaver, 7 October 1923, Meany Letterpress Book (1922-1923); Meany, *History of the State of Washington*, revised edition (New York: The Macmillan Company, 1924), Chapter XXXII, "Evidence of recent Advance." The anecdote on President Harding is on pp. 363-364.
22. George P. Brett to Meany, 20 May 1925; Meany to Brett, 22 June 1925. Italics are those of present author.
23. Brett to Meany, 30 June 1925; "Annual Statement of Royalty Account," The Macmillan Company, Publishers, to Meany, 28 July 1928 and 29 July 1929. The present author's

copy of the *History of the State of Washington*, revised edition, was printed in 1950 (fifth printing).

24. C.W. Smith, "Report of the *Washington Historical Quarterly*, 1925-1926," (quotation "but from distant," p. 1, "a comparison," pp. 1-2); C.W. Smith Papers, University of Washington Archives.
25. A detailed discussion of these authors appears in Frykman, "Development of the *Washington Historical Quarterly*, 1906-1935," *Pacific Northwest Quarterly*, 128-129.
26. *Ibid.*, 128; "News Department," *Washington Historical Quarterly* 17 (January 1926): 77, 78; "The Pacific Rim," *ibid.*, (April 1926): 83-125, introduces the symposium and the papers discussed.
27. Meany, "History and Science," *ibid.*, 19 (April 1928): 83-89; Charles A. Beard, "Fresh Air in American Letters," *The Nation* 124 (18 May 1927): 560 (quotation).
28. Meany, "History and Science," *Washington Historical Quarterly* 19 (April 1928): 83, 84 (quotation "Yes, I know about that," pp. 83-84; quotation from Byers, p. 83).
29. *Ibid.*, 83.
30. *Ibid.*, 84, 87 (quotations from Freeman and Meany found on p. 84; from Sarton on p. 87).
31. *Ibid.*, 87.
32. Frykman, "Development of the *Washington Historical Quarterly*," 128, 129; "Fourth List of Members of the History of Science Society, Elected from August 1, 1927 to December 1, 1928," *Isis, International Review Devoted to the History of Science and Civilization*, 12 (1929): 181; Arthur M. Schlesinger, Sr., "An American Historian Looks at Science and Technology," *ibid.*, 36 (October 1946): 162-166.
33. Meany to Mrs. Eliza Ferry Leary, 17 January and 6 February 1921, Meany Letterpress Book (1920-1921); Meany to Robert S. Boyus, 8 February 1921 (quotation), *ibid.*
34. *Seattle Post-Intelligencer*, 20 and 23 February 1921; Meany to James A. Wood, 20 February 1921, Meany Letterpress Book (1920-1921), expresses his gratitude for the editorial; Meany to Hon. Wesley L. Jones, 26 February 1921, *ibid.*; Meany to Arthur R. Priest, 26 February 1921, *ibid.*
35. Meany to Mrs. Eliza Ferry Leary, 10 December 1922, Meany Letterpress Book (1922-1923); "Washington's Birthday 1923-1924," and "Washington's Birthday 1925-1926," Meany Scrapbook: Washington's Birthday, Meany Papers.
36. Meany to Mrs. W.A. Barrows, 11 November 1920, Meany Letterpress Book (1920-1921); notes by Edmond S. Meany on Armistice Day, written on 18 February 1926 (quotation "Kept tradition alive"), Meany Papers.
37. Henry Suzzallo to Meany, 3 March 1924; Mitchell V. Charnley to Meany, 28 April 1924 (quotations). Information on dedication of the columns is found in the *Seattle Post-Intelligencer*, 23 April 1921.
38. *Seattle Post-Intelligencer*, 3 May 1924 (quotation, "glowing tribute"); *Seattle Times*, 2 May 1924 (quotation, "service as the ideal alumnus"); Printed letter, "The Committee," by Matthew W. Hill to _____, n.d., found in *Edmond S. Meany, 1862-1935, Tributes, II* (scrapbook). That the automobile was a Buick is established by Meany in a note of appreciation to Clarence B. Bagley (Meany to "Dear Friends," n.d., but May, 1924), C.B. Bagley Papers, University of Washington Archives; Meany to Mrs. Gus Hensler, 10 May 1926.
39. The popularity of pageantry in the 1920s is discussed by Constance D'Arcy Mackay in "The Rebirth of American Pageantry," *The American Magazine of Art* 17 (June 1926): 303-304. For current discussion see the following: Karal Ann Marling, *George Washington Slept Here: Colonial Revivals and American Culture, 1876-1986* (Cambridge: Harvard University Press, 1988); Wilbur Zelinsky, *Nation into State: The Shifting Symbolic Foundations of American Nationalism* (Chapel Hill: University of North

Carolina Press, 1988); and David Glassburg, *American Historical Pageantry, The Uses of Tradition in the Early Twentieth Century* (Chapel Hill: University of North Carolina Press, 1990).

40. Frank C. Doig, "The Wayfarer—America's Passion Play," *Washington Journal of Education* 1 (May 1922): 286-287; *Seattle Post-Intelligencer*, 1 June, 23, 24, 31 July 1921, and 23 July 1922; Meany to Montgomery Lynch, 29 July 1921, Meany Letterpress Book (1921-1922); Meany to Lynch, 16 March 1923, *ibid.*, (1922-1923).
41. *Official Program, "Americanus," produced in the University of Washington Stadium, 23-28 July 1923, written and produced by Prof. Edmond S. Meany and Montgomery Lynch, under auspices of Americanus Pageant Society acting for the Associated Students, University of Washington* (Seattle: Pioneer Printing Company, 1923). Meany was the author and Lynch directed the production, as attested by the letterhead of the Americanus Pageantry Society used in Lynch to Meany, 14 May 1923. See also, Meany to Lynch, 16 March 1923, Meany Letterpress Book (1922-1923). A copy of the pageant is available in the Northwest Collection, University of Washington Libraries. Reference to Seattle as "The Pageant City" is found in a handbill advertising "Americanus," Meany Papers; Meany to Darwin M. Meisnest, 21 July 1923, Meany Letterpress Book (1922-1923).
42. Meany, "Americanus" script, mimeograph, Meany Papers.
43. *Ibid.*, pp. 1,2 (quotation "The Great Spirit," p. 1; and other quotations on p. 2).
44. *Ibid.*, 7-8.
45. *Ibid.*, 10-12 (quotation on p. 12).
46. Meany, "From America to Europe," *ibid.* The second of two stanzas from p. 11 of the "Americanus" script is quoted.
47. *Ibid.*, 13.
48. *Seattle Times*, 23 (quotations) and 24 July 1923; *Seattle Post-Intelligencer*, 24, 28, and 29 July 1923.
49. Meany to Darwin M. Meisnest, 24 (quotations), 28 July and 13 August 1923, Meany Letterpress Book (1922-1923); Meisnest to Meany, 8 August 1923.
50. *Seattle Times*, 10 March 1925; *Seattle Post-Intelligencer*, 27 May 1925.
51. Memorandum of Conference Regarding Puget Sound Navigation Company Radio Program, held at University Faculty Club, 23 May 1929, Meany Papers; *Seattle Times*, 3 June 1929; *Seattle Post-Intelligencer*, 3 June 1929; Meany, "When Puget Sound was Discovered," radio script, 3 June 1929, Meany Papers; *Seattle Times*, 1 July 1929; Meany, "When Uncle Sam Surveyed Puget Sound," radio script, 1 July 1929, Meany papers; *Seattle Times*, 22 June 1929 (quotation).
52. Radio scripts cited above, and Meany, "When the Early Settlers Built Blockhouse Forts," radio script for program on 26 August 1929, which closely followed the text in Meany, *History of the State of Washington* (revised edition), Chapters 19 and 20; *Seattle Times*, 26 August 1929. All quotations are from Meany, "When Early Settlers Built Blockhouse Forts."
53. Meany to C.W. Smith, 30 September 1929, Director of Libraries Papers, University of Washington.
54. Meany to Smith, 6 January and 7 February 1927, and 23 November 1928 (quotation), *ibid.*; Smith to Hamilton Platt, 20 December 1926, 25 February 1927, *ibid.*; the Swan Papers are described in Lucile McDonald, *Swan Among the Indians: Life of James G. Swan, 1818-1900* (Portland: Binfords and Mort, Publishers, 1972), vii-ix.
55. Meany to Charles W. Smith, 30 September 1929, Director of Libraries Papers.
56. *Ibid.*

57. *Seattle Times*, 2 October 1929; *University of Washington Daily*, 2 October 1929, clipping in *Edmond Stephen Meany, 1862-1935 Tributes II*. These newspapers incorrectly reported Meany's injury as a fractured leg. Meany affirmed that it was a broken knee in a letter to Mrs. Peter Jensen, 7 January 1929 [should be 1930]. Mrs. E.C. Richards to Meany, n.d., reported that the accident was discussed even on street cars. Numerous messages of condolence are found among the incoming file for October, 1929, including one from Governor Hartley, 3 October 1929.
58. Meany to Mrs. Peter Jensen, 7 January 1929 [should be 1930]; Meany to Mr. and Mrs. James S. Bushnell, 6 November 1929; Meany to David Starr Jordan, 13 December 1929, volume 8, Education 1919-1942, Jordan Correspondence, Stanford Collection, Stanford University Library; interview with Edmond S. Meany, Jr., 6 March 1975.
59. A series of letters between C.W. Smith and F.W. Howay reveal Smith's editorial assistance to Meany. See, Smith to Howay, 24 October 1929, and 11 February 1930, and also Howay to Smith, 29 October 1929, 11 January and 21 February 1930 (all found in Director of Libraries Papers); Meany to Smith, 13 December 1929, *ibid.*; Meany to Mr. and Mrs. James Bushnell, 6 November 1929; *Seattle Post-Intelligencer*, 5 October 1929, clipping in *Edmond Stephen Meany, 1862-1935, Tributes*, II; *Seattle Times*, 21 October 1929.
60. *Seattle Times*, 15 and 16 September 1920; Meany to Mrs. William Kelly, 17 September 1920, Meany Letterpress Book (1920-1921).
61. Meany, Notes on Thomas Mercer Meany, 15 July 1928, Meany Papers, Folder 31-25 (106-2-75-10); Meany to Samuel Hill, 16 November 1920, Meany Letterpress Book (1920-1921).
62. Meany to Colin H. Livingstone, 13 November 1920, *ibid.*; interview with Edmond S. Meany, Jr., 6 March 1975; *The Mountaineer* 17 (15 December 1924): 7, 70, 71.
63. W.W. Seymour, "Chimney Rock to Mount Stuart," *The Mountaineer* 18 (15 December 1925): 21, 22 (quotation "never was a campfire program" p. 21; "he launched into," pp. 21-22). "Members of the 1925 Summer Outing," *ibid.*, 63. On the "Blockhouse War" see Meany, *History of the State of Washington*, 183.
64. Meany, "Ned," *The Mountaineer* 18 (15 December 1925), 56; "Members of the 1926 Outing," *ibid.*, 19 (December 1926): 42; "Members of the 1927 Summer Outing," *ibid.*, 20 (15 December 1927): 16; "Members of the 1928 Summer Outing," *ibid.*, 21 (15 December 1928): 19; Meany to James S. Bushnell, 24 August 1929; for evidence of the 1930 outing, see Meany to Frederick Jackson Turner, 5 September 1930; Meany's notes on a visit to Garibaldi Park [British Columbia], cover the 1931 outing (Meany Papers).
65. Mother [Mrs. Edmond S. Meany] to "Boys of Mine," 4 August 1925; Mrs. Edmond S. Meany to Ned, 8 August 1926; Lizzie Meany to Edmond S. Meany, 11 August 1926; interviews with Edmond S. Meany, Jr., 6 and 7 March 1975; Lizzie Meany to Ed [Meany], 5 August 1923.
66. Interview with Edmond S. Meany, Jr., 7 March 1975.
67. *Ibid.*; Meany to Samuel Hill, 26 November 1920, Meany Letterpress Book (1920-1921), reveals that Ned had undergone an appendectomy the previous day.
68. Joseph T. Bradley, in his interview with the present author on 16 December 1969, stated that there was an "academic community a bit north of the campus, running from 15th to 18th and from 45th to about Ravenna Boulevard, where most of these people resided. They hadn't moved to Laurelhurst yet, and they were a real close community." Interview with Edmond S. Meany, Jr., 7 March 1975.

69. *Seattle Post-Intelligencer*, 2 July 1919; Myra L. Phelps, *Public Works in Seattle: A Narrative History of the Engineering Department, 1875-1975* (Seattle Engineering Department, 1978), 34, 46, 47.
70. Interview with Edmond S. Meany, Jr., 7 March 1975. Corroboration of Edmond S. Meany, Jr.'s recollection that the house was turned around some time in 1924 is found by comparing the Meany address listed in *The Mountaineer* 16 (15 December 1923), 100, with *ibid.*, 17 (15 December 1924), 7 (supplement); Meany to R.C. Smith, 28 June 1928; Meany to J. Arthur Younger, 19 September 1928. The new home address was 4024 Ninth Avenue, NE.
71. Meany to Frederick Jackson Turner, 21 September 1923 (quotation "rather disconcerting"), Meany Letterpress Book (1922-1923); Turner to Meany, 27 September 1923 (quotation "a flood of sunshine"); Ray Allen Billington, *Frederick Jackson Turner: Historian, Scholar, Teacher* (New York: Oxford University Press, 1973), 5, 386.
72. Diploma: Doctor of Letters degree, College of Puget Sound, Meany Papers; Meany to R. Lester Kelly, 22 May 1926; Meany to Edwin C. Starks, 23 November 1927.
73. Gates, *First Century,* 158-160, 175.
74. M. Lyle Spencer to Meany, 12 May 1928; Frederick M. Padelford to Meany, n.d., lists salary figure for 1930-1931; Gates, *First Century,* 158-160, 175. As late as January, 1937, President L.P. Seig deplored the lack of a retirement system and warned that many faculty were being forced to retire without adequate income. See, *Report of the Board of Regents of the University of Washington to the Governor of Washington; Twenty-fourth Biennium* (Bulletin of the University of Washington, General Series, No. 457, 2 January 1937), 12.
75. *Seattle Post-Intelligencer*, 23 February 1929 (quotations "visibly moved," and "international viewpoint"); Meany to Gilbert Chinard, 8 September 1930 (quotation, "one of the great days").
76. *Seattle Star*, 3 February 1930, clipping in *Edmond Stephen Meany, 1862-1935, Tributes, II.*

Notes for Epilogue

1. *Seattle Times*, 9 February 1930, clipping in *Edmond Stephen Meany, 1862-1935, Tributes, II.* Italics are those of present author.
2. Joseph Daniels to Meany, 12 May 1930; Meany to Mrs. Maud S. Jensen, 26 January 1931 (quotation); Meany to Miss Soester [*sic*] I. Anthony, 26 February 1934; Meany to W.P. Bonney, 7 December 1934.
3. Meany to J.M. Howell, 23 and 25 March 1920, Meany Letterpress Book (1918-1920); Meany to Harry B. McElroy, 18 July 1920, ibid., (1920-1921); Meany to Clarence D. Martin, 17 December 1934. The work remained in manuscript according to the "Bibliography of Edmond Stephen Meany," 1935, MS., University of Washington Library. Governor Martin acknowledged that he had been a student of Meany's in his tribute at the latter's death. See, *Aberdeen World*, 22 April 1935, clipping in *Edmond Stephen Meany, 1862-1935, Tributes, I.*
4. Meany, *Washington From Life* (Seattle: Printed by Frank McCaffrey, Dogwood Press, 1931); Meany, *The Washington Statue, A Keepsake of Washington's Birthday Observance in the Commons at the University of Washington, Seattle, February 22, 1933* (Seattle: Printed By Frank McCaffrey, Dogwood Press, 1933); Meany, *Lincoln Esteemed Washington* (Seattle: Frank McCaffrey, 1933); E.S. Meany, Jr., commentary on Floyd Fessler's articles on E.S. Meany, *Seattle Star*, 10 February 1930, Meany Papers; Meany, "History of the University of Washington," 107 p. incomplete MS., Meany Papers.

5. George Frykman, "Development of the *Washington Historical Quarterly*, 1906-1935: The Work of Edmond S. Meany and Charles W. Smith, *Pacific Northwest Quarterly*" 70 (July 1979): 130. "Cost Ascertainment," Post Office Department. Photostatic copy of report signed by C.W. Smith, publisher, regarding mailing of the *Washington Historical Quarterly*, 8 Oct. 1934, Box 1, *Washington Historical Quarterly* Papers, Manuscript Division, University of Washington Library.
6. *University of Washington Daily*, 18 February 1932, clipping in *Edmond Stephen Meany, 1862-1935, Tributes, II.*
7. Charles M. Gates, *The First Century at the University of Washington, 1861-1961* (Seattle: University of Washington Press, 1961), 179, 180; E.S.M. [Meany] to Frederick Merk, 4 June 1932 (quotation "deemed worthy"); Meany to C. Eden Quainton, 31 October 1932.
8. *Seattle Post-Intelligencer*, 19 and 20 March 1934; Meany to H.H. Gowen, 2 April and 9 June 1934.
9. E.S. Meany, Jr., remarked in the interview of 7 March 1975, that his father realized that department chairmen no longer could be autocrats. Professor Meany sought consensus as often as possible, the son said, "but there may have been some occasions when he felt very strongly about something and could not go along with what the department advised." Meany's anxieties are expressed in a draft of a letter possibly never sent: Meany to Ned and Dorothy [Meany], n.d., but January 1933, or later, Meany Papers.
10. *Seattle Post-Intelligencer*, 28 January, 23 September 1930; *University District Herald*, 15 April 1930, clipping in *Edmond Stephen Meany, 1862-1935, Tributes, II;* Meany to John E. Burkheimer, 31 October 1931; *Seattle Times*, 13 November 1931 (quotations "clicking movie cameras," and "One of the most distinguished citizens"), and 15 November 1931; Meany to John R. Winans, 19 November 1931, indicates Meany had no financial interest in the hotel; Meany to Walter N. Sage, 23 November 1931 (quotation "but a bigger one").
11. Meany to City Editor, *The Seattle Times*, 16 August 1923, Meany Letterpress Book (1922-1923); *New York Times*, 26 August 1923; James T. Flexner, *George Washington in the American Revolution (1775-1783)* (Boston: Little, Brown and Company, 1967), 28; "News Department," *Washington Historical Quarterly* 18 (April 1927): 159; Meany to Howard T. Lewis, 7 November 1927.
12. M. Lyle Spencer to Meany, 10 October 1930, and 12 March 1931; Meany to Francis O'Reilly, 9 May 1931; Meany to Mrs. Fanny O'Brien, 28 March 1931; Meany to The President, White House, 18 September 1931; Meany to Mrs. J.B. Bowman, 18 September 1931 (quotation); David Lynn to Meany, 11 December 1931.
13. Joseph Daniels to M. Lyle Spencer, 7 March 1929, Meany Papers; M. Lyle Spencer to James B. Stewart, 7 March 1929, *ibid.*; *Seattle Times*, 22 February 1932; *Seattle Post-Intelligencer*, 23 February 1932; Meany Scrapbook, "Washington Bicentennial, 1932," Meany Papers.
14. *University of Washington Daily*, 3 and 7 October 1930; Meany to Herbert T. Condon, 30 September 1933; *University of Washington Daily*, 20 February 1935.
15. Meany to Sid Patzer, 9 May 1934.
16. "Members," *The Mountaineer* 20 (15 December 1927): 64-73; Ben C. Mooers, "Fleeting Glimpses of Edmond S. Meany," *ibid.*, 50 (28 December 1956): 33; Joseph T. Hazard, always eager to praise Meany's work with The Mountaineers, was silent on the latter's lukewarm attitude toward national park and ecological proposals. See Hazard, "The First Twenty-Five Years, 1906-1930," *The Mountaineer* 50 (28 December 1956): 9-13; *University of Washington Daily*, 20 January 1926, clipping in *Edmond*

Stephen Meany, 1862-1935, Tributes, II; *The Mountaineer* 20 (15 December 1927): 63-73 lists "Six Peakers" for the first time. Meany was one of 33 out of Seattle's 653 members who were given that designation. In 1934, Meany was again joined by 33 other active members as "Six Peakers" but 40 others, out of 451 Seattleites, had climbed a large number of peaks, *The Mountaineer* 27 (December 1934): 39-52.

17. "Members of the Summer Outing, 1929," *ibid.*, 22 (December 1929): 18; Lydia Lovering Forsyth, "A Word Portrait of Edmond S. Meany," *ibid.*, 50 (28 December 1956): 26-31; "Members of the Summer Outing—Glacier National Park," *ibid.*, 27 (December 1934): 8; *University of Washington Daily*, 23 April 1935, clipping in *Edmond Stephen Meany, 1862-1935, Tributes, I.*
18. E.S. Meany, Jr., commentary on Floyd Fessler's articles on E.S. Meany, *Seattle Star*, 3-15 February 1930, see especially 14 February 1930; Forsyth, "A Word Portrait of Edmond S. Meany," *The Mountaineer* 50 (28 December 1956): 26-31.
19. *Ibid.*, 26.
20. *Ibid.*, 28 (quotation "He set high standards"), and 29 (quotation, "To Professor Meany").
21. Fred W. Ball, "The Story of Meany Ski Hut," *ibid.*,(28 December 1956): 55, 56; "The Mountaineers—Seattle: Treasurer's Report for the Year Ending October, 31, 1928," *ibid.*, 21 (15 December 1928): 54-55; Mrs. Stuart P. Walsh, "Skiing and the Ski Hut," *ibid.*, 21 (15 December 1928): 45-48; Henry Landes, "A Geographical Dictionary of Washington," Bulletin 17 (Washington Geological Survey, 1917), 271; "Meany Crest," picture and caption in *The Mountaineer* 23 (15 December 1930), frontispiece; *University of Washington Daily*, 4 February 1932, clipping in *Edmond Stephen Meany, 1862-1935, Tributes, II.*
22. Joseph T. Hazard's analysis of the 151 charter members demonstrates that the group was middle class and professional. See, Hazard, "The First Twenty-Five Years, 1906-1930," *The Mountaineer* 50 (28 December 1956): 6-9; Arthur R. Winder, "The Second Twenty-Five Years, 1931-1956," *ibid.*, 15-16; Dee Molenaar, *The Challenge of Rainier, A Record of Explorations and Ascents, Triumphs and Tragedies on the Northwest's Greatest Mountain* (Seattle: The Mountaineers, 1971), xiii, xiv, 289, 290; Varne Denham, "The First Golden Years of Climbing," *The Mountaineer* 50 (28 December 1956): 73-74.
23. [J. Arthur Younger], a report on mortgages, 11 April 1932, Folder 31-30, 106-2-75-10, Meany Papers; Meany to Republican State Headquarters, 16 September 1932; Meany to *Post-Intelligencer* Christmas Fund, 5 December 1932.
24. *University of Washington Daily*, 23 April 1935, clipping in *Edmond Stephen Meany, 1862-1935, Tributes, I*; *Seattle Times*, 22 April, 1935.
25. *Seattle Post-Intelligencer*, 23, 24, 25, and 27 April 1935; *Seattle Times*, 22 April 1935; *University of Washington Daily*, 30 April 1935, clipping in *Edmond Stephen Meany, 1862-1935, Tributes, I*; Matthew W. Hill, "In Memorium Bro. Edmond S. Meany, Past Master, St. John's Lodge No. 9, F. and A.M., read at the Lodge, May 25, 1935. . . ." (Seattle, [1935]), Northwest Collection, University of Washington Library. According to the memorial, Meany had been a Mason since 1891.
26. *University of Washington Daily*, 22 and 23 April 1935 (quotation), clipping in *Edmond Stephen Meany, 1862-1935, Tributes, I.*
27. *Cathlamet Eagle*, 25 April 1935, clipping in *ibid.*
28. *Yakima Republic*, 23 April 1935, *ibid.*; see also, the *Toppenish Review*, 26 April 1935, *ibid.*, for similar sentiments.
29. "Student Body Pays Tribute to Meany," *University of Washington Daily*, 26 April 1935, clipping in *Edmond Stephen Meany, 1862-1935, Tributes, I;* Herbert T. Condon and

others, "Faculty Approves Tribute to Prof. Edmond Meany," *University of Washington Daily*, 25 April 1935, *ibid., II* (quotation "a benediction"); *Seattle Argus*, 27 April 1935, *ibid., I* (quotation "down through the lives").

30. *Oregonian* (Portland), 24 April 1935, *ibid.*
31. Charles H. Carey's statements are a part of "Tributes to Professor Meany," *Washington Historical Quarterly* 26 (July 1935): 173.
32. *University of Washington Daily*, 3 October 1935, clipping in *Edmond Stephen Meany, 1862-1935, Tributes, II* (quotations "Traditions," and "I will strive"); Lee Paul Seig, "Edmond S. Meany: The Value of a Man," *Washington Historical Quarterly* 26 (July 1935): 163-164; *Seattle Post-Intelligencer*, 5 October 1935.
33. A number of tributes are chronicled in clippings found in *Edmond Stephen Meany, 1862-1935, Tributes II*; McMahon became executive officer of the Department of History immediately upon Meany's death. Gary A. Lundall to Frykman, 20 April 1983, letter in possession of current author; *University of Washington Daily*, 30 April 1935, clipping in *Edmond Stephen Meany, 1862-1935, Tributes, II.*
34. On Merrill Jensen, see *Directory of American Scholars*, Sixth Edition, vol. I, History, 313; "University Publications," *Pacific Northwest Quarterly* 27 (January 1936), inside back cover.
35. *Seattle Post-Intelligencer*, 4 May, and 9 October 1935; interview with Edmond S. Meany, Jr., 7 March 1975; [J. Arthur Younger] a report on mortgages, 11 April 1932, Meany Papers.
36. Program of the "Meany Hall Dedication Festival: February 7-March 21, 1975" (copy in possession of the author). *Seattle Post-Intelligencer*, 8 February 1975.

About the Author

George A. Frykman is professor emeritus of history at Washington State University, where he taught for thirty-seven years, retiring in 1987. In addition to his teaching duties, Frykman, while at the university, served at various times as chief of the social sciences division of the library, as assistant to the dean of the graduate school, and as chair of the university senate. In 1985 he was appointed Washington State University centennial historian and authored the university's centennial volume, *Creating the People's University: Washington State University, 1890-1990* (WSU Press, 1990). Frykman is also the author of numerous articles and is the editor, along with David Stratton, of *The Changing Pacific Northwest: Interpreting Its Past* (WSU Press, 1988). Dr. Frykman lives in Pullman.

INDEX